Legal Writing

Aspen Coursebook Series

Legal Writing

3E

Richard K. Neumann, Jr.
Professor of Law
Maurice A. Dean School of Law
Hofstra University

J. Lyn Entrikin
Professor of Law
William H. Bowen School of Law
University of Arkansas at Little Rock

Sheila Simon
Former Lt. Governor of Illinois

Wolters Kluwer

Printed in the United States of America.

1 2 3 4 5 6 7 8 9 0

ISBN 978-1-4548-3097-9

Library of Congress Control Number: 2014960144

About Wolters Kluwer Law & Business

Wolters Kluwer Law & Business is a leading global provider of intelligent information and digital solutions for legal and business professionals in key specialty areas, and respected educational resources for professors and law students. Wolters Kluwer Law & Business connects legal and business professionals as well as those in the education market with timely, specialized authoritative content and information-enabled solutions to support success through productivity, accuracy and mobility.

Serving customers worldwide, Wolters Kluwer Law & Business products include those under the Aspen Publishers, CCH, Kluwer Law International, Loislaw, ftwilliam.com and MediRegs family of products.

CCH products have been a trusted resource since 1913, and are highly regarded resources for legal, securities, antitrust and trade regulation, government contracting, banking, pension, payroll, employment and labor, and healthcare reimbursement and compliance professionals.

Aspen Publishers products provide essential information to attorneys, business professionals and law students. Written by preeminent authorities, the product line offers analytical and practical information in a range of specialty practice areas from securities law and intellectual property to mergers and acquisitions and pension/benefits. Aspen's trusted legal education resources provide professors and students with high-quality, up-to-date and effective resources for successful instruction and study in all areas of the law.

Kluwer Law International products provide the global business community with reliable international legal information in English. Legal practitioners, corporate counsel and business executives around the world rely on Kluwer Law journals, looseleafs, books, and electronic products for comprehensive information in many areas of international legal practice.

Loislaw is a comprehensive online legal research product providing legal content to law firm practitioners of various specializations. Loislaw provides attorneys with the ability to quickly and efficiently find the necessary legal information they need, when and where they need it, by facilitating access to primary law as well as state-specific law, records, forms and treatises.

ftwilliam.com offers employee benefits professionals the highest quality plan documents (retirement, welfare and non-qualified) and government forms (5500/PBGC, 1099 and IRS) software at highly competitive prices.

MediRegs products provide integrated health care compliance content and software solutions for professionals in healthcare, higher education and life sciences, including professionals in accounting, law and consulting.

Wolters Kluwer Law & Business, a division of Wolters Kluwer, is headquartered in New York. Wolters Kluwer is a market-leading global information services company focused on professionals.

for Lillianna and Alexander
RKN Jr

for Meg, Hobbes, and Ben
JLE

for Reilly and Brennan
SS

Summary of Contents

Contents

Chapter 7: Policy and Why Courts Care about It   47

Chapter 8: Selecting the Right Authority   53

Chapter 9: Working with Statutes   69

Chapter 10: Working with Cases   89

2 The Process of Writing

Chapter 11: Getting to Know Yourself as a Writer   99

Chapter 12: Inside the Process of Writing   105

Chapter 13: How Professional Writers Plan Their Writing   115

Office Memoranda

Organizing Analysis

Chapter 18: Varying the Sequence and Depth of Rule Explanation and Rule Application   153

Chapter 19: Advanced CREAC: Organizing More Than One Issue   161

Chapter 20: Working with CREAC in First Drafts and in Later Drafts   167

5 # Working Effectively with Details

Informal Analytical Writing

The Shift to Persuasion

Contents

Chapter 28: Writing a Motion Memorandum   253

8   Telling the Client's Story

Chapter 29: The Statement of the Case in a Motion Memo or Appellate Brief   267

Chapter 30: Developing a Persuasive Story   271

Chapter 31: Telling the Story Persuasively   277

9   Making the Client's Arguments

Chapter 32: The Argument in a Motion Memo or Appellate Brief   287

Chapter 33: Point Headings and Subheadings   297

10   Appellate Briefs and Oral Argument

Chapter 34: Appellate Practice   311

Chapter 35: Writing the Appellate Brief 315

Chapter 36: Handling Standards of Review 321

Chapter 37: Questions Presented 333

Chapter 38: Making Policy Arguments 345

Chapter 39: Oral Argument   351

Appendices

Index   411

Acknowledgments

From Richard K. Neumann, Jr:

Thank you to Lyn Entrikin and Sheila Simon for the special collaboration that has produced this book and its website. Thanks also to Anne Kringel, Coleen Barger, Mary Beth Beazley, Robin Boyle, Ralph Brill, Jen Gundlach, Derek Kiernan-Johnson, Amy Langenfeld, Jan Levine, Pam Lysaght, Terry Pollman, Ruth Anne Robbins, Amy Stein, Judy Stinson, and Ed Telfeyan for their advice. For research assistance and suggestions, thanks to Elizabeth Brehm, Raf Cheema, Jennifer Garber, Rachael Ringer, Michelle Gordon, Caitlin Locurto, Samuel Lui, Nina Ovrutsky, Laura Schaefer, Matt Weinick, and Frances Zemel. Thanks also to Barbara Dillon, Alex Fiore, Francis Forde, Angelina Ibragimov, Felicia Leo, Alex Leonard, Danielle Manor, Gariel Nahoum, Jody-Ann Tyrell, and Jason Weber for their many suggestions as well. And for sharing their thoughts about professional use of email, we are grateful to the following members of the bar: Elizabeth Brehm, Heather Canning, Mirel Fisch, Evgeny Krasnov, Adam Kahn, Melissa Manna, Ronald Meister, Madelyn Mostiller, and Jane Sovern.

Lill and Alex have taught me much about how to learn and about how textbooks can become both lighter *and* deeper. At the keyboard I have often wondered what kind of book they might want to learn from in future years, whatever they study.

From J. Lyn Entrikin:

Thank you to Coleen Barger for her wise counsel, and for offering helpful suggestions for the updated chapter on citing and quoting. Many thanks to Matthew Stromberg for allowing us to reprint a portion of his office memo for the exercise on citation placement. Thank you to Mary Algero, Mary Beth Beazley, Ralph Brill, Brad Clary, Sue Leimer, Jan Levine, Pam Lysaght, Anthony Niedwiecki, Craig Smith, Terry Pollman, Suzanne Rowe, and Judy Stinson for their friendship, leadership, and encouragement over the years.

Thanks also to the following former law students and colleagues for responding to our survey about how lawyers use email for day-to-day correspondence with clients and other lawyers: Adam Andersen, Shanelle Dupree, David Jack, Skye Johnson, David C. Jung, Victoria Malony, Matthew Stromberg, Kelly Trussell, Megan Walawender, Eric Weslander, and Craig West.

Thank you especially to Richard Neumann and Sheila Simon for inviting me to become a co-author of this project and for their continued patience and encouragement throughout my learning process. To Meg, Hobbes, and Ben, thank you for your ongoing love and inspiration, and for always believing in me.

From Sheila Simon:

Thank you to Susan Williams and Ramon Escapa, who contributed long and often tedious hours to this book. Jayne McCarroll and Linda Kalloran are the stars who turned scripts into moving images for the book's website. Thanks to many people who gave ideas and energy, including Peter Alexander, Levi Burkett, Delio Calzolari, Amy Campbell, Bruce Ching, Laura Cox, Brannon Denning, Andrea Jones, Elizabeth Kee, Hannah Kelley, Sue Liemer, Melissa Marlow, Matt Rokusek, Hollee Temple, Tim Ting, and Melissa Weresh. Thanks also to the many students who allowed me to consider using their writing, particularly Elizabeth Gastélum, Nate Bailey, Joanne Olson, and Caroline Borden. I am grateful to Richard Neumann for the opportunity to work with him. I have learned from Richard far more than I have contributed to this book.

Thanks to my husband, Perry Knop, for his constant encouragement. And our daughters, Reilly and Brennan Knop, are my best source of learning about teaching. We were on to something with Barbie Math Bath!

From Richard, Lyn, and Sheila:

At Wolters Kluwer, we are grateful to George Serafin for suggesting the concept of this book; to Carol McGeehan, Richard Mixter, and Mike Gregory for their help in brainstorming its possibilities; and to Dana Wilson for her skill, insight, and diplomacy while managing us through many editorial difficulties.

We are also grateful to the anonymous reviewers who read drafts of the manuscript and subsequent editions for Wolters Kluwer and made many valuable suggestions. (It really is anonymous; you know who you are, but we don't.)

We are especially grateful to the Writers' Colony at Dairy Hollow in Eureka Springs, Arkansas, for providing a place of solitude and support designed for writers of all kinds. It is especially meaningful that parts of a book about writing were written among writers in a colony set aside for writers.

Copyright Acknowledgments

Permission to reprint copyrighted excerpts from the following is gratefully acknowledged:

Calvin and Hobbes ©1993 Watterson. Reprinted with permission of Universal Uclick. All rights reserved.

Ellie Margolis, *Teaching Students to Make Effective Policy Arguments in Appellate Briefs*, 9 Perspectives 73 (2001).

Carrie Newcomer, *Don't Push Send* from *The Geography of Light* 2008.

Legal
Writing

1 Writing and Professional Work

§ 1.1   Writing as a Professional

Becoming a professional is a long and gradual process. It began the first time you opened a law school textbook and will continue for many years to come.

Of all the qualities that make someone an effective professional, perhaps the most important are integrity, good judgment, and the ability to facilitate the best outcomes for clients. You expect that from your doctor, and your clients will expect it of you. Clients pay lawyers to *get results*.

In college, students write to satisfy requirements such as writing a term paper or demonstrating knowledge in an exam. Lawyers, however, write to *make things happen*. A lawyer writes an appellate brief, for example, to persuade a court to rule in favor of the lawyer's client. If the lawyer succeeds, the client wins.

Writing is so essential to the practice of law that a good writer has an enormous advantage over a lifetime career. Law firm hiring partners often say that the two most important factors in deciding whether to hire a job applicant are the quality of the applicant's writing sample and the extent to which the applicant conveys professionalism when interviewed. Once you have a job, "excellent writing skills are a form of future job security."[1] A person who has supervised 400 lawyers at a major corporation has said that if you write well, "you are more likely to get good grades in law school [and] become a partner in your law firm, or receive comparable promotions in your law department or government law office."[2] Good writing is a strength. If you are a better writer than other lawyers, your clients will have an advantage.

---

[1] Mark E. Wojcik, 3 Persps. 7 (1994).
[2] Richard S. Lombard (formerly Exxon general counsel), *Remarks, in* ABA Section of Legal Educ. & Admissions to the Bar, *Lost Words: The Economical, Ethical and Professional Effects of Bad Legal Writing* 54 (Occasional Paper No. 7, Aug. 5, 1993).

Young lawyers often say that the most valuable skills for them are communicating professionally, both in writing and orally, as well as researching the law while solving problems in a professional manner. In the law school course for which you are reading this book, you will learn all these skills.

In law, what counts is what works. Legal writing is put to practical tests in the real world. But that does not mean that all lawyers must write in the same way or in the same style. Most legal writing tasks can be done effectively in a variety of ways. As you learn legal writing, try to assess your own personal strengths and weaknesses—so that you can develop ways of writing that take advantage of your strengths and minimize the effect of your weaknesses. Students sometimes say that they learn a lot about themselves in the legal writing course.

§ 1.2 A Professional Audience

Your audience is all the people who will read the documents you write: supervising lawyers such as law firm partners as well as judges and lawyers outside your law firm or organization. They all share three characteristics.

First, the typical reader must make a decision and reads your document to find the material necessary for that decision. Your reader wants and needs your help. The more helpful you are, the better lawyer you are. Your reader can also think in the other direction. If you are not helpful, you are not doing a good job of lawyering.

Second, your typical reader is a busy person who must read quickly and does not have time to read twice. Your writing must communicate so clearly and concisely that your reader will quickly understand all your analysis. Your writing must be *efficient* for the reader.

Third, the typical reader is skeptical by nature and for good reason. Badly made decisions harm people. Your reader learned long ago to make decisions only if they are based on a foundation of solid reasoning from accurate analysis of law and facts. One way for a reader to do that is to look for gaps or weaknesses in your analysis. If the reader cannot find any, you have done a good job. But if the reader does find gaps or weaknesses, you will not be believed. Your readers are not being unkind when they do this. Part of their job is to protect clients that way. Skepticism leads to better decisions.

You will be a better writer if, while writing, you think frequently about your reader's needs and sensibilities. This is called audience sense.

§ 1.3 Memos and Briefs

An *office memorandum* analyzes a legal issue objectively. It answers a question about how the law treats certain facts. The reader will be a supervising lawyer, such as a partner in a law firm.

A lawyer writes a *motion memorandum*, also called a *trial brief*, to persuade a trial court to decide an issue in favor of the lawyer's client. A lawsuit starts in a trial court, and the memo's audience is the trial judge.

A lawyer writes an *appellate brief* to persuade an appellate court to affirm or reverse the decision of a lower court. An appellate brief's audience is all the judges who will decide the appeal.

§ 1.4 Predictive Writing and Persuasive Writing

In an office memo, you *predict* objectively how a court would decide a legal issue on which you are writing. In a motion memo or appellate brief, you try to *persuade* the court to make a decision favorable to your client.

Here is an example of predicting: Suppose your client runs a website from which ringtones can be downloaded into cell phones. Your client asks, "If we copy the ringtones sold by the telephone company, and if we then sell them for a lower price, will we get into trouble?" Because you will think precisely about the law, your mind will translate "will we get into trouble?" into questions like these:

- Does the phone company own a copyright or have some other property interest in its ringtones?
- If the answer is yes, would a court order the client to pay damages to the phone company if the client copies its ringtones?

Other issues could grow out of the facts, but these two illustrate predictive thinking.

Suppose the client does copy the phone company's ringtones and the phone company sues. In the trial court, you might ask the judge to compel the phone company to respond in discovery or to grant summary judgment. If you lose at trial, you might appeal to a higher court. In all these situations, you will try to persuade a judge or judges to decide in favor of your client. You will do so by telling the client's story in a compelling way and by making logical arguments to support your position. Lawyers persuade primarily through storytelling and argumentation.

§ 1.5 How to Use This Book and Its Website

Different people learn differently, and we have designed the book and the website to accommodate as many learning styles as possible. The book alone explains everything you need to know, but the website provides some enhancements.

Although we cannot sit with you individually and talk, we try to come as close to that as we can in a book. We have also written the book in an informal style. We try to explain what you need to know without creating distance between you and the book.

When you write memoranda and briefs in this course, **please do *not* imitate the informality of this book**. Memoranda and briefs are formal documents. For example, in this book we sometimes use contractions (two words merged into one with an apostrophe), but **contractions do not belong in formal documents**. And we use italics and dashes more than you should. In formal memoranda and briefs, italics and dashes have a place for emphasis, but not often.

On the other hand, we have tried to write the book in a style that illustrates some of the most important features of legal writing—clarity, precision, conciseness, and vividness. When you find those characteristics in any writing, they are worth imitating.

The card inside this book has instructions for redeeming your access code and getting into the website, where you will find:

- videos that help explain (with a touch of humor) some of the most fundamental aspects of legal writing
- checklists from several chapters that you can print from the website to help you improve your writing throughout the course
- articles on Writing Exam Answers and other subjects

Part 1

Legal Rules and Their Sources

2 Inside a Rule of Law

§ 2.1 The Inner Structure of a Rule

A rule is a formula for making a decision. For example: "A person who drives a motor vehicle at a speed greater than a posted speed limit is guilty of speeding." Here's how this rule would look as a formula:

drives + motor vehicle + faster than a posted speed limit
= guilty of speeding

Suppose that you receive a speeding ticket and appear in court to contest it. The police officer would testify, and you would testify. If any bystanders saw what happened, they might testify.

Listening to the testimony, the judge would be interested in three things. Were you driving something? Was it a motor vehicle (not a bicycle or a glider)? And were you traveling faster than the speed limit posted by the side of the road? That is because the judge will decide your case exactly according to the speeding rule's formula.

Most rules have three components:

1. **A test.** In the speeding example, the test is *driving a motor vehicle faster than a posted speed limit*. A test is a list of elements or factors.
2. **A result that occurs when the test is satisfied.** In the speeding example, the result is *guilty of speeding*.
3. **A causal term that determines whether the result is mandatory, prohibitory, discretionary, or declaratory.** (We will explain these in a moment.) In the speeding example, the result is declaratory: You are declared guilty.

Some rules also have a fourth component:

4. **One or more exceptions that, if satisfied, would prevent the result, even if the test has been satisfied.** For example, if the rule above contained the words "unless the motorist reasonably believes it necessary to exceed the speed limit in order to prevent injury to a person or substantial damage to property," that would be an exception. Often an exception is expressed in a dependent clause beginning with *unless* or *except* or *in the absence of*.

§ 2.2   Two Types of Tests

A test is based on either elements or factors.

Elements Tests. A rule that has an elements test could be called *an elements rule* or *a rule with elements*. They mean the same thing. An elements test is satisfied only if *all* the items in the list are satisfied.

Let's return to the speeding rule at the beginning of this chapter. To figure out whether you are guilty, compare each of the phrases in the first line to the facts. You are guilty if you were behind the wheel and operating the controls (*drives*), the thing you were driving was a car (*motor vehicle*), and you were driving perhaps 60 miles per hour when you passed a sign by the side of the road that said "Speed Limit 45" (*faster than a posted speed limit*).

But you are not guilty if you were in the passenger seat (*not driving*) regardless of how fast the car travelled. An elements test is satisfied only if *all* the elements are present in the facts.

Factors Tests. A rule that has a factors test could be called *a factors rule* or *a rule with factors*. Factors are criteria that function as guidelines for making a decision.

In a given set of facts, some factors might tilt in favor of enforcing the rule, and other factors might tilt against enforcing it. In applying a factors test, a court weighs all the factors together, which is why some factors tests are also called balancing tests. The test is satisfied if the factors, taken as a whole, tilt in the direction of enforcing the rule.

Factors usually do not have equal weight. In a five-factor test, for example, the factors would not be worth 20 percent each. In a hypothetical set of facts, for example, that five-factor test might come out like this: Factors 1 and 2 might tilt slightly against enforcing the rule. Factors 3 and 4 might not matter because no facts are relevant to them. They might matter with some other set of facts but not these. Factor 5 might tilt overwhelmingly in favor of enforcing the rule.

Looking at these factors as a group, Factor 5 would be decisive. With these factors and these facts, a court will probably enforce the rule.

Comparing Elements Tests and Factors Tests. Elements tests are rigid. *Every* element is essential, and *every* element must be satisfied. If any element—even just one of them—is not satisfied, the whole test is not satisfied, and a court will refuse to enforce the rule. Most of the rules you will encounter in the first year of law school have elements tests.

A factors test is flexible. Usually none of the individual factors is essential. Some might tilt in favor of enforcing the rule, and some might tilt against. A court weighs them as a group. If those that tilt in favor of enforcing a rule outweigh those that tilt against, a court will enforce the rule. If the opposite is true, a court will not enforce it. What if they are equal and on balance tilt neither one way nor the other? Often a tie means not enforcing the rule, but to be sure, you would need to look carefully at the way the test is worded.

§ 2.3   Four Types of Causal Terms

A **mandatory rule** requires someone to act and might be expressed in words like "shall" or "must" in the causal term. "Shall" means "has a legal duty to." "The court shall grant the motion" means the court has a legal duty to grant it.

A **prohibitory rule** forbids someone to act and is generally expressed by the words "may not" or "shall not" in the causal term.

A **discretionary rule** gives someone the power or authority to do something. That person has discretion to act but is not required to do so. You might see words like "may" or "has the authority to" in the causal term.

A **declaratory rule** simply states (declares) that something is true. That might not seem like much of a rule, but the consequences of the declaration can be serious. The rule at the beginning of this chapter is declaratory: "A person who drives a motor vehicle at a speed greater than a posted speed limit is guilty of speeding." If all the elements of that declaration are satisfied, other rules are activated. If you are speeding, a police officer can give you a ticket because another discretionary rule elsewhere in the law gives police the authority to do that. A court can sentence you to a fine because another discretionary rule gives courts power to impose penalties for speeding. And in many states, a mandatory rule requires the motor vehicle department to impose points on your driver's license.

A declaratory rule places a label on a set of facts (the elements or factors). The rule's power is what that label permits or requires people to do (the police officer to give you a ticket, and so on). Often the declaration is expressed by the word "is" or "means" in the causal term. But other words could be used there instead. You have to look at what the rule *does*. If it simply states that something is true, it is declaratory. If it does more than that, it is another kind of rule.

"Shall" and "shall not" can be confusing if you are not careful. Legislatures and lawyers are sometimes careless with these words and use them just for emphasis. When you see them in a statute, ask yourself whether the sentence where they occur requires someone to act (a mandatory rule) or forbids them to act (a prohibitory rule). If the sentence neither requires conduct nor forbids it, it might create a discretionary or declaratory rule. Again, you have to look at what the rule *does*.

Here are examples illustrating the four types of rules:

mandatory   A person driving a motor vehicle *shall* stop at a stop sign or a red traffic light.

prohibitory   A person *shall not* drive a motor vehicle in this state unless licensed to do so by the Department of Motor Vehicles.

discretionary   A person driving a motor vehicle *may* turn right after coming to a complete stop at a red traffic signal and yielding the right-of-way to pedestrians and other motor vehicles, unless a sign erected by the highway department prohibits doing so.

declaratory   A person who violates any section of the Vehicle Code is guilty of an infraction.

§ 2.4 Analyzing a Rule to Figure Out What It Means

Analyzing a rule is a three-step process.

§ 2.4.1 *Step 1:* Break Down the Rule into Its Parts

Take apart the rule by diagramming it. List and number the elements or factors in the test. Identify the causal term and the result. If there is an exception, identify it, and if the exception has more than one element or factor, list and number them as well.

In Step 1, *you do not care what the words mean.* You only want to know the structure of the rule. You are breaking down the rule into parts small enough to understand each one. Let's take the discretionary rule in § 2.3 and run it through Step 1. Here is the rule diagrammed:

Elements in the Test:
If
    (1) a person driving a motor vehicle
    (2) comes to a complete stop
    (3) at a red traffic signal and
    (4) yields the right-of-way to pedestrians
       and other motor vehicles,

Causal Term:
the driver may

Result:
turn right

Exception:
unless a sign erected by the highway
department prohibits doing so.

You do not need to lay out the rule exactly this way. You can use any method of diagramming that breaks up the rule so you can understand it. The point is to break up the rule visually so that it is no longer a blur of words and you can see *separately* the elements or factors in the test, the causal term, the result, and any exception.

When can you combine the causal term and result? You can do it whenever that would not confuse you. If you can understand the following, you can combine them, at least with this rule:

Causal Term and Result:
the driver may turn right

§ 2.4.2 *Step 2:* Look at Each Part Separately

Many rules seem baffling at first. Step 1 breaks the rule down into smaller parts. In Step 2, look at each of those parts separately to figure out what each means. Examine the details. Figure out the meaning of each element or factor, the causal term, the result, and any exception. If you are not certain what a word means, look it up in a legal dictionary or read other material your teacher has assigned. Because you are looking at smaller parts now, the figuring out becomes easier.

Decide now what kind of rule you have. Is it an elements rule or a factors rule? Is it mandatory, prohibitory, discretionary, or declaratory?

§ 2.4.3 *Step 3:* Put the Rule Back Together in a Way That Helps You Use It

Sometimes that means rearranging the rule so that it is easier to understand. For example, when you first read the rule, if an exception came at the beginning and the elements came last, rearrange the rule so the elements come earlier and the exception last. It will be easier to understand that way. For many elements rules—though not all of them—the rule's inner logic works like this:

What events or circumstances set the rule into operation?
(These are the elements or factors.)

When all the elements or factors are present, what happens?
(The causal term and the result supply the answer.)

Even if all the elements are present, could anything else prevent the result?
(An exception, if the rule has any.)

Usually, you can put the rule back together by creating a flowchart and trying out the rule on some hypothetical facts to see how it works. A flowchart is essentially a list of questions. You will be able to make a flowchart because of the diagramming you did earlier in Step 1, which not only breaks the rule down so that it can be understood, but also permits putting it back together so that it is easier to apply. The flowchart below comes straight out of the diagram in Step 1 above.

Elements

1. Were you driving a motor vehicle?
2. Did you come to a complete stop?
3. Did you do that at a red traffic signal?
4. Did you yield the right-of-way to pedestrians and other motor vehicles?

Exception

Did a sign erected by the highway department prohibit turning right on a red light?

Causal Term and Result

(if all the elements questions are answered "yes" and if the exception question is answered "no")
You may turn right.

Step 3 helps you add up everything to see what happens when the rule is applied to a given set of facts.

Assume that you are being tried in traffic court for making an illegal turn at a red light. The police officer testifies that you were driving a car (*element #1 satisfied*) and that this happened at a red traffic light (*element #3 satisfied*). You are representing yourself. (No lawyer represents you.) On cross-examination, you ask the police officer the following:

Q: Did I come to a complete stop before turning right?
A: Yes. (*element #2 satisfied*)
Q: Did any pedestrians have a "walk" signal?
A: No. (*starting element #4*)
Q: Did any approaching cars have a green light?
A: No. (*element #4 satisfied*)
Q: Did a sign at this intersection prohibit right-turn-on-red?
A: No. (*exception does not apply*)

A few minutes later, this happens:

You: Your Honor, the evidence satisfies all the elements in the test that gives me discretion to turn right on a red light, and the evidence does not substantiate the exception to that rule. Therefore, I was legally permitted to turn right.
Judge: Not guilty! Charge dismissed!

§ 2.4.4   The Three Steps Summarized

Here are the steps (explained above) in analyzing a rule:

Step 1 Break the rule down into its parts (*§ 2.4.1*).

Step 2 Look at each of those parts separately (*§ 2.4.2*).

Step 3 Put the rule back together in a way that helps you use it (*§ 2.4.3*).

Exercise 2-A. Four Rules for Law School Exams

Consider the following rules:

The compelling circumstances rule

declaratory (handwritten)

TEST (handwritten) / *result* (handwritten) / *CT* (handwritten)

Compelling circumstances include serious illness or an emergency in which the student's or a family member's health or property is endangered, but do not include nervousness, fatigue, oversleeping, or forgetting an examination's time or place. — *exception* (handwritten)

The excused exam rule

discretionary (handwritten)

— *result* (handwritten)

The dean of students may excuse a student from taking an examination at the scheduled time and place if the student or someone acting on the student's behalf asserts that compelling circumstances prevent the student from functioning effectively during the exam, and if the dean of students receives evidence documenting that compelling circumstances exist.

The makeup exam rule

mandatory (handwritten)

— *result* (handwritten)

The registrar shall schedule a makeup examination for an appropriate date and time, considering both the student's compelling circumstances and the school's need to compute final grades for all students in a timely manner.

The electronic devices rule

prohibitory (handwritten)

result (handwritten)

A student is not permitted to have any electronic device in the exam room other than a laptop computer on which the school's information technology department has installed exam software. — *exception* (handwritten)

Part 1. For each rule, label the test, the causal term, and the result. If the rule has an exception, label that as well. You might find this easier if you use different color inks or highlighters.

Part 2. For each rule, decide whether it is mandatory, prohibitory, discretionary, or declaratory.

Part 3. For each rule, decide whether the test is based on elements or factors.

Exercise 2-B. A Rule on Late Papers

Below is a rule that appears in a teacher's syllabus—not *your* teacher's syllabus.

If a student submits a paper after the deadline, the student's grade on that paper will be reduced five per cent for every hour the paper is late unless the student submits written proof that the student or a member of the student's family had been hospitalized or otherwise gravely at risk within 24 hours before the deadline.

Use the three-step process in § 2.4 to analyze the rule. Identify any parts of it that need further definition. What questions would you ask of this teacher to make sure you understand the full meaning of each part of the rule?

More about Rules

3

I try not to break the rules but merely to test their elasticity.

—*Bill Veeck*

§ 3.1 Remedies, Causes of Action, and Affirmative Defenses

Most of the rules you will study in law school define causes of action or affirmative defenses, which together determine whether a party can get a remedy.

A plaintiff sues to get a *remedy*. A remedy (also called *relief*) is what the law can do to solve a problem. The most common remedy is damages—money, paid by someone responsible for causing harm, to compensate the person who suffered the loss. But damages are not the only remedy. Sometimes a court will order a party to do something that does not involve paying money.

A harm the law will remedy is called a *cause of action* or a *claim*. If a plaintiff cannot prove a cause of action, the plaintiff cannot get a remedy. Even if a plaintiff does prove a cause of action, a court will not order a remedy if the defendant proves an *affirmative defense*.

For example, when a plaintiff proves that a defendant intentionally confined him and that the defendant was not a law enforcement officer acting within the scope of an authority to arrest, the plaintiff has proved a cause of action called *false imprisonment*. Here is the rule:

> False imprisonment consists of (1) a confinement (2) of the plaintiff (3) by the defendant (4) intentionally (5) where the defendant is not a sworn law enforcement officer acting within that authority.

But if the defendant can prove that she caught the plaintiff shoplifting in her store and restrained him only until the police arrived, she might have an affirmative defense called a *shopkeeper's privilege*. When a defendant proves all the elements of a shopkeeper's privilege, a court will not award the plaintiff damages, even if he has proved false imprisonment. Here is the rule:

> A shopkeeper or a shopkeeper's employee is not liable for false imprisonment when (1) the shopkeeper or shopkeeper's employee (2) has reasonable cause to believe that (3) the plaintiff (4) has shoplifted (5) in the shopkeeper's place of business and (6) the confinement occurs in a reasonable manner, for a reasonable time, and only to the extent needed to detain the plaintiff for law enforcement purposes.

§ 3.2   Where Rules Come From (Sources of Law)

Our legal system has two primary sources of law: statutes and case law.

§ 3.2.1   Statutes

Legislatures create rules of law by enacting statutes such as the Freedom of Information Act, which gives you the right to read and copy certain government documents. The federal legislature—Congress—enacts federal statutes. Each state has a legislature of its own to enact state statutes.

In addition, some rules of law are found in materials that resemble statutes but were not enacted by legislatures. Statute-like provisions include constitutions, administrative regulations, and court rules. Administrative regulations are issued by government agencies, and court rules are adopted usually, but not always, by courts.

§ 3.2.2   Case Law

American law is derived from English law. In England, courts existed before legislatures gained the power to make law. Without legislation, those courts not only enforced law but also created the law they were enforcing. The main tool English courts used in this process was a rule called *stare decisis*, Latin for "let stand that which has been decided," or, more loosely, "follow the rules courts have followed in the past." A past court decision is a *precedent*, which later courts, within limits, are required to take into account. Courts record their decisions in judicial opinions. Lawyers use the words *cases, case law, decisions, opinions,* and *precedents* interchangeably to refer to these decisions and to the opinions that explain them. This judge-made law is called common law.

In modern American law, the common law continues to exist to the extent it has not been superseded by legislation. Most of what you will study in the course on Torts, for example, is common law because legislatures have enacted only a few statutes on the subject. For a common law issue, the rules come exclusively from case law. Courts, having created the common law, can change it and periodically do, in decisions that enforce the law as changed.

In addition, many statutes have ambiguities, and often we do not know what a statute means until the courts interpret it—through judicial decisions applying the statute to specific facts. If the statute is unclear, we have to read the case law to find out what it means. By interpreting the statute, courts essentially finish the process of law creation that the legislature started by enacting the statute in the first place.

Thus, courts make law in two ways. They created the common law centuries ago and continue to change it. And when they interpret statutes, they add meaning to what the legislature has enacted.

Each state has its own courts enforcing that state's law, and in addition the federal government has courts throughout the country enforcing federal law. Federal courts include general trial courts (the United States District Courts), intermediate appellate courts (the United States Courts of Appeals), and a final appellate court (the United States Supreme Court). The Courts of Appeals are divided into thirteen Circuits.

Most large and medium-sized states have a similar structure: a general trial court, an intermediate appellate court, and a final appellate court. Smaller states might not have an intermediate appellate court. Both federal and state systems also include specialized courts, such as the United States Tax Court or a state's family court. Court names differ from state to state.

§ 3.3   Some Questions about Rules

1. Must the elements or factors always be stated before the rest of the rule? No. If you have a simple causal term and result together with a complicated test listing many elements or factors, you can put the test last. For example:

> Common law burglary is committed by breaking and entering the dwelling of another in the nighttime with intent to commit a felony therein.[1]

If the elements were listed first, this rule would be a lot harder to understand.

---

[1] This was the crime at common law. Because of the way its elements are divided, it does a good job of illustrating several different things about rule structure. But the definition of burglary in a modern criminal code will differ.

2. If a rule has lots of elements or factors, or if they are complicated or ambiguous, how can you make it clear where one ends and the next begins? You can enumerate:

> Common law burglary is committed by (1) breaking and (2) entering (3) the dwelling (4) of another (5) in the nighttime (6) with intent to commit a felony therein.

3. With an elements rule, how can you tell what the elements are? Think of each element as an integral fact, the absence of which would prevent the rule's operation. If you can think of a scenario that has a realistic chance of occurring in real life, and if in that scenario part of what you believe to be one element could be true but another part not true, then you actually have two or more elements.

For example, is "the dwelling of another" one element or two? A person might be guilty of some other crime, but he is not guilty of common law burglary when he breaks and enters the restaurant of another, even in the nighttime and with intent to commit a felony therein. The same is true when he breaks and enters his own dwelling. In each instance, part of "the dwelling of another" is present, and part is missing. "The dwelling of another" thus includes two elements: the nature of the building (a residence) and the identity of its resident (not the defendant).

Often you cannot know the number of elements in a rule until you have consulted the judicial decisions that interpret it. Is "breaking and entering" one element or two? The cases define "breaking" in this sense as the creation of a gap in a building's protective enclosure, such as by opening a door, even when the door was left unlocked and the building was thus not damaged. The cases further define "entering" for this purpose as placing inside the dwelling any part of oneself or any object under one's control, such as a crowbar. Can a person "break" without "entering"? Yes. If you open a window by pushing it up from outside the building, and if, before you do anything else, the police appear and arrest you, you "broke" by opening the window, but you did not enter. "Breaking" and "entering" are therefore two elements. But to know that, you would have to read the judicial decisions that define these terms.

4. With a factors rule, how can you tell what the factors are? If the factors are in a court decision, the court will usually tell you. The following, from a recent Supreme Court case, is typical.

> We here consider an indigent's right to paid counsel at [a civil contempt proceeding, in light of what] the Constitution's Due Process Clause requires in order to make a civil proceeding fundamentally fair. *Mathews v. Eldridge*, 424 U.S. 319 (1976). . . . As relevant here those factors include (1) the nature of "the private interest that will be affected," (2) the comparative "risk" of an "erroneous deprivation" of that interest with and without "additional or substitute procedural

safeguards," and (3) the nature and magnitude of any countervailing interest in not providing "additional or substitute procedural requirement[s]." *Id.*[2]

If the test is in a statute, the factors will be listed there. For example, this Illinois statute guides a court's discretion in deciding who should receive custody of a child:

§ 602. Best Interest of Child.[3]

(a) The court shall determine custody in accordance with the best interest of the child. The court shall consider all relevant factors including:

(1) the wishes of the child's parent or parents as to his custody;

(2) the wishes of the child as to his custodian;

(3) the interaction and interrelationship of the child with his parent or parents, his siblings and any other person who may significantly affect the child's best interest;

(4) the child's adjustment to his home, school and community;

(5) the mental and physical health of all individuals involved;

(6) the physical violence or threat of physical violence by the child's potential custodian, whether directed against the child or directed against another person;

(7) the occurrence of ongoing or repeated abuse as defined in Section 103 of the Illinois Domestic Violence Act of 1986, whether directed against the child or directed against another person;

(8) the willingness and ability of each parent to facilitate and encourage a close and continuing relationship between the other parent and the child;

(9) whether one of the parents is a sex offender; and

(10) the terms of a parent's military family-care plan that a parent must complete before deployment if a parent is a member of the United States Armed Forces who is being deployed.

5. What if you read a rule that does not specify *who* has a legal duty or is prohibited from doing something or has discretion to act? For example:

A motion for a new trial must be filed no later than 28 days after the entry of judgment.[4]

"Shall" means "has a legal duty to." Here, it is a legal duty to file this kind of motion "no later than 28 days after the entry of judgment." Who has that duty? The rule does not say. You need to figure it out from the context. A judgment is the document

---

[2] *Turner v. Rogers*, 131 S. Ct. 2507, 2517 (2011).
[3] 750 Ill. Comp. Stat. Ann. § 5/602(a) (West Supp. 2014).
[4] Fed. R. Crim. P. 59(b).

that terminates a lawsuit, for example, after a trial. Who would want a new trial? The loser might want another chance to win. If that person wants a new trial, she has a legal duty to file a motion for one no later than 28 days after entry of judgment.

6. When you find the word *or* in a list of elements, what does it mean? It usually means that an element can be satisfied in more than one way. Here is an example:

> A person shall not drive or park on a public street a motor vehicle to which license plates issued by a government motor vehicle department are not attached.

Here it is again, with *or* underlined and the elements enumerated:

> A person shall not (1) drive or park (2) on a public street (3) a motor vehicle (4) to which license plates issued by a government motor vehicle department are not attached.

The first element can be satisfied by doing *either* of two acts: driving on a public street or parking on a public street. It is not necessary to do both. One is enough. Why would a rule be created this way?

Suppose a police officer found a parked car without license plates and a person nearby with keys to the car. The officer did not see the person drive the car and therefore cannot issue a citation for driving a motor vehicle without license plates. But it's a fair inference that the person parked the car, and the officer can reasonably issue a citation for that. A legislature enacting this statute would want to stop people from *driving* motor vehicles without license plates. It would not care much about parking them. Penalizing parking is a way of indirectly penalizing driving in situations where the police do not have sufficient evidence that the car was driven without license plates or who drove it.

Thus you can violate this rule in either of two ways. You can drive a motor vehicle without license plates on a public street. Or you can park it on a public street. The *or* creates alternative ways of satisfying the first element.

Exercise 3-A. Nansen and Byrd

Part 1. With the aid of §§ 16 and 221(a) of the Criminal Code (below), outline the rule in § 220 into a list of elements and exceptions. Annotate the list by adding definitions for the elements and for any exceptions you might come across.

Criminal Code § 16

When a term describing a kind of intent or knowledge appears in a statute defining a crime, that term applies to every element of the crime unless the definition of the crime clearly indicates that the term is meant to apply only to certain elements and not to others.

Criminal Code § 220

A person is guilty of criminal sale of a controlled substance when he knowingly sells any quantity of a controlled substance.

Criminal Code § 221(a)

As used in section 220 of this code, "sell" means to exchange for goods or money, to give, or to offer or agree to do the same, except where the seller is a licensed physician dispensing the controlled substance pursuant to a permit issued by the Drug Enforcement Commission or where the seller is a licensed pharmacist dispensing the controlled substance as directed by a prescription issued by a licensed physician pursuant to a permit issued by the Drug Enforcement Commission.

Part 2. You have interviewed Nansen, who lives with Byrd. Neither is a licensed physician nor a licensed pharmacist. At about noon on July 15, both were arrested and charged with criminal sale of a controlled substance. Nansen has told you the following:

> Byrd keeps a supply of cocaine in our apartment. He had been out of town for a month, and I had used up his stash while he was gone. I knew that was going to bend Byrd completely out of shape, but I thought I was going to get away with it. I had replaced it all with plaster. When you grind plaster down real fine, it looks like coke. For other reasons, I had decided to go to Alaska on an afternoon flight on July 15 and not come back. Byrd was supposed to get back into town on July 16, and by the time he figured out what had happened, I would be in the Tongass Forest.
>
> But on the morning of the 15th, Byrd opened the door of the apartment and walked in, saying he had decided to come back a day early. I hadn't started packing yet—I wouldn't have much to pack anyway—but I didn't know how I was going to pack with Byrd standing around because of all the explaining I'd have to do. I also didn't want Byrd hanging around the apartment and working up an urge for some cocaine that wasn't there. So I said, "Let's go hang out on the street."
>
> We had been on the sidewalk about ten or fifteen minutes when a guy came up to us and started talking. He was dressed a little too well to be a regular street person, but he looked kind of desperate. I figured he was looking to buy some drugs. Then I realized that that was the solution to at least some of my problems. I took Byrd aside and said, "This guy looks like he's ready to buy big. What do you think

he'd pay for your stash?" Byrd looked reluctant, so I turned to the guy and said, "We can sell you about three ounces of coke, but we have to have a thousand for it." When the guy said, "Yeah," Byrd said, "Wait here" and ran inside the apartment building. A thousand was far more than the stuff was worth.

Byrd walked out onto the stoop with the whole stash in his hand in the ziplock bag he kept it in, and while he was walking down the steps, about ten feet away from me and the guy who wanted to buy, two uniforms appeared out of nowhere and arrested Byrd and me.

The "guy" turned out to be Officer D'Asconni, an undercover policeman who will testify to the conversation Nansen has described. The police laboratory reports that the bag contained 2.8 ounces of plaster and 0.007 ounces of cocaine. When you told Nansen about the laboratory report, he said the following:

I didn't think there was any coke in that bag. What they found must have been residue. I had used up every last bit of Byrd's stuff. I clearly remember looking at that empty bag after I had used it all and wondering how much plaster to put in it so that it would at least look like the coke Byrd had left behind. I certainly didn't see any point in scrubbing the bag with cleanser before I put the plaster in it.

Part 3. Will Nansen or Byrd be convicted of criminal sale of a controlled substance?

Criminal Code § 221(b)

As used in section 220, "controlled substance" includes any of the following: . . . cocaine. . . .

Criminal Code § 10

No person shall be convicted of a crime except on evidence proving guilt beyond a reasonable doubt.

Using your annotated outline of elements, decide whether each element can be proved beyond a reasonable doubt, and whether any exceptions are satisfied. Then predict whether Nansen or Byrd will be convicted.

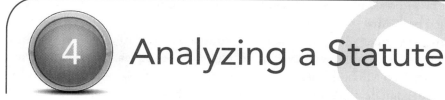

4 Analyzing a Statute

Elizabeth: Wait! You have to take me to shore. According to the Code of the Order of the Brethren. . . .

Captain Barbossa: First, your return to shore was not part of our negotiations nor our agreement so I "must" do nothing. And secondly, you must be a pirate for the pirate's code to apply and you're not. And thirdly, the code is more what you'd call "guidelines" than actual rules. Welcome aboard the Black Pearl, Miss Turner.

—*Pirates of the Caribbean: The Curse of the Black Pearl*

§ 4.1   A Statute's Structure

Statutes are different from anything else you have ever read. A statute does not describe or explain anything. It has no story or characters. Almost every word in a statute is part of a legal rule. And most of the rules in statutes are written in an abstract way because they apply to many people and different sets of circumstances. That is one of the reasons statutes can be so difficult to understand.

Statutes are groups of legal rules. A statute makes much more sense once you look for the individual rules and outline the statute to separate it into its parts. Lawyers call that process *statutory analysis*.

§ 4.2   Outlining a Statute

Lawyers deal with statutes and rules of one kind or another almost every day. While many law school courses introduce you to common law and case analysis, you might be surprised by how often statutes and rules come into play in solving your clients' legal problems.

Outlining a statute helps you break it down into its separate rules to figure out how each of them operates and how they work together. Once you learn how to analyze a statute this way, you will find it useful for the rest of your career. Whenever you read an unfamiliar and complicated statute or rule, use this method to help you figure out how it applies to your client's case.

§ 4.2.1   *Step 1:* Decide How Many Legal Rules Are in the Statute

As Chapter 2 explains, every legal rule is one of the following: mandatory, prohibitory, discretionary, or declaratory. Look carefully at the statute to identify what types of rules it contains. Look for specific requirements, prohibitions, permissions, and declarations. Those lead you into the individual rules within the statute.

In Step 1, do not worry about what the words actually mean. That comes later in Step 2. In Step 1, just try to separate one rule from another. List each rule separately so they can be outlined one by one.

For example, how many rules are in the following statute? (The answer might be one, or it might be more than one.)

> (a) Any person having an interest in land including the structures, buildings, and equipment attached to the land, including without limitation, wetlands, rivers, streams, ponds, lakes, and other bodies of water, who lawfully permits the public to use such land for recreational, conservation, scientific, educational, environmental, ecological, research, religious, or charitable purposes without imposing a charge or fee therefor, or who leases such land for said purposes to the commonwealth or any political subdivision thereof or to any nonprofit corporation, trust or association, shall not be liable for personal injuries or property damage sustained by such members of the public, including without limitation a minor, while on said land in the absence of wilful, wanton, or reckless conduct by such person.[1]

When you first read a statute like this one, it can look overwhelming. But you can bring order to the sea of words by using a step-by-step, analytical approach. Once the statute is outlined so you can see its inner rule structure, you can more easily apply it to a client's legal problem.

The statute quoted above has one very complicated rule, which includes one exception.

---

[1] MASS. GEN. LAWS ANN. ch. 21, § 17C (West 2010).

The rule protects an owner of land, wetlands, and improvements from civil liability to members of the public, including minors, for personal injury or property damage that occurs on the land. The rule applies in only two sets of circumstances: either the owner allows the public to use the property for certain purposes at no charge, or the owner leases the property to a state[2] or local government, or to a nonprofit corporation, for one of the same purposes. Even if all of the rule's elements are met, the statute provides an exception if certain kinds of conduct by the property owner cause injury to a member of the public on the land.

§ 4.2.2 *Step 2:* Analyze Each Rule to Determine What It Means

For each rule you have identified in the statute, use the method explained in Chapter 2 to take the rule apart to determine what it means. First, break the rule down into its parts (see § 2.4.1). Second, look at each of those small parts separately (§ 2.4.2). And third, put the rule back together in a way that helps you use it (§ 2.4.3).

Here, you have only one rule, but it has a complicated structure. To reveal the rule's structure, look for the connecting words between each sub-part of the rule and underline them. When you use this process to analyze the statute quoted in § 4.2.1, here is the outline you end up with. The connectors are underlined.

Elements

1. any person having an interest in land, <u>including</u>:[3]
   (a) attached structures, buildings, and equipment, <u>and</u>
   (b) wetlands, rivers, streams, ponds, lakes, and other bodies of water
2. who does <u>one</u> of the following:
   (a) lawfully permits the public to use the property without charge or fee <u>or</u>
   (b) leases the property to
       (i) the commonwealth or any political subdivision, <u>or</u>
       (ii) to a nonprofit corporation, trust, or association

---

[2] The statute's language refers to "commonwealth," the term used in Massachusetts, Pennsylvania, and Virginia law when referring to the state itself. The other states refer to their governments by the more familiar term "state" government.

[3] The first part of the statute applies to any person who has "an interest in land including the structures, buildings, and equipment attached to the land, including without limitation, wetlands, rivers, streams, ponds, lakes, and other bodies of water." From the first part of this wording, we know the person must have an interest in *land*. The rest of the wording following "including" simply *defines* exactly what the statute means by the term *land*. This is an example of an *inclusive* definition that gives a non-exhaustive list of examples. In this case, *land* is defined broadly to include any improvements ("structures, buildings, and equipment attached"), and any marshes, streams, and bodies of water on the land ("wetlands, rivers, streams, ponds, lakes, and other bodies of water"). This second element's two subparts are joined together with the word "and" to illustrate that the statutory term "land" has a more general meaning than a reader might otherwise give it.

3. for <u>one</u> of the following purposes:
   - (a) recreational,
   - (b) conservation,
   - (c) scientific,
   - (d) educational,
   - (e) environmental,
   - (f) ecological,
   - (g) research,
   - (h) religious, <u>or</u>
   - (i) charitable

Causal term

shall not

Result

be liable for personal injuries or property damage sustained by such members of the public (including minors) while on said land

Exception

in the absence of wilful, wanton, or reckless conduct by such person

Now look at the rule to see what it *does*. Although the causal term includes "shall not," this rule is a *declaration* that under certain circumstances, a landowner is not liable for personal injuries or property damage to those whom she allows to use the property for certain purposes listed in the statute.

The rule's elements require that for the owner to be absolved of liability, the property must be used for certain purposes (recreational, conservation, scientific, educational, environmental, ecological, research, religious, or charitable), and only if the land is open to the public at no charge, or if it is leased to nonprofit corporations, trusts, or associations for one of those purposes. If the land is used for some other purpose, or if it is leased to a private individual or a for-profit corporation, the statute does not protect the landowner from civil liability for injuries or property damage, even if a user is on the owner's land for one of the purposes listed in the rule.

The *exception* means that even if all the elements of the declaration are satisfied, the statute does not prevent civil liability by the landowner if her wilful, wanton, or reckless conduct causes harm to a member of the public. In other words, if the landowner's bad conduct (worse than simple negligence) causes the injury, she cannot avoid liability.

Now, let's apply the statute to a set of specific facts.

Assume that your client owns 160 acres of farmland surrounding a farm pond. This landowner allows children to swim in the pond for free whenever they wish. A neighbor's eight-year-old son drowns one afternoon while swimming in the pond without adult supervision. Is the landowner liable to the child's parents for wrongful death?

Applying the rules in the statute as outlined, we can easily figure out that the four elements of the declaration are met: The client *owns an interest in land* together with the farm *pond* (element 1). The landowner allows members of the *public*, including *minors*, to use the property *without charge* (element 2(a)) for swimming, which is a *recreational purpose* (element 3(a)). Without more, we can apply the causal term and the result to predict that the client will not be liable.

But wait. There's more. The statute includes an exception if the landowner's "wilful, wanton, or reckless conduct" caused the child's injury. As far as we know from the facts given in the hypothetical, the owner's *conduct* had nothing to do with the child's drowning. While the child's parents might argue that the owner was *reckless* by not supervising the swimming children, you might consider arguing that your client's failure to act was not reckless *conduct*. The outcome will turn on how the court interprets the statutory word *conduct*.

What do the terms "wilful, wanton, or reckless conduct" mean? To find out, you would look for definitions elsewhere in the statute. If the statute does not provide definitions for its terms, you would research how the cases in your jurisdiction have interpreted the words in the statute.

§ 4.2.3 The Two Steps Summarized

Here are the two steps (explained above) in outlining a statute:

Step 1 Decide how many legal rules are in the statute (§ 4.2.1).

Step 2 Analyze each rule in the statute to figure out what it means (§ 4.2.2):
    (a) Break the rule down into its parts (§ 2.4.1).
    (b) Look at each of the parts separately to figure out what it does (§ 2.4.2).
    (c) Put the rule back together in a way that helps you use it (§ 2.4.3).

Exercise 4-A. Uniform Commercial Code and Unconscionability

Outline Uniform Commercial Code § 2-302(1), which appears below.

If the court as a matter of law finds the contract or any term of the contract to have been unconscionable at the time it was made the court may refuse to enforce the contract or it may enforce the remainder of the contract without the unconscionable clause, or it may so limit the application of any unconscionable clause as to avoid any unconscionable result.

Exercise 4-B. Outlining a Dram Shop Liability Statute

Outline the Arkansas dram shop liability statutes, which appear below.

Ark. Code Ann. § 16-126-103. In cases where it has been proven that an alcoholic beverage retailer knowingly sold alcoholic beverages to a minor or sold under circumstances where such retailer reasonably should have known such purchaser was a minor, a civil jury may determine whether or not such knowing sale constituted the proximate cause of any injury to such minor, or to a third person, caused by such minor.

Ark. Code Ann. § 16-126-104. In cases where it has been proven that an alcoholic beverage retailer knowingly sold alcoholic beverages to a person who was clearly intoxicated at the time of such sale or sold under circumstances where the retailer reasonably should have known the person was clearly intoxicated at the time of the sale, a civil jury may determine whether or not the sale constitutes a proximate cause of any subsequent injury to other persons. For purposes of this section, a person is considered clearly intoxicated when the person is so obviously intoxicated to the extent that, at the time of such sale, he presents a clear danger to others. It shall be an affirmative defense to civil liability under this section that an alcoholic beverage retailer had a reasonable belief that the person was not clearly intoxicated at the time of such sale or that the person would not be operating a motor vehicle while in the impaired state.

Ark. Code Ann. § 16-126-105. Except in the knowing sale of alcohol to a minor or to a clearly intoxicated person, the General Assembly hereby finds and declares that the consumption of any alcoholic beverage, rather than the furnishing of any alcoholic beverage, is the proximate cause of injuries or property damage inflicted upon persons or property by a legally intoxicated person.

Exercise 4-C. Applying a Dram Shop Liability Statute

After outlining the statute in Exercise 4-B, use your outline to predict the outcome of the following case:

Joe Atkinson played basketball for his high school team. Even at the young age of 16, he was 6′4″. College basketball scouts had already offered him scholarships to play basketball, so he owned several college sweatshirts and baseball caps bearing college logos.

On the day of the accident, Joe rode his bike to a retail liquor store. Wearing a sweatshirt bearing the name of the local university, he went inside and paid cash for a six-pack of beer and a bottle of Mogen David 20/20 wine. The liquor store cashier did not ask Joe for identification before ringing up the sale.

In the parking lot behind the liquor store, Joe drank half the bottle of MD 20/20 and strapped the paper bag holding the six-pack onto the back of his bike. A few minutes later, on his way to a friend's house, he rode into an intersection against a red light. A motorcycle travelling through the intersection on a green light collided with his bike, knocking both Joe and the six-pack off the bike and onto the pavement. Joe was thrown from the bike, sustaining severe injuries.

Is the liquor store liable to Joe for his injuries? Does the store have any affirmative defense? If the case goes to trial, will the jury have discretion to decide whether the liquor store's sale of beer and wine to Joe was the proximate cause of his injuries? Using your outline, explain your answers.

5 Analyzing a Judicial Opinion

§ 5.1 The Contents of a Judicial Opinion

When law teachers refer to "a case," they mean a judicial opinion through which a court announces and explains a decision. While occasionally a judge issues a ruling or decision orally from the bench, almost all significant decisions in a case are reduced to writing and added to the court's record of the case in the form of a written opinion. If a party challenges the opinion on appeal, the reviewing court focuses its attention on the trial court's written opinion to evaluate its legal reasoning.

Most (but not all) judicial opinions typically include each of the following ten ingredients:

1. Case name and citation
2. Legal issue or issues to be decided by the court
3. Factual story (what happened *before* the lawsuit)
4. Procedural story (what happened *during* the lawsuit)
5. Legal rule or rules
6. Legal arguments by each side
7. Holding on each issue
8. Legal reasoning used to reach each holding
9. Dicta (statements not directly related to the holding or legal reasoning)
10. Disposition or Outcome (the court's order or remedy)

When you first look at a judicial opinion, it can seem intimidating and mysterious. Reading the opinion is a lot easier if you identify and label each of its ingredients as you read. That process is called *case analysis*—it breaks down the opinion into smaller chunks so you can understand its parts more easily. It also helps you see how the parts of a case are related to each other and produce the court's decision.

The *case name* is made up of the names of the plaintiff and defendant, separated by "v." for "versus." The case's *citation*, located at the top of the opinion just after the case name, includes the volume number of the reporter in which the opinion is published, the reporter's standard abbreviation, and the page number in that volume where the opinion begins. The citation often includes more than one reporter reference. It also includes, in a parenthetical, an abbreviation identifying the specific court that decided the case and the year it was decided. In legal research, every opinion published by a court can be located by using the case citation; thus it is essential to understand how to decipher one early in your first year of law school.

The court's opinion begins *after* the court's syllabus (if any) and after the headnotes, if you are reading the opinion as printed in a West reporter or on Lexis or Westlaw. Nearly always, the syllabus and headnotes are written not by the judges but by the court's staff or the publisher's editors. *Never* cite or quote a syllabus or a headnote. They are not parts of the judicial opinion. They are only research aids for lawyers who want to scan them quickly to get an idea about the facts and issues in the opinion before reading it in detail.

Just after the syllabus and headnotes, the last name of the judge who wrote the opinion generally appears. That is where the court's opinion begins, often with the *factual story*. Who are the parties? What did they and others do that led to the dispute? The court knows the facts of the story from what the parties alleged in their pleadings, or from the witnesses' testimony, or from other evidence the parties presented to the court. Depending on the procedural status of the case, it can be challenging to separate the factual story from the next part.

The *procedural story* is often described next. Lawyers and judges usually call this part of the opinion the *procedural history* or *procedural posture*. After the lawsuit was filed, what have the parties' lawyers done so far? What orders has the judge already issued in the case? For example, a motion to dismiss the complaint may have been denied. Or the court may have granted partial summary judgment on one of the claims. Or the jury may have reached a verdict following a trial.

A court might ascribe a procedural step to one of the parties ("The *defendant* moved to dismiss"). The court would mention that because the procedural step a lawyer takes to raise an issue determines how the court will decide it.

The court's opinion might also identify the *legal issue* or *issues* to be decided and the *legal arguments* made by each side. An <u>*issue*</u> *is a question the court must answer because the lawyers disagree about it*. Sometimes the issues are not stated explicitly, and you will need to read the opinion carefully to figure out what legal issues the court has resolved.

For each of the legal issues, the opinion will generally state or imply the *holding* as well as the *legal rule* the court has applied in reaching the holding. Many students find it difficult to distinguish the holding on an issue from the legal rule the court applied. While the legal rule is stated in the abstract, the holding is stated in terms of the specific facts of the case that the court considers in determining the result. For example:

legal rule	A sign posted in a public place that prominently displays a message prohibiting smoking applies to both tobacco products and e-cigarettes.
holding	A pedestrian on a city sidewalk who inhales and exhales water vapor from an e-cigarette does not violate a prohibition against smoking in a public place when the "No Smoking" sign is posted in the courtyard of a public community college building and displays its message in lowercase 14-point type.

A court also explains the *legal reasoning*—sometimes called the *rationale*—for its decision. The legal reasoning will show how the court applied the legal rule to the relevant facts of the case to reach its holding. The reasoning used to decide the legal issue in light of the facts becomes an important aspect of the case's precedential value in future cases. For example, the court may use either broad or narrow reasoning to decide the case. If the reasoning is broad and general, the case might set a precedent that will apply to many future cases, even with somewhat different facts. But if the court's reasoning is narrowly framed to apply to the specific facts of the case before it, lawyers will have more trouble convincing a court to follow the decision as precedent in a future case that involves significantly different facts.

The court's legal reasoning sometimes includes its interpretation of the legal rule in light of the *policy* the rule advances. A legal rule's policy includes the public purpose it serves or the goal it is designed to accomplish. For example, public safety is the policy reason supporting laws that prohibit driving while under the influence of alcohol. When a court sentences a drunk driver who injured a young pedestrian on her way home from school, it might explain that the policy reason for the rule prohibiting drunk driving is to prevent harm to innocent victims by alcohol-impaired drivers.

Somewhere in the opinion, the court might include *dicta*, which is a discussion of legal rules, policies, or reasoning that are not necessary to support a holding on a disputed issue in the case. Often a court will discuss matters outside the issues that are central to the decision it must make. If the court provides this kind of background discussion in an opinion, it is not considered binding precedent because it is not part of the legal analysis the court has actually used to resolve the *disputed* legal issue.

In determining the holding of a case, think carefully about the issues the parties have brought before the court for a decision. If the court includes ancillary information that is not part of the legal analysis required to resolve the parties' dispute, it is part of the court's *opinion*, but not its *holding* on the legal issues. It takes lots of practice to learn how to distinguish case holdings from dicta, but you will gain confidence in your ability to do so with experience and effort.

An opinion usually ends with the *disposition* or *outcome*. If the opinion is from a trial court, the outcome is typically an order granting or denying a motion of some kind. But if the opinion has been issued by an appellate court, like those commonly included in law school casebooks, the court may affirm or reverse the lower court's decision. An opinion may include many other kinds of dispositions or outcomes. Generally you can find the disposition of the case at the very end of the court's opinion.

In an appellate court, several judges decide the issues together as a group, usually by voting following a private conference to discuss the case. For example, if an appellate court has seven justices, which is common for the highest state appellate courts, a majority decision is reached if at least four judges agree on the outcome and the legal reasoning. One of the judges in the majority will write the opinion for the court and circulate it to the other judges for review so that it accurately reflects the group's reasoning.

What if one or more of the judges on an appellate court disagree with the majority? A judge who disagrees with some aspect of the decision may write a *dissenting opinion* explaining that the judge thinks the court reached the wrong result. Sometimes a judge will write a *concurring opinion* if the judge agrees with the disposition or outcome reached by the majority of the court but would have used different reasoning to get there. Concurring and dissenting opinions often shed light on the issues and the majority's legal reasoning, but they are never binding precedent. Only the majority opinion speaks with that authority.

Use care when reading cases to distinguish the reasoning of the court's majority opinion from language or reasoning in a dissent or concurrence. A minority opinion will begin with a reference to the name of the author, such as *Smith, J., dissenting*, whose separate opinion will follow. It is wrong to cite part of a dissenting or concurring judge's opinion as though it reflects the holding of the court. It never does.

§ 5.2   Reading Aggressively in Law School

Most people read passively most of the time—breezing through paragraphs, understanding some or most of what appears on the page, and guessing about the rest. You cannot succeed in law school that way.

In college, most assigned reading is in textbooks. Textbook authors try to write in a way that communicates efficiently to their audience, which is primarily undergraduate students. College textbooks are secondary sources of information because the authors have compiled and synthesized information from various other original sources in an organized, easy-to-understand way.

Law school is different. Law students read mostly judicial opinions and statutes, which are primary sources of law. A judge writing a judicial opinion does not wonder, "How should I write this opinion so a first-year law student can easily understand it?" A judge instead writes primarily for a professional audience of lawyers and judges— who quickly understand legal wording and concepts that may baffle law students. Nor are statutes and court rules written for the purpose of helping law students comprehend what they mean.

Several studies have shown that an important part of success in the first year of law school is learning to read analytically, the way experienced lawyers do.[1] Experienced lawyers do not glide from one sentence to the next, waiting for meaning to jump off the page. Instead, they read *aggressively*, dissecting the opinion as they go through it.

Aggressive reading is pulling apart, in your mind, what appears on the page and wringing meaning out of it. Consciously or unconsciously, aggressive readers engage in silent dialogs with themselves about what they are reading. They ask themselves questions, which they then try to answer. For example:

"Why is the judge emphasizing that fact?"
(A passive reader isn't curious.)

"What's preventing me from understanding that paragraph?"
(A passive reader ignores the paragraph without trying to figure it out.)

"What does that phrase mean? What must I do to find out?"
(A passive reader just skims over the phrase.)

Who is in charge—the reader or the page? For a passive reader, the page is in charge because the passive reader lets words hide their meaning. An aggressive reader refuses to allow words to do that. An aggressive reader interrogates until the words give up and confess what they mean.

Aggressive reading is one of the most important skills for success in law school. You can start learning how to read aggressively by carving up judicial opinions, looking for the ingredients listed at the beginning of this chapter, and marking each ingredient using highlighters or handwritten notes in the margin. Experienced lawyers identify the ingredients quickly and almost unconsciously. Because of their experience, they no longer need to brief cases or write notes in the margin. For example, they instantly recognize where the factual and procedural story ends and where the legal reasoning begins. They also interpret judicial opinions to find meaning at every step along the way.

You will learn much faster by looking up unfamiliar legal terminology in a good legal dictionary. Also look up any word or phrase that seems to be used in an unusual way. A legal *term of art* is a word or phrase that has a special meaning in the legal profession. Some terms of art obviously have a special meaning to lawyers, such as *stare decisis* and *res ipsa loquitur*. But other terms are deceptive. They look like words you have seen many times before, but they mean something different in the law. Examples include consideration, claim, damages, negligent, and relevant. While reading this way takes extra time at first, it will pay off many times over in the long run.

Claim= a harm the law will remedy

---

[1] *See* Ruth Ann McKinney, Reading Like a Lawyer: Time-Saving Strategies for Reading Law Like an Expert (2d ed. 2012); *see also* Leah M. Christensen, *Legal Reading and Success in Law School: An Empirical Study*, 30 Seattle U. L. Rev. 603 (2007); Laurel Currie Oates, *Beating the Odds: Reading Strategies of Law Students Admitted Through Alternative Admissions Programs*, 83 Iowa L. Rev. 139 (1997).

Before long, with practice, you will understand much more from reading judicial opinions, and they will take less time to read. But getting there will take time and discipline.

Exercise 5-A. Analyzing a Judicial Opinion

Read *Conti v. ASPCA*, reprinted below, and find each of the ingredients as they occur (if anywhere) in the court's opinion. Mark up the text generously, with highlighting and margin notes, so you can discuss your analysis in class. Look up every unfamiliar word in a legal dictionary, as well as every familiar word that is used in an unfamiliar way.

Conti v. ASPCA

353 N.Y.S.2d 288 (N.Y. City Civ. Ct. 1974)

Rodell, J.

Chester is a parrot. He is fourteen inches tall, with a green coat, yellow head and an orange streak on his wings. Red splashes cover his left shoulder. Chester is a show parrot, used by the defendant ASPCA in various educational exhibitions presented to groups of children.

On June 28, 1973, during an exhibition in Kings Point, New York, Chester flew the coop and found refuge in the tallest tree he could find. For seven hours the defendant sought to retrieve Chester. Ladders proved to be too short. Offers of food were steadfastly ignored. With the approach of darkness, search efforts were discontinued. A return to the area on the next morning revealed that Chester was gone.

On July 5, 1973 the plaintiff, who resides in Belle Harbor, Queens County, had occasion to see a green-hued parrot with a yellow head and red splashes seated in his backyard. His offer of food was eagerly accepted by the bird. This was repeated on three occasions each day for a period of two weeks. This display of human kindness was rewarded by the parrot's finally entering the plaintiff's home, where he was placed in a cage.

The next day, the plaintiff phoned the defendant ASPCA and requested advice as to the care of a parrot he had found. Thereupon the defendant sent two representatives to the plaintiff's home. Upon examination, they claimed that it was the missing parrot, Chester, and removed it from the plaintiff's home.

Upon refusal of the defendant ASPCA to return the bird, the plaintiff now brings this action in replevin.

[If the parrot] is in fact Chester, who is entitled to its ownership?

The plaintiff presented witnesses who testified that a parrot similar to the one in question was seen in the neighborhood prior to July 5, 1973. He further contended that a parrot could not fly the distance between Kings Point and Belle Harbor in so short a period of time, and therefore the bird in question was not in fact Chester.

The representatives of the defendant ASPCA were categorical in their testimony that the parrot was indeed Chester, that he was unique because of his size, color and habits. They claimed that Chester said "hello" and could dangle by his legs. During the entire trial the court had the parrot under close scrutiny, but at no time did it exhibit any of these characteristics. The court called upon the parrot to indicate by name or other mannerism an affinity to either of the claimed owners. Alas, the parrot stood mute.

Upon all the credible evidence the court does find as a fact that the parrot in question is indeed Chester and is the same parrot which escaped from the possession of the ASPCA on June 28, 1973.

The court must now deal with the plaintiff's position, that the ownership of the defendant was a qualified one and upon the parrot's escape, ownership passed to the first individual who captured it and placed it under his control.

The law is well settled that the true owner of lost property is entitled to the return thereof as against any person finding same.

This general rule is not applicable when the property lost is an animal. In such cases the court must inquire as to whether the animal was domesticated or ferae naturae (wild).

Where an animal is wild, its owner can only acquire a qualified right of property which is wholly lost when it escapes from its captor with no intention of returning.

Thus in *Mullett v. Bradley* (24 Misc. 695) an untrained and undomesticated sea lion escaped after being shipped from the west to the east coast. The sea lion escaped and was again captured in a fish pond off the New Jersey coast. The original owner sued the finder for its return. The court held that the sea lion was a wild animal (ferae naturae), and when it returned to its wild state, the original owner's property rights were extinguished.

In *Amory v. Flyn* (10 Johns. 102) plaintiff sought to recover geese of the wild variety which had strayed from the owner. In granting judgment to the plaintiff, the court pointed out that the geese had been tamed by the plaintiff and therefore were unable to regain their natural liberty. . . .

The court finds that Chester was a domesticated animal, subject to training and discipline. Thus the rule of ferae naturae does not prevail and the defendant as true owner is entitled to regain possession.

The court wishes to commend the plaintiff for his acts of kindness and compassion to the parrot during the period that it was lost and was gratified to receive the defendant's assurance that the first parrot available would be offered to the plaintiff for adoption.

Judgment for defendant dismissing the complaint without costs.

Exercise 5-B. Distinguishing Holdings, Dicta, Rules, and Reasoning

In a New Jersey case,[2] a truck driver sent text messages back and forth to a friend while he was driving home from work. Distracted by the text messages, he swerved across the center line and collided with an oncoming motorcycle, seriously injuring the motorcyclist, who sued both the truck driver and his friend for negligence. One of the legal issues was whether the sender of a text, here the friend, could be held liable to the injured motorcyclist when the text message distracted the truck driver and led him to collide with another vehicle.

The trial court granted summary judgment for the sender of the text, and the plaintiff motorcyclist appealed. The parties disagreed about whether a "remote texter" like the friend owed a legal duty to a third-party driver or occupant of a motor vehicle if the texter knew that the recipient truck driver would most likely read the text message while driving.

The following passages are edited from the appellate court's opinion. Determine whether each passage is a **holding**, **dicta**, a **legal rule**, or **legal reasoning**. Be prepared to explain your answers in class.

1. Whether a duty of care exists is generally a matter for a court to decide, not a jury.
2. A passenger who distracts a driver can be held liable for the passenger's own negligence in causing an accident. In other words, a passenger in a motor vehicle has a duty "not to interfere with the driver's operations."
3. The public interest requires fair measures to deter dangerous texting while driving.
4. Because the necessary evidence to prove breach of the remote texter's duty to the plaintiff is absent in this record, the trial court properly granted summary judgment for defendant.
5. In New Jersey, the use of a wireless telephone or electronic communication device by an operator of a moving motor vehicle on a public road or highway violates the Traffic Code, unless the telephone is a hands-free wireless telephone, or the electronic communication device is used hands-free.
6. One does not actually have to be the person who threw a rock to be liable for injury caused by the rock.
7. In a lawsuit alleging that a defendant is liable to a plaintiff because of the defendant's negligent conduct, the plaintiff must prove four things: (1) that the defendant owed a duty of care to the plaintiff, (2) that the defendant breached that duty, (3) that the breach was a proximate cause of the

---

[2] *Kubert v. Best*, 75 A.3d 1214 (N.J. Super. Ct. App. Div. 2013).

plaintiff's injuries, and (4) that the plaintiff suffered actual compensable injuries as a result. The plaintiff bears the burden of proving each of these four "core elements" of a negligence claim.

8. A person should not be held liable for sending a wireless transmission simply because some recipient might use his cell phone unlawfully and become distracted while driving. Whether by text, email, Twitter, or other means, the mere sending of a wireless transmission that unidentified drivers may receive and view is not enough to impose liability.

9. The sender of a text message can potentially be liable if an accident is caused by texting, but only if the sender knew or had special reason to know that the recipient would view the text while driving and thus be distracted.

10. The New Jersey public has learned the dangers of drinking and driving through a sustained campaign and enhanced criminal penalties and civil liability.

6 Reading a Case for Issues, Rules, and Determinative Facts

§ 6.1 How to Identify Issues, Rules, and Determinative Facts

Many facts are mentioned in an opinion just to provide background, continuity, or what journalists call "human interest." Other facts might be related to the court's thinking but are not crucial. The most important facts are the ones that *caused* the court to come to its decision.

This last group—the *essential* or *determinative facts*—are essential to the court's decision because they determined the outcome. If they had been different, the decision would have been different. They lead to the rule of the case—the rule of law for which the case stands as precedent—and discovering that rule is the most important goal of reading cases. Of course, when several issues are raised together in a case, the court must make several rulings, and an opinion may thus stand for several different rules.

The determinative facts can be identified by asking the following question: *If a particular fact had not happened, or if it had happened differently, would the court have made a different decision?* If so, it is one of the determinative facts. This can be illustrated with a decision that has nothing to do with law.

Suppose you are trying to find a place to live while attending law school. A rental agent has just shown you an apartment. The following are also true:

A. The apartment is located half a mile from the law school.
B. It is a studio apartment (one room plus a kitchenette and bathroom).
C. The building appears to be well maintained and safe.
D. The apartment is at the corner of the building, and windows on two sides provide ample light and ventilation.

   E. It is on the third floor, away from the street, and the neighbors do not appear to be disagreeable.

   F. The rent is $900 per month, furnished.

   G. You have a widowed aunt, with whom you get along well and who lives alone in a house 45 minutes by bus from the law school. She has offered to let you use the second floor of her house during the school year. The house and neighborhood are safe and quiet, and the living arrangements would be satisfactory to you.

   H. You have taken out loans to go to law school.

   I. You neither own nor have access to a car.

   J. Reliable local people have told you that you are not likely to find an apartment that is better, cheaper, or more convenient than the one you have just inspected.

Which facts are *essential* to your decision? For example, if the apartment had been two miles from the law school (rather than a half-mile), would your decision have been different? If the answer is no, fact A could not be determinative. It might be part of the factual mosaic and might explain why you looked at the apartment in the first place, but you would not base your decision on it.

The determinative facts, the issue, the holding, and the rule all depend on each other. In the apartment hypothetical, for example, if the issue were different—say, "How should I respond to an offer to join the American Automobile Association?"—the selection of determinative facts would also change. In fact, the only determinative one would be fact I: "You neither own nor have access to a car." You will often use what the court tells you about the issue or the holding to fill in what the court has not told you about the determinative facts, and vice versa.

Courts often do not explicitly state the issue, the holding, or the rule for which the case stands as precedent, and courts do not usually label the determinative facts as such. Whenever a court gives less than a full explanation, we have to use what is explicitly stated to pin down what is only implied.

If the court states the issue but does not identify the rule or specify which facts are determinative, you might discover the rule and the determinative facts by answering the following questions:

Who is suing whom over what series of events and to get what relief?
What issue does the court say it intends to decide?
How does the court decide that issue?
On what facts does the court rely in making that decision?
What rule does the court enforce?

Facts from a case can often be reformulated to be more general than the court described them. In the apartment hypothetical, for example, a generalized reformulation of fact G might be the following: "You have a rent-free alternative to the apartment, but the alternative would require 45 minutes of travel each way plus the expense of public transportation." Why would you generalize the facts in this way?

The generalized version of the facts can supply a guide to deciding later cases where the factual details are similar but not identical. For example, suppose a later case involves a person who is a member of the clergy in a religious organization that has given her a leave of absence to attend law school. Assume that she may continue to live rent-free in the satisfactory quarters the religious organization has provided, but getting to the law school would require walking for 15 minutes and then riding a subway for 30 minutes, at the same cost as a bus ride. Isn't this really the same situation as the aunt's house, but with different details? The generalized reformulation covers *both* sets of facts.

§ 6.2 Formulating a Narrow, Middling, or Broad Rule

When a court does not state a rule of the case, you might be able to formulate the rule by converting the determinative facts into elements of a rule. Often, you can interpret the determinative facts narrowly (specifically) or broadly (generically). Notice how different formulations of a rule can be extracted from the apartment example. If the student decides to stay with the aunt, a narrow rule formulation might be the following:

> A law student who has a choice between renting an apartment and living in the second floor of an aunt's house should choose the latter when the student has had to borrow money to go to law school and when the apartment's rent is $900 per month but the aunt's second floor costs nothing except for bus fares.

Because this rule is limited to the specific facts in the hypothetical, it can directly govern only a tiny number of future decisions, if any at all. For example, it will not directly govern the member of the clergy described above.

Although the clergy member might be able to reason by analogy from the narrow rule, she would not be directly governed by it. Analogy is indirect. A broader rule would directly govern *both* situations:

> A student on a tight budget should not pay rent when a nearly free alternative is available.

An even more general formulation would govern an even wider circle of applications:

> A person with limited funds should not lease property when there is a satisfactory and nearly free alternative.

The following, however, is so broad as to be meaningless:

> A person should not spend money unnecessarily.

Exercise 6-A. Isolating Determinative Facts and Formulating a Rule

Part 1. Read *Conti v. ASPCA* (Exercise 5-A on page 38). Identify the determinative facts, and summarize them in one paragraph.

Part 2. After identifying the determinative facts in *Conti v. ASPCA*, write a narrow version of the rule as well as a broad version of the rule for which the case stands.

Exercise 6-B. The Cow and the Swimming Pool

A farmer's swimming pool was damaged when one of his cows, a 300-pound heifer—which everyone describes as an ordinary and gentle cow accustomed to life outside a barn—strayed from the pasture where she was grazing. She wandered into the farmer's unfenced yard and stepped on the canvas cover over the farmer's swimming pool. The cow fell through, damaging the pool cover and the pool itself. The farmer filed a claim under his homeowner's insurance policy, seeking reimbursement for the repair costs. The insurer denied the claim and cited the following provision from the insurance policy, particularly the words underlined below:

> This policy does not insure against loss from wear and tear; marring or scratchings; deterioration; inherent vice; latent defect; mechanical breakdown; rust; mold; wet or dry rot; contamination; smog; smoke from agricultural smudging or industrial operations; settling, cracking, shrinkage, bulging or expansion of pavements, patios, foundations, walls, floor, roofs or ceilings; birds, vermin, rodents, insects or <u>domestic animals</u> . . . .[1]

Part 1. Assume you represent the farmer in a suit against the insurer. You will argue that the exclusion does not apply here. Formulate a rule from *Conti v. ASPCA* (Exercise 5-A on page 38) that supports that argument.

Part 2. Now assume you are on the other side of the case, representing the insurer. Formulate a rule from *Conti v. ASPCA* that supports an argument that the policy does exclude coverage in the farmer's case.

---

[1] *Smith v. State Farm Fire & Cas. Co.*, 381 So. 2d 913, 914 (La. Ct. App. 1980).

Policy and Why Courts Care about It

7

In the Bookstore

Time: August.
Place: the campus bookstore.
Student approaches the cashier counter, carrying a big pile of books.
Behind the counter stands a store clerk.

Student: I'd like to return these books.
Clerk: Do you have a receipt?
Student: No.
Clerk: *[points to sign]* The rule is *[reading sign aloud]* "No returns without a receipt."
Student: *[frustrated]* But I just bought them.
Clerk: *[looks at sign]* It doesn't say, "except when you just bought them."
Student: But I just bought them.
Clerk: Maybe I should rephrase the rule: "If you have a receipt, you may return the books." You don't have a receipt, so you may not return the books. Sorry.
Student: Look, I bought them half an hour ago. When I got back to my dorm room, there was an email from the registrar saying they switched me into a different section, where the teachers are different, and those teachers assigned different books. I don't have any choice in this. I'm a first-year law student, and all the courses are required. They assign me to a section. I need completely different books for five courses.
Clerk: *[in a snide tone]* Did your dog eat your receipt?
Student: No. I just can't find it. Don't you ever lose things?
Clerk: Not within a half hour. A rule's a rule. Sorry.

Student: But every rule has a purpose. What's the purpose of this rule?

Clerk: To protect the store from people who bring in books they found or stole or bought more cheaply elsewhere. A rule's a rule.

Student: But a rule should be applied in a way that's consistent with the rule's purpose. I can prove that I didn't find or steal them or buy them more cheaply elsewhere. I bought them half an hour ago from that clerk over there.

Second Clerk: *[looks up]* I did ring up a sale to you. I don't remember what books you bought. I just scan the bar codes. Bring them over here and let's see if my register recorded the book titles.

[The two clerks compare the books to the register's record and explain to a supervisor who has wandered over.]

Supervisor: *[to student]* We'll take all these books back and give you credit toward the books you need to buy now. The only reason we can do this is because we're confident that in these circumstances you actually did buy these books from us. Don't assume in the future that you can return things without a receipt.

§ 7.1   What Is Policy?

// the purpose of the rule

Notice the method through which the student won this argument. The student showed store employees that the purpose of the rule could be accomplished without enforcing the rule in the most obvious way. Instead, the store enforced the rule in a novel way—by treating the second clerk's memory and the store's internal records together as the equivalent of a receipt. If the student had not been able to persuade store employees to interpret their rule in light of its purpose, the student would have lost the argument.

Every rule of law, whether found in a statute or a case, has a purpose—a reason for being. That purpose is called the rule's *policy* or the *policy behind the rule*. Some policies are obvious. Why is it illegal to drive while intoxicated? You probably already know the answer.

Other policies are more complicated, and understanding them requires some special knowledge. Why is your internet service provider (ISP) not liable for defamation if you send email messages to a million people accusing Britney Spears of stealing another singer's style? (She did *not* do that.) An ISP provides access to the internet. Every email message is sent through the sender's ISP and received through the recipient's ISP. And every website is accessible through the website owner's ISP.

Congress enacted a statute exempting ISPs from liability for publishing defamatory material. If every ISP had to read and screen every email message that a website transmitted or made accessible through its equipment, the internet would suddenly become very slow and very expensive to use. And ISPs often would not be able to tell what is defamatory and what is not.

Policy also exists in a wider sense—not tied to one specific rule. A broad policy might lead the law to adopt many separate rules. For example, courts everywhere like solutions that are easily enforceable, promote clarity in the law, are not needlessly complex, and do not allow true wrongdoers to profit from illegal acts.

Other policy considerations may differ from state to state. In many Sunbelt states, for example, public policy favors development of land by building homes and businesses, while in states like Vermont policy prefers preservation of the environment and agriculture. Some states favor providing tort remedies even if additional lawsuits slow down courts, although in others the reverse is true.

§ 7.2   Why Courts Care about Policy

It is revolting to have no better reason for a rule of law than that so it was laid down in the time of Henry IV. It is still more revolting if the grounds upon which it was laid down have vanished long since, and the rule simply persists from blind imitation of the past.

—*Justice Oliver Wendell Holmes*

Law is not just rules. It is rules *plus* their policies. To understand a rule, it is not enough to know its elements, results, and exceptions. You also need to know what the law is trying to accomplish through the rule.

Whenever there is doubt about what a rule means or how it should be applied, the rule's purpose provides one solution to the problem. If you are not sure what a rule *means,* choose the meaning that is most consistent with its purpose. If you are not sure *how to apply* the rule, apply it in whatever way is most consistent with its purpose. If you know the rule but not its purpose, you do not really know what to do with the rule. And if rules did not have policies, they could be arbitrary and might cause more harm than good.

Policy is also important in a different context. When the law does not yet have a rule on a given subject and courts or legislators have to decide what rule to adopt, they consider the policies the law already has for other rules, and they try to choose a rule that achieves those policies. Policy thus is valuable not only in interpreting and enforcing results consistent with existing rules, but also in adopting of new rules.

Policy as an extra layer of analysis might seem like a burden. "Why can't we just have rules and stop there?" you might ask. We cannot stop there because lawyers and judges will always have questions about what a rule means and how to apply it, and we have to know a rule's policy to resolve those questions. And you can understand and write about law more easily and more effectively—in this course and on exams in other courses—if you frequently ask yourself questions like, "What is the law trying to accomplish through this rule?" and "Why does this rule exist?"

Every rule of law makes more sense when we understand why it exists.

§ 7.3 How to Recognize Policy in a Judicial Opinion

A rule itself does not tell you its policy. You have to look in the judicial decisions and statutes that are the sources of most law, or in commentaries on the law, such as law review articles. Sometimes, courts openly say something like "The policy behind this rule is . . . ." But more often a court will discuss policy without calling it policy—for example, by explaining what would happen if the rule did not exist. The rule's purpose is to prevent that from happening. With some practice, you will be able to spot a policy discussion in a judicial decision—and write about it in this course.

In the case below, a court used policy to decide whether to adopt a new rule.

Ash v. New York University Dental Center
564 N.Y.S.2d 308 (App. Div. 1st Dep't 1990)

Ellerin, J.

The issue before us in this dental malpractice action is the validity of an agreement that plaintiff Arthur Ash was required to sign as a precondition to obtaining treatment at defendant New York University Dental Center which prospectively exculpated the various defendants from any liability for negligence in treating plaintiff.

Plaintiff seeks to recover for injuries suffered as a result of his aspiration, during dental treatment, of two dental crowns, which became lodged in his right lung and required surgical removal. Plaintiff [needed] substantial dental work which would cost over $6,000[, and he therefore sought treatment at the clinic associated with the defendant's dentistry school], where the work could be done [by dentistry students under supervision] for $3,000. . . .

When plaintiff arrived at the clinic . . . , he was required to sign a form containing the following provision: "In consideration of the reduced rates given to me by New York University, and in recognition of the risks inherent in a clinical program involving treatment by students, I hereby release and agree to save harmless New York University, its trustees, doctors, employees and students from any and all liability, including liability for its and their negligence, arising out of or in connection with any personal injuries (including death) or other damages of any kind which I may sustain while on its premises or as a result of any treatment at its Dental Center or infirmaries."

[P]laintiff testified that he believed the signing of this form was an insignificant registration procedure and he was never told, nor did he imagine, that he was relinquishing any of his legal rights. . . .

. . . There is no decision of the Court of Appeals [the state's highest court] that expressly deals with this precise issue. . . .

It is clear that the State's substantial interest in protecting the welfare of all of its citizens, irrespective of economic status, extends to ensuring that they be provided with health care in a safe and professional manner. Toward that end, the State carefully regulates the licensing of physicians and other health care professionals and monitors such activities to prevent untoward consequences to the public from "the ministrations of incompetent, incapable, ignorant persons." A similar concern for the enforcement of established minimum standards of professional care provides the underlying rationale for a cause of action for malpractice in favor of those who have been subjected to substandard care. Unquestionably public clinics such as defendant, which are used primarily by those who are unable to pay the rapidly escalating fees for private medical and dental care, play an important role in delivery of such care to those who may not otherwise be able to obtain it. However, important as this role is, it cannot serve as a basis for excusing such providers from complying with those minimum professional standards of care which the State has seen fit to establish. It is the very importance of such clinics to the people who use them that would create an invidious result if the exculpatory clause in issue were upheld—i.e., a de facto system in which the medical services received by the less affluent are permitted to be governed by lesser minimal standards of care and skill than that received by other segments of society.

There is, of course, no public policy against allowing patients of such clinics to agree to fewer amenities, longer waits or greater inconvenience in exchange for lower prices than they would pay elsewhere. Nor is there any public policy against such a clinic limiting itself to certain types of care or refusing to perform certain procedures. There cannot, however, be any justification for a policy which sanctions an agreement which negates the minimal standards of professional care which have been carefully forged by State regulations and imposed by law. . . .

The fact that defendant New York University Dental Center is a clinical program associated with an educational institution does not alter this conclusion. Defendant, of course, has a substantial interest in providing its students with clinical experience as part of their education. However, this interest cannot negate the State's overriding concern in seeing that defendants fulfill their equally important obligation to their patients. That obligation includes ensuring that students are sufficiently prepared and supervised so that the treatment which is provided to human patients is at least at the minimally acceptable reasonable level of skill and care. If defendants cannot fulfill this obligation, they must not hold themselves out as being providers of dental care. . . .

Other jurisdictions which have addressed attempts by health care professionals to relieve themselves of liability, particularly to those who stand in a disadvantageous bargaining position, have arrived at a conclusion similar to the one we have reached.

[For example, i]n *Emory Univ. v. Porubiansky* ... the Supreme Court of Georgia refused to enforce a very similar contract in a setting identical to the one herein, stating: "A contract between a medical practitioner and patient must be examined in light of the strong policy of the state to protect the health of its citizens and to regulate those professionals that it licenses. ..."

This court was able to create new law only because existing law had a gap in it. How do we know there is a gap? The fifth paragraph tells us: "There is no decision of the Court of Appeals [the state's highest court] that expressly deals with this precise issue." The court used policy as a guide in filling that gap.

Exercise 7-A. A Cell Phone in Class

This rule appears in a course syllabus:

A student who uses any form of electronic communication during class will be counted as absent for the entire class.

Before class, a student set his cell phone to vibrate. During class, a friend in the parking lot sent him a text message saying the student's car was being stolen. The teacher spotted the student reading the message and marked him as absent. The student protested.

Under this rule as written, who was right? Who *should* be right? How would policy considerations affect your answers?

8 Selecting the Right Authority

This chapter explains how to select the right legal authorities for your legal issues. The next two chapters explain how to use the two most important kinds of authority: statutes (Chapter 9) and cases (Chapter 10).

In reading this chapter, remember that the federal government and each state have separate bodies of law, which in most respects are independent of each other. Before selecting legal authorities to use in your case, your first step is to answer the following questions:

- What *law* applies: federal or state? If state law applies, which one?
- Which *kind of court* will decide your issue: federal or state? If state, which one?
- What *level of court* will decide the issue: trial court, intermediate appellate court, or the highest appellate court?

Keep these questions in mind as you read this chapter.

§ 8.1   The Hierarchy of Authority

Primary authority is the law itself. Its words are the words of the law. Cases and statutes are the primary authorities most often used in legal reasoning. Others are constitutions, court rules, and administrative regulations. Primary authority is the product of a legislature, a court, or some other government entity empowered to make or determine law.

Secondary authority is commentary that explains the law but is not the law itself. Examples are law review articles, treatises, and other reference materials written by legal scholars. Secondary authority is only a summary, description, or analysis of what a private person or group believes the law is (or should be). The author of secondary authority may know a lot about the law but lacks the power to create law itself.

From its name, you might think primary authority is always the best authority. While that is often true, identifying the best legal authority for resolving a particular dispute depends on the source of the primary authority and its relationship to the nature of the legal issue and the jurisdiction of the court that will decide it.

Courts use a complicated set of preferences—called the *hierarchy of authority*—to determine which authority they will follow. You can follow the hierarchy of authority more easily if you visualize it this way:

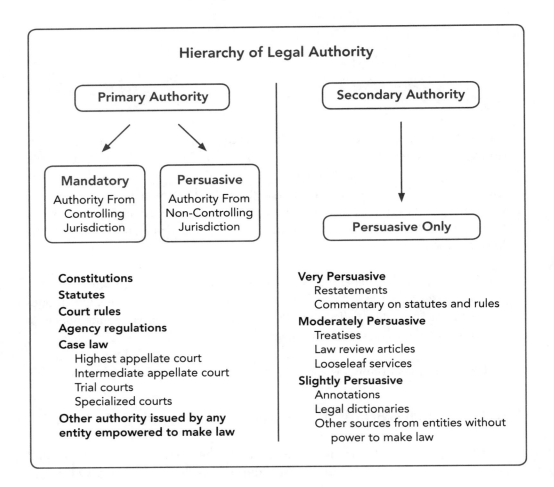

§ 8.1.1 Primary Authority

Primary authority (on the left side of the diagram above) is the law itself—constitutions, statutes, cases, rules, and regulations. But not all primary authority is *mandatory authority* that your court *must* follow. Primary authority is *mandatory* only if issued by the federal or state government whose law controls the legal question.

Mandatory primary authority includes case precedents issued by appellate courts that have jurisdiction over the trial court that will decide the question. A trial court must follow those precedents because those courts have power to affirm or reverse the decision if the losing party challenges it on appeal.

For either state or federal courts, some mandatory primary authority outranks other mandatory primary authority. For example, a constitution prevails over all other forms of primary authority from the same jurisdiction. The reason is that a constitution is the fundamental law creating a government in the first place. If a state legislature enacts a statute that is inconsistent with the state or federal constitution, a court can strike it down. Similarly, a court's power to create and reinterpret common law in its judicial decisions is subservient to the constitution and statutes of the government of which that court is a part.

A statute trumps an administrative regulation from an agency in the same jurisdiction because statutes give administrative agencies the power to adopt regulations. In federal courts, federal statutes trump court rules because the authority of nearly all federal courts is a matter of federal statutory law, except the U.S. Supreme Court, which is created by the U.S. Constitution.[1]

Statutes generally control over case law because a legislature's power to enact new law or amend existing law prevails over the courts' power to interpret or reinterpret statutes and common law. And case law from appellate courts prevails over inconsistent case law from lower courts.

What happens if two mandatory authorities of the same rank are inconsistent with each other—for example, what if one state statute preserves a cause of action for alienation of affection, while another statute from the same state abolishes it? The court will first try to *reconcile* the two inconsistent authorities by applying interpretive canons. (See Chapter 9.) If they cannot be reconciled, dates matter in deciding which one controls. A more recently enacted statute generally prevails over an older one. Similarly, a more recent case prevails over an earlier one issued by the same court.

For precedent to be mandatory in a trial court, the precedent must have been made by an appellate court to which the trial court's decision could be appealed. A federal circuit is made up of the U.S. Court of Appeals for that circuit and the federal district courts that are geographically within the circuit.[2] A party can appeal a decision of a federal district court in that circuit to the court of appeals in the same circuit.

For example, the U.S. Court of Appeals for the Third Circuit decides appeals from federal trial courts in Delaware, New Jersey, and Pennsylvania. The U.S. Court of Appeals for the Sixth Circuit hears appeals from federal trial courts in Kentucky,

---

[1] U.S. Const. art. III, § 1.
[2] You can find a map of the federal circuits in your legal research textbook or materials, or in the front pages of any volume of the Federal Reporter, Third Series (F.3d). Or you can download a map online from http://www.uscourts.gov/uscourts/images/CircuitMap.pdf showing the geographic boundaries of each circuit and the federal districts within them.

Michigan, Ohio, and Tennessee. A Sixth Circuit opinion is mandatory authority in a U.S. District Court in Ohio because the Sixth Circuit can reverse that trial court's decision on appeal. The same Sixth Circuit opinion is mandatory primary authority for issues decided by other panels of the Sixth Circuit, which is bound by its own prior decisions.

But that same Sixth Circuit opinion is merely persuasive primary authority to a U.S. District Court in Pennsylvania. That is because the Third Circuit—not the Sixth—hears appeals from federal trial courts in Pennsylvania. And that opinion is only persuasive primary authority in the Third Circuit and in the U.S. Supreme Court, which is superior to all federal circuit courts.

On the other hand, U.S. Supreme Court decisions are mandatory primary authority on issues of federal law in every court, including state courts. That is because the Supreme Court has the power to reverse a decision by any court on any issue of federal law. But for state courts, U.S. Supreme Court decisions are not mandatory on issues of state law. For state law issues, the final authority is the state's highest court.

As you will learn in the Civil Procedure course, federal courts have diversity jurisdiction over state law issues when the parties are citizens of different states. In such a case, a federal trial court must also follow primary authority issued by the state in question—including state statutes and state appellate court precedents governing that state law issue. As a general rule, federal law governs over state law when the two are inconsistent.[3] But when a federal court decides an *issue of state law*, the federal court must follow the law of that state. Similarly, state courts sometimes decide issues of federal law. When they do, the state court must follow federal statutes and case law issued by federal courts interpreting those statutes.

A state trial court sometimes decides issues governed by the law of a different state. This could happen, for example, if a car accident occurs in Wyoming but the lawsuit is brought in Montana, perhaps because the defendant lives there. The Montana court must apply Wyoming law because the accident occurred in Wyoming. For that lawsuit, Wyoming statutes and cases will be mandatory authority in a Montana court.

§ 8.1.2 Applying the Hierarchy of Primary Authority

Mandatory primary authority. To apply some of these principles, let's try an example. Assume you represent a client who lives in Madison, Wisconsin, while attending the university there. While she was attending a Blue Man Group performance in Chicago, Illinois, someone stole her car from the parking lot. Your client has since learned from her Facebook friends that a student from Knox College

---

[3] U.S. Const. art. VI, cl. 2.

in Galesburg, Illinois, was spotted driving her car. She has asked you to sue to recover the car or its fair market value. How do you find the best authority for predicting the outcome?

Remember the questions listed at the beginning of this chapter:

- What *law* applies: federal or state? If state law applies, which one?

In a civil case for return of a stolen car, or for compensatory damages for the value of the stolen car, *state tort law* will govern the issues. But the tort law of which state? Because the car was stolen in Chicago, the claim arose there, and therefore Illinois tort law will most likely control the issue.

- Which *kind of court* will decide your issue: federal or state? If state, which one?

We know that the client lives in Wisconsin, and the theft occurred in Illinois. Civil procedure rules give her a choice where she files suit. Assuming the defendant who stole the car lives in Illinois, a federal court there would have diversity jurisdiction, but only if the amount at issue exceeds the jurisdictional threshold, currently $75,000.[4] You would need to know whether the stolen car is a brand new Porsche or a 1995 Dodge Neon. Unless the car's fair market value exceeds the jurisdictional threshold for diversity jurisdiction in federal court, your client most likely will sue in state court in Illinois, where the car was stolen.

- What *level of court* will decide the issue: trial court, intermediate appellate court, or the highest appellate court?

No matter where the plaintiff files her lawsuit, we know it will be in a trial court. Which primary authorities are best in that trial court? For issues of Illinois tort law, common law (found in case law) generally controls. Whether the plaintiff sues in a Wisconsin or an Illinois trial court, the court will be required to follow appellate court decisions interpreting the tort law of Illinois, where the car was stolen. If Illinois has enacted any statutes governing civil remedies for car theft, the trial court would be required to follow that mandatory primary authority as well.

What if the car is a brand new Porsche 911 worth $90,000, which exceeds the $75,000 threshold for federal diversity jurisdiction? Then the plaintiff might decide to file suit in a federal district court. Would that change the best primary authority? No, it would not. Whether your client sues in federal or state court, the car theft involves the same issue of Illinois tort law. A federal court deciding a state law issue must follow

---

[4] 28 U.S.C. § 1332(a)(1) (2012).

state law, just the same as if a state court were to decide the issue. Here, that includes relevant Illinois cases and statutes—the same mandatory authority that would govern a state trial court.

But if a federal trial court rules against your client, the U.S. Court of Appeals for the Seventh Circuit would decide the appeal. Does that mean a Seventh Circuit decision would be mandatory authority for the federal trial court? Generally no, because a federal appellate court never has the final say over issues of state law. A Seventh Circuit decision on an issue of Illinois tort law would be only persuasive primary authority, even for a federal trial court in the same circuit. The reasons for this complicated relationship between state law and federal courts are addressed in the Civil Procedure course, and are beyond the scope of this introduction to primary authority.

Nonmandatory primary authority. *Persuasive primary authority* may or may not be followed, at the court's election. For that reason, it is *nonmandatory*. Persuasive primary authority usually comes from a court that lacks the power to make law for the jurisdiction whose law controls the issue. In the example we just discussed, the trial court might cite a Michigan appellate court case involving a car theft from a concert parking lot in Ohio. That case is *primary* authority because a Michigan appellate court can create Michigan common law. But it would not be *mandatory* because an issue of Illinois tort law is not controlled by either Michigan or Ohio law. The Michigan appellate case qualifies only as *persuasive primary authority* in this example because it was issued by a court that has no power to make Illinois law.

Just how persuasive is nonmandatory primary authority? If a court opinion is not mandatory authority, its persuasive value depends on several factors. One of the most important is how *factually analogous* the persuasive authority is compared to your case. The more factually similar the Michigan appellate court case is to the facts of your case, the more persuasive it will be for the trial court resolving your client's issue.

Other important factors are when the nonmandatory primary authority was decided, and whether it reflects a prevailing trend in the law. A trial court will be more persuaded by another jurisdiction's case if it has been issued recently, or if it reflects a modern trend in developing the law.

Let's try another example. Suppose Wyoming law controls. And suppose the issue involves Wyoming common law, and no Wyoming statute has changed it. Wyoming Supreme Court decisions would be mandatory primary authority for this issue. But suppose those cases, for one reason or another, do not clearly settle the issue, which means there is a gap in Wyoming law.

To fill the gap in Wyoming law, the state trial court might consider persuasive authority from other state supreme courts that have decided the same common law issue. Those cases are primary authority because courts have the power to make law in their own states. But in Wyoming, they are only persuasive (nonmandatory) because Wyoming courts are not required to obey decisions from other state courts.

A Wyoming court might follow the reasoning of a South Carolina court on a similar common law issue, but only if the Wyoming court is *persuaded* that the South Carolina court's reasoning does a good job of filling a gap in Wyoming law. If the Wyoming court concludes that the other state court's opinion is not very helpful for some reason, it can disregard that case. While it is still persuasive primary authority, it is nonmandatory because the Wyoming court has a choice whether to follow it or not.

Section 8.3 explains more about how you can use nonmandatory primary authority. But first, we need to show how primary authority differs from secondary authority. Before reading the next subsection, look back at the diagram on page 54 to review what you have already learned about primary authority.

§ 8.1.3   Secondary Authority

As we explained in § 8.1, secondary authority explains the law but is not the law itself. For that reason, mandatory authority always trumps secondary authority. But in the hierarchy of authority, persuasive (nonmandatory) primary authority and secondary authority start out approximately equal in value. A court can either follow them or ignore them.

The most significant categories of secondary authority are restatements, which are formulations of the common law issued by the American Law Institute; treatises written by scholars; and articles and similar material published in law reviews and other periodicals.

Restatements are the most influential and persuasive form of secondary authority. Since 1923, the American Law Institute has commissioned scholars to draft restatements of the common law of contracts, property, torts, and several other fields. The purpose of a restatement is to express scholarly consensus about the common law. When a restatement is no longer up-to-date, a second or third version supersedes it. Thus, the Restatement (Third) of Torts will soon replace the Restatement (Second) of Torts, finalized in the late 1970s. A restatement consists of a series of black-letter rules organized into sections, followed by commentary and illustrations. They are often cited by courts when deciding novel issues of state common law.

The persuasive value of a *scholarly treatise* depends on the author's reputation and whether the treatise has been kept up to date. Some outstanding treatises have been written by Wigmore (on evidence), Corbin (on contracts), Williston (on contracts), Prosser and Keeton (on torts), and Sutherland (on statutory interpretation). Some treatises are multivolume works, and some double as student hornbooks. In your law library, you will find subject-matter specific treatises that comprehensively address many legal issues in detail. If you have a gap in the law, a treatise can reveal how other courts have handled the issue, and it can lead you to persuasive primary authority from other states.

Law reviews print two kinds of material: articles (written by scholars, judges, and practitioners), and comments and notes (written by students). If an article is especially thorough and insightful, or is authored by a respected scholar, it may influence a court and might therefore be worth citing. Most articles, however, do not fit that description. The fact that an article has been published does not necessarily mean that it is influential. For example, a student comment or note influences a court in only the most unusual circumstances. But even when law review material would not influence a court, it might stimulate your thinking about the legal issue, and its footnotes can help you find cases, statutes, and other primary authority.

Legal dictionaries, encyclopedias, digests, and annotations are also secondary authorities, but generally they are not very persuasive.[5] Their true function is to provide researchers with background information and to help them find primary authority. Dictionaries are often helpful in defining statutory terms, and courts regularly cite *Black's Law Dictionary* in particular to reveal the legal meaning of undefined statutory terms. The other kinds of less persuasive secondary authority collect, analyze, and summarize case law on specific topics or issues. Use them to find primary authority relevant to your issue, and carefully analyze those authorities to find the ones that are most persuasive for your legal issue.

§ 8.2 How Courts Use Dicta

When citing to a court's opinion as primary authority, only the holding and the legal reasoning necessary to support it (including rules of law) are mandatory authority in future cases. Comments in an opinion that go beyond what is needed to state and support the court's holding are *obiter dicta*—a Latin term that means words said in passing.[6] Because *dicta* is not a holding or support for a holding, it cannot be mandatory authority.

Why do courts bother to write dicta in the first place? Often, dicta adds clarity to an opinion. Here are some examples:

- A court may want to make clear what the case is *not*: "If the plaintiff had presented evidence of injury to his reputation, he might be entitled to damages." But because that evidence was not before the court, whatever the court says about it is dicta, not a holding.

---

[5] Years ago, lawyers and judges cited legal encyclopedias and dictionaries more often because genuine legal authority was more difficult to find, especially in newer or smaller states. You will still see that done occasionally in older opinions printed in your casebooks, and in some recent opinions from states lacking centuries of precedent. But generally legal encyclopedias and annotations are no longer considered acceptable or persuasive sources to cite as secondary authority.

[6] Although in Latin *dictum* is the singular and *dicta* is the plural, *dictum* is falling into disuse among lawyers and judges. More often, *dicta* is used for both the singular and the plural forms.

- The court may want to illustrate possible ways to generalize its decision to analogous situations: "When a minor is at the controls of a power boat—or for that matter a car or an airplane—she is subject to the standard of care expected of a reasonable adult." If the quote comes from a case dealing with injuries caused by a power boat when operated by a minor, it is part of the holding because it defines the legal standard for liability in that case. But the statement is merely dicta for similar cases involving cars and airplanes operated by minors.

- The court may make a suggestion to a lower court for proceedings on remand: "Although the parties have not appealed the issue of punitive damages, that issue will inevitably arise on retrial. We believe it necessary to point out that punitive damages are available only if the plaintiff proves that the defendant acted with malice." Because the issue of punitive damages was not disputed in this appeal, whatever the court says about the elements of proof on remand is merely dicta (although the trial court is highly likely to follow that dicta on remand).

Sometimes dicta is unintended. A judge might get carried away with extravagant wording in an opinion, or might formulate the issue, the rule, or the determinative facts in a way that makes it unclear whether a particular comment is within the scope of the holding. Sometimes the holding is difficult to distinguish from dicta. Even when a judge carefully defines the issue, rule, and determinative facts, readers can reasonably disagree whether a particular statement in an opinion is necessary to the resolution of the issue and therefore part of the holding.

Sometimes a court decision gives two separate and independent grounds for a holding, either of which is sufficient by itself to support the result. When that happens, neither alternative ground is dicta. Both were the legal basis of the decision, even if only one was necessary to support it. If the decision is challenged on appeal, the appellate court will affirm if either ground supports the trial court's result.

It is not wrong to refer to dicta in your legal analysis, but it is wrong to use it inappropriately. Dicta can never take the place of a holding, and it is inappropriate to treat it as though it could. When you refer to dicta, identify it that way. For example: "The court said in dicta that the same standard of care would apply to minors who operate cars and airplanes." A holding is introduced differently: "The court held that a minor who takes the controls of a power boat is subject to the same standard of care expected of a reasonable adult." Or: "The court decided that the minor was liable to the injured passenger." Dicta is only talk by the court. A holding is the court's decision about the facts in the case.

§ 8.3 How Courts React to Precedent from Other Jurisdictions

In § 8.1.2, we explained nonmandatory primary authority, including opinions from other jurisdictions that address the same legal issue. If you cite a Missouri case to a Kansas court, how will the Kansas judge react? If you are in a federal court in the Ninth Circuit, how will the court react if you cite precedent from the Eighth Circuit? These are the two most common situations when case law from another jurisdiction might be cited as persuasive primary authority—an opinion from another state (if your case will be decided by a state court) or from another federal circuit (if your case will be decided by a federal court).

Courts rely on cases from other jurisdictions only for guidance, and only when a gap appears in mandatory authority governing that issue. A gap exists when a jurisdiction's law does not fully settle an issue.

Courts can fill a gap in mandatory authority in two situations. One occurs when the unresolved issue is the kind normally resolved by common law. Because courts developed the common law, they continue to fill its gaps, and they are often guided by precedent from other jurisdictions when they do.

The second gap-filling situation occurs when a mandatory statute governs the issue, but the statute is so unclear that the court must decide what it means. In effect, the court fills the gap by interpreting how the statute applies in that situation. This kind of opinion is sometimes known as *statutory precedent* because the court's interpretation of an unclear statute in effect becomes part of the mandatory authority in that jurisdiction (unless, of course, the legislature amends the statute to clarify or modify its meaning).

But not every type of statutory precedent is persuasive in this situation. For example, opinions interpreting another state's statute might persuade your court, but only if the other statute is very similar to the statute in your case. If the two statutes are *identical*, statutory precedent from the other state can be especially persuasive. Two statutes can be virtually identical even if they have minor differences in wording that do not affect their meaning. But when the *substance* of the two statutes differs, statutory precedent from the other state has little or no persuasive value. If the two statutes take radically different approaches to solving the same problem, the other state's statutory precedent is usually irrelevant.

If your state has no statute on the issue, statutory precedent from other states has no value at all. If your state treats the issue as a matter of common law, the court will consider only precedent from other states that also address the issue in common law.

What generally impresses a court when you cite case law from other jurisdictions?

First, a court that must fill a gap will want to know the *majority rule*. A majority rule is a rule adopted by the majority of states (or circuits) that have considered the issue (not the number of specific courts or cases). A rule can be a majority rule even if most other jurisdictions have not yet addressed it. For purposes of determining the majority rule, each state or circuit is counted only once. When a jurisdiction has not addressed an issue before, the court will want to know how most other courts have resolved the issue, even if the issue is a novel one and most jurisdictions have not addressed it at all. The majority rule is often very persuasive, although some courts will decide to follow the *minority rule* if a substantial number of other courts have taken a different but well-reasoned position on the issue.

Second, if a majority of states or circuits follows one rule but there is a modern trend in favor of adopting a minority rule (in other words, the number of jurisdictions following the majority rule is falling), a gap-filling court would want to know that too. A modern-trend minority rule might be more appropriate for current conditions than an older majority rule that is declining in favor.

Third, a precedent case will be more persuasive to a gap-filling court if sound reasoning supports its solution to the issue. Careful and thoughtful legal reasoning impresses a court looking for precedent to follow.

§ 8.4 How to Use Persuasive Authority to Fill a Gap in Mandatory Law

How do you fill a gap in the law of the jurisdiction that will decide your case? First, establish a foundation for the court by showing that the gap exists because no mandatory authority fully resolves the issue. Second, use persuasive authority to fill the gap.

§ 8.4.1 *Step 1:* Establish the Foundation

Because persuasive precedent is used most often to help fill gaps in a jurisdiction's mandatory law, you must first convince the court that a gap exists that must be filled in order to resolve the issue before it. To establish the foundation, define the gap and specify how the mandatory law fails to resolve the controversy.

A particularly deep gap occurs when an issue is one of "first impression" in the state or circuit that will decide the case. "First impression" means that the courts in that jurisdiction have never before had occasion to address the issue.

Another type of gap occurs when cases from the jurisdiction's highest court are questionable due to age or poor reasoning. But be careful: A precedent is not infirm just because it is old or just because you dislike its reasoning. Age weakens precedent when society or culture has so changed that the precedent no longer represents contemporary public policy on the issue. And sometimes a more recent precedent case is questionable because it has been criticized in other courts' opinions or in treatises or law review articles.

If other states have statutes on the question and your state does not, that does not necessarily mean a gap exists in the law. Your state's courts might reason that when the state legislature has not enacted a statute to resolve the issue, the legislature in effect has deferred the issue to the courts for resolution by common law.

In summary, to establish the foundation for filling a gap, do *all* of the following:

- State the legal issue precisely.
- Explain what related issues the jurisdiction's law *has* decided.
- Identify the gap by demonstrating what the law *has not yet* decided.

63

The following example concisely establishes a foundation in the first sentence:

> No court in this state has decided whether the sale of a newly built home implies a warranty of habitability. However, a common law warranty of habitability has been recognized, as a matter of common law, in a growing number of states.

Here, the gap is clear: The state has no case law addressing whether the sale of a newly built home implies a warranty of habitability.

But things are not usually this clear cut. For example, the state courts might have decided cases that have nibbled around the edges of the issue, or cases to which analogies could be made, or cases setting out public policy, or even cases that give the false impression of having resolved the question, but in dicta. If so, the foundation is not complete until you have explained—in as much detail as the reader would need in order to agree with you—why the issue is still unresolved by the jurisdiction's law. For example:

> No reported decision in this state has determined whether a violation of § 432 is negligence per se. But the neighboring states of Colorado and Arizona have enacted similar statutes. [Explain why they are similar.] Courts in those states have interpreted those statutes to mean . . . .

Here, the state legislature has enacted a statute, but the courts have not yet decided a certain aspect of its meaning (whether a violation of the statute amounts to negligence per se). The foundation is established by the first sentence, which explains that no case in that state has decided the issue.

Avoid lecturing the reader on basic principles in evaluating legal authority. A lawyer or judge already understands that when mandatory law does not exist on the issue, persuasive precedents are the next best alternative for filling the gap. Just show that the gap exists, and then move to fill it.

§ 8.4.2 *Step 2:* Fill the Gap

Once you establish the foundation, summarize the persuasive authority. For example, "Sixteen states have adopted this cause of action, and four have rejected it." Then explain the persuasive authority in detail. Include not only precedent from other jurisdictions, but also highly persuasive secondary authority. A court convinced that a gap in law exists will often consult relevant restatement provisions, scholarly treatises, and law review articles. But keep your focus on the case law. The views of commentators generally play a secondary role in gap-filling.

§ 8.4.3   The Two Steps Summarized

Follow these two steps when using persuasive authority to fill a gap in your jurisdiction's law relevant to your legal issue:

Step 1 Establish the foundation by doing all of the following (§ 8.4.1):
- State the legal issue precisely.
- Explain what related issues the jurisdiction's law *has* decided.
- Identify the gap by demonstrating what the law *has not yet* decided.

Step 2 Fill the gap (§ 8.4.2).

§ 8.5   How to Select Persuasive Precedent to Fill a Gap

When selecting precedent to fill a gap in a jurisdiction's law, how do you decide which precedents are most persuasive? Once you have found a precedent case you plan to use, answer the following questions in approximately this order:

1. Is the precedent case factually on point with your case, or if not, can you make a sound analogy to the facts of your case? If the precedent opinion is easily distinguished on its facts, it will not persuade your court to follow it.

2. How good is the precedent's reasoning? Is the logic of the holding sound? Is it careful, thoughtful, and complete? Does it reach a just result? Well-reasoned precedents that reach just results persuade.

3. Which court decided the case? Was the precedent issued by the highest court in its jurisdiction? If so, it will be more persuasive. Or is it from a court that your jurisdiction's courts have treated as unusually influential in past decisions? Is the precedent from a state where relevant conditions are similar to those prevailing in your state? For example, a state whose economy is heavily based on manufacturing might be more persuaded by precedents from a state with a similar economic base, especially if the legal issue involves a labor dispute or an issue about job safety.

4. Is the policy reasoning of the precedent case consistent with public policy in your jurisdiction? For example, some state supreme courts have historically been leaders in creating new tort causes of action. If your state only reluctantly recognizes new torts, your court is unlikely to find precedents from those states persuasive.

5. How have other reported opinions treated the precedent? Have later courts discussed the precedent case or its legal rule with approval or with skepticism? Is it part of a general trend or a widely accepted body of law? Or is it a lonely straggler that other courts seem to be leaving behind?

6. How recent is the precedent case? Judges often treat recent opinions as more authoritative than older ones, simply because changing social conditions sometimes mean that a traditional legal rule is no longer suitable. On the other hand, a court may be wary of following a very recent precedent that other courts have not yet considered, or that has not yet been tested through experience. That is especially true if the precedent addresses a novel issue or an issue of first impression in your jurisdiction.

Exercise 8-A. Distinguishing Between Primary and Secondary Authority

Decide whether each of the following research materials is primary or secondary authority.

1. An administrative regulation issued by the Arkansas Department of Wildlife and Fisheries governing how to obtain a hunting license
2. A definition of "burglary" in *Black's Law Dictionary*
3. Rule 56 of the Federal Rules of Civil Procedure
4. An *American Law Reports* annotation collecting cases about liability for texting while driving
5. A trial court decision granting summary judgment to the defendant in a fraud case
6. A federal statute known as the Affordable Care Act
7. A provision of the Restatement (Second) of Torts defining the "concert of action" theory of liability
8. An opinion of the U.S. Court of Appeals for the Eighth Circuit deciding an issue of Missouri law
9. A regulation issued by the U.S. Fish and Wildlife Service defining the word "take" as used in the federal Migratory Bird Treaty Act, which makes it unlawful to take any migratory bird except as permitted by the agency's regulations
10. A paragraph from Prosser and Keeton's treatise explaining proximate cause

Exercise 8-B. Distinguishing Between Mandatory and Persuasive Authority

You represent a client who has been prosecuted in federal court for possessing marijuana with intent to distribute, in violation of federal criminal statutes. Law enforcement officers found marijuana growing in the corner of an uncultivated field on her small family farm in Grinnell, Iowa, which she inherited from her grand-parents. Your client lives with her partner in the old farmhouse, which is surrounded by a fence enclosing a large yard and a garden. The fenced yard covers about an acre of land. Your defense theory is that your client was never in "possession" of marijuana as defined by the statute because she did not know it was growing in the corner of an uncultivated field, located a half mile from the farmhouse.

First, determine whether each of the following is mandatory or persuasive primary authority. Second, for those you decide are persuasive authority, determine whether each one is highly persuasive, moderately persuasive, or slightly persuasive.

Before answering, review the questions at the beginning of this chapter. If you need more information to answer the questions, consult the resources mentioned in this chapter to find what you need. Use your legal research materials to identify the federal circuit in which Iowa is located.

1. A decision of the U.S. Court of Appeals for the Sixth Circuit interpreting the term "possession" as used in federal criminal statutes prohibiting a felon from possessing a firearm.
2. A regulation of the U.S. Fish and Wildlife Service defining "possession" for purposes of the Endangered Species Act.
3. A federal court rule determining whether a prejudicial statement by a criminal defendant is admissible against her at trial.
4. A decision of the Iowa Supreme Court defining "possession" as used in state criminal statutes prohibiting possession of marijuana with intent to sell.
5. A published decision from a different federal trial judge in Iowa defining the term "possession" in a case involving similar facts.
6. An Iowa criminal statute defining "possession" for purposes of prohibiting possession of burglary tools.
7. A North Dakota Supreme Court decision holding that a criminal defendant could not be found guilty for possession of marijuana without knowledge that the prohibited substance was either on his person or within the curtilage of his dwelling.
8. A decision by the U.S. Court of Appeals for the Tenth Circuit affirming a conviction of a Kansas farmer for possession of marijuana with intent to distribute, in violation of the same federal statute, after the local sheriff spotted a patch of marijuana growing in a corner of his garden.

Exercise 8-C. Using the Hierarchy of Authority

You are working on a case now pending in the U.S. District Court for the District of Nevada, located in the Ninth Circuit. You have been asked to find out whether a defendant who unsuccessfully moved to dismiss the case for insufficient service of process can later file a motion to dismiss for failure to state a claim on which relief can be granted.

Your legal research has located the following authorities, each of which squarely addresses your legal issue. Based only on the information provided in this exercise, make a preliminary ranking of the authorities in order of their respective mandatory and persuasive value in resolving the issue.

> *Catdog v. Amundsen*—U.S. Court of Appeals for the Fourth Circuit, 2008
> *Great Basin Realty Co. v. Rand*—Nevada Supreme Court, 2002
> Matthewson's treatise titled *Federal Courts* (published last year)
> *Wilkes v. Jae Sun Trading Corp.*—U.S. Court of Appeals for the Ninth Circuit, 1977
> *Pincus v. McGrath*—U.S. Supreme Court, 1953
> *Mader v. City of Las Vegas*—U.S. District Court for the District of Nevada, 2013
> Federal Rule of Civil Procedure 12(b) (revised last year)
> *Barking Pumpkins Records, Inc. v. Sepulveda*—California Supreme Court, 2009
> *Garibaldi v. City of Boulder*—U.S. Court of Appeals for the Tenth Circuit, 2007
> *Ott v. Frazier*—U.S. Court of Appeals for the Seventh Circuit, 1935

9 Working with Statutes

[T]he statutes of this Commonwealth . . . do not always mean what they say.

—*Henry David Thoreau*

§ 9.1 How Courts Interpret Statutes

Chapter 4 explains how to outline a statute. This chapter explains how to determine what the words and phrases in a statute mean. If an appellate court has issued an opinion interpreting a statute, the statute means whatever the court held that it means, at least for lower courts whose decisions could be appealed to that court.

In the absence of an authoritative appellate court decision interpreting a statute, most judges begin by considering the *plain language* of a statute. Unless the statute itself defines terms differently, a court will interpret the words of the statute to carry the meaning most readers would give it. Courts generally assume that legislatures use words as nonlawyers would use them except where legal or other specialized terminology is needed. They reason that a statute's plain language best represents what the legislature intended when it enacted the statute.

As we know from experience, however, most statutory language is not as plainly written as lawyers and judges would like. Legislatures often draft statutes that apply to a wide range of situations and varying circumstances. When a legislature enacts a statute, it is nearly impossible to predict all the factual situations that will be within the statute's scope. Moreover, the legislative process is inherently characterized by compromise. When introduced in the legislature, a bill may be written in plain language. But throughout the political process of negotiation and compromise, the final language of the bill may be amended several times to appease various constituencies.

Ambiguities can creep in because more general language may garner votes for the bill. As a result, statutory language is often difficult to understand and apply to a specific set of facts.

§ 9.1.1   Judicial Approaches to Statutory Interpretation

When a court cannot determine the meaning of a statute from the language itself, or when a court decides that applying the plain language would reach an *absurd result*, the court will turn to other interpretive tools to sort out what a statute means. But judges vary in what interpretive tools they find persuasive. Each judge tends to adopt one or more of the following policy preferences when interpreting statutes:

- Intentionalism
- Purposivism
- Textualism

Intentionalism. The traditional approach used by judges in interpreting unclear statutes is to ascertain the *legislative intent*. Intentionalists consider a wide range of informational sources in an effort to figure out what the legislators who enacted the statute actually had in mind. A judge who follows this approach might be persuaded, for example, by the legislative history of a statute, which might include a formal report issued by the legislative committee that first considered the bill and proposed certain amendments, or a statement of the bill's sponsor when it came before the legislature for a vote.

A well known illustration of the intentionalist approach is the following quote from the U.S. Supreme Court: "It is a familiar rule that a thing may be within the letter of the statute and yet not within the statute, because not within its spirit nor within the intention of its makers."[1]

Purposivism. Other judges are skeptical about the traditional approach to statutory interpretation because they question any judicial effort to search for the enacting legislature's subjective intent. Instead, a purposivist judge will consider a wide variety of information in an effort to identify the *statutory purpose*. Occasionally, the legislature will include a statement of legislative purpose or a list of legislative findings in the statute itself. When it does, a purposivist judge will give particular consideration to that statement. More often, however, a judge tries to identify the legislative purpose by reviewing evidence that is extrinsic to the statute's wording, such as legislative history.

A purposivist perspective is influenced, for example, by the social context of the legislation. The statute commonly known as the USA PATRIOT Act ("Uniting and

---

[1] *Holy Trinity Church v. United States*, 143 U.S. 457, 458 (1892).

Strengthening America by Providing Appropriate Tools Required to Intercept and Obstruct Terrorism") was enacted by Congress shortly after September 11, 2001. A purposivist judge interpreting that legislation would be strongly influenced by the purpose it sought to achieve—deterring future attacks on American soil by foreign-based terrorists.

At first, it might seem that the *purpose* of a statute is not much different than the legislative *intent*. But the two judicial approaches reflect different perspectives. A purposivist judge would want to understand what public problem, mischief, or evil a statute was enacted to address, or more generally the goal the legislature sought to achieve—a purpose external to the words of the statute itself. On the other hand, an intentionalist judge would be more interested in interpreting the specific words of the statute in light of what the legislator who drafted and sponsored the bill actually intended the bill to accomplish, and what those who voted for the bill actually thought it meant.

Textualism. In contrast to the other two perspectives, a textualist judge primarily focuses on textual cues intrinsic to the words and literal context of the statute itself. Textualist judges consider not just the specific words whose meaning is disputed, but also the statute as a whole. The judge might also consider how the same terms are used elsewhere in the same overall statutory scheme, reasoning that the legislature would not use the same terminology in different statutes to mean different things.

A textualist judge generally disregards evidence of subjective legislative intent, and is less influenced by the public purpose the legislation was designed to accomplish. The focus is on the words themselves, read in context. However, textualist judges often refer to extrinsic evidence in the form of dictionaries (both legal and general) to interpret ambiguous terms not otherwise defined in the statute itself.

As you gain more experience reading judicial opinions that interpret statutes, try to figure out which of these interpretive perspectives the author used to sort out the meaning of a black-letter statute or rule.

§ 9.1.2 Canons of Statutory Interpretation

If a court cannot figure out the meaning of a statute based on its plain language, the court generally relies on one or more *canons of statutory interpretation*. A canon is a general guideline the courts have developed over time to help them figure out what unclear statutes mean. Although scholars have criticized the use of canons, courts continue to use them regularly to interpret unclear statutes. Depending on the judge's interpretive perspective (§ 9.1.1), she may be more likely to rely on some canons than others.

Canons are almost always judge-made rules of law, and you must prove them with legal authority, usually mandatory case law. However, sometimes they appear in the statutes themselves. For example, a few appear in 1 U.S.C. §§ 1-8. State statutes also include an assortment of canons, and states vary as to how many and which canons are codified in statute. Some state legislatures have even enacted statutes that overrule one or more of the traditional common law canons of statutory interpretation.[2] Be sure to check the statutes of your jurisdiction before researching the case law.

Courts employ a large number of canons of statutory interpretation, but these are some of the most common ones:

- A remedial statute should be liberally construed to address the harm the legislature intended to remedy.
- Criminal statutes should be narrowly interpreted in favor of the accused (*rule of lenity*).
- The expression of one thing implies the exclusion of alternatives (*expressio unius est exclusio alterius*).
- A general term following a list of specific terms will be construed in a manner consistent with the common features of the specific terms (*ejusdem generis*).
- Statutory words and phrases should be construed in the context of the entire enactment of which they are a part.
- Different statutes on the same subject (*in pari materia*) should be construed together.
- Statutes in derogation of the common law are strictly construed.
- A statute is presumed to operate prospectively only, unless the legislature has clearly expressed an intent to apply it retroactively.
- A strong presumption exists in favor of the constitutionality of a statute.
- A state statute patterned on another state's statute carries the interpretation the other state's courts have given it (*borrowed statute rule*).
- When a statute has been interpreted by the courts and the legislature has not later amended it, the legislature is presumed to have acquiesced in the judicial interpretation.

§ 9.2 How to Discuss Statutes in Writing

Writing about a statutory question focuses on the *words of the statute* because most courts agree that a legislature signals its intent primarily through the words it enacts. For that reason, you should directly quote the crucial statutory term or phrase (inside quotation marks) in the relevant sections of your office memorandum or brief. Those words should be the most important focus of your brief answer, legal analysis, and conclusion.

---

[2] *E.g.*, Kan. Stat. Ann. § 77-109 (1997); 1 Pa. Cons. Stat. Ann. § 1928(a) (West 2008).

In Exercise 9-A below, two courts repeatedly discuss variations of a single word in the controlling statutes: "carry," "carries," and "carrying" a firearm.

Because statutes are drafted to govern a wide range of circumstances, you might need to reformulate a rule expressed entirely in statutory language before you can easily apply it. (Chapters 2, 3, and 4 explain how.) But be careful when reformulating the statutory language into a more useful expression of the rule. If you oversimplify or distort the rule, trouble awaits. Quoting the key phrases of the statute helps.

From there, use the canons to the extent they reveal what the statute means for your issue. Only rarely will all of the canons do that. If one fails to help, skip it and use others. In Exercise 9-A below, you can see examples of the canons in use.

Exercise 9-A. The Statutory Canons in Action

Title 18 U.S.C. § 924(c)(1) provides that "any person who, during and in relation to any crime of violence or drug trafficking crime . . . for which the person may be prosecuted in a court of the United States, uses or *carries a firearm* . . . shall, in addition to the punishment provided for such crime of violence or drug trafficking crime . . . be sentenced to a term of imprisonment of not less than 5 years." *Id.* (emphasis added.)

Many of the canons of statutory interpretation are illustrated in the two cases that follow, which interpret the statutory words "*carries a firearm.*" As you read the opinions, identify each canon in the margin where the author considers it in interpreting the statute. Explain the interpretive perspective used by the author of each opinion.

United States v. Foster

133 F.3d 704 (9th Cir. 1997)

KOZINSKI, Circuit Judge.

What does it mean to "carry a gun"? . . .

Leon Foster and Sandra Ward manufactured methamphetamine. In 1989 the police got wise to them, pulled Foster over while he was driving his pickup truck and arrested him. In his truck bed, in a zipped up bag under a snap-down tarp, they found a loaded 9 mm semiautomatic and a bucket. Inside the bucket were a scale, plastic baggies, and some hand-written notes with prices.

Foster and Ward were convicted of conspiracy to manufacture and distribute methamphetamine in violation of 21 U.S.C. §§ 841(a)(1) and 846. Foster was also convicted of possessing methamphetamine, in violation of 21 U.S.C. § 844, and of carrying a firearm during and in relation to a drug trafficking crime, in violation of 18 U.S.C. § 924(c)(1). . . .

. . . Was Leon Foster carrying a gun when he drove with it in his truck bed?

. . . "Carry" has two differing relevant uses. It may mean to transport or even to arrange for something to be transported: "I had to carry my piano all the way across the country." But it may also mean to hold an object while moving from one place to another: "I carried that ball and chain wherever I went." This narrower sense applies particularly to weapons. If I were to say "Don Corleone is carrying a gun"—or even just "Don Corleone is carrying"—you would understand that the Don has a sidearm somewhere on his person. A synonym for carry in this sense is to "pack heat." Criminals who pack heat are obviously much more dangerous than those who do not.

In our caselaw, we first adopted the broad definition of "carry" as transporting in *United States v. Barber*, 594 F.2d 1242 (9th Cir. 1979). Interpreting section 924(c)(1)'s predecessor, we said "[i]n ordinary usage, the verb 'carry' includes transportation or causing to be transported. Nothing in the legislative history indicates that Congress intended any hypertechnical or narrow reading of the word 'carries.'" *Id.* at 1244. After [the Supreme Court's decision in *Bailey v. United States*, 516 U.S. 137 (1995)], we switched to the narrower (packing heat) sense in *United States v. Hernandez*, 80 F.3d 1253 (9th Cir. 1996). We held that "in order for a defendant to be convicted of 'carrying' a gun in violation of section 924(c)(1), the defendant must have transported the firearm on or about his or her person. . . . This means the firearm must have been immediately available for use by the defendant." *Id.* at 1258 (citations omitted). A number of recent cases follow the *Hernandez* definition. . . .

We can also speculate[*] as to what purpose a prohibition on carrying a gun during and in relation to a violent or drug trafficking crime might serve. Using or carrying guns makes those crimes more dangerous. A drug dealer who packs heat is more likely to hurt someone or provoke someone else to violence. A gun in a bag under a tarp in a truck bed poses substantially less risk. . . .

On balance, the arguments point to the narrower definition: It fits the more specific dictionary definition, follows *Bailey* more closely, harmonizes better with the full statute, and flows from the likely purpose of section 924(c)(1). . . . A final argument for the narrower definition is the rule of lenity. Where a criminal law is ambiguous, we are wary of imposing criminal liability for conduct that the law does not clearly prohibit. *See Bifulco v. United States*, 447 U.S. 381, 387 (1980). . . .

---

[*] [*Court's footnote*] There is mercifully little legislative history on "carry" to burden our discussion. The original version of the section was added as a floor amendment by Representative Poff. *See United States v. Anderson*, 59 F.3d 1323, 1327 (D.C. Cir. 1995) (en banc). The general aim of the section seems to have been to ensure that violent criminals receive longer sentences, and to deter the use of guns. *See* 114 Cong. Rec. 22,231 (1968) (remarks of Representative Poff); *see also id.* at 22,230 (remarks of Representative Casey) and at 22,234 (remarks of Representative Harsha). The only references to "carry" concerned a proposed amendment to delete the word, apparently because it might affect people such as policemen who were authorized to carry a gun, then committed an assault without using the gun. "Carry" was deleted from Representative Casey's version of section 924(c)(1), but eventually Representative Poff's version, "carry" included, passed. *See United States v. Ramirez*, 482 F.2d 807, 814 (2d Cir. 1973).

The rule of lenity applies only where a statute has resisted the ordinary tools of statutory interpretation. *See Hanlester Network v. Shalala*, 51 F.3d 1390, 1397 (9th Cir. 1995) ("Canons of statutory construction, such as the Rule of Lenity, are employed only where 'reasonable doubt persists about a statute's intended scope even *after* resort to the language, and structure, legislative history and motivating policies of the statute.'") (citations omitted) (emphasis in original). We think these ordinary tools of interpretation point to the narrow definition; at worst (for Mr. Foster) they leave the scope of section 924(c)(1) in doubt. If Congress wants us to put people like Leon Foster in prison for a longer time, it can re-write the law to give us clearer instructions, perhaps by using the word "transport" in section 924(c)(1) as it does in various other sections of the firearm statutes.

We reaffirm our holding in *Hernandez* and its progeny that "in order for a defendant to be convicted of 'carrying' a gun in violation of section 924(c)(1), the defendant must have transported the firearm on or about his or her person. . . . This means the firearm must have been immediately available for use by the defendant." *Hernandez*, 80 F.3d at 1258. . . .

Shortly after the Ninth Circuit decided *Foster*, the United States Supreme Court came to the opposite conclusion in the following case.

Muscarello v. United States
524 U.S. 125 (1998)

Justice BREYER delivered the opinion of the Court.

A provision in the firearms chapter of the federal criminal code imposes a 5-year mandatory prison term upon a person who "uses or carries a firearm" "during and in relation to" a "drug trafficking crime." 18 U.S.C. § 924(c)(1). The question before us is whether the phrase "carries a firearm" is limited to the carrying of firearms on the person. We hold that it is not so limited. Rather, it also applies to a person who knowingly possesses and conveys firearms in a vehicle, including in the locked glove compartment or trunk of a car, which the person accompanies. . . .

We begin with the statute's language. . . . Although the word "carry" has many different meanings, only two are relevant here. When one uses the word in the first, or primary, meaning, one can, as a matter of ordinary English, "carry firearms" in a wagon, car, truck, or other vehicle that one accompanies. When one uses the word in a different, rather special, way, to mean, for example, "bearing" or (in slang) "packing" (as in "packing a gun"), the matter is less clear. But, for reasons we shall set out below, we believe Congress intended to use the word in its primary sense and not in this latter, special way. . . .

This Court has described the statute's basic purpose broadly, as an effort to combat the "dangerous combination" of "drugs and guns." *Smith v. United States*, 508 U.S. 223, 240 (1993). And the provision's chief legislative sponsor has said that the provision seeks "to persuade the man who is tempted to commit a Federal felony to leave his gun at home." 114 Cong. Rec. 22231 (1968). . . .

From the perspective of any such purpose (persuading a criminal "to leave his gun at home") what sense would it make for this statute to penalize one who walks with a gun in a bag to the site of a drug sale, but to ignore a similar individual who, like defendant Gray-Santana, travels to a similar site with a similar gun in a similar bag, but instead of walking, drives there with the gun in his car? How persuasive is a punishment that is without effect until a drug dealer who has brought his gun to a sale (indeed has it available for use) actually takes it from the trunk (or unlocks the glove compartment) of his car? It is difficult to say that, considered as a class, those who prepare, say, to sell drugs by placing guns in their cars are less dangerous, or less deserving of punishment, than those who carry handguns on their person.

We have found no significant indication elsewhere in the legislative history of any more narrowly focused relevant purpose. . . .

We are not convinced by petitioners' remaining arguments to the contrary. First, they say that our definition of "carry" makes it the equivalent of "transport." Yet, Congress elsewhere in related statutes used the word "transport" deliberately to signify a different, and broader, statutory coverage. The immediately preceding statutory subsection, for example, imposes a different set of penalties on one who, with an intent to commit a crime, "ships, transports, or receives a firearm" in interstate commerce. 18 U.S.C. § 924(b). Moreover, § 926A specifically "entitles" a person "not otherwise prohibited . . . from transporting, shipping, or receiving a firearm" to "transport a firearm . . . from any place where he may lawfully possess and carry" it to "any other place" where he may do so. . . .

[P]etitioners say that our reading of the statute would extend its coverage to passengers on buses, trains, or ships, who have placed a firearm, say, in checked luggage. To extend this statute so far, they argue, is unfair, going well beyond what Congress likely would have thought possible. They add that some lower courts, thinking approximately the same, have limited the scope of "carries" to instances where a gun in a car is immediately accessible, thereby most likely excluding from coverage a gun carried in a car's trunk or locked glove compartment. See, e.g., [*United States v. Foster*, 133 F.3d 704, 708 (9th Cir. 1998)] (concluding that person "carries" a firearm in a car only if the firearm is immediately accessible). . . .

In our view, this argument does not take adequate account of other limiting words in the statute—words that make the statute applicable only where a defendant "carries" a gun both "during *and* in relation to" a drug crime. § 924(c)(1) (emphasis added). Congress added these words in part to prevent prosecution where guns "played" no part in the crime. See S. Rep. No. 98-225, at 314, n. 10. . . .

[P]etitioners argue that we should construe the word "carry" to mean "immediately accessible." And, as we have said, they point out that several Courts of Appeals have limited the statute's scope in this way. See, e.g., *Foster*, supra, at 708. . . . That interpretation, however, is difficult to square with the statute's language, for one "carries" a gun in the glove compartment whether or not that glove compartment is locked. Nothing in the statute's history suggests that Congress intended that limitation. And, for reasons pointed out above, . . . we believe that the words "during" and "in relation to" will limit the statute's application to the harms that Congress foresaw.

Finally, petitioners and the dissent invoke the "rule of lenity." The simple existence of some statutory ambiguity, however, is not sufficient to warrant application of that rule, for most statutes are ambiguous to some degree. Cf. *Smith*, 508 U.S. at 239 ("The mere possibility of articulating a narrower construction . . . does not by itself make the rule of lenity applicable"). "The rule of lenity applies only if, 'after seizing everything from which aid can be derived,' . . . we can make 'no more than a guess as to what Congress intended.'" *United States v. Wells*, 519 U.S. 482 (1997). . . . To invoke the rule, we must conclude that there is a "'grievous ambiguity or uncertainty' in the statute." *Staples v. United States*, 511 U.S. 600, 619, n.17 (1994). . . . Certainly, our decision today is based on much more than a "guess as to what Congress intended," and there is no "grievous ambiguity" here. The problem of statutory interpretation in this case is indeed no different from that in many of the criminal cases that confront us. Yet, this Court has never held that the rule of lenity automatically permits a defendant to win. . . .

For these reasons, we conclude that the petitioners' conduct falls within the scope of the phrase "carries a firearm." The decisions of the Courts of Appeals are affirmed. . . .

Justice GINSBURG, with whom the CHIEF JUSTICE, Justice SCALIA, and Justice SOUTER join, dissenting.

. . . I would read the words to indicate not merely keeping arms on one's premises or in one's vehicle, but bearing them in such manner as to be ready for use as a weapon. . . .

For indicators from Congress itself, it is appropriate to consider word usage in other provisions of Title 18's chapter on "Firearms." . . .

Section 925(a)(2)(B), for example, provides that no criminal sanction shall attend "the transportation of [a] firearm or ammunition carried out to enable a person, who lawfully received such firearm or ammunition from the Secretary of the Army, to engage in military training or in competitions." . . .

. . . "Courts normally try to read language in different, but related, statutes, so as best to reconcile those statutes, in light of their purposes and of common sense." *McFadden*, 13 F.3d at 467 (Breyer, C. J., dissenting). So reading the "Firearms" statutes, I would not extend the word "carries" in § 924(c)(1) to mean transports out of hand's reach in a vehicle.

Section 924(c)(1), as the foregoing discussion details, is not decisively clear one way or another. The sharp division in the Court on the proper reading of the measure confirms, "[a]t the very least, . . . that the issue is subject to some doubt. Under these circumstances, we adhere to the familiar rule that, 'where there is ambiguity in a criminal statute, doubts are resolved in favor of the defendant.'" *Adamo Wrecking Co. v. United States*, 434 U.S. 275, 284-285 (1978) . . . ; see *United States v. Granderson*, 511 U.S. 39, 54 (1994) ("[W]here text, structure, and history fail to establish that the Government's position is unambiguously correct—we apply the rule of lenity and resolve the ambiguity in [the defendant's] favor."). "Carry" bears many meanings, as the Court and the "Firearms" statutes demonstrate. The narrower "on or about [one's] person" interpretation is hardly implausible nor at odds with an accepted meaning of "carries a firearm." . . .

The narrower "on or about [one's] person" construction of "carries a firearm" . . . fits plausibly with other provisions of the "Firearms" chapter, and it adheres to the principle that, given two readings of a penal provision, both consistent with the statutory text, we do not choose the harsher construction. . . .

Exercise 9-B. Plagiarism and the Board of Bar Examiners

Hardy and Tisdale were enrolled in a law school Legal Writing course. On the first assignment of the semester, Tisdale wrote a draft of the first half of his paper before Hardy did, and Hardy asked to see it. That was forbidden by the course rules because the assignment's due date had not yet arrived. Tisdale showed Hardy what he had written anyway and let Hardy borrow the flash drive on which Tisdale's work was stored.

Hardy copied Tisdale's work onto his own laptop. He then changed as many of the words as he could. When he was finished, the first half of the two papers had approximately the same organization, although about 80% of the words were different—similar, but different.

Tisdale and Hardy then had a falling out. Each of them said unkind things about the other's choice of ringtone, clothing, sports loyalties, and career goals. They stopped speaking to each other. On the due date, they submitted their papers.

The teacher instantly recognized the similarity between the first half of Hardy's paper and the first half of Tisdale's. In the second half of Hardy's paper, the teacher noticed phrases that did not "sound like" him. The teacher had a vague memory of having seen those phrases previously somewhere else. The teacher logged onto Lexis and then onto Westlaw, typing in the suspect phrases from Hardy's paper and looking for sources in which they might appear. (This is one way a teacher can easily check a student's paper for plagiarism.) The teacher found a number of instances where Hardy had copied passages word for word from sources he did not cite and without quote marks around the copied words.

When confronted with all this, Hardy claimed that by changing most of the words in Tisdale's draft he had not misrepresented someone else's work as his own, and that the plagiarism in the second half of his paper was not deliberate. He said that while researching he must have written down the phrases in question, then misplaced the cites, and later assumed that the words in his notes were his own. The teacher properly rejected that explanation and gave Hardy a failing grade for the course. The law school suspended him for a year. (Tisdale was also punished, but Hardy poses the issue here.)

After a year, Hardy returned to the law school that had suspended him. Last spring, he graduated. He has applied for admission to the Wisconsin bar.

In every state, an applicant for admission to the bar must prove to the bar examiners that she or he has the type of character needed to practice law. After passing the bar examination, the applicant must fill out a detailed character questionnaire and submit supporting documents, including an affidavit from the applicant's law school. A false, misleading, or incomplete answer on the questionnaire is itself grounds for denying the application for admission. Every state's questionnaire asks, among other things, whether the applicant has ever been accused of academic dishonesty, and the law school's affidavit must answer the same question.

On his questionnaire, Hardy described what he had done and what the school had done. And in its affidavit, the law school reported—as it must—the same thing.

What will happen when Hardy applies for admission to the Wisconsin bar?

The statute-like provisions governing admission to the bar are usually found in a state's court rules, as well as the rules of the agency or board designated to review the character of bar applicants. The primary difference between a court rule and a statute is that court rules are adopted by courts, while statutes are enacted by legislatures. Otherwise, court rules and statutes are drafted and interpreted using the same skills explained in this chapter.

Your research has found the following:

1. SCR 40.06, a Wisconsin Supreme Court Rule;
2. BA 6.01, 6.02, and 6.03 of the Wisconsin Board of Bar Examiner Rules, all of which govern applications for admission to the bar;
3. *In re Radtke*, a Wisconsin case interpreting BA 6.03; and
4. five out-of-state cases, each interpreting a statute or court rule quoted in the case.

Wisconsin Supreme Court Rules

SCR 40.06 Requirement as to character and fitness to practice law

(1) An applicant for bar admission shall establish good moral character and fitness to practice law. The purpose of this requirement is to limit admission to those applicants found to have the qualities of character and fitness needed to

assure to a reasonable degree of certainty the integrity and the competence of services performed for clients and the maintenance of high standards in the administration of justice.

. . .

(3) An applicant shall establish to the satisfaction of the board that the applicant satisfies the requirement set forth in sub. (1). . . .

. . .

(5) The dean of a law school in this state shall have a continuing duty to report to the board any information reflecting adversely upon the character and fitness to practice law of an applicant for bar admission. . . .

Rules of the Wisconsin Board of Bar Examiners

BA 6.01 Standard of character and fitness. A lawyer should be one whose record of conduct justifies the trust of clients, adversaries, courts and others with respect to the professional duties owed to them. A record manifesting a deficiency in the honesty, diligence or reliability of an applicant may constitute a basis for denial of admission. The Supreme Court Rules place on the applicant the burden of producing information sufficient to affirmatively demonstrate the character and fitness appropriate for bar admission.

BA 6.02 Relevant conduct or condition. The revelation or discovery of any of the following should be treated as cause for further inquiry before the Board decides whether the applicant possesses the character and fitness to practice law:

. . .

    (b) academic misconduct

. . .

    (d) acts involving dishonesty or misrepresentation

. . .

BA 6.03 Use of information. The Board will determine whether the present character and fitness of an applicant qualifies the applicant for admission. In making this determination through the processes described above, the following factors should be considered in assigning weight and significance to prior conduct:

    (a) the applicant's age at the time of the conduct

    (b) the recency of the conduct

    (c) the reliability of the information concerning the conduct

    (d) the seriousness of the conduct

    (e) the mitigating or aggravating circumstances

    (f) the evidence of rehabilitation

    (g) the applicant's candor in the admissions process

    (h) the materiality of any omissions or misrepresentations

    (i) the number of incidents revealing deficiencies

In re Radtke v. Board of Bar Examiners

601 N.W.2d 642 (Wis. 1999)

We review . . . the decision of the Board of Bar Examiners (Board) declining to certify that Terry George Radtke satisfied the character and fitness requirement for admission to the Wisconsin bar. . . .

We determine that the Board properly concluded . . . that Mr. Radtke failed to meet his burden . . . to establish the requisite moral character and fitness to practice law. . . .

Prior to his graduation from Marquette University School of Law in May 1998, Mr. Radtke was a lecturer in the Department of History at University of Wisconsin-Milwaukee (UWM) from August 1984 to May 1991. [I]n the fall of 1990 he had prepared a paper and submitted a version of it for publication to a number of journals, including the *Business History Review*. He explained that the paper . . . "did not include several key cites to secondary sources in the bibliography and paraphrased several sources that were not quoted." He stated that he "simply forgot to include the necessary footnotes in the paper" and asserted that the allegation that he had engaged in "professional plagiarism" arose from a letter the editors of *Business History Review* sent to the UWM History Department chair about the missing citations. . . .

. . . In respect to the alleged plagiarism, Mr. Radtke asserted that he had not provided source citations to materials quoted in his paper and to various facts . . . , most of which he had taken from secondary articles. He acknowledged that he should have mentioned those articles as sources.

. . . Mr. Radtke's descriptions of his paper were at variance with the evidence. . . . Mr. Radtke deliberately had copied a substantial portion—more than half—of his article from other people's work, presented it as his own, and lied to the Board.

. . . Mr. Radtke minimized his conduct by characterizing what he did as "paraphras[ing] several sources that were not quoted" and having "simply forgot[ten] to include the necessary footnotes" and "several key cites to secondary sources in the bibliography." The argument that if he had intended to plagiarize, he would not have set forth text from scholarly journals verbatim, thereby running the risk of detection by any person knowledgeable in the field, is disingenuous. . . .

Mr. Radtke has failed to establish that any of the Board's findings is clearly erroneous. Each of the foregoing findings of fact is adequately supported by the credible evidence and the reasonable inferences that can be drawn from it. . . .

Mr. Radtke's final argument . . . asserted that the Board erred in concluding that his unprofessional conduct and incomplete and untruthful disclosures were relevant to his character and fitness because it failed to take into consideration each of the nine factors listed in BA 6.03. We find no merit to that argument. First, Mr. Radtke incorrectly stated that the Board considered only two factors—the seriousness of his conduct and his candor in the admission process. In fact, the Board also explicitly considered the lack of evidence of his rehabilitation and the materiality of his omissions in the admission process. Second, we rejected the same argument in *Saganski v. Board of Bar Examiners*, 595 N.W.2d 631 (Wis. 1999), holding that it is sufficient that the Board consider those BA 6.03 factors that are applicable to the conduct of the applicant.

[W]e affirm the Board's determination declining to certify Mr. Radtke's character and fitness for bar admission. [In considering] the effect Mr. Radtke's conduct in the plagiarism incident and in the bar admission application process has on his eligibility to reapply for bar admission . . . , we take into account Mr. Radtke's professional record during the eight years following the plagiarism incident. Mr. Radtke . . . admitted his mistake in the submission of his article for publication and took full responsibility for it, subsequently published the article with proper footnotes, published a book, completed his doctoral thesis and obtained his doctorate, and earned a law degree. He did all of that without any allegation of questionable conduct.

While Mr. Radtke's recent characterizations of the plagiarism incident and the impact it had on his professional employment cause great concern . . . , we determine that Mr. Radtke should be permitted to reapply for bar admission. [A] one-year period is the appropriate time for him to wait before reapplying.

In re Howard

855 N.E.2d 865 (Ohio 2006)

On August 16, 2004, Micheal Habib Howard applied to register as a candidate for admission to the practice of law in Ohio. . . .

On review, we agree that this applicant has not shown that he is a proper candidate for admission to the practice of law in this state.

An applicant has the burden to prove by clear and convincing evidence that he or she possesses the requisite character, fitness, and moral qualification for admission to the practice of law. Gov. Bar R. I(11)(D)(1). An applicant's record of conduct must justify "the trust of clients, adversaries, courts and others with respect to the professional duties owed to them" and demonstrate that the applicant "satisfies the essential eligibility requirements for the practice of law" as defined by law. Gov. Bar R. I(11)(D)(3). To ensure that the record does not manifest "a significant deficiency in the honesty, trustworthiness, diligence or reliability" of an applicant, the rule lists several factors that weigh against approval . . . .

This applicant's bar examination and admission materials are saturated with these three ethical impediments. First, the applicant has a troubling criminal record of misdemeanor convictions. . . . Of equal concern are the many other times that the applicant was accused of criminal conduct, even though the charges were dismissed. . . .

At the hearing, the applicant assured the panel that when he decided to become a lawyer, he had changed his lifestyle and turned over a new leaf. The board was not convinced, noting that the applicant had been charged with four crimes in 2001, just about the time he was accepted into law school. We share the board's skepticism.

The applicant also has a significant record of academic misconduct. On June 2, 2003, after his purported reformation, the applicant was suspended for a semester from the University of Toledo College of Law because he plagiarized material for a writing assignment. While an undergraduate, the applicant was also issued a "letter of warning" for copying another student's homework assignment during the 1995 autumn quarter at the Ohio State University. . . .

Evidence also suggested that the applicant had not been forthright and candid when he initially discussed his law school honor-code violation with members of the bar association. [H]e first suggested that his plagiarism involved only an initial draft of a paper and that he had not understood that copying was unacceptable in his preliminary work. The applicant's law professor, however, confirmed to the committee that the applicant had plagiarized material in both the draft and the final version of his paper. . . .

In summary, the board concluded:

> [T]he past record of conduct of the applicant . . . seems to reflect a pattern of disregard for the law and action that involves deceit or misrepresentation. These concerns are only magnified by the seemingly evasive and less than candid demeanor of the applicant during the hearing. . . . The Board, therefore, concludes that the applicant does not currently possess the requisite character, fitness and moral qualifications for admission to the practice of law.

We adopt the board's findings and recommendation to disapprove applicant's request. We make no finding as to whether the applicant can rehabilitate his character, fitness, and moral qualification, however, or as to when rehabilitation might permit him to reapply as a candidate for admission pursuant to Gov. Bar R. I(2). . . .

In re Worthy

991 N.E.2d 1131 (Ohio 2013)

Michele Yulana Worthy of Beavercreek, Ohio, is a January 2013 graduate of the University of Dayton School of Law and has applied to register as a candidate to sit for the February 2013 bar exam. . . .

... Worthy received her undergraduate degree from the Ohio State University in the spring of 2009 and worked as an assistant teacher for one year before beginning her law studies at the University of Dayton in the fall of 2010.

During Worthy's senior year of college, ... she fell short on funds following an illness that caused her to miss work. She and a friend planned to shoplift designer jeans from a store and then sell them, but they were caught shoplifting by the store's security officers. ... This offense has since been expunged from Worthy's record.

... As an undergraduate, Worthy submitted a paper for one of her courses that included material plagiarized from a website. [S]he had not reported this incident on her application to register as a candidate for admission to the bar ....

The [hearing] panel [of the Board of Commissioners on Character and Fitness] found that Worthy had engaged in two instances of dishonesty when faced with minor emergencies—shoplifting when she was short on cash and plagiarizing when she fell behind in a college course. The panel also found that she had intentionally failed to disclose her plagiarism on her application to register as a candidate for admission to the bar. ...

The ... [Board of Commissioners] was not convinced that Worthy understood the significance of her failure to disclose and explain the circumstances of her academic probation on her law-school application and her application to register as a candidate for admission to the bar. ...

While the board believed that Worthy had learned from her mistakes and that she might be able to satisfy the character-and-fitness standards in the near future, it found that she had failed to demonstrate that she currently possesses the requisite character, fitness, and moral qualifications to be approved for admission to the practice of law in Ohio. We agree. ...

... [We] disapprove [Worthy's] application [for admission to the bar]. However, we believe that with time, Worthy may be able to prove that she meets the requisite qualifications, and we therefore permit her to reapply for the July 2014 bar exam, at which time she will be subject to a new character-and-fitness investigation.

In re White

656 S.E.2d 527 (Ga. 2008)

In October 2005, Willie Jay White applied to sit for the Georgia Bar Exam. As part of the application process, White submitted a request for certification of fitness to practice law. The Board to Determine Fitness of Bar Applicants ("Board") denied White certification of fitness to practice law, and White appealed. ...

... White ... had submitted a paper at the end of his second year of law school that was a virtually verbatim reproduction of sections of five previously published sources, none of which was cited in the paper. ...

... White ... deliberately took sections of five previously published works, typed them word-for-word into his computer, made minute changes in citations and wording, and ... submitted it to his professor as his own work.

... The hearing officer specifically found that White's explanation of the plagiarism incident was not credible, that he had not yet accepted full responsibility for his actions, and that he did not currently possess the character and fitness required of a prospective member of the State Bar. The hearing officer recommended final denial of White's application for certification of fitness to practice law, and the Board adopted ... [the] recommendation.

The applicant bears the burden of establishing that he or she is fit to practice law.[†] ...

... White intentionally submitted a wholly plagiarized paper in his advanced torts class at the end of his second year of law school. From the time the plagiarism was first discovered through the application and investigation process by the Board and up to the present day, White has failed to offer a plausible explanation of his actions. As a result, he has never accepted full responsibility for what he did, and he has not yet been rehabilitated.

Our independent review of the record confirms not only the factual findings of the hearing officer and the Board, but also that White presently lacks the integrity, character, and moral fitness required for admission to the Georgia Bar. Accordingly, the Board properly denied his application for certification of fitness to practice law, and we affirm the Board's judgment.

In re Widdison
539 N.W.2d 671 (S.D. 1995)

[The applicant has graduated from law school and applied for admission to the bar of this state.]

[During his] second year of law school, he wrote and submitted a casenote for law review publication [which] included ... material from secondary sources which he had failed to cite. ... The faculty advisor ... assigned [the applicant] a failing grade in the law review course. ...

[After the applicant took the final exam in the course on Worker's Compensation, the professor discovered two students' examination answers] were strikingly

---

[†] [*Court's footnote*] [T]his Court's primary responsibility in reviewing fitness applications, like the Board's, is "to the public to see that those who are admitted to practice are ethically cognizant and mature individuals who have the character to withstand the temptations which are placed before them as they handle other people's money and affairs" and ... doubtful cases "must be decided in favor of the public's protection." [Citation omitted.]

similar. . . . [T]he professor assigned a failing grade to each examination[, one of which was the applicant's].

[The applicant] has the burden of proving by clear and convincing evidence his qualifications for admission to practice law in this state. . . . One of those qualifications is that he "be a person of good moral character." SDCL 6-16-2. SDCL 16-16-2.1 defines "good moral character" as including, but not limited to, "qualities of honesty, candor, trustworthiness, diligence, reliability, observance of fiduciary and financial responsibility, and respect for the rights of others and for the judicial process." That statute also provides that "[a]ny fact reflecting a deficiency of good moral character may constitute a basis for denial of admission." SDCL 16-16-2.1 (emphasis added). Good moral character is a prerequisite to practice law in every state. . . .

"The state bears a special responsibility for maintaining standards among members of the licensed professions" such as attorneys at law. [Citations omitted.] . . . The same zeal to protect the public from the unfit within the bar must also be applied to the unfit who would seek to enter the bar. . . .

[The applicant] has not met his burden of proving good moral character. [We affirm the order denying his application for admission to the bar], with leave to reapply at a future date provided [the applicant] is able to rectify his character deficits and show he has gained an understanding of, and the ability to put into practice, the qualities of honesty, candor, and responsibility required [of lawyers].

In re Zbiegien

433 N.W.2d 871 (Minn. 1988)

[The petitioner has graduated from law school and has applied for admission to the bar of this state.]

[In a law school seminar in products liability, the petitioner submitted a draft paper that] was plagiarized in large part from the works of other authors. Nearly all of the first 12 pages were taken verbatim or nearly verbatim from a number of law review articles without proper citation in the endnotes. In addition, some endnotes were taken from other sources in such a way as to give the appearance that they were petitioner's own work. Several other portions of the paper were paraphrased or had words or phrases omitted or substituted for the originals as they appeared in various published sources. Again, no proper citation was given. . . . [The petitioner received] a course grade of "F". . . .

[The petitioner] admitted the extensive plagiarism . . . both in the form of direct quotes not properly indented and footnoted and paraphrased passages not appropriately credited to the original sources. [He said that his computer printer had not been printing properly, and he did not proofread the paper as it came out of the printer because at the time his wife was disabled from an auto accident, and his teenage son had run away from home.] . . .

The [State Board of Law Examiners, however,] found that not only had petitioner plagiarized a substantial amount of text and footnotes taken verbatim, or nearly verbatim, from various published sources without proper identification [but also] that the alleged computer problems did not explain away the plagiarism. . . .

Petitioner appeals from that determination. . . .

Rule II.A of the Minnesota Rules of the Supreme Court for Admission to the Bar provides that an applicant must establish good character and fitness to the satisfaction of the Board.

"Good character" is defined as "traits that are relevant to and have a rational connection with the present fitness or capacity of an applicant to practice law." Definition 4, Minn. R. Admis. Bar (1986). . . .

Plagiarism, the adoption of the work of others as one's own, does involve an element of deceit, which reflects on an individual's honesty. . . . The petitioner clearly plagiarized large sections of his paper. . . .

It is the view of this court that [this] petitioner's conduct, wrongful though it was, does not demonstrate such lack of character that he must be barred from the practice of law. He has been punished [already in practical terms because the Board's investigation has delayed his admission to the bar] for over a year. [In dealing with law school officials and when testifying before the Board, the petitioner was filled with genuine remorse and shame.] We . . . believe that this conduct will not be repeated. We hold that, under the facts and circumstances of this case petitioner will not be barred from the practice of law. . . .

KELLEY, J. (dissenting):

. . . When this court admits an applicant to the practice of law, it certifies to the public that . . . it knows of no reason why the applicant-admittee does not possess the character which the profession demands of all admitted attorneys in this state. We judge an applicant's character by the standard that it must reflect those traits of integrity, honesty and trustworthiness necessary for a lawyer to possess when he or she represents clients, when dealing with professional peers, and when appearing before the courts. Yet, in this case, notwithstanding that we know that this petitioner has . . . recently engaged in outright dishonesty by plagiarizing and claiming as his own the intellectual works of others with no attempt at appropriate attribution of source, the majority would conclude, even as it condemns the petitioner's conduct, that he has been "punished" enough by the delay in his admission. . . .

[D]enial of admission . . . has not as its purpose punishment but rather protection of the public and the integrity of the legal system. . . .

Even though I would deny the petition, I would not foreclose forever, petitioner's admission to the Bar. I would, however, require that he prove that after a reasonable period of time had elapsed he then . . . demonstrates that from the experience he has learned to conduct his affairs in a manner that this court can, with confidence, certify to the public that his character does reflect traits of integrity and trustworthiness.

10 Working with Cases

§ 10.1 Eight Skills for Working with Cases

If you find mandatory precedent on point—a case from the highest court in your jurisdiction deciding your issue on facts that exactly mirror yours—the legal issue is probably so straightforward that it requires little or no hard thinking. But that is rare. More often, you will need to predict what a court would do using at least some of the following skills:

1. Evaluating a precedent case according to the hierarchy of authority and its mandatory or persuasive value (Chapter 8)
2. Isolating a precedent opinion's determinative facts, and framing its holding either broadly or narrowly (Chapter 6)
3. Analogizing precedent cases on their facts (§ 10.2)
4. Distinguishing cases on their facts (the opposite of analogizing) (§ 10.2)
5. Identifying policy reasoning (§ 10.3)
6. Synthesizing fragmented authorities into a unifying rule that reconciles them (§ 10.4)
7. Reconciling conflicting or adverse authority (§ 10.5)
8. Testing the results for realism (§ 10.6)

The first two skills are explained earlier in this book. The others are explained in this chapter.

§ 10.2   Analogizing and Distinguishing Precedent Cases

If two cases are so factually parallel that the reasoning a court used to decide the first case should also govern the second, the cases are *analogous*. *Distinguishing* is showing that the facts of two cases are so fundamentally different that they should be decided differently. Both analytical skills support the policy of ensuring that the common law is both predictable and fair.

For example, assume that your older brother graduated from high school and went to a large public university, and your parents bought him a used car. Four years later, you graduate from high school and plan to attend a small liberal arts college. You might argue that the situations are *analogous*, and if your brother got a car, you should get one, too.

But your parents might reason differently. They might say that your older brother needed a car to get around a huge university campus. But in your case, you can easily navigate your small college campus on foot without a car. Besides, your private college tuition is much more costly than your brother's tuition at a public university. Your parents might reason that the situations are so different that it would be unfair for you to expect to be treated the same as your older brother. In that case, your parents would be pointing out that the two situations are *distinguishable*.

Lawyers and judges are skilled at both analogizing and distinguishing cases. That is because the common law was developed entirely through case precedent and the principle of *stare decisis*, which both rely heavily on analogous reasoning to resolve legal issues.

A court is most likely to apply the same legal rule and reasoning to a new set of facts if it is persuaded that a previous case involving the same or similar facts was decided that way. Consistency in decision making helps make the law predictable. If judges decided cases based on what they thought was the fair result in each case without considering precedent, lawyers would have a much harder job predicting the outcome of a client's legal problem.

Analogize and distinguish cases using these three steps:

Analogizing and Distinguishing Cases

Step 1   Make sure the legal issue in the precedent case is the same as the issue you are trying to resolve.

Step 2   Identify the precedent's determinative facts (§ 6.1). Do not look for mere coincidences between the precedent's facts and yours. Look instead for facts on which the precedent court's decision relied, and which were crucial to the outcome.

Step 3   Compare the precedent's determinative facts to the facts of your case. If they match, you have an analogy, and you can use the precedent to predict the same outcome in your case. If not, the precedent is distinguishable from your case because the crucial facts differ.

Let's consider an example to show how these steps work.

The precedent. A landlord failed to repair a residential tenant's toilet for one week, in violation of the local housing code. A court held that the tenant could withhold her next monthly rent payment and use the money to repair the toilet herself.

Our facts. The owner of a refrigerated warehouse failed to maintain the refrigeration device, causing the commercial tenant's fruits and vegetables to spoil. The lease obligates the landlord to provide refrigeration. The tenant wants to withhold the next rent payment and use the money to repair the refrigeration device.

Step 1 Is the legal issue the same? Yes. In both, the issue is whether the tenant may deduct the cost of repairs from the rent payment.

Step 2 What were the determinative facts in the precedent?
- Landlord/tenant relationship
- Toilet problem
- Landlord violated housing code obligation to repair

Step 3 Compare the precedent's determinative facts to the facts in the current problem.

Precedent Facts	Our Facts
• Landlord/tenant relationship	• Same
• Toilet problem	• No toilet issue
• Landlord violated housing code	• No code governs commercial leases

Does the analogy fail because a residential toilet is not the same as a commercial refrigeration device, and because commercial leases are not governed by a statute like the housing code? In both cases, the equipment that failed was essential to the tenant's purpose for leasing the property. And in both cases, the landlord had an obligation (whether by law or under the lease agreement) to maintain the equipment that failed. Once we think about the two situations that way, Steps 2 and 3 might look analogous after all. Notice how they change below from those above.

Step 2 What were the determinative facts in the precedent?
- Landlord/tenant relationship
- Essential equipment failed (toilet)
- Landlord violated obligation to repair (housing code)

Step 3 Compare the precedent's determinative facts to the facts in the current problem.

Precedent Facts	**Our Facts**
• Landlord/tenant relationship	• Same, but a commercial lease
• Essential equipment failed	• Same—refrigeration essential
• Landlord violated obligation to repair	• Same—violated lease obligation to repair

In both cases, the landlord had an obligation to maintain something essential to the tenant's reason for occupying the rented space. The obligation arose from different sources, but an obligation is an obligation, whether imposed by statute (the housing code) or by contract (the lease). Although we cannot be certain that the outcome would be the same in both cases, drawing the analogy greatly increases the chances that if one tenant could deduct the cost of repairs from the rent payment, then the other tenant can, too.

If you were representing the landlord in the second case, how might you distinguish the facts of your case from the precedent? You might emphasize the difference between a residential tenant and a commercial tenant, and the difference between a repair obligation as a matter of statute (the housing code) and a repair obligation by contract (the lease). Or perhaps the commercial lease has another provision requiring the commercial tenant to immediately make the necessary repairs to mitigate damages, and then to bill the landlord for the out-of-pocket expense rather than deducting it from the next rent payment.

Even when two cases seem factually similar, experienced lawyers can find ways to distinguish them to persuade a court that the outcome in the second case should not be the same as the outcome in the precedent. The court will ultimately decide which party's arguments are most persuasive. The lawyer's job is to predict whether the judge will analogize or distinguish the precedent case.

§ 10.3 Identifying Policy Reasoning

What could a court do that would satisfy not just the elements of a rule but also the reason why the rule exists in the first place—its policy, as explained in Chapter 7? The hypothetical in § 10.2 illustrates how policy analysis interacts with other skills discussed in this chapter.

Policy explains why the precedent case was governed by a housing code and the second case was not. Parties to a commercial lease can bargain with each other to protect themselves. If a commercial tenant needs refrigeration, the tenant can insist that the lease be written to require the landlord to provide it. But residential tenants often lack knowledge and market power to negotiate the terms of an apartment lease. If you have ever signed a lease, did it occur to you to negotiate for a provision requiring the landlord to fix the toilet or the stove or the heating system? Most likely not. The legislature has therefore enacted a housing code to protect residential tenants from landlords who might otherwise refuse to make repairs reasonably necessary for day-to-day living.

How do you find out what the law's policies are? Sometimes they will be expressly stated in the statutes themselves. (See § 9.1.1.) More often, policy discussions can be found in precedent cases, either expressly stated or implied. Courts do not often say, "We adopt this rule to achieve the following policies." More typically, a case will discuss the types of policy concerns the court is trying to address, the useful things the legal rule would accomplish, or the dangerous things that would happen without the rule. When a court talks about any of these concerns, the court is discussing policy, even if it never uses that word to describe it.

§ 10.4   Synthesis

Case synthesis is the process of unifying the reasoning of several opinions into a whole that stands for an overall legal rule or an expression of policy. By focusing on the common reasoning and generalized facts of a group of cases, synthesis finds and explains collective meaning that is not apparent from any single case read in isolation. Synthesis is plausible to a legal reader if it is logical, reasonable, and consistent with public policy. To test a synthesized rule, be sure it explains the court's reasoning and result in each of the synthesized precedents.

A synthesis does more than describe several cases, one by one. Do not synthesize by "mini-briefing" Case A, Case B, Case C, and finally Case D, and then stop. That is nothing more than a description of your raw materials.

To turn a description of several cases into a unified synthesis, step back and ask yourself what the cases really have in common under the surface. Identify the common threads of reasoning or policy that appear in all four cases, tie the threads together, and organize the analysis around the threads themselves—rather than around the individual cases. The reader cares more about the common threads than about the individual cases. In a synthesis, each individual case is important only to the extent it illustrates something about one of the common threads in legal reasoning.

It may turn out that Case B sets out the most convincing explanation to prove whatever element is in dispute. Cases A and D agree, and perhaps they are the only cases from other jurisdictions that have decided the issue. Case C may be a much older decision from the same state as the deciding court. It may support the same rule, but its reasoning may be less complete than in Case B, also from our state. An effective synthesis would explain Case B in detail, using Cases A and D to show that other states agree. Case C might be omitted entirely, or it might be mentioned with a brief citation and a concise explanatory parenthetical.

When working out a synthesis, make that clear to the reader. First, summarize the synthesis in an opening sentence:

> Although the Supreme Court has not ruled on the question, the trend in the appellate courts is to hold that a trial court may dismiss a criminal complaint if any of three kinds of government misconduct occurs.

A synthesis like this could take many pages to prove because you would later need to show that

- the Supreme Court really has not ruled on the issue (*You would discuss Supreme Court cases that come close and show how those cases do not resolve the issue*)
- appellate courts have held that each kind of government misconduct is grounds for dismissal (*You would write a separate synthesis for each kind of misconduct*).

When in your mind you develop or discover a rule synthesis, you will usually do it from the bottom up. First, work with the details of each case until you see their analogous features that suggest a synthesis. When you explain your synthesis in writing to your reader, do the reverse. Begin by summarizing the synthesis, and then explain how the details of each case support it. Your first draft might not do that very well because your thinking develops as you write. (Writing is thinking.) But later drafts should reflect the top-down explanation that will make the most sense to your reader.

§ 10.5   Reconciling Authority

Reconciling authority is a hybrid of some of the other skills discussed in this chapter. If two cases on the surface seem to conflict with each other, you might be able to demonstrate that the conflict does not exist because the two decisions, on closer examination, actually stand for the same rule, espouse the same policy, or can be harmonized in some other way. Done that way, reconciliation has much in common with synthesis. Sometimes you might be able to reconcile precedents by showing that one opinion is really analogous to another, even if the similarity is not apparent at first glance. If you can reconcile cases in a plausible way, they are not distinguishable.

§ 10.6   Testing for Realism

The last skill in working with cases is *testing the result of your reasoning to see whether it would seem realistic to the judicial mind.* For example, would your reasoning seem reasonable to the typical judge? Does it reach a just result? Or would it produce impractical consequences?

Experience at judging creates what Roscoe Pound once called "the trained intuition of the judge,"[1] an instinct for how the law ought to treat each set of facts. If the result of your reasoning would strike the judicial mind as impractical, many judges will reject it, even if you have effectively used all the other skills. If you do not test your result for realism, your analysis will be *formalistic* because it will do nothing more than comply with the letter of the law. Because the law is hardly ever certain, a skeptical judge can always fold back your reasoning and make analogies you did not make, build other syntheses, and so forth. Even worse, the judge might adopt the analogies, syntheses, and other constructs proposed by your adversary.

Karl Llewellyn wrote that "rules *guide*, but they do not *control* decision. There is no precedent that the judge may not at his need either file down to razor thinness or expand into a bludgeon."[2] To test for realism, you need to understand how the judicial mind operates. That understanding may take a long time for you to develop fully, but you are learning it now through the decisions you read in casebooks and through the writing you do in this course.

Although lawyers often write arguments based on equity, justice, and reasonableness, they *never put in writing* the kind of testing described in this section. How could you possibly reduce to writing a test for realism? If a lawyer concludes that the result of her or his reasoning would be inconsistent with the judge's trained intuition, the lawyer simply starts over again and builds a different analysis that a judge would accept.

Exercise 10-A. To Google or Not to Google?

You are sitting in your Contracts class, listening intently, while the professor introduces a hypothetical. One of the factors that would influence the result is the relative distance to deliver a product from Cincinnati, Ohio, to either Columbus, Ohio, or Lexington, Kentucky. You think you know which way is faster, but you will get more accurate information if you use your laptop to check Google Maps.

Before you consult Google Maps while sitting in Contracts class, you recall the following:

- The syllabus allows computers in class, if used "only for purposes associated with the class."
- Last year the same Contracts professor noticed a student bidding on eBay during class. After that, the professor prohibited students from using laptops in class for the rest of the year, and everyone else in class resented the person who was caught.

---

[1] Roscoe Pound, *The Theory of Judicial Decision*, 36 HARV. L. REV. 940, 951 (1923).
[2] KARL N. LLEWELLYN, THE BRAMBLE BUSH 180 (1930).

- This semester, your Civil Procedure professor posted a message from a student about the Seventh Circuit's website providing information on standards of review. The professor's posting thanked the student for locating and sharing such useful information.

Use the skills of working with precedent to predict what the Contracts professor will do if you use Google Maps, following these steps:

1. Fill in the table printed below to see whether it helps you make a prediction. In the second and third columns, write a narrow and a broad interpretation of the rule applied in each precedent.
2. Synthesize by weighing the information together to determine whether the precedents combine to support one rule, a rule with an exception, or more than one rule.
3. Tentatively predict the result if you use Google Maps in Contracts class, based on the rule or rules you just synthesized.
4. Assess your tentative prediction by imagining arguments that can be made for each side. Would a narrow or broad interpretation of the rule lead to different results? Does your case include facts that seem significantly different from the precedent cases?
5. Weigh the arguments for the competing results, as a judge would. Which side is more likely to win, and why? This answer will be your final prediction.

It may help your legal analysis to draw a table like this one on a separate page, filling in the spaces for each precedent. After considering your entries in the table, does this visual diagram help synthesize a rule you can use to predict the result?

Case Synthesis Table

Precedent	Mandatory or persuasive?	Narrow reading	Broad reading	Policy
Syllabus rule				
Last year's eBay incident				
Internet value in Civ. Pro. class				

Part 2

The Process of Writing

11 Getting to Know Yourself as a Writer

§ 11.1 Product and Process

A writing course focuses on improving both the written *product* and the *process* of creating it. An office memo is an example of product. What should it look like? What should it accomplish? The process of writing is what you do at the keyboard while creating the memo, including what you are thinking while you type.

Process is much harder to learn than product. Product is tangible. It can be seen and held in the hand, and a sample office memo, like the one in Appendix A, can be discussed in class to learn what makes it effective or ineffective. Process is much harder to observe because it happens mostly in your mind. Imagine a teacher sitting next to you as you write. The teacher would have a difficult time figuring out what you are doing—and you might want the teacher to leave.

There are many different effective processes of writing. If you put the 50 best-selling book authors in America into one room and asked them how they write, they would probably give you 50 different answers. But most effective writing processes share a few basic traits, which we discuss in this and later chapters of this book.

Beyond that, finding the process that works best for you can happen through experimenting by *doing* while simultaneously *thinking* about what you are doing. Reflecting on what you do and how you do it is the most effective way of improving your process of writing.

§ 11.2 What Do You Do When You Write?

How do you go about writing? How did you write in the past, and how are you doing it in law school? Be honest with yourself. If asked how you write, it might be tempting to say that you use exactly the process someone recommends—simply because it is human nature to confuse what you set out to do with what you actually do. For most people, it takes serious reflection to separate the two. If you are open and self-critical about your process, you can improve it more quickly.

What do you *like* about the way you write? What *frustrates* you? What seems to cause the frustration? What would you like your process to be? What might it take for you to accomplish that? What methods have you tried to get there?

When teachers ask individual students questions like these, often the students themselves do most of the brainstorming—because they know themselves better than anybody else can know them and because they really want to find a process that works well for them. That means that you do not need to wait until your next conversation with your teacher to work on your writing process. You can brainstorm with another thoughtful student. Or, while writing, you can have an internal dialog with yourself about what is working in your process and why.

§ 11.3   Voice

Voice is a personal quality in a person's writing, something that speaks from the page in that writer's own way. Most people have only a slight voice in their writing—and prefer not to write in a way that is unique. There is nothing wrong with that.

Some students enter law school with distinctive written voices of their own. In legal writing courses, they learn that their writing must conform to a number of professional standards. Does that mean that you can no longer write in a voice that is yours? No, but you might need to adapt it to a professional situation. Your voice in professional documents will grow into something different from what it was before law school, but it will still be distinctively yours—although recognizably professional. Most people who enter law school with distinctive written voices say later, after they have developed a professional voice, that they like the professional version.

§ 11.4   Confidence

Learning a skill at a higher level of proficiency, with new requirements, can make you feel as though you have lost the competency you thought you had before. Most students feel at least some of that uncertainty while learning to write at a professional level. The feeling of doubt is sharpest near the beginning. But gradually—very gradually—it is replaced with a feeling of *strength*. By the end of the legal writing course, many students feel much stronger as writers than ever before because they have *become* stronger. For now, please remember this: If in the weeks ahead you fall into doubt about your writing abilities, it will be because you are quickly learning a lot. *It does not necessarily mean you are a bad writer. You might be a good one. Once you absorb what you are learning and start producing professional writing—and that can happen—your prior confidence can return and might be stronger than before because you would now be reaching for mastery.*

Many law students and young lawyers report that while learning legal writing they felt discouraged, but that later they experienced a first moment of validation. That moment might have come late in a semester, when a legal writing professor told them that they had done something really well. Or it might have come in a summer or part-time job, when a supervising lawyer complimented them on a well-written memo. Or it might have come in court when a judge leaned over the bench and said, "It was a pleasure to read your brief, counselor." That first moment of validation was the beginning of the recognition of *mastery*. Mastery was not yet complete; it would take much longer for that to happen. But it had begun.

Many students and young lawyers also say that they wished someone had told them while they were working so hard in legal writing that a moment marking the beginning of mastery would eventually come. That is why we are telling you now that if you are like most students—and even if you feel deeply discouraged along the way—that moment *can* eventually come.

§ 11.5 Learning Styles and Writing

This section explains three frequently discussed learning styles. Most people have some of the characteristics of two or all three styles.

Rather than classify your learning style one way or another, you might figure out which style or styles reflect your strengths and whether other styles illustrate strengths you want to try to develop. To become effective at learning writing or any other skill, it helps to identify your strengths so you can capitalize on them. But it also helps to identify areas where you need to grow so you can consciously work on that goal.

Auditory/sequential learners, or ASLs, absorb information most efficiently by listening. They would rather hear driving directions than look at a map. They tend to think in words rather than pictures. "Sequential" in "auditory/sequential" refers to thinking in a series of ideas that add up to a progression to larger conclusions, like this:

Traffic Stop Arrest
(If the police violate the Constitution during a search or interrogation, any resulting evidence or confession will be inadmissible at trial.)

if		*then*
police seize stolen property and get a confession	→	both need justification
probable cause for police to stop the car in traffic	→	police had legal authority to stop the car
no probable cause to search trunk	→	evidence found there will be inadmissible
driver consented to search	→	evidence admissible based on consent
driver in custody after stolen property found in trunk	→	*Miranda* warnings required
driver knowingly & voluntarily waived *Miranda* rights	→	confession admissible
evidence and confession admissible	→	***driver will be convicted of possessing stolen property***

Visual/spatial learners, or VSLs, absorb information most efficiently by seeing—either reading words or looking at pictures, diagrams, or demonstrations. They would rather look at a map than listen to someone give driving directions. More than other people, they think in images, although they also think in words. When reading a story, they often "see" the action in their minds, as though watching a movie, or they create a mental diagram of the relationships among the people involved. "Spatial" in "visual/spatial" refers to several aspects of thinking, among them a tendency to start from an idea and branch out in several directions, sometimes simultaneously, like this:

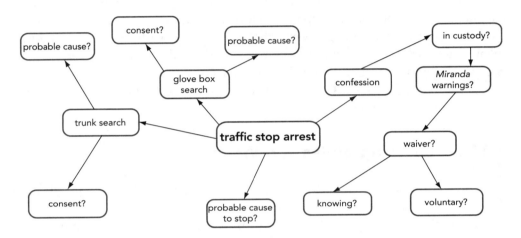

Tactile/kinesthetic learners, or TKLs, absorb information most efficiently through action. They learn best by doing something rather than by reading or hearing about it or looking at it, especially when doing so involves use of the sense of touch. They also learn well from experience. They would rather explore than look at a map or hear directions. They often think through doing because activity creates insights. While studying, TKLs often feel a desire to move about or do something with their hands because motion is thought.

Imagine that you buy something complicated, perhaps a PC with monitor, keyboard, printer, and speakers. Connecting everything and learning how to use it will be difficult. Inside the boxes are owner's manuals. If you have auditory/sequential strengths, your first instinct might be to read carefully the text in the manuals. If you have visual/spatial strengths, you might look first at the diagrams in a manual and consult the text only if the diagrams do not tell you what you need to know. If you have tactile/kinesthetic strengths, you might toss the manuals aside and start fiddling with the equipment until you have figured out how to install it and how to use it.

This example is somewhat of an oversimplification, but researchers sometimes use it to illustrate differences among the three learning styles. Manufacturers know about learning styles. They put lots of diagrams in manuals for VSLs, and for TKLs they sometimes include a separate one- or two-page insert with essential information, titled something like "If You Hate Manuals, Use This."

When it comes to writing, people with auditory/sequential strengths tend to focus on the details, and in legal writing, they might intuitively understand how to show the steps of their reasoning in a logical sequence. Regardless of learning style, most students need to improve at explaining their reasoning steps *in depth.*

People with visual/spatial strengths might more quickly understand an entire situation. They might see the big picture at once. They can seem to sculpt a document rather than writing it from beginning to end. A leading researcher in this field says the following:

> For visual-spatials, writing is a lot like painting a picture. They may paint with broad strokes at first, filling in the details as they refine their pictures. In a painting, there's no particular order. You can start in the middle and work toward either end, or you can start at the end and work toward the beginning. I know a VSL who's a superb writer. . . . She cannot show anyone her rough drafts because they are full of holes. These are real gaps in the flow of writing where the picture hasn't formed yet. Being nonsequential in her thinking, she skips around the text, filling in the parts that are clear in her mind, and leaving large, gaping holes. Sometimes these holes are filled in her dreams, as her unconscious supplies the missing words or missing pieces of the picture.[1]

Less is known about TKLs and writing, except that some people with tactile/kinesthetic strengths say that writing helps them think because of the physical activity involved, especially when typing. Some describe this as thinking through their fingers.

In legal writing, *all* of these strengths can be valuable. You can continue to build your skills around the ones you already have. It is not necessary to build up the others equally. No one is perfect or equally rounded, and all of us have uneven strengths. Many of the most famous writers can describe in abundant detail where they are weak in the writing process. And everyone can become more effective by identifying areas where they are not strong and by trying to improve there.

Much of education is based on the erroneous assumption that all learners are auditory/sequential. A teacher stands at the front of the room and talks. Students are supposed to sit still for long periods of time. Most textbooks are masses of words with few or no diagrams. In law school, an exception to all this is in skills courses, where students learn to do things, like write memos or cross-examine witnesses.

---

[1] LINDA KREGER SILVERMAN, UPSIDE-DOWN BRILLIANCE: THE VISUAL-SPATIAL LEARNER 300 (2002).

Some researchers include learning style categories other than those discussed here, for example *verbal* (learning through reading and writing) and *oral* (learning through talking). These overlap with some of the categories explained earlier in this section. Researchers are still discovering new aspects about learning styles, and much remains to be discovered.

If you want to know more about your learning style or styles, you might look at the books and articles listed in the footnote[2] and do an internet search for the phrase "learning style." The books, articles, and websites explain how people with various learning styles can study more effectively and create more productive learning environments for themselves.

---

[2] Ann L. Iijima, The Law Student's Pocket Mentor: From Surviving to Thriving 59-76, 103-106 (2007); Michael Hunter Schwartz, Expert Learning for Law Students (2d ed. 2008); Robin A. Boyle & Rita Dunn, *Teaching Law Students Through Individual Learning Styles*, 62 Alb. L. Rev. 213 (1998); M.H. Sam Jacobson, *Learning Styles and Lawyering: Using Learning Theory to Organize Thinking and Writing*, 2 J. ALWD 27 (2004); M.H. Sam Jacobson, *How Law Students Absorb Information*, 8 Legal Writing 175 (2002); M.H. Sam Jacobson, *A Primer on Learning Styles: Reaching Every Student*, 25 Seattle U. L. Rev. 139 (2001).

12 Inside the Process of Writing

Learning how to write like a lawyer is the beginning of learning how to make professional decisions. Partly those are analytical decisions, such as determining how a statute affects the client. And partly they are practical decisions, such as how to communicate most effectively to the reader.

§ 12.1 Five Phases of Writing

Writing happens in five phases:

1. researching authorities and analyzing what you find (see § 12.3)
2. organizing your raw materials into an outline (§ 12.4)
3. producing a first draft (§§ 12.5-12.6)
4. rewriting it through several more drafts (§ 12.7)
5. polishing it (§ 12.9)

Writing teachers say that writing is recursive and not linear. Writers rarely, if ever, start at the beginning, write until they get to the end, and then stop (which would be in a line, or linear). And they do not go through the five phases of writing in strict order, finishing one phase before starting the next one (which would also be linear).

Instead, writers often circle back (recursively) to reopen something already done and redo some aspect of it. You will, for example, continue to analyze while organizing, writing the first draft, and rewriting, although much of the analytical work comes at the beginning. While writing the first draft, you might decide to go back and rewrite something you wrote a few pages ago. While rewriting, you might reorganize.

Still, it helps to think about writing in the five phases listed above. Each phase is a different *kind* of work, requiring somewhat different skills.

§ 12.2   Managing Time

Suppose your teacher distributes an assignment and sets a deadline three weeks later for submitting your work. On the day you receive the assignment, you have two options.

The first is to toss it aside when you get home and not to think about it for at least two weeks, leaving only the last few days before the deadline to do the entire job. Many students did this in college and turned in their first draft as their final product. When they try it again in law school, the result is usually disappointing because law school writing requires much more preparation and many more drafts. When you are learning professional skills, each new task will usually take longer to accomplish than you might think because the complexities of the task are not immediately apparent. (Later, with experience, you will get much better at predicting how long it will take to get things done.)

The other option is to start working right away so you have the full three weeks to get the job done. Some students have very good internal clocks that pace them through the work without having to set a schedule for themselves. But for most students, time will get out of control unless they schedule. In this sense, planning the work includes

- *estimating* how long it will take you to do the research, analyze the results, organize your raw materials, produce a first draft, rewrite it through several more drafts, and polish it, and
- *budgeting* your time so that you can do each one of these tasks well.

When you first get the assignment, it can seem huge and intimidating. But once you break it down into a group of smaller tasks, it is not as big any more, and it seems much more doable. Here is what Amy Stein,[1] a legal writing professor, tells her students:

> When I ask students if they have made a schedule for completing their work, they often look at me as if I have asked them to split the atom. Taking a series of complicated tasks and breaking them into manageable pieces is the best way that I know of to deal with the panic that comes from feeling that I have too much to do in too little time. Preparing a calendar will provide a master plan for all tasks, both work and play. . . .
>
> Building a schedule requires a certain amount of honesty. Students must know their own strengths and weaknesses and be able to answer several questions. . . . Do

---

[1] Amy R. Stein, *Helping Students Understand That Effective Organization Is a Prerequisite to Effective Legal Writing*, 15 Persps. 36, 37 (2006).

you work best in short, intense bursts or longer sessions? Where do you work the best? Are you a procrastinator? Are you a morning person or a night person? A morning person should schedule research in the morning and thirty minutes on the elliptical bike at night. . . .

. . . It is marvelously satisfying to cross off what you have accomplished.

§ 12.3   Researching and Analyzing

Researching is finding relevant authority, such as statutes and cases. Your teacher has probably assigned a research textbook that explains how.

Analysis is deciding which authorities to rely on (Chapter 8), figuring out what they mean (Chapters 9 and 10), and how they govern the client's facts (Chapter 16). Students and lawyers often print out the authorities that research suggests might be relevant and mark them up while reading and rereading them, identifying the most significant passages. For statutes, it helps to outline them as you read (Chapter 4).

§ 12.4   Organizing Your Raw Materials into an Outline

For two reasons, good organization is crucial in legal writing. First, legal writing is a highly structured form of expression because rules of law are by nature structured ideas. The structure of a rule controls the organization of its application to facts—and thus the organization of a written discussion of the rule and its application.

Second, your writing is measured by how well you educate a reader and convince the reader that you are right. Well-organized writing helps a reader understand you and your thinking. Organize so that you lead the reader through the steps in your reasoning.

Many students find that organizing in legal writing is especially challenging. That is why it takes several chapters in this book to explain how to plan and organize (see Chapter 13 and Chapters 16 through 20).

§ 12.5   Producing a First Draft

Many students treat the first draft as the most important phase of writing. But that is wrong: the first draft is often the *least* important phase. Most of the rest of writing does much more to produce an effective final product. And on a computer, first-draft writing might not be separate from rewriting. That is because of the ease with which you can interrupt your first draft and go back to rewrite something you initially wrote only a few minutes ago.

The only purpose of a first draft is to get something written so you can start rewriting. The first draft *has no other value*. A first draft accomplishes its entire purpose merely by existing.

It need not even be good. You can write what Anne Lamott calls "shitty first drafts":

> All good writers write them. This is how they end up with good second drafts and terrific third drafts. . . . I know some very great writers, . . . who write beautifully. . . . Not one of them writes elegant first drafts. All right, one of them does, but we do not like her very much. . . .
>
> Almost all good writing starts with terrible first efforts. Start by getting something—anything—down on paper. A friend of mine says that the first draft is the down draft—you just get it down. The second draft is the up draft—you fix it up. . . . And the third draft is the dental draft, where you check every tooth. . . . [2]

Do your first draft as early as you possibly can. You cannot start rewriting (§ 12.7) until you have a first draft.

You do not have to write the first draft from beginning to end. You can start with any part of the document that you feel ready to write, no matter where in the document it will be. You can write the middle before you write the beginning, for example. If your mind is mulling over a certain part of the document, start writing that part. You can write the rest later.

§ 12.6   Overcoming Writer's Block

Suppose you sit down to write your first draft, but nothing happens. You stare at the computer screen, and it seems to stare right back at you. This does *not* mean you are an inadequate writer. Writer's block happens to everybody from time to time, even to the very best writers. What can you do to overcome it? Here are some strategies:

1. Do something unrelated for a while. Prepare for class, do the dishes, or jog. While you are doing something else, your unconscious mind will continue to work on the first draft. After a while, ideas will pop into your conscious mind unexpectedly, and you will need to sit down and start writing again. But be careful: In law, you are usually writing against a deadline, and doing something else cannot go on for too long.

2. If the first paragraphs of a document are blocking you, start somewhere else. The reader starts at the beginning, but you do not have to. A common cause of writer's block is starting to write at the beginning. The beginning of a document is

---

[2] Anne Lamott, Bird by Bird 21-22, 25-26 (1994).

often the hardest part to write. And in each part of the document, the first paragraph is often the hardest to write. One of the reasons is that if you are not sure exactly what you will say, you will not know how to introduce it at the beginning.

3. Use writing to reduce your fear. The most effective way to reduce anxiety is to start writing early—long before your deadline—and to keep on working steadily until you have finished. If you start early, you will lose less sleep and be a happier writer. Many students procrastinate because they worry about writing. But procrastination *increases* anxiety and puts you further and further behind. The only way to break this cycle is to get started on writing so you can bring the task under control.

4. Do not expect perfection in first drafts. If you are chronically blocked when you try to do first drafts, it might be because you expect yourself to produce, in your first draft, a polished final version. That is expecting too much. Even well-known novelists cannot do it. Really bad first drafts are just fine. Keep reminding yourself that the first draft is the *least* important phase of writing. You can afford to write horribly in the first draft because you can fix everything during rewriting.

5. Start writing while researching and analyzing. While you are reading a case, words you would like to say might flash through your mind. Type them or write them down. As you do, sentences might start coming to you. You sat down to research and analyze, but now you are writing. When you run out of steam while writing, go back to researching and analyzing.

Experienced writers keep their computer on or a notepad handy while reading statutes, cases, and other authority because reading, thinking, and writing are all part of a single process. To read is to trigger thinking, which can trigger writing. It does not matter that you are writing without consulting your outline. You can figure out later where to put what you are writing into the document.

6. Separate yourself from distractions. If you are distracted by roommates or by the temptation to watch television or play computer games, leave the distractions in one place while you work in another.

§ 12.7 Rewriting

There is no such thing as good writing. There is only good rewriting.

—*Justice Louis Brandeis*

A first draft is for the writer. You write to put your thoughts on the page. But in subsequent drafts, the focus shifts to the reader. How much will *this* reader need to be told? Will this reader understand what you say without having to read twice?

To answer these questions while you read your first draft, pretend to be the reader for whom you are writing. Keep in mind the needs and sensibilities of the professional reader described in § 1.2 at the beginning of this book. Does your writing help this pragmatic person solve a problem? Will this skeptical person see issues that you have not addressed? Will this busy person become impatient wading through material of marginal value? Will this careful person be satisfied that you have written accurately and precisely?

You will do a better job of impersonating the reader if, between drafts, you stop writing for a day or two, clear your mind by working on something else, and come back to do the next draft both "cold" and "fresh." Obviously, that cannot happen if you put off starting the project and later have to do the whole thing frantically at the last minute. To make sure that you have time to rewrite, start on an assignment as soon as you get it, and then pace yourself, working at regular intervals within the time allotted.

With computers, there might not be a clear dividing line between writing a first draft and rewriting it. A writer working on the sixth page of a first draft can interrupt that to rewrite part of page three; return to page six to continue first-draft writing; interrupt that again to make changes in the introduction on page one; then return to page six for more first-drafting; and so on. The writer keeps moving back and forth because while one part of the brain is working on page six, another part is thinking about other pages. This is *recursive* rather than *linear* writing. You have finished a draft when you feel it is more or less complete, even if you know you will need to return to it for more rewriting.

Most of the writing you will do in the practice of law can be made effective in three to five drafts. The paragraphs you are reading now are a fifth draft. (Some parts of this book, however, required 10 or 12 drafts.)

To experience what the reader will experience, some writers read their drafts out loud, which can alert you to wording problems. Bad phrasing often sounds terrible when you say it. Other writers can get the same effect without speaking because they have developed the ability to "hear" in their minds a voice saying the words they read.

While rewriting, you can test your draft for effectiveness by using the checklists in this book. Look for section titles that include the words "Ways to Test."

Don't be afraid to cut material from your first draft. The fact that you have written something does not mean that you have to keep it.

Eventually, you will notice, after putting the writing through several drafts, that the problems you find are mostly typographical errors and small matters of grammar, style, and citation. When that happens, you have moved from rewriting into polishing (§ 12.9), and the project is almost finished.

For many people, rewriting "is the hardest task of all."[3] Set aside a lot of time for it. Sometimes during rewriting, things will seem discouraging because you will discover

---

[3] Peter Elbow, Writing with Power: Techniques for Mastering the Writing Process 121 (1981).

that problems you thought you had solved earlier are still there. At other times, when you piece things together well, you might experience relief, even exhilaration.

Rewriting may be the hardest phase of writing, but parts of it can be turned into a game. Read the preceding sentence again. While we were writing this book, the second part of that sentence—"parts of it can be turned into a game"—went through the following evolution:

1st draft: . . . there are ways of causing parts of rewriting to include the kinds of fun many people enjoy while playing games.

2d draft: . . . parts of rewriting can be turned into something that includes the fun of a game.

3d draft: . . . parts of it can be turned into a game.

How did this keep getting shorter and more clear?

Convoluted language was made simpler. Concepts that did not add understanding were taken out. If games are usually fun, what meaning does the word *fun* add to the word *games*? Rewriting tightened the draft by finding ways to say the same thing more vividly in fewer words.

Look again at the first-draft version above. During rewriting, you would notice its weakness in either of two ways. You might reread it and ask, "What's that supposed to mean? What was I trying to say?"

Question 7 in § 21.5 lists variations of the verb *to be*, which usually weakens writing. Your writing will become stronger and livelier if you try to replace *is, are, was,* and other forms of *to be* with action verbs. That does not always work, but if you look for opportunities to do it, you will find some ways to make your writing stronger. The weakness in the first draft example above begins with "there are," which is a variant of the verb *to be*.

How can you find all the places where you have used variations of the verb *to be*? Use the "find" feature in your word processor to search for *is, are,* and *was*. Every time you find one, consider replacing the word with an action verb. Sometimes that will strengthen your writing, and sometimes it will not. Decide one way or the other. You can make a list of words that cause you trouble and do this for each of them.

Although rewriting focuses on the sentence level, it should also consider the big picture. Is your organization natural and effective? As you reread and rewrite, do you have doubts about your analysis? Do not limit yourself to "surface-level changes," but instead use rewriting as "an opportunity to re-see [your] work" as a whole.[4]

---

[4] Patricia Grande Montana, *Better Revision: Encouraging Students to See Through the Eyes of the Legal Reader*, 14 LEGAL WRITING 291, 292 (2008).

Do not confuse rewriting with polishing (§ 12.9). If all you do is fix typographical errors, awkward wording, grammatical errors, and errors in citation form, you are only polishing, and you have skipped rewriting completely. Rewriting is hard because much of it involves reimagining your first draft and reexamining the decisions you made there. Experienced writers report that they can really enjoy rewriting because of what they can achieve there. "The pleasure of revision"—another name for rewriting—"often arises when you refine what you intend to say and even discover that you have more to say, a new solution, a different path, a better presentation."[5] Research on the writing process has shown that experienced writers use rewriting for deep rethinking, and usually they reorganize the earlier draft.[6]

§ 12.8   Using Writing to Help You Think

Writing is thinking.

—Deirdre McCloskey

[T]here is no better way to master an idea than to write about it.

—Robert H. Frank

[L]earning to write as a lawyer is another way to learn to think as a lawyer.

—Terrill Pollman

Writing and rewriting will help you expand and refine your analysis. The writing process and the thinking process are inseparable. You cannot write without rethinking what you are trying to say.

Wherever you are in writing—in the first draft, in rewriting, or even in polishing—do not be afraid to change your mind about your analysis of the law and the facts. Most writers have abandoned ideas that seemed valuable at first but nevertheless proved faulty when—in the end—they "wouldn't write."

Most writers have experienced the reverse as well: sitting down to write with a single idea and finding that the act of writing draws the idea out, fertilizes it, causes it to sprout limbs and roots, and to spread into a forest of ideas. The amount of thought

---

[5] Christopher M. Anzidei, *The Revision Process in Legal Writing: Seeing Better to Write Better*, 8 LEGAL WRITING 23, 44 (2002) (emphasis added).
[6] *Id.* at 40.

reflected in a good final draft is many times more than the amount in the first draft because the writing process and the thinking process are inseparable, each stimulating and advancing the other.

§ 12.9 Polishing

This is the last phase. Allow a day or more to pass before coming back to the writing to polish it. If you are away from it for at least a day, you will come back fresh and be able to see things you would otherwise miss.

Print the document so you can see it exactly the way the reader will see it. Readers often see problems on the printed page that are not so obvious on a computer screen. Before returning to the computer to fix problems, mark up the printed copy. This is sometimes called "a red-pen proofread," although you could use another color.

Is your document formatted so that it is visually attractive and easy on a reader's eyes? Does the document look dense and cramped? If it is, add white space in appropriate places. Appendix E explains how to identify and fix document design problems like these.

Take one last look for wording that does not say clearly and unambiguously what you mean. This is the biggest reason for waiting at least a day. When you wrote the words, they seemed clear because at that moment you knew what you were trying to say. But after some time has passed, you are no longer in that frame of mind. If you are not sure what the words mean or what you intended them to mean, fix them.

And take one last look for wording that can be tightened up. Can you say it equally well in fewer words? If you can, do so.

Look for awkward wording, typographical and grammatical errors, and errors in citation form. Use your word processor's spellcheck function. Make sure the pages are numbered.

Now your job is done.

§ 12.10 Plagiarism

Plagiarism is using other people's words or ideas as though they were your own. You commit plagiarism if you lift words or ideas from *anywhere* else and put them into your own work without quotation marks (for words) and citations (for words or ideas).

You already know the ethical and moral reasons not to plagiarize. You heard them before law school. Here are three more reasons:

First, you'll feel better about yourself if you do not steal words or ideas from someone else. You can have professional self-respect and pride in your own work only if you do it yourself. If you plagiarize, you will not have the satisfaction of knowing that you accomplished something important on your own merits—which, together with professional self-respect, is one of life's most important pleasures. Do not deprive your-self of it.

Second, it is so easy for a teacher to catch plagiarism that you should assume you will be caught. A teacher can take some of your words and search for them in any of the legal research databases to find the case or article from which they were taken. Many teachers routinely do that. Teachers can also electronically search other students' papers for words like yours. A teacher who designed your assignment and grades the other students' papers knows where *all* the ideas came from. Even if you copy the structure of your paper from another student, that can be plagiarism, and a teacher who grades both papers will notice it.

Third, your writing actually gains value from appropriate citation to the sources of words and ideas. Much of what you write will have credibility *only* if you show exactly where words and ideas come from. Proper attribution of ideas will allow your reader to rely on your work and to give you credit for ideas that are truly yours.

13 How Professional Writers Plan Their Writing

In college, students are sometimes told that they should do all the organizational work in an outline before starting the first draft. Professional writers rarely do that. Before starting the first draft, you need an organization to work from, but it can be flexible. During the first draft and during rewriting, experienced writers typically *reorganize* as they write. Chapter 20 explains a fluid outlining method that helps you write.

§ 13.1 Myths about Outlines

If you dislike outlining, it may be that you were taught an unnecessarily rigid outlining method. In college, you might have been told that before you can start writing, you must make an outline with roman numerals, capital letters, and arabic numerals, like this (from a paper on the effectiveness of professional schools):

I. Legal Education
    A. The First Year
        1. Large Classes
        2. The Casebook Method of Teaching
        [and so on]
    B. The Second and Third Years
    [and so on]
II. Medical Education

This is a linear outline. It starts in one place and goes straight from I to II and later from III to IV to the end, with lower-level layers for detail along the way. It outlines the kind of paper you might have written in college and might write for a second- or third-year seminar in law school. Here, the student has chosen and researched an important topic. The end product—the paper the student eventually submits—might be very effective organized this way.

But differentiate between an *end product's* organization, and the *method* through which a writer organizes the *first* draft. The end product and the method through which a writer *begins* are not the same thing. If the student starts with a linear outline on the first day of writing, that outline might make writing more difficult. Many professional writers do *not* plan their work by doing a linear outline in advance. Here's why:

Suppose you are sitting at the keyboard thinking about the project you are working on. Valuable thoughts are running through your mind. At that moment, you are in the groove. Ideas are flowing. This mental state—which some social scientists call "flow"—does not happen every day, but you are lucky enough to be in it at this moment. You look at your linear outline (like the one above) and try to find a place to put one of the ideas you have in mind. While you are trying to find a place for that idea, all the other ideas in your mind recede. They seem to fly away. And it is hard to find a place in the outline for the one idea that is left because when you made the outline, that idea had not yet occurred to you. Trying to deal with your outline has obstructed the flow of ideas.

Or the situation is different: You are not in flow. You have not written anything yet. But you have made a linear outline. You stare at it and ask yourself, "What should I write under roman numeral I and before letter A?" Five minutes later, you have not been able to answer that question. You are focused on writing what the outline tells you to write first, but your imagination is dry. The outline hurts you. If you were not trying to satisfy it, your mind might start thinking about some other part of the project, and ideas would start coming. But as long as you are staring at the outline, your mind shuts down. In fact, "one of the only virtues of linear outlining is that it looks neat, and that very virtue is its downfall. By working to make sure the outline is neat, we effectively cut off any additions or inserts, and new ideas. After all, we do not want to mess up our neat outline."[1]

The principal myth about outlining is that a linear outline helps *everyone* write better. Linear outlining helps some writers, but it hurts others. It might help those who naturally think in a linear fashion. If you do not naturally think that way, a linear outline made before writing might inhibit you from starting to write and might obstruct the flow of ideas while you write. (If the idea of flow interests you, you might look at some of the books in the footnote.[2])

Linear outlining can also interfere with what writing teachers call the recursive nature of writing. Writing as a process does not go neatly from one step to the next.

---

[1] HENRIETTE ANNE KLAUSER, WRITING ON BOTH SIDES OF THE BRAIN 48 (1987).
[2] *See* MIHALY CSIKSZENTMIHALYI, FINDING FLOW (1998); MIHALY CSIKSZENTMIHALYI, FLOW: THE PSYCHOLOGY OF OPTIMAL EXPERIENCE (1990); MIHALY CSIKSZENTMIHALYI, BEYOND BOREDOM AND ANXIETY (1975); SUSAN A. JACKSON & MIHALY CSIKSZENTMIHALYI, FLOW IN SPORTS (1999); OPTIMAL EXPERIENCE (Mihaly Csikszentmihalyi & Isabella Selega Csikszentmihalyi eds., 1988); SUSAN K. PERRY, WRITING IN FLOW (2001).

It goes back and forth from one aspect of writing to another and in several directions at once (see Chapter 12). The process through which writers create can be messy. A messy process is fine as long as it leads to a neat and orderly final product.

This is why many students resist outlining in college. Outlining can seem like an arbitrary and useless requirement. But you still need to organize what you will say, and you will need to create an outline—but maybe not the way you were taught to do it in college.

§ 13.2 A Method Used by Many Professional Writers to Plan Their Writing

Organizing really means two things: For the writer, organizing is structuring the document. This is part of the *process* of writing explained in Chapters 11 and 12. For the reader, however, organization should be *visible in the product* so the reader does not get lost. Thus, you will organize before the first draft, just to get the writing started in a coherent way. You will also reorganize during the first draft and later during rewriting—so the reader can understand.

Sometimes the original organization works well and does not need much reworking. But often you will need to do a lot of reorganizing while rewriting until you find a structure that works. When you reorganize a lot, that does not necessarily mean you have been making mistakes and are now fixing them. Most of the time, reorganizing happens because the act of writing teaches you the analysis you are trying to write. *Writing is thinking.* You cannot rewrite without rethinking what you are trying to say. Reorganizing is a natural part of rewriting.

This makes outlining easier because it does not have to be perfect the first time. Before a first draft, you can do a quick-and-dirty *fluid outline*. Then in later drafts, you can reorganize, if necessary, to meet the reader's expectations. With experience, you will gain foresight. Your first drafts will become more organized, and you will need to do less and less reorganizing in later drafts. But even the most experienced writers reorganize a lot of what they write.

Before a first draft: Make a fluid outline, which is just a flexible collection of lists on scratch paper or on your computer. Your raw materials (cases, facts, hypotheses, and so on) flow through it and into your first draft.

Begin by identifying the issues. For each issue, identify the rule or rules of law that control the answer. Then make a list (either on paper or on your computer screen) of everything you found through research that proves a rule is accurate, and another list of everything that supports your application of the rule to the facts. With practice, you might not even make lists; you might just make piles of your photocopies or print-outs.

As you write about an issue during your first draft, cross off things on your list (or move things out of your pile). When you have crossed off everything on your list, go on to the next issue. When you have done all the issues, you have completed a first draft of the Discussion if you are writing an office memo, or the Argument if you are writing a motion memo or appellate brief. Chapter 20 explains how to do all this effectively.

Many professional writers organize this way: by making lists or piles, knowing that they will be finished when everything is crossed out or a pile is empty. This method is only a suggestion. If you develop a different procedure that works better for you, use yours instead.

In later drafts: Linear outlines are not inherently bad. Although linear outlines might obstruct producing a first draft, they can help to improve later drafts during rewriting. To do that, you would create *a post-draft linear outline*—a linear outline of what you have *already* written. That might seem strange, but for many writers it works. *A finished product should be organized the way a linear outline is—even if you used a fluid outline to produce your first draft.*

To find out whether this method would work for you, print out a copy of your draft and read it, asking yourself whether you have incorporated a linear outline into your writing without realizing you were doing so. If the answer is yes, that increases the odds that you have organized effectively.

At each point in your draft where you state an important conclusion or start a new topic, write a heading reflecting that. You can handwrite the headings in the margins of your printed draft. The headings will resemble the items that would be listed in a linear outline. For example, if you were writing a seminar paper on the topic partially outlined at the beginning of this chapter, you would write in the margin "The Casebook Method of Teaching" at the point where you finish talking about whether large classes work well and are about to start talking about casebooks.

After you have done this to your entire draft, step back and look at your headings. For the moment, look at the headings alone and ignore the rest of your draft. You are trying to see the big picture. Are the headings in a logical order? Do they cover everything? Do they lay out the analysis in a way that would be clear to the reader? If you answer yes to these questions, you might have a good organization—and you have now produced good headings, which you can insert into your draft if they would help guide the reader.

But if any of the answers is no, use the cut-and-paste feature of your word processor to rearrange portions of your draft. Then reread everything to make sure that individual sentences and paragraphs still work well in their new locations. You might need to reword some things.

§ 13.3   Some Other Methods Used by Professional Writers to Plan Their Writing

Some writers outline by writing on sticky notes and putting them on a wall. The outline can be reshuffled by moving the notes around.

Some outline by making flowcharts in which the things to be written about appear in boxes or ovals with arrows showing their relationship to each other and the order in which they will be discussed. For some very visual writers, this accurately reflects how they think about what they are writing.

A few outline with mind-mapping software like Inspiration.

And some outline the linear way, with roman numerals, as illustrated at the beginning of this chapter. It has worked well for them, and they are happy with it.

Experiment with outlining processes until you find a method that works well with the way you most effectively work and think. The end result—the organization the reader sees—should be the best one for the material you are explaining to the reader. But the process of creating that organization should be the one that works best for you. As with so much else in writing, the result is for the reader, but the *process* of creating the result is for you.

Part 3

Office Memoranda

Writing an Office Memorandum

§ 14.1 Structure of an Office Memorandum

Form follows function.

—*Louis Sullivan (architect)*

A lawyer writes an office memorandum to determine how the law will treat a client's situation. Typically a junior lawyer will write a memo to answer a supervisor's legal question. The supervising lawyer, often a law firm partner, might know the law generally, but not necessarily how the law treats the specific facts and issues in the case that triggered the legal question. The supervisor might use the contents of the office memo to advise the client or to plan a lawsuit or other action undertaken on the client's behalf. In the office memo, you will present the legal research and analysis in a format that most efficiently helps your busy reader resolve the client's legal problems.

Purpose. Imagine that you are writing to the typical supervising lawyer described in § 1.4. Your supervisor will read your memo for the purpose of making a decision for a client and will probably be under some pressure, especially time pressure. This hypothetical busy person will be both careful and skeptical by nature.

Good legal writers learn to *anticipate* the questions a reader silently asks about the client's legal situation *before the reader even becomes consciously aware of those questions*. To do that, you must understand the legal analysis so well that you can prepare for the questions your hypothetical reader will formulate while reading, and answer them in the appropriate place to keep your reader from becoming skeptical.

Format. Office memo format varies from law office to law office, and even from case to case. But a typical office memorandum includes some combination of the following components, though not always in this order:

1. Memorandum heading
2. Issue or Issues
3. Brief Answer
4. Facts
5. Discussion (or Legal Analysis)
6. Conclusion (which may include Recommendations)

A sample office memo is in Appendix A. You might want to put a sticky note or bookmark there now to help you move back and forth in the book easily while reading this chapter.

Some components of an office memo might seem repetitive of others. But a busy supervising lawyer rarely reads your entire memo from front to back. Rather, a lawyer reads only the part of the office memo needed for the immediate task ahead. For example, just before meeting with a client to advise about alternatives, the supervising lawyer might scan the Issue and the Brief Answer, and if time allows perhaps the Conclusion. When preparing a motion memorandum based on your office memo, she will study the Facts and the Discussion more carefully. Each memo component serves a specific purpose for your reader, depending on the task immediately at hand and the time available to review your work product.

Heading. The memorandum heading usually includes the word MEMORANDUM centered at the top of the page. The entries that follow identify the recipient (usually your supervisor), the writer (you), the date, and a brief reference to the subject matter.

The date in the memorandum heading is essential because you may learn additional facts after that date that may change the outcome of your analysis. The information you include in the reference line is also important because your employer is likely to file your office memo away for possible use in a later case involving similar facts and legal issues. For that reason, your entry should concisely refer to the subject matter of the memo, not just the specific case number, client name, or caption of the case your memo addresses.

Your memorandum heading should be carefully edited. Your reader forms a first impression about your professionalism and work ethic based on the heading. Pay careful attention to format, spacing, spelling, and punctuation so you immediately gain your reader's confidence in the quality of your written work.

Issue. Just after the heading, the Issue states the legal question that the memorandum resolves, along with the relevant factual context. A good issue statement should provide as much information as possible about the determinative facts. Cases rarely involve pure questions of law. Integrating the legal question with the relevant facts helps the reader quickly grasp the unique aspects of the client's case.

As a general rule, write the Issue as a question that invites a "yes" or "no" answer. For example, a good Issue might ask whether the client has a viable cause of action under a specific legal theory, such as negligence, based on the most salient facts.

Brief Answer. Immediately following the Issue, the Brief Answer begins by concisely stating your conclusion in a way that directly responds to the Issue. In most cases you should qualify your prediction to reflect how certain (or uncertain) you are about the outcome. Only rarely can you accurately predict the result a court will reach on a legal issue, and every set of facts is unique. For that reason, it is risky to predict any outcome with absolute certainty. On the other hand, some questions lend themselves to more confident predictions than others. It is perfectly acceptable to give a qualified Brief Answer such as "Probably not" or "Most likely yes."

The Brief Answer also includes a short summary of the analysis supporting your prediction. Give the essence of the legal reasoning, the essential facts on which your conclusion depends and a brief explanation showing how the rule applies to those key facts. The Brief Answer should provide a snapshot of your reasoning—no longer than one concise paragraph, without citing any legal authorities. Your detailed legal analysis and citations to the supporting legal authorities will appear later in the Discussion.

The following illustrates the Issue and Brief Answer components of an office memo analyzing a legal question about trademark law:

Issue

Will trademark law allow plaintiff Donald Trump to recover damages from the defendant for advertising its manufactured firewood using the phrase "You're fired!", which Mr. Trump is known for repeating on his television show for dramatic effect?

Brief Answer

Most likely not. Under trademark law, the words "You're fired!" qualify as generic or descriptive terms. They lack the secondary meaning required for trademark protection. Many others have used the phrase as a business name or slogan before Trump became known for doing so. Trump can claim trademark protection to prevent the commercial use of his photograph while pointing an index finger and saying, "You're fired!" But he cannot claim trademark protection for the words alone.

Here the Issue isolates the core facts crucial to the answer: the well-known businessman and celebrity Donald Trump, his television show, and the words "You're fired!" The Brief Answer directly responds ("most likely not"), along with a concise summary of the writer's legal reasoning.

Statement of Facts. The Facts include the events and circumstances legally relevant to the Issue. A _relevant fact_ is one that influences the outcome of the legal issue. A _determinative fact_ is a relevant fact that is so critical that it might alone dictate the outcome of the legal issue.

How should the Facts be organized? Organize to help your reader. Often the Facts are stated chronologically, but sometimes organizing them by topic or subject matter would be more helpful instead. Emphasize dates and times only if they are determinative or necessary to avoid confusing the reader. For example, a date might be determinative if the issue is whether a complaint was filed within the statute of limitations.

If your supervisor is thoroughly familiar with the factual background, this part of the memo might be short. You want to remind the supervisor about the essential facts rather than enumerate every factual detail.

But be sure to include any fact you mention in your Discussion section. State both what you know _and what you do not yet know_ about the client's situation. Sometimes you will later learn additional facts that lead to a different legal outcome. If your legal analysis leads you to a fact question that you need to resolve before you can reach a reasoned conclusion, include a notation in your Facts so your supervising lawyer can ask for that information.

The Facts should never include legal analysis or even references to the applicable legal rule. But a good Statement of Facts includes every fact that is determinative or relevant to the legal issues.

Discussion or Analysis. The Discussion (sometimes called the Analysis) is the largest and most complex part of the office memo. It explains and justifies the prediction set out in the Brief Answer. Chapter 16 explains how to write predictively in the Discussion section of an office memo. Chapters 17 through 20 explain step by step how to organize the Discussion.

If the Discussion is especially complex or analyzes several issues, break it up with subheadings, preferably written as complete sentences. Subheadings help the reader locate relevant portions of the Discussion and provide an outline for your legal analysis.

Conclusion. Lawyers follow different practices concerning the Conclusion. Some include it only if the analysis is so complicated that a reader would find a summary of the reasoning helpful. Others always include it. If your teacher asks you to include a Conclusion, summarize the points in the same order you presented them in the Discussion or Analysis section without citing legal authority. Sometimes the Conclusion is a good place to explain what you believe the lawyer or client should do next.

§ 14.2   Which Part of the Memo to Write First

One lawyer might write the Discussion before writing anything else, on the theory that the other components of the memorandum will be shaped by the insights gained while putting the Discussion together. For example, writing the Discussion first could help you identify which information to include in the Facts. Another lawyer might start by writing the Facts because they seem easier to describe and summarize. A third lawyer might be flexible, starting with whatever component of the office memo first begins to take shape in the lawyer's mind, sometimes drafting two or more components simultaneously and rewriting each one to dovetail with the other.

One way of overcoming writer's block is to just start writing whatever part of the memo you are thinking about at the time. It is not necessary to write the parts in order from beginning to end. In fact, it is often more effective to do just the opposite.

Writing is thinking. If your mind is already thinking about one part of the memo, you are beginning to write even if your fingers have not yet touched the keyboard. As you begin writing, your thinking deepens and becomes more focused on the issue and the relevant facts. Insights will come as you write because your subconscious mind is already working out the legal reasoning for you. *Just get started.*

§ 14.3   An Office Memo's Audience

You are primarily writing an office memo to your supervisor, although others might eventually read it (including the client or your supervisor's co-counsel).

If you were sitting at a conference table in your law office looking your supervisor in the eye while explaining your research and analysis, you would choose your words and tone to communicate with that one person. In an office memo, you are doing the same thing, but in writing. In a first-year writing course, how can you write to a hypothetical supervisor when you do not yet have one of your own?

Think of someone you know whose intelligence, wisdom, and judgment you deeply respect. In your mind, let this person play the role of your supervising lawyer. In your first draft, write as though you are explaining your research and analysis to her. Assume that she is educated in the law even if that is not true. The point is to write to a real human being who would be engaged with the subject matter when reading your document.

In later drafts, you are really writing to two people: your imagined supervisor and your teacher. While your reader is knowledgeable about the law, do not assume that the reader knows what you know about the case and how the law applies. Even the most capable and experienced supervising lawyers rely on junior associates to identify the determinative facts of a client's case, research and analyze the applicable law, and apply the law to the facts to predict the outcome.

Exercise 14-A. Reading and Revising an Office Memo

Part 1. In Appendix A, read *only* the Issues, Brief Answers, and Conclusion. Do not read the Facts or the Discussion section. Then write one paragraph, in your own words, concisely advising the client about the results of the writer's analysis. (Assume your client is not a lawyer or a sophisticated business person.)

Part 2. After completing Part 1, read the Facts and Discussion sections in Appendix A. Did your perception and understanding of the case change after reading the details? Explain how. Revise the paragraph you wrote to the client in Part 1 to incorporate your insights from reading the detailed components of the memo.

Part 3. Now assume you are a senior associate revising the junior associate's memo. Rewrite the Issues, Brief Answers, and Conclusion in Appendix A to better convey the legal issue, the determinative facts, and the legal reasoning leading to the predicted outcome. Frame the Issue as a "yes" or "no" question, and be sure the Brief Answer directly responds with a qualified one- or two-word answer before giving a concise summary of the key facts and legal reasoning. Revise the Conclusion to concisely summarize the legal argument in the same sequence as the Discussion.

15 Interviewing the Client

Client representation starts with an interview. A person who wants a lawyer's help calls to make an appointment. The secretary finds a convenient time and asks what the subject of the interview will be. The person calling says, "I've just been charged with a crime," or "I signed a contract to buy a house and now the owner won't sell." At the time of the appointment, that person and the lawyer sit down and talk. If the visitor has confidence in the lawyer, the visitor may become a client.

During that conversation, the lawyer learns what problem the prospective client wants solved, the client's goals in getting it solved, and what the client knows factually about the problem. The lawyer also learns about the client as a person and gives the client a reciprocal opportunity to learn about the lawyer. Then or later, the lawyer and client also negotiate the contract through which the client hires the lawyer, but here we focus on the main parts of the interview: building a relationship with the client and fact-gathering.

§ 15.1   Clients and Lawyers

Most clients are not really interested in hiring "a lawyer." They want to hire a genuine and caring human being who can do legal work well.

You probably dislike it when a doctor treats you in a detached way as a case of flu, rather than as a person who has the flu. A doctor who treats you as a human being with flu-like symptoms might spend enough time with you to learn that you also have other symptoms inconsistent with the flu, and that you have a different disease that should be treated differently. If you have never been a lawyer's client, you can imagine what clients experience during lawyer interviews simply by remembering how you have experienced contact with professionals such as doctors.

Treating the client as a person is called "client-centered lawyering,"[1] which means focusing your efforts around what the client wants rather than what you assume the client should want. Your client has hired you to accomplish the *client's* goal. And many clients can collaborate actively with you along the way, brainstorming with you about how to solve problems.

You are obligated to keep secret whatever the client tells you in private, which is the lawyer's duty of confidentiality.[2] There are exceptions. For example, the client may give the lawyer permission to reveal the client's confidences to other people. And a lawyer may reveal the client's confidences if necessary to prevent the client from committing a serious crime. States differ in defining these and other exceptions to the duty of confidentiality.

§ 15.2   The Interview

After the sort of pleasantries that people exchange when meeting each other, the lawyer says something like "How can I help you?" or "Let's talk about what brings you here today," or "My secretary tells me the bank has threatened to foreclose on your mortgage. You're probably worried. Where shall we begin?"

§ 15.2.1   Learning What the Client Knows

Do not label the problem in your own mind until you have heard most of the facts. A client who starts by telling you about a dispute with a landlord might have claims for defamation and assault rather than a claim for breach of a lease obligation.

Do not leap in with questions as soon as the client has told you the nature of the problem. Give the client a full opportunity to tell you whatever the client wants to talk about before you intervene. Many clients want to make sure from the beginning that you hear certain things about which the client feels deeply. If you obstruct this process, you will seem remote, even bureaucratic, to the client. And if you listen to what the client wants to tell you, you may learn a lot about the client as a person and about how the client views the problem.

In the beginning, encourage the client to present the facts in the way the client thinks best. After a while (sometimes pretty quickly), the client will want you to take the lead by asking questions.

Most clients will not mind if you take notes on a pad of paper, if you first explain that you want to be sure to remember everything the client tells you. But keep listening

---

[1] David A. Binder, Paul Bergman, Paul R. Tremblay & Ian S. Weinstein, Lawyers as Counselors: A Client-Centered Approach (3d ed. 2011).
[2] Model Rules of Prof'l Conduct, R. 1.6(a) (2013).

while you write, and make eye contact often. You might feel comfortable taking notes on your laptop, but consider whether your client would feel comfortable as well. The computer screen places a barrier between you and your client at a time when you want to encourage interaction.

§ 15.2.2 The Art of the Question

Explore the various aspects of the problem in detail with the client. On each topic, start with broad questions ("Tell me what happened the night the nuclear reactor melted down") and gradually work your way toward narrow ones ("Just before you ran from the control panel, what number on that dial was the needle pointing to?"). But do this gradually. If you jump too quickly to the narrow questions, you will miss a lot of information. Ask broad questions until you are not getting useful information anymore. Then go back and ask narrow questions about the facts the client did not cover. While the client is answering the broad questions, you can note on a pad the topics you will need to explore later using narrow questions.

Word your questions carefully. How you ask questions has a lot to do with the quality and quantity of the information you get. A good question does not confuse, does not provoke resistance, and does not distort memory. One of the marks of an effective lawyer is the ability to ask the right questions in the most productive way.

What are the qualities of a good question? First, it seeks information that you really need to know. Second, it is phrased in a way most likely to produce valuable information. Some words help jog the client's memory and encourage answers, while other words confuse, cloud memory, or provoke resistance. Third, a good question is asked in a useful sequence with other questions. When you start exploring various aspects of the problem in detail, try to take up each topic in logical order. Sometimes other questions have to be asked and answered first. And ask one question at a time. If you ask two at a time, only one of them will be answered. Too much skipping around confuses you and the client.

Keep asking questions until you have all the details: when, where, who, how, and why. Get precise answers. "Last week" is not good enough. You need "Thursday, at about 11 A.M., in the truck stop parking lot." If the client tells you about a conversation, ask who else was present, what else was discussed, how long the conversation lasted, how it started, how it ended, what words each participant used, and so on. You will need these details to analyze the situation. In nonprofessional life, vagueness and approximation are usually enough in conversations. But experienced lawyers know that only precision works.

Before the interview ends, make sure you understand the timeline of events from beginning to end: What happened first, what happened next, what happened just after that, and so on.

§ 15.2.3　Listening and Talking

The ability to listen well is as important in the practice of law as the ability to talk well. The popular image of a lawyer is a person talking—to juries, to judges, to adversaries, to reporters. But in the end, the lawyer who succeeds is the one who also knows how to listen. If you do not listen carefully, you might as well not have asked the question. Knowledge is strength, and in the practice of law one of the most important means of gaining knowledge is to listen carefully.

When communicating with clients, talk and write in plain English. If you have to use a legal term of art, explain its meaning in an uncondescending way. Use concrete, precise language rather than vague generalities. Behave in ways that encourage clients to tell you things that you need to know, and to ask you questions about things that make them anxious.

§ 15.2.4　How to Conclude

Clients often want the lawyer to predict immediately whether the client will win or lose. Do not even try to make that prediction. You must research the law and might need more facts. And you need to think about it. Hasty predictions are often inaccurate.

But clients want assurance. What can you give them? Usually, it is enough to explain what work you will do next. A client might not realize that lawyers do not know all the answers right away. But we *do* know how to find the answers. You can convey to your client that you take the problem very seriously and want to do something to help.

As a client leaves your office, two questions are typically running through her mind: Will this lawyer be able to accomplish what I want? And did this lawyer truly *hear me* and *understand me*? The law and the facts might prevent you from accomplishing what the client wants. But nothing should prevent you from hearing everything the client says, acknowledging the client's concerns, and understanding the client as a person.

16 Predictive Writing in an Office Memorandum

§ 16.1 Predicting in Writing

When a client hires a lawyer, the client often asks the lawyer to start making predictions pretty quickly: "Will I win?" "Is it worth fighting for this?" "Can the other side get away with that?" This chapter explains how to predict. You might reread § 1.2 at the beginning of this book on the difference between predictive writing and persuasive writing. It is short and will help you here.

A lawyer predicts for either of two reasons. One is to help *the client* make a decision knowing how the law will respond ("if the client constructs her estate in this way, it will not be taxed"). The other is to help *the lawyer* make a tactical or strategic decision ("we can plead this claim because it will survive a motion to dismiss").

Predictive writing is sometimes called *objective writing*, but objectivity only partly describes it. Any writing that makes a disinterested report of the law can be called objective. Predictive writing does more than that. It foretells how the law will resolve a particular controversy. Sometimes an office memo predicts explicitly, and sometimes it predicts implicitly:

explicitly: Ms. Olmstead will probably be awarded damages for trademark infringement.

implicitly: Ms. Olmstead probably has a cause of action for trademark infringement.

These two statements mean essentially the same thing. You can say it either way, unless you work in an office that prefers one or the other.

The first step in predicting is to develop arguments for each side on every issue. Think of the reasons why your client should win. And think of the reasons why the opposing party should win. To predict which arguments will persuade a court, you need to know the arguments the court will hear from each side. Then evaluate each argument by asking yourself whether it will probably persuade a judge. Bearing those evaluations in mind, how would a court rule on each issue? Then step back and consider the matter as a whole. In light of your predictions on each individual issue, how will the court decide the entire controversy?

§ 16.2 An Example of the Predictive Process: Taylor and Garrett

Assume that in our jurisdiction the crime of common law burglary has been codified in the following form and renamed burglary in the first degree:

> **Criminal Code § 102.** A person commits burglary in the first degree by breaking and entering the dwelling of another in the nighttime with intent to commit a felony therein.

This part of the statute is preceded by a definitions section:

> **Criminal Code § 101.** Definitions:
>
> (a) A "breaking" is the making of an opening, or the enlarging of an opening, so as to permit entry into a building, or a closed off portion thereof, if neither the owner nor the occupant has consented thereto.
>
> (b) A "closed off portion" of a building is one divided from the remainder of the building by walls, partitions, or the like so that it can be secured against entry.
>
> (c) A "dwelling" is any building, or closed off portion thereof, in which one or more persons habitually sleep.
>
> (d) An "entering" or an "entry" is the placing, by the defendant, of any part of his body or anything under his control within a building, or a closed off portion thereof, if neither the owner nor the occupant has consented thereto.
>
> (e) "Intent to commit a felony therein" is the design or purpose of committing, within a building or closed off portion thereof, a crime classified in this Code as a felony, if the defendant had that design or purpose both at the time of a breaking and at the time of an entering.
>
> (f) "Nighttime" is the period between sunset and sunrise.
>
> (g) A dwelling is "of another" if the defendant does not by right habitually sleep there.

The legislature has also enacted the following:

> **Criminal Code § 10.** No person shall be convicted of a crime except on evidence proving guilt beyond a reasonable doubt.
> **Criminal Code § 403.** A battery causing substantial injury is a felony.

Assume—just to make things simpler—that none of these sections has yet been interpreted by the courts, and that you are therefore limited to the statute itself. That is a very unusual situation. You will typically be working with judicial decisions that have interpreted the statute.

Taylor and Garrett are students who have rented apartments on the same floor of the same building. At midnight, Taylor was studying, while Garrett was listening to a Radiohead album with his new four-foot concert speakers. Taylor had put up with this for two or three hours, and finally she pounded on Garrett's door. Garrett opened the door about six inches, and when he realized that he could not hear what Taylor was saying, he stepped back into the room a few feet to turn the volume down, without opening the door further. Continuing to express outrage, Taylor pushed the door fully open and strode into the room. Garrett turned on Taylor and ordered her to leave. According to Taylor, she felt this to be "too much" and punched Garrett so hard that he suffered substantial injury.

The punch was a felonious battery under Criminal Code § 403. *Is Taylor also guilty of burglary in the first degree under Criminal Code § 102?* Your first reaction might be "no," and your reasoning might be something like this: "That's not burglary. Burglary happens when somebody gets into the house when you're not around and steals all the valuables. Maybe this will turn out to be some kind of trespass." But in law a satisfactory answer is never just "yes" or "no." An answer includes a sound *reason*, and regardless of whether Taylor is guilty of burglary, this answer is wrong because the reasoning is inadequate. The answer can be determined only by applying all the relevant rules to the facts. Anything else is a guess.

A lawyer might start *thinking* predictively in the following way. These would be the lawyer's *thoughts*:

> First-degree burglary (from § 102) has six elements and no exceptions. In § 101, the legislature defined each of the elements as well as some terms used in defining the elements. Taylor is guilty only if each element is proved beyond a reasonable doubt (§ 10). So I'll make a list of the elements and annotate each element with relevant facts:
>
> 1. *breaking*: When Taylor pushed the door back, she enlarged an opening into Garrett's apartment, which is a closed off portion of a building, and neither Garrett nor the landlord consented to that.

2. *and entering*: Taylor "entered" by walking into the apartment, which neither Garrett nor the landlord consented to.

3. *the dwelling*: Nothing suggests that Garrett doesn't habitually sleep in his own apartment. He was there at midnight, although he obviously wasn't sleeping at the time. It's a dwelling.

4. *of another*: And it isn't Taylor's dwelling. She lives down the hall.

5. *in the nighttime*: Midnight is in the nighttime.

6. *with intent to commit a felony therein*: Taylor committed a felony under § 403 when she hit Garrett. The issue is when she formed the intent to do that. Because of the way § 101(e) defines this element, it isn't satisfied unless she had the intent to hit him both when she did the breaking *and* when she entered Garrett's apartment. If she formed the intent to hit him *after* she entered, the element isn't satisfied. Here are the arguments:

> *guilty:*   Taylor was already furious, and she walked right over and punched Garrett, without hesitation.

> *not guilty:*   After Taylor's breaking and entering and before the punch, Garrett turned on her and ordered her to leave, and she'll testify that she was reacting to what he did. She felt it to be "too much." She may have been angry when she pushed the door open and walked in, but anger doesn't necessarily include an intent to hit somebody. She isn't guilty unless the evidence proves beyond a reasonable doubt that she formed that intent before or during the breaking and entering—not afterward.

The not guilty argument looks better. It creates reasonable doubt that undermines the guilty argument (unless the jury decides she's not telling the truth).

So the prosecution can prove every element except the last one. And since they'll be missing an element, she'll be acquitted.

This is how a lawyer might *think*. But if you were asked to *write* that prediction in the Discussion portion of an office memorandum, you might write something like the following. (This Discussion is relatively simple because it does not evaluate any judicial opinions.)

Discussion

Taylor will probably be acquitted of first-degree burglary because the evidence does not show beyond a reasonable doubt that she had formed the intent to commit a felony when she broke and entered Garrett's apartment. The evidence will prove, however, that she committed the other five elements of first-degree burglary. Under § 102 of the Criminal Code, a person is guilty of burglary if he or she (1) breaks and (2) enters (3) the dwelling (4) of another (5) in the nighttime (6) "with intent to commit a felony therein." Under § 10, she can be convicted only "on evidence proving guilt beyond a reasonable doubt."

The prosecution will easily prove the third, fourth, and fifth elements. Section 101(c) defines a dwelling as "any building, or closed off portion thereof, in which one or more persons habitually sleep." Nothing suggests that Garrett does not habitually sleep in his own apartment. That apartment is, to Taylor, the dwelling of another. Section 101(g) would define it as her dwelling only if she habitually slept there and had a legal right ("by right") to do so. Neither is true. These events transpired between sunset and sunrise, which satisfies § 101(f)'s definition of nighttime.

Taylor's pushing open Garrett's door was a breaking. A breaking includes, among other things, "the enlarging of an opening, so as to permit entry into . . . a closed off portion" of a building "if neither the owner nor the occupant has consented thereto." Crim. Code § 101(a). Garrett's apartment is a "closed off portion" of a building, which is defined by § 101(b) as "one divided from the remainder of the building by walls, partitions, or the like so that it can be secured against entry." It would be difficult to imagine an apartment that is not thus divided from the building in which it is located. During the incident in question, Garrett opened his front door about six inches after Taylor knocked on it to complain of noise. When she pushed open the door and walked into his apartment moments later, he immediately ordered her out. The initial opening of six inches would not have been enough to admit Taylor, and Garrett's prompt order to leave shows beyond a reasonable doubt that he had not consented to her opening the door farther. And nothing suggests that Taylor had consent from an owner of the apartment, who might have been someone other than Garrett.

Taylor's walking into Garrett's apartment was an entry, which § 101(d) defines as "the placing, by the defendant, of any part of his body or anything under his control within a building, or a closed off portion thereof, if neither the owner nor the occupant has consented thereto." Taylor walked into Garrett's apartment, and the circumstances do not show consent to an entry for the same reasons that they do not show consent to a breaking.

But the prosecution will not be able to prove beyond a reasonable doubt that Taylor had already formed the intent to assault Garrett at the time she broke and entered. Section 101(e) defines "intent to commit a felony therein" as "the design or purpose of committing, within a building or closed off portion thereof, a . . . felony, if the defendant had that design or purpose both at the time of a breaking and at the time of an entering." Taylor will testify that when Garrett turned around and ordered her to leave while she was protesting his noise, she found this to be "too much" and punched him. A reasonable explanation is that her intent was formed after she was already in Garrett's apartment. No words or action on her part show that she had the intent to punch Garrett before she actually did so. Although, in her anger, she might have contemplated an assault before or when she broke and entered, there is a difference between considering an act and having the "design or purpose of committing" it. Her actions before she struck Garrett show no more than an intent to complain.

Thus, unless the jury decides that Taylor is not telling the truth, she will be acquitted of first-degree burglary because the evidence does not show beyond a reasonable doubt that she had the intent to commit a felony when she pushed open Garrett's door and walked into his apartment.

This material could be organized effectively in other ways, too. *Resist the temptation to copy uncritically the style of this example.* It might not be appropriate to your assignment or to your own approach to the analysis. The issues here are not difficult, and the facts given are few. The writing you do in law school will require both more extensive discussion and deeper analysis than in this example.

§ 16.3   How to Test Your Writing for Predictiveness

While rewriting, ask yourself the following questions.

1. Have you refused to hide from bad news? If the client's case is weak, it is better to know that now. Predictive writing is frank diagnosis. Advocacy has another time and place.

2. Have you edited out waffling? Your readers will expect you to take a position and prove it. Mushy waffling with words like "seems," "appears," and their synonyms makes your advice less useful to clients and supervising lawyers. Supervisors and judges are grateful for concreteness, whether or not they agree with you. If somebody disagrees with you, lightning will *not* strike you down on the spot. (It is not waffling to say that "the plaintiff probably will win an appeal" or "is likely to win an appeal." No prediction can be a certainty.)

3. Have you told the reader whether your prediction is qualified in any way? For precision, a prediction should at least imply how confident you are of it. Is the underlying rule a matter of "settled law," and are the facts clear-cut? If your prediction is qualified, state precisely the variables on which the prediction is based, such as "The defendant will probably prevail unless . . . ."

4. Have you concentrated on solving a problem, rather than on writing a college essay? A college essay is a vehicle for academic analysis—analysis to satisfy curiosity—rather than practical problem-solving for clients. Legal writing is practical. Solve the problem you were asked to solve. Solve it completely. But do not insert into your writing essays not essential to solving the problem. Here is an example of writing that *does not* solve a problem:

> Common law courts developed the crime of burglary because in the middle ages, with no police and no electric lights, life was much more dangerous at night. People bolted their doors and windows when the sun went down, but they still felt vulnerable because of the advantage darkness gave to criminals. The courts classified burglary as a felony with the same punishment as murder (execution by hanging) so that people could sleep at night with some sense of security. Modern statutes have reduced the punishment to imprisonment. They often retain something like the common law formulation of burglary as the most serious form of the crime. Lesser statutory forms might omit some of the elements of common law burglary and might be called second- or third-degree burglary or breaking and entering.

This is interesting. It even explains why Goldilocks would not be charged with common law burglary. She got into the bears' house during the daytime, and she did not have a felonious intent, even if she later ate their porridge and slept in their beds. But it does not help predict whether Taylor will be convicted, and therefore, it does not belong in Taylor's predictive memo.

Part 4

Organizing Analysis

CREAC: A Formula for Structuring Proof of a Conclusion of Law

17

This and the following chapters explain how to structure the Discussion section of an office memo as well as the Argument section of a motion memo or appellate brief.

§ 17.1 The Need to Organize with Care (Kendrick and Jordan)

After a long day in the library studying for exams, Jordan and her friends walked to the student lounge, bought cans of apple juice from vending machines, poured the juice into clear plastic cups, sat down, and chatted. One of the group suggested that before going back to the library to study for a few more hours, they have a contest to see which of them could do the most convincing job of pretending to be drunk. Kendrick, who was eating pizza nearby, took out his cell phone and, without Jordan's knowledge, filmed her while she was clearly winning the contest.

Kendrick posted the video on YouTube under the title "Jordan Drunk in the Student Lounge." Nothing on the YouTube page suggested that she was not actually drunk.

The next day Jordan received a very attractive job offer from a law firm. Like many job offers, this one was conditioned on a background check. Among other things, the firm searched the internet for websites on which Jordan's name appeared. When the firm came across the YouTube video, it rescinded the offer. Jordan tried to persuade the firm that she had not actually been drunk and that she'd had nothing to do with putting the video on YouTube. But by then the firm had filled the position with another applicant. Other firms that had interviewed Jordan did not return her phone calls, and she thinks that is because they have done background checks of their own.

Jordan has hired your law firm, which is not the one that rescinded the job offer. Your supervisor has decided that a lawsuit would make sense only if YouTube would be liable for posting the video. You and your supervisor have already determined that Jordan will win a lawsuit against Kendrick for defamation and invasion of privacy. But suing Kendrick alone will not help because it will be years before he earns enough money to compensate Jordan.

A television station would be liable under your state's common law of defamation and invasion of privacy if it had broadcast the video with the title Kendrick posted on YouTube. And a newspaper or magazine would be similarly liable if it had published still frames from the video with the same caption. Your supervisor has asked you to research whether the federal Communications Decency Act of 1996 would prevent recovery against YouTube, which is not a television station, newspaper, or magazine. After reading the statute and the case law interpreting it, you believe that Jordan could not recover against YouTube.

When you write the Discussion section of an office memo or the Argument in a motion memo or appellate brief, what will you say first? What will you say after that? How will you organize the many things you have to say? And in how much detail will you say them? Those questions are answered in this and the following chapters.

§ 17.2   A Formula for Organizing Analysis

A supervising lawyer reads an office memo to prepare for making a decision. So does a judge who reads a motion memo or appellate brief. They will make different kinds of decisions. The lawyer will decide how to advise the client or handle the client's case. The judge will decide how to rule on a motion or appeal. But both look for tightly structured analysis that makes your conclusion seem inevitable.

§ 17.2.1   CREAC

The reader who must make a decision understands your analysis most easily if you organize it using the following formula—or some variation of it.

CREAC Organization

To prove a conclusion of law:

C — State your **Conclusion**.

R — State the primary **Rule** that supports your conclusion.

E — **Explain** and prove the rule by analyzing legal authority.

A — **Apply** the rule's test (elements or factors) to your facts.

C — *(optional)* If explaining or applying the rule is complicated, sum up by restating your **Conclusion.**

What do the ingredients in the CREAC[1] formula mean?

C: The **Conclusion** of law is your determination of how the law treats certain facts. It is what you are trying to prove. In predictive writing, it can be expressed as a determination ("The Communications Decency Act prevents recovery against YouTube") or as a prediction ("Jordan probably will not be able to recover against YouTube for defamation or invasion of privacy").

R: The **Rule** is the primary one on which you rely in reaching your conclusion. Other rules might also be involved, but this is the main one on which your analysis rests.

E: Rule **Explanation** is proof—using authority such as statutes and cases—that the main rule on which you rely really is the law in the jurisdiction involved. The reader needs to know for certain that the rule exists in the jurisdiction, and that you have expressed it accurately. Explain how the authority supports the rule, analyze the policy behind the rule, and counteranalyze reasonable arguments that might contradict your interpretation of the rule. A subsidiary rule might help explain the main rule. A subsidiary rule guides application of the main rule or works together with it in some way important to your analysis. For example, a conviction in a criminal case requires proof beyond a reasonable doubt. In the Discussion on pages 136–138, notice how that rule of evidence interacts with the main rule that defines first-degree burglary.

A: Rule **Application** is a demonstration that the rule + the facts = your conclusion. Explain why your result is what the law has in mind, using legal authority, policy considerations, counteranalyses, and any subsidiary rules needed.

---

[1] The CREAC formula is identical to the paradigm for structuring proof of a conclusion of law—often called just *the paradigm*—which first appeared in Richard K. Neumann, Jr., Legal Reasoning and Legal Writing: Structure, Strategy, and Style 111-125 (1990), and which has continued to be called *the paradigm* in subsequent editions of that book.

C: Depending on the complexity of your analysis, you might need to state your **Conclusion** again. If your treatment of a given issue is three pages long, the reader probably needs a sentence or two at the end wrapping up by restating the conclusion you have just proved. On the other hand, if your analysis is two paragraphs long, the reader might not need to be reminded; you can just go on to the next issue without restating something you said only a few sentences earlier.

Although the CREAC formula *helps* you organize, it will take some effort to learn how to use it effectively. But once you have learned that, writing will become easier because you will not have to struggle to figure out how to organize a mass of information. The CREAC formula will organize it for you.[2]

§ 17.2.2   Why Readers Prefer CREAC Organization

Your readers will be practical and busy people who read your memo or brief to help them make a decision. Because skepticism results in better decisions, readers will be skeptical about what you say. To present your thinking effectively, organize it to meet the ways that law-trained readers tend to process information. Here is what things look like from the typical reader's point of view:

State your **conclusion** first because a practical and busy reader needs to know what you are trying to support before you start supporting it. If you state your conclusion only after the analysis that supports it (or in the middle of that analysis), some or all of your reasoning will seem pointless to the reader, who does not yet know what you are trying to prove. Effective writers usually state their conclusions boldly at the beginning of a Discussion or Argument. This may take some getting used to because it differs from the way writing is often done in college. And in conversation, aggressively stating a controversial conclusion before explaining its background data and reasons can seem opinionated or arrogant.

Far from being offended, however, the reader who has to make a decision is grateful not to be kept in suspense. That kind of reader becomes frustrated and annoyed while struggling through sentences without understanding their relevance because the writer has not yet stated the proposition the writer intends to prove.

Next, state the **rule** because, after reading a conclusion of law, a skeptical lawyer or judge instinctively wants to know what principle of law requires that conclusion. After all, a core idea of law is that things are to be done according to the rules.

Then **explain** and prove the rule because the reader will refuse to follow you until you establish that the rule really is controlling law and you educate the reader on how the rule works. The skeptical lawyer or judge will not accept a rule statement as genuine unless it is proved with authority. You need to do all this *before* you apply the rule

---

[2] The formula explained here is designed for practical writing in office and motion memos and appellate briefs. For exams, use the IRAC organization explained in the article on Writing Exam Answers on this book's website.

to your facts because the reader will not accept the rule until you show that it is law and how it operates.

Then **apply** the rule. Once you have done that, you have proved a conclusion of law.

If what you have said is complicated, restate your **conclusion** to wrap things up.

§ 17.3 Rule Explanation and Rule Application

You can see many examples of rule explanation and rule application in your casebooks. Judicial opinions usually start with a statement of the facts of the case. After that, a court will typically begin discussing the law. In the legal discussion, you can often see exactly where the court stops explaining the law generally and starts applying the law to the facts of the dispute. If you were to draw a line across the page at that point, above the line would be rule explanation and below it would be rule application. If the opinion decides several issues, you might find a dividing point for each issue. If you want to get some practice in recognizing the difference between rule explanation and rule application, you might try looking for this dividing point when you read cases for other courses. The more recent the case, the more apparent the dividing point will be. Older cases tend to be somewhat less organized.

Authority, policy, and counteranalyses can appear both in rule explanation and in rule application. Sometimes authority used in rule explanation might reappear in rule application, but for a different purpose.

For example, suppose that *Alger v. Rittenhouse* held that a boat crew who caught a shark became its owner, to the exclusion of the fisherman who hooked but lost the shark an hour earlier. In your case, ranchers trapped a wild mustang in their corral. The mustang immediately jumped over the fence and galloped onto land owned by your client, who captured it. In rule explanation, you can use *Alger* to prove that your jurisdiction has adopted the rule that a wild animal becomes the property of the first person who reduces it to possession. And in rule application, you can use *Alger* again—this time to show that your client satisfies that rule because her facts are analogous to those of the boat crew, and that she thus owns the mustang.

A rule's *policy* is the rule's reason for being (Chapter 7). Each rule of law is designed to accomplish a purpose, such as preventing a particular type of harm. When courts are unsure what a rule means or how to apply it, they interpret the rule in the way most consistent with the policy behind it. Thus, policy can be used to show both what the rule is (in rule explanation) and how to apply it (in rule application).

A *counteranalysis* evaluates the arguments that could reasonably be made against your conclusion. Counteranalyses can appear in rule explanation or in rule application. In the comic strip below, it is what Calvin (the boy) refuses to do even though prompted by Hobbes (the tiger). In predictive writing, the counteranalysis is an objective evaluation of each reasonable contrary argument, with an honest assessment of its strengths and weaknesses. You must say whether your conclusion can withstand attack. And you must consider the possibility that other analyses might be better than the one you have selected.

In persuasive writing in a motion memo or appellate brief, a counteranalysis is called a *counterargument*. It does not objectively consider contrary points of view. It argues against them, stressing their weaknesses and showing their strengths to be unconvincing. Calvin might be more comfortable writing persuasively rather than objectively.

§ 17.3.1   How to Explain a Rule

To explain a rule, do the following:

1. Prove that the rule is law in the jurisdiction where the dispute will be decided. If the jurisdiction adopted the rule by statute, quote the key words of the statute, and show how the courts' interpretation of the statute is consistent with your understanding of it. If the rule is part of the jurisdiction's common law, prove that with cases. If the jurisdiction has a gap in its law on this subject, show how cases from other jurisdictions would persuade local courts to adopt the rule you are using.

2. Prove that you have stated the rule accurately. Sometimes whatever you say to prove that the rule is law also shows that you have stated it accurately. Sometimes you will need to add some extra discussion to give the reader confidence that you have not misstated the rule.

3. Explain how the rule operates. Some information about how courts have interpreted and applied the rule will give the reader an overview before you start rule application. But do not include information irrelevant to your issue.

4. Explain the policy behind the rule—if that would help the reader understand the rule. What is the law trying to accomplish through the rule? You do not need to explain the policy behind the cause of action for negligence. Every lawyer learned in the first year of law school that the policies behind negligence are to deter people from behaving in ways that are unreasonably dangerous to others and to compensate those who are injured through others' unreasonably dangerous behavior. But the reader might not know the policy behind the rule that a judge is not allowed to ask jurors to explain how they reached their verdict. That might need to be explained so that the reader can see how your analysis of the rule is consistent with its policy.

5. If any arguments could reasonably challenge your explanation of the rule, show why they are not persuasive in the counteranalysis. If you cannot do that, consider changing your mind.

6. If any subsidiary rules are essential to the analysis, prove and explain them as well. A subsidiary rule is one that operates with the primary rule to resolve the issue. Usually, less explanation is needed for subsidiary rules because they are less important. Not all subsidiary rules need to be explained in rule explanation.

§ 17.3.2 How to Apply a Rule

To apply a rule to your facts, do the following:

1. State, in summary, what happens when you compare the facts to the rule. Here are some examples:

All of these elements are supported by the facts.

Ms. McGillicuddy did everything the law of adverse possession requires of her.

Cobb did not proximately cause Crawford's injury, although the facts support the other elements of negligence.

None of these elements are supported by the facts.

2. Show, in detail, why that result occurs. Go through the rule's elements—all of them. But concentrate on the elements that are difficult to analyze, and allocate less space to others. Use legal authority to support your analysis. Show how the facts are equivalent or analogous to those in precedent cases.

3. Unless it is obvious, show how the result is consistent with the rule's policy. See paragraph 4 in § 17.3.1.

4. If any arguments could reasonably challenge your application of the rule, show why they are not persuasive in a counteranalysis. If you cannot do that, consider changing your mind.

> ## Exercise 17-A. Changing Planes in Little Rock

Wong has sued Keating in an Arkansas state court. Wong has never lived in Arkansas, and none of the events that led to *Wong v. Keating* happened in that state. But Wong sued in Arkansas because his lawyer has confidence in the juries there. The only time Keating has ever set foot on the ground in Arkansas was for 45 minutes while changing planes at the Little Rock airport. The only way for Keating to get to Shreveport, Louisiana, where she had a job interview, was to fly into Little Rock on one flight and then fly from Little Rock to Shreveport on another. During those 45 minutes, while Keating was walking in the airport from her incoming gate to her outgoing gate, a process server, acting on Wong's behalf, served Keating with a summons and complaint in *Wong v. Keating*. Keating has moved to dismiss on the ground that Arkansas has no personal jurisdiction over her. Wong claims that service in Arkansas gives Arkansas personal jurisdiction over Keating.

Below is an analysis of this issue. Find the components of the CREAC formula set out in the box in § 17.2.1.

> Arkansas has personal jurisdiction over Keating. Under the Due Process Clause of the Fourteenth Amendment, a state is authorized to exercise personal jurisdiction over a defendant who is served with a summons while the defendant is voluntarily inside the state. *Burnham v. Superior Court*, 495 U.S. 604 (1990). That is true even if service of the summons is the only connection between the state and the plaintiff, the defendant, or the plaintiff's claim. It is true when a defendant does not reside in the state, is only traveling through the state, and has no connection to the state except for the trip during which the defendant was served. *Id.* at 617-619, 635-639. And it is true even when none of the events or circumstances alleged in the plaintiff's complaint happened in the state. *Id.* at 620-621.
>
> The defendant in *Burnham* was a New Jersey resident who had traveled on business to southern California and then to northern California to visit his children. The plaintiff was the defendant's wife, who had him served in a divorce action while he was in northern California. Four justices of the Supreme Court joined in an opinion by Justice Scalia and reasoned that, under precedent going back two centuries, a state has "the power to hale before its courts any individual who could be found within its borders." *Id.* at 610. Another four justices joined in an opinion by Justice Brennan and reasoned that the defendant's presence in the state at the time of service was a purposeful availment that satisfies the minimum contacts requirements of *International Shoe v. Washington*, 326 U.S. 310 (1945). The ninth justice (Stevens) concurred separately on the ground that both rationales were correct. Because there was no majority opinion, it is not settled which rationale supports the rule, although the rule had the unanimous support of all nine justices.
>
> Regardless of the rationale, service on Keating in the Little Rock airport created personal jurisdiction in Arkansas. Keating was present in Arkansas at the moment of service. The process server's affidavit is evidence of that, and Keating

concedes it. Moreover, she does not claim that she did not know she was in Arkansas or that she was in the state under duress. She bought her airline ticket knowing she would have to change planes in Little Rock, and her presence was therefore voluntary.

Keating argues, however, that she was not in Arkansas long enough to be subject to the state's jurisdiction, even if she was served in Arkansas. She points out that the *Burnham* defendant had traveled to California to conduct business there and visit his children, spending nights in hotels and purposely availing himself of the benefits of the state. Keating contends that this case is distinguishable from *Burnham* because her destination was Louisiana rather than Arkansas, and because she was on the ground in Arkansas for less than an hour and only for the purpose of getting to Louisiana.

This case cannot be distinguished from *Burnham*. The Scalia opinion stressed that the state's jurisdiction extends to any visitor, "no matter how fleeting his visit." *Id.* at 610. And the Brennan rationale would treat Keating's decision to use the Little Rock airport for a connecting flight as purposeful availment supporting minimum contacts because Keating gained a benefit from her presence in Arkansas. Any other result would be unsupportable policy in an era of modern travel. There is no practical way to craft a rule that would clearly distinguish between a presence in the state that is too short to support personal jurisdiction and a presence that is long enough, which is why the Supreme Court held in *Burnham* that any presence is long enough if the defendant is served while physically present.

Moreover, Keating's presence in Arkansas was not limited to her 45 minutes inside the airport. She might have been validly served while either of the airplanes on which she flew was on the tarmac or even in the air over Arkansas. Service of process on a passenger in an airplane that flew over Arkansas but never landed in the state has been sustained because at the moment of service, the passenger was inside Arkansas even though not on the ground. *Grace v. MacArthur*, 170 F. Supp. 442 (E.D. Ark. 1959). The *Grace* court reasoned that there is no real difference between a passenger on an airplane that passes through Arkansas airspace and a passenger who travels through the state by train or bus without disembarking. *Id.* at 447.

Thus Arkansas has personal jurisdiction over Keating, and her motion to dismiss should be denied.

18

Varying the Sequence and Depth of Rule Explanation and Rule Application

§ 18.1 Varying the CREAC Formula to Suit Your Needs

The CREAC formula set out on page 145 can be varied in two ways. First, you can vary the **sequence** in which the components appear. The next section in this chapter explains how. Second, in rule explanation and in rule application, you can vary the **depth** to suit the amount of skepticism you expect from the reader. Later sections in this chapter explain how.

In addition, when you have more than one issue or subissue, you can **combine** separate CREAC analyses into a unified explanation of several issues and sub-issues. Chapter 19 explains how.

§ 18.2 Varying the Sequence

In some situations, you might vary the sequence of the CREAC formula's components—for example, by stating the rule first and the conclusion second—although the order should not be illogical or confusing. Think long and hard before deciding to vary the sequence in the box on page 145. If you do vary it, you should be able to give a good reason for doing so. Because of the reader's needs, described in § 17.2.2, *rule explanation should be completed before rule application begins.* In an office memo, variations in sequence usually do not work well. They are more useful in motion memos and appellate briefs, where varying the sequence might fit into a strategy of persuasion.

§ 18.3   When to Vary the Depth of Rule Explanation or Rule Application

Depending on the situation, rule explanation or rule application can be very short, very long, or somewhere in between. In one instance, rule explanation might need to be only a sentence, while rule application might require three pages. In another instance, the reverse might be true. Or each of them might be four or five pages long—or four or five sentences long. How can you tell how much depth is needed? Ask yourself three questions:

First, *how much depth will convince the reader that your conclusion is correct?* That depends on the reader's level of skepticism, which in turn depends on how complicated the issue is and how important it is to the decision the reader must make.

Second, *how much depth will convince your reader that she does not personally need to read the authorities on which you rely?* This second question poses a need-to-read test: You have not gone into enough depth if your reader would find it hard to agree with you without reading the authorities you have cited. A reader's need to consult the statutes and cases depends on the context. A reader is more likely to feel that need with a crucial and difficult issue than with a simple, peripheral, or routine one.

Third, *how much depth would help the reader make an informed decision?* If the reader were to go to the statutes and cases, would she be startled to find things you have left out? Part of your job is choosing what to leave out. The reader is counting on you to cut out the things that do not matter. But do not leave out so much that the reader is deprived of some of the information needed to make the decision.

Do not explore an issue in more depth than a reader would need. Your reader is a busy person, almost as intolerant of too much explanation as too little. If you include a great deal of detail about peripheral issues or about routine propositions with which your reader will easily agree, she can feel stuck in quicksand.

Students often underestimate the skepticism of legal readers. If you are not sure how much analysis to include, err on the side of making a more complete analysis until you have gained a better sense of your reader's expectations.

Rule explanation and rule application can each be developed in a way that is *comprehensive* or *substantiating* or *conclusory*. The rest of this chapter explains how, using the facts from Jordan's possible claim against YouTube introduced in § 17.1.

§ 18.4   Comprehensive Analysis

A comprehensive explanation includes whatever analyses are needed to satisfy a reader's aggressive skepticism. This is the full treatment. In the example below, notes in the margin show where each component of the CREAC formula begins. Can you locate policy discussions and counteranalyses?

Conclusion   YouTube has been immunized by federal law from liability for the video and words posted by Kendrick on YouTube's website.

Rule   Under the Communications Decency Act of 1996, a defendant is immune from liability if (1) the defendant is a "provider or user of an interactive computer service," which the statute defines to include a website; (2) the plaintiff has pleaded a state law claim; (3) the claim requires the plaintiff to prove that the defendant is a "publisher or speaker of any information"; and (4) the information at issue in the plaintiff's claim was "provided by another information content provider," which the statute defines to include a person, other than the defendant, who puts information on the defendant's website. 47 U.S.C. § 230(c)(1), (e)(3), (f)(2), (f)(3) (2012). The immunity test is in § 230(c)(1), (e)(3). The other subsections are definitional.

Rule Explanation   In the leading case interpreting these subsections of § 230, a
begins   plaintiff sued America Online, alleging that AOL allowed users to post anonymous messages on its website that defamed him and put his life in jeopardy. *Zeran v. Am. Online, Inc.*, 129 F.3d 327 (4th Cir. 1997). According to the complaint, the messages purported to be advertisements for "Naughty Oklahoma T-Shirts" with what the court described as "offensive and tasteless slogans related to the April 19, 1995, bombing of the Alfred P. Murrah Federal Building in Oklahoma City." *Id.* at 329. The messages said that viewers could purchase the t-shirts by calling the plaintiff's home telephone number. Although the plaintiff knew nothing about this and was not selling t-shirts of any kind, so many outraged people called him at home that at times he "was receiving an abusive phone call approximately every two minutes." *Id.* Several calls included threats to his life, and he had to seek police protection. *Id.* The plaintiff alleged that AOL was slow to remove these messages from its site, and that every time one was removed, another was posted, which AOL failed to prevent. *Id.*

The Fourth Circuit held that the Communications Decency Act barred the plaintiff's claims against AOL. *Id.* at 339. Even though the messages defamed him, AOL was immunized because, in the words of § 230(c)(1), (1) AOL is a "provider . . . of an interactive computer service"; (2) the plaintiff's defamation and negligence claims were based on state law; (3) publication is an element of defamation, requiring the plaintiff to prove that AOL is a "publisher or speaker of . . . information"; and (4) the information at issue in the plaintiff's claim was "provided by another information content provider," the anonymous poster. *Zeran*, 129 F.3d at 332. Section 230 even immunized AOL from liability for delays in removing the messages after the plaintiff informed the company of their defamatory character and their effect on him. *Zeran*, 129 F.3d at 339.

The plaintiff in *Zeran* argued that a website is no different from the publisher or distributor of a newspaper, book, or magazine, which would be liable for defamatory words it publishes. But the court held that even though a website is easily analogous to a print publisher, Congress had immunized websites anyway. "By its plain language, § 230 creates a federal immunity to any cause of action that would make service providers liable for information originating with a third-party user of the service," such as the unknown person who posted the false messages about the plaintiff. *Zeran*, 129 F.2d at 330.

Other Circuits have interpreted § 230 in the same way. *Doe v. GTE Corp.*, 347 F.3d 655 (7th Cir. 2003) (holding Internet service provider immune from liability for a user's invasion of plaintiff's privacy); *Batzel v. Smith*, 333 F.3d 1018 (9th Cir. 2003) (holding website operator immune for defamatory email message posted on its website); *Ben Ezra, Weinstein, & Co. v. Am. Online, Inc.*, 206 F.3d 980 (10th Cir. 2000) (holding AOL immune for inaccurate information posted on bulletin boards about stocks).

According to the statute's legislative history, Congress added subsections 230(c)(1) and (e)(3) to overrule a case that held that Prodigy could be liable for defamatory statements posted on one of its bulletin boards. S. Rep. No. 104-230, at 194 (1996); H.R. Conf. Rep. No. 104-458, at 194 (1996); 141 Cong. Rec. H84691-70 (1996). The case was *Stratton Oakmont, Inc. v. Prodigy Services Co.*, 1995 WL 323710 (N.Y. Sup. Ct. May 24, 1995).

In the statute itself, Congress enunciated the reasons for this immunity: "to promote the continued development of the Internet" and "to preserve the vibrant and competitive free market that presently exists for the Internet and other interactive computer services, unfettered by Federal or State regulation." 47 U.S.C. § 230(b)(1) & (2). "Congress recognized the threat that tort-based lawsuits pose to freedom of speech in the new and burgeoning Internet medium. . . . Section 230 was enacted, in part, to maintain the robust nature of Internet communication and, accordingly, to keep government interference in the medium to a minimum." *Zeran*, 129 F.3d at 330. People like the plaintiff in *Zeran* would be left without a remedy, but Congress considered the vitality of the Internet to be more important than insuring recovery by every plaintiff aggrieved by information distributed over the Internet. *Id.*

Rule Application begins

Here, YouTube can satisfy the immunity test in subsections 230(c)(1) and (e)(3). First, YouTube operates a website. It is therefore, in the statute's words, "a provider or user of an interactive computer service."

Second, defamation and false light invasion of privacy are state law claims. The immunity provisions of § 230 were enacted to prevent defamation claims against websites when the defamatory words were not generated by the website operator. That is why defamation claims failed in *Zeran* and *Batzel*. *Doe* treated invasion of privacy claims the same way.

Third, publication by the defendant is an element of both defamation and false light invasion of privacy. Thus, both claims would require Jordan to prove that YouTube was, in the statute's words, the "publisher or speaker of [the] information" that defamed her and invaded her privacy.

Finally, that information was not provided by YouTube. Instead, it was, in the statute's words, "provided by another information content provider." That was Kendrick.

This result is consistent with Congress's purpose in enacting the immunity provisions in § 230. As a practical matter, YouTube cannot review every video posted on its website without incurring business expenses so great that they could easily make the website unprofitable and cause weeks or months of delay in posting video clips that are the very reason for YouTube's existence. If the law imposed liability on YouTube for failing to conduct these investigations, the site could be forced to shut down. Congress did not immunize interactive computer service providers like websites from all informational liability, but only liability for information provided by others, like Kendrick. They remain liable for information that they generate themselves.

Even though a television station, newspaper, or magazine would have been liable under state law for defamation and false light invasion of privacy for publishing Kendrick's video with the words that he posted on YouTube, § 230 immunizes it from these state law claims. The courts have uniformly enforced the distinction between internet service providers and conventional media.

Conclusion (again)   Thus, Jordan will not be able to recover from YouTube.

§ 18.5 Substantiating Analysis

A substantiating analysis goes less deeply into the writer's reasoning. It supports the conclusion but without comprehensive detail. A substantiating analysis works when the reader is less skeptical because the issue is not central to the problem you are addressing. A substantiating analysis would be inadequate if the issue is crucial or difficult. A substantiating analysis might look like this:

Conclusion   YouTube is immune from liability for the video and words Kendrick posted on YouTube's website.

Rule   A defendant is immune if (1) the defendant is a "provider or user of an interactive computer service," including a website; (2) the plaintiff has pleaded a state law claim; (3) the plaintiff must prove that the defendant is a "publisher or speaker of any information"; and (4) the information was "provided by another information content provider," defined to include a third party who puts information on the defendant's website. 47 U.S.C. § 230(c)(1), (e)(3), (f)(2), (f)(3) (2012).

Rule Explanation begins

In the leading case interpreting these subsections of § 230, a plaintiff sued America Online for allowing anonymous postings on its website that defamed him and jeopardized his life. *Zeran v. Am. Online, Inc.*, 129 F.3d 327, 339 (4th Cir. 1997). The Fourth Circuit held that AOL was immune because (1) AOL was a "provider . . . of an interactive computer service"; (2) the plaintiff's defamation and negligence claims grew out of state law; (3) to prove defamation, the plaintiff had to prove that AOL was a "publisher or speaker of . . . information"; and (4) the information was "provided by another information content provider," the anonymous poster. *Id.* (quoting § 230(c)(1)). Section 230(f)(3) defines "another information content provider" to include a third party who puts information on the defendant's website.

Other circuits have interpreted § 230 in the same way. *Doe v. GTE Corp.*, 347 F.3d 655 (7th Cir. 2003); *Batzel v. Smith*, 333 F.3d 1018 (9th Cir. 2003); *Ben Ezra, Weinstein, & Co. v. Am. Online, Inc.*, 206 F.3d 980 (10th Cir. 2000). In the statute itself, Congress enunciated the reasons for this immunity: "to promote the continued development of the Internet" and "to preserve the . . . free market that presently exists for . . . interactive computer services, unfettered by Federal or State regulation." 47 U.S.C. § 230(b)(1) & (2).

Rule Application begins

YouTube can satisfy the immunity test in § 230(c)(1) and (e)(3). First, YouTube operates a website and is therefore "a provider or user of an interactive computer service." Second, defamation and false light invasion of privacy are state law claims. Third, both claims require Jordan to prove that YouTube was the "publisher or speaker of [the offending] information." Finally, that information was "provided by another information content provider" (Kendrick). § 230(f)(3).

This result is consistent with the congressional purpose of the immunity provisions. YouTube cannot practically review every video posted on its website, and if the law imposed liability on YouTube for failing to do so, the site could be forced out of business.

What in the comprehensive explanation in § 18.4 is missing here? If you and your supervisor were trying to figure out whether to sue YouTube, would the substantiating analysis be sufficient?

§ 18.6 Conclusory Analysis

A conclusory analysis does no more than allude to some of the more important reasons supporting your conclusion. The CREAC formula components are all included in the example below, but in abbreviated form except the rule itself. The only rule explanation is the statutory citation that proves the rule.

A conclusory analysis is appropriate *only* when the reader will easily agree with you, or when the point is not important to your analysis. In those situations, a reader would find a more detailed analysis tedious.

Conclusion	YouTube is immune from liability for the video and words Kendrick posted on YouTube's website.
Rule	A defendant is immune if (1) the defendant is a "provider or user of an interactive computer service," including a website; (2) the plaintiff has pleaded a state law claim; (3) the plaintiff must prove that the defendant is a "publisher or speaker of any information"; and (4) the information was "provided by another information content provider," including a third party who puts information on
Rule Explanation	the defendant's website. 47 U.S.C. § 230(c)(1), (e)(3), (f)(2), (f)(3) (2012).
Rule Application begins	YouTube can satisfy this test. First, YouTube operates a website and is therefore "a provider or user of an interactive computer service." Second, defamation and false light invasion of privacy are state law claims. Third, both claims require Jordan to prove that YouTube was the "publisher or speaker of [the] information" in question. Finally, that information was "provided by another information content provider," Kendrick.

§ 18.7 Cryptic Analysis

Beginning students sometimes write analyses so cryptic as to be less than conclusory.

> Jordan will not be able to recover from YouTube because it satisfies all four requirements under the Communications Decency Act of 1996 and is therefore immune from Jordan's claim. 47 U.S.C. § 230(c)(1), (e)(3), (f)(2), (f)(3) (2012).

This example omits the rule on which the conclusion is based, and it does not show in any way how the rule applies to the facts. It would *never* satisfy a skeptical reader.

19 Advanced CREAC: Organizing More Than One Issue

§ 19.1 Introduction

If you have more than one issue, the reader will need a separately structured CREAC proof for each one. That can happen when

- more than one element of a rule is at issue (see § 19.2)
- more than one claim or defense is at issue (see § 19.3)
- a dispute involves separate but related issues (see § 19.4)

Each issue will have its own conclusion. When you add all those conclusions together, you get an ultimate conclusion. When you organize your writing, you will state the ultimate conclusion first, which will cover all the issues—like a big umbrella:

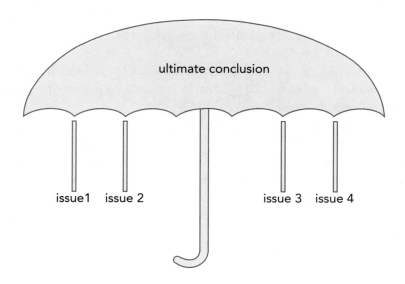

ultimate conclusion

issue1   issue 2   issue 3   issue 4

§ 19.2   How to Organize When More Than One Element or Factor Is at Issue

If you need to resolve more than one element of a test, you will have an ultimate conclusion for the rule as a whole, together with a conclusion for each individual element—in this instance from the test for adverse possession:

Ultimate Conclusion	Melrose will probably be able to gain title through adverse possession to the land known as the Ironwood Tract.
Conclusions on Issues	*Element 1* Melrose has been in actual possession of the Ironwood Tract.
	Element 2 Melrose possessed the land continuously for at least ten years.
	Element 3 Melrose possessed it openly and notoriously for the entire ten years.
	Element 4 Melrose's possession has been hostile to the owner's rights.
	Element 5 Melrose possessed the land under a claim of right or title.

When you write this analysis out, your opening or umbrella passage will state the ultimate conclusion ("Melrose will probably be able to gain title to the client's Ironwood Tract") and the essence of the reason ("because she has satisfied all the elements of adverse possession"). Your umbrella passage will also recite the *rule* on which the ultimate conclusion is based (the test for adverse possession, which has five elements). The umbrella passage will at first seem to be an incomplete CREAC structure because it will not define the elements or apply them to facts. But the discussion of the each element will provide that. The umbrella passage simply covers and organizes the subordinate proofs of the elements.

The umbrella passage also sets out a roadmap for what follows. It tells the reader what issues you will consider, their relative importance, and sometimes the order in which you will consider them.

Your umbrella passage will be followed by CREAC-structured discussions for the elements—a separate CREAC for each element. Each element is an issue for which you will have a separate *conclusion*. You will define each element through a definitional or other declaratory *rule*. For example, the first elements rule is a definition: "Actual possession means exclusive occupation of the land." You will prove the definition through authority in *rule explanation*. And you will apply the definition to the facts in *rule application*.

§ 19.3   How to Organize When More Than One Claim or Defense Is at Issue

Suppose your supervisor wants to know whether the client will be awarded damages in a tort case. You need to figure out whether the client has a cause of action (one issue or a cluster of issues). And you anticipate that the defendant will raise the affirmative defense of sovereign immunity. Although this situation is more complex than when several elements of a single rule are in dispute, you will handle it in the same way (see § 19.2).

Build an umbrella CREAC structure, and underneath it prove each of the conclusions through separate CREAC-structured analyses. For example, the ultimate conclusion might be that the client will be awarded damages because she has a cause of action (first conclusion) and the defendant has waived sovereign immunity (second conclusion). Thus:

Ultimate Conclusion	The client will be awarded damages.	
Conclusions on Issues	*The claim*	The client can prove negligence.
	Element 1	The defendant owed the client a duty.
	Element 2	The defendant breached it.
	Element 3	The client suffered injury.
	Element 4	The breach proximately caused the injury.
	The defense	The defendant has waived the affirmative defense of sovereign immunity.

Because negligence has four elements, the first issue is divided further into the four sub-issues shown above. At the beginning of your analysis of Issue 1, include an umbrella passage limited to whether the client has a cause of action for negligence.

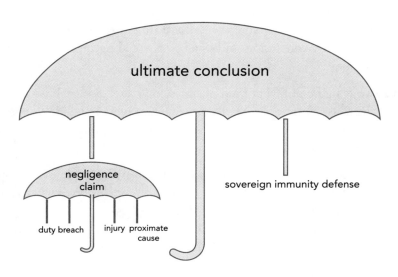

§ 19.4   How to Organize Other Types of Separate but Related Issues

Suppose someone sues your client, and your supervisor wants to know whether the lawsuit can be dismissed on forum selection grounds (because it was brought in the wrong court). You will have to resolve some or all of the following issues: (1) Does this court have subject matter jurisdiction over this kind of case? (2) Does this court have personal jurisdiction over your client? (3) Is this court the right venue for this lawsuit? To resolve these issues, you will use the same umbrella CREAC structure explained in § 19.2:

Ultimate Conclusion	The court will not dismiss this lawsuit on forum selection grounds.
Conclusions on Issues	*Issue 1* The court has subject matter jurisdiction.
	Issue 2 The court has personal jurisdiction over our client.
	Issue 3 The court is the proper venue.

Here, too, if an issue involves a test with more than one element, you will include an umbrella passage limited to that issue.

§ 19.5   How to Work with Multi-Issue Situations

Many students feel confused at first by multi-issue situations. But within a few weeks, you might begin to gain confidence in organizing this way. Within a year or two, most students instinctively think in structured proofs because it becomes second nature. This section provides some suggestions for getting to that point.

Step 1 While researching and planning your writing, ask yourself how many issues you have. If you have a hard time identifying issues, ask yourself how many conclusions of law a court would need to reach to resolve the dispute.

Step 2 Now, figure out what kind of issues you have. For each issue, is it part of the cause of action, part of a defense, part of a procedural requirement, or something else? Identifying the type of issue will help you choose one of the structures described in this chapter.

Step 3 Select one of the multi-issue structures explained in this chapter, and adapt it to your case. Make a list of every conclusion of law you will prove in your memo or brief, like the lists of issues earlier in this chapter. Organize the conclusions logically—for example, elements of a cause of action first, then defenses. Treat this list of conclusions as the beginning of an outline. Chapter 20 explains how to complete this outline and turn it into a memo or brief.

Step 4 At the beginning of an umbrella passage, use a roadmap paragraph to explain your umbrella CREAC to the reader. An introductory roadmap paragraph outlines your discussion so the reader knows what to expect as you explain the details. It states your ultimate conclusion ("The client should be awarded damages," for example) and then states the conclusions on subissues that support that ultimate conclusion. If some elements of a test are at issue and others are not, the roadmap paragraph is the place to make that clear. Most judges say that a well-written roadmap paragraph is essential in helping them understand what you are trying to say.[1] Here is a typical roadmap paragraph, which you might use to introduce the discussion outlined in § 19.3:

> The client will be awarded damages for destruction of its warehouse. The evidence supports all four of the elements of negligence. The defendant owed a duty to the plaintiff to keep the loading dock clear and breached that duty by leaving explosive materials on the loading dock overnight. The client's injury, destruction of its warehouse, is uncontested. The property damage was proximately caused by the defendant's breach when the materials it left on the loading dock exploded. In addition, sovereign immunity has been waived by § 419 of the Highways Code.

After reading this umbrella paragraph, the reader knows that you will discuss each of these issues in detail later in your analysis.

Step 5 Use headings to show your reader where your analysis of each issue begins. Lawyers and judges will not read your work from beginning to end. They will read parts of it at a time, and headings help them find the parts they need. If you are writing an office memo, look at the way headings are used in Appendix A. If you are writing a persuasive memo or an appellate brief, you will write point headings, which are explained in Chapter 33.

---

[1] Kristen K. Robbins, *The Inside Scoop: What Federal Judges Really Think About the Way Lawyers Write*, 8 LEGAL WRITING 257, 273 (2002).

Working with CREAC in First Drafts and in Later Drafts

20

§ 20.1 Using CREAC to Outline and to Begin Your First Draft

The CREAC formula explained in the preceding chapters can help you organize your legal analysis. It will also help keep your material from getting out of control. Getting used to writing with the CREAC formula takes some effort, but once you are used to it, organizing your writing becomes much easier *because the formula shows you where to put things*.

This section describes one method of working with CREAC. It is only a suggestion for the first time you write. If you develop a different process that works better for you, use that instead.

In the method described here, you will label everything so that you know where it goes and then plug it into whatever variant of the formula best fits your situation. The first time you try this method, it might seem a little awkward. But by the second or third time, it will begin to feel more natural because it fits the way people instinctively work and takes less effort than other methods of organizing.

Step 1 **Figure out how many issues you have.** You will analyze each using a separate CREAC structure. Chapter 19 explains how.

Step 2 **For each issue, identify the rule that is central to and governs the answer.** You might also use other rules, but for the moment focus on the rule that—more than any other—compels your answer.

Step 3 **Inventory your raw materials**. For each issue or subissue, sort everything you have into two categories: rule explanation and rule application. Some methods of sorting may work better for you than others, and over several writing assignments you might experiment to find the method that best fits the way you write.

One method is to go through your notes and write "RE" in the margin next to everything that you might use in rule explanation, and "RA" next to everything you might use in rule application. Some ideas or authorities might be useful in both rule explanation and rule application. Write "RE/RA" on them. If you have several issues, you can work out a shorthand for marking them separately, such as "#3 RE" for "rule explanation on issue 3" or "#1 RA" for "rule application on issue 1." If you have printed out cases, write these notations next to each part of the case that you will use. Go through your facts, too, marking the ones that are important enough to talk about during rule application.

Step 4 **Think about how all these things add up.** If you have not yet drawn a conclusion, do it now. If you decided previously on a conclusion, check it against your raw materials to see whether it still seems like the best conclusion.

Step 5 **Make a fluid outline.** Your notes are now complete enough to be organized into some variation of the CREAC formula. You can do that by making the fluid outline described in § 13.2.

For each issue, take a piece of paper and write four headings on it, using abbreviations for the CREAC components (for example: "concl," "rule," "RE," and "RA"). You can do this on a computer instead if you feel more comfortable typing than writing.

Under "concl," write your conclusion for that issue in whatever shorthand will remind you later what your thinking was (for example: "no diversity—Wharton citizen of Maine"). Under "rule," do something similar. Under "RE," list your raw materials for rule explanation. For each item listed, do not write a lot—just enough to remind you at a glance of everything you have. Under "RA," do the same for rule application. Make sure that everything you have on that issue is listed on that page. *This is your outline page for the issue.*

Suppose that for rule explanation on a certain issue you have listed six resources (cases, facts, and so on). You have not yet decided the order in which you will discuss them when you explain the rule. In most situations, that decision will be easier and better if you do *not* make it while outlining. The best time to decide is just before you write that issue's rule explanation in your first draft. *You do not need to know exactly where everything will go before you start the first draft.* When you decide, just write a number next to each item ("1" next to the first one you will discuss, "2" next to the second, and so on).

Step 6 **Start writing.** Choose the issue you feel most comfortable writing about. Put that issue's outline page (from Step 5) where you can see it while you work. Using what you have on the outline page, write a complete sentence stating your conclusion for that issue. Then write the other CREAC components.

As you cover each thing listed on the issue's outline page, cross it off. When everything has been crossed off, go on to another issue, and use the same process to write it.

Your first draft probably will not use everything that you listed on your outline pages. Some material will not seem as useful while you are writing as it did when you were sorting. But do not throw anything away yet. During rewriting, you might change your mind and decide to use it after all.

§ 20.2 How to Test Your Writing for Effective Organization

While reviewing your work, ask yourself the following questions:

1. Have you organized around tests and elements, rather than around cases? Readers will be frustrated if you dump before them the cases you found in the library. A mere list of relevant cases, with a discussion of each, does not help a decisionmaker, who needs to understand how the *rules* affect the facts. The law is the rules themselves, and a case merely proves a rule's existence and accuracy. Teachers sometimes call this problem *case-by-case-itis*. It is easy to spot in a student's paper: The reader sees a series of paragraphs, each devoted to a single case. Instead, organize around *ideas*, such as issues, arguments, or a test's elements or factors.

2. Have you collected closely related ideas in one place, rather than scattering them? If you have three reasons why the defendant will not be convicted, first list them all in one place, and then explain each separately. The reader looking for the big picture cannot follow your analysis if you introduce the first reason on page one; mention the second for the first time on page four; and surprise the reader with the third on page six. If you have more than one item or idea, listing them in a roadmap paragraph at the beginning helps the reader keep things in perspective. It also forces you to organize and evaluate your thoughts. Roadmap paragraphs help tell the reader where you are going.

3. Have you accounted for all the issues and discussed them in logical order? If you have several issues, have you organized them so the reader understands how everything fits together?

4. For each issue and subissue, have you stated your conclusion? If so, where? State it precisely so the reader knows from the very beginning what you intend to demonstrate. In an office memo, your conclusions will be predictions, either expressed ("Kolchak will probably be acquitted of robbery") or implied ("The evidence does not establish beyond a reasonable doubt that Kolchak is guilty of robbery").

5. For each issue and subissue, have you stated the rule or rules supporting your conclusion? If so, where? Do not merely describe the cases and assume your reader will figure out what rule they stand for. Formulate a credible rule, and prove it by analyzing the authority.

6. For each issue and subissue, have you explained the rule? If so, where? See § 17.3.1 for how to evaluate your rule explanation.

7. For each issue and subissue, have you applied the rule to the facts? If so, where? See § 17.3.2 for how to evaluate your rule application.

8. Have you completed rule explanation before starting rule application? Before you start rule application, the reader needs to know that you have accurately stated the rule and that it really is law. If you do not do those things first during rule explanation, many readers will find it harder to agree with your rule application. You might use some authorities first in explaining the rule and again in applying the rule. But that does not mean rule application and rule explanation can be mixed.

9. In both rule explanation and rule application, have you explained your reasoning fully? Explain each step in your reasoning. Do not leave anything out. One way to discipline yourself to do this well is to ask yourself "Why is that true?" about each statement you make. Then make sure your writing completely answers that question.

10. Have you created a post-draft linear outline to test your organization? A post-draft linear outline is explained in § 13.2.

Part 5

Working Effectively with Details

21 Writing Effective Paragraphs and Sentences

This chapter explains how to structure paragraphs and sentences to help the reader easily see your reasoning. Paragraphs are the building blocks of your legal analysis. Sentences are the bricks and mortar. Your reader will struggle to understand unless you pay careful attention to structuring your analysis block by block and brick by brick.

§ 21.1   Paragraphs Reveal the Organizational Details

Most readers subconsciously use paragraph divisions to learn how a writer's thoughts fit together. They assume that each paragraph substantiates or explores a separate and distinct idea or subject. They also assume that the first or second sentence in each paragraph states or implies that idea or subject and shows how it relates to matters already discussed in previous paragraphs. To the extent that you frustrate these assumptions, your writing will be less helpful to the reader and therefore less influential.

An effective paragraph has the following five characteristics:

- *Unity:* It proves one proposition or covers one subject. Material more relevant to other propositions or subjects has been relocated.
- *Completeness:* It includes whatever is needed to prove the proposition or cover the subject.
- *Internal coherence:* Ideas are expressed in a logical sequence that the reader can follow without having to mentally edit the paragraph while reading.
- *Readable length:* It is neither so long that the reader gets lost, nor so short that valuable material is underdeveloped or trivialized.

- **Thesis or topic sentence:** An effective paragraph announces or implies its purpose at the outset. Its first or second sentence states or implies its thesis or topic and, if necessary, makes a transition from the preceding material.

§ 21.2 Descriptive and Probative Paragraphs

The way you write a paragraph depends on whether you are *describing* something or *proving* something. Compare these paragraphs:

Descriptive	Probative

Descriptive

In January in Death Valley, the average high temperature is about 65°, and the average low is about 37°. Spring and fall temperatures approximate summer temperatures elsewhere. In April and in October, for example, the average high is about 90°, and the average low about 60°. July is the hottest month, with an average high of about 116° and an average low of about 87°. The highest temperature ever recorded in Death Valley was 134° on July 10, 1913. Average annual rainfall is about 1½ inches.

Probative

The climate in Death Valley is brutal. At Furnace Creek Ranch, the highest summer temperature each year reaches at least 120° and in many years at least 125°. The highest temperature recorded in Death Valley—134°—is also the highest recorded anywhere on earth.[1] In the summer sun, a person can lose four gallons of perspiration a day and—in 3% humidity—die of dehydration.

A *topic* is a subject or category of information, such as "Death Valley weather." After reading the descriptive paragraph, you know some weather details about Death Valley. Descriptive paragraphs give factual information about things. If a descriptive paragraph confuses a reader, she might ask, "What is this paragraph about?"

A *thesis* or *proposition*, on the other hand, begins a probative paragraph with a statement that can be proved or disproved—such as "the climate in Death Valley is brutal." After reading the probative paragraph, you have a reaction to that proposition. You might agree or disagree. A probative paragraph should try to *prove*

---

[1] Previous editions of this book said that Death Valley's 134° temperature was the second highest ever recorded on earth, the highest being 136° recorded in the Sahara Desert. But in 2012, the World Meteorological Organization disqualified the 136° Sahara temperature because of measurement errors. That leaves Death Valley the record holder as "the world's hottest place." World Meteorological Org., *Press Release No. 956* (Sept. 13, 2012), http://www.wmo.int/pages/mediacentre/press_releases/pr_956_en.html (last visited Nov. 15, 2014).

something about the subject matter or topic. If a probative paragraph confuses, the reader might ask, "What is this paragraph supposed to prove?"

Probative and descriptive writing often appear in the same legal document. In an office memo, for example, the Facts are mostly descriptive, and the Discussion is mostly probative.

Even in probative writing, some paragraphs are more descriptive than others. If it takes three pages to prove a particular proposition, at least a few paragraphs in those three pages will describe the raw materials involved—facts, cases, or statutes, for example. Proving a proposition means explaining *how* the relevant legal authority and determinative facts support it. Most readers need a description of those raw materials before you can convincingly explain how they prove something when artfully woven together.

§ 21.3 Proposition Sentences, Topic Sentences, and Transition Sentences

The first or second sentence of a probative paragraph is the *proposition sentence* because it clearly states the proposition. The rest of the paragraph should prove the proposition.

In contrast, a descriptive paragraph provides details about a topic. The first or second sentence is the *topic sentence*, which identifies the topic by expressly stating it or implying it. If the context implies the topic, sometimes the topic sentence can be omitted from the paragraph. But in most cases, including a topic sentence helps the reader understand by revealing your internal organization step by step.

Although in descriptive writing a topic can often be implied, in probative writing the proposition should be expressly stated. *A practical reader needs to know what you are trying to prove before you start proving it.* Law-trained readers are always practical because they must make decisions after reading a lot of material in a limited amount of time. Careful paragraph structure is an important part of helping your reader understand your information as quickly and efficiently as possible.

Both descriptive and probative paragraphs are much more effective if they include *transition words or phrases* to show the reader how each paragraph is connected to the material before or after it. Transitions are the mark of a professional writer, who thoughtfully adds connections between each block of writing to help the reader follow what she is communicating. A transition most often appears at the beginning of a paragraph but may also appear at the end, serving as a bridge to the next paragraph or topic. Often the first sentence of a paragraph can both state a proposition or topic and make a transition.

Section 22.3, paragraph 2, gives several examples of transitions you can use to make your writing flow more clearly.

§ 21.4   How to Test Your Paragraphs for Effectiveness

In first drafts, paragraphs are seldom structured well. To identify the paragraphs in need of improvement, ask yourself the following questions.

1. Does each paragraph serve just one purpose? Prove one proposition or describe one topic. Remove and relocate material that is more relevant to other propositions or topics.

2. Have you told the reader each paragraph's proposition (if probative) or its topic (if descriptive) near the beginning? If your reader has to wait until later in the paragraph to learn its proposition or topic, the reader may need to read the paragraph two or three times to figure out its purpose. However, a topic sentence may not be necessary if the topic is clearly implied by the context.

3. Have you broken up long paragraphs so the reader does not get lost inside them? Your reader will be confused by paragraphs that wander on aimlessly or endlessly, addressing multiple topics. As a general rule, paragraphs in an office memo or brief should not exceed a half-page of double-spaced text.

A busy reader relies on paragraph divisions to take a momentary mental breath before proceeding to the next thought. Think about a case you recently read in one of your casebooks that had unusually long paragraphs.[2] You probably felt tired and confused by trying to understand its internal organization and reasoning. That is how a lawyer or judge feels when navigating a legal document with paragraphs that are too long.

A paragraph that is too long probably lacks *unity* as well because it includes two or more topics or propositions. Writers of long paragraphs often shift topics without realizing it. If you tend to write paragraphs longer than a half-page, look for the natural topic shifts inside the paragraph. After identifying each individual topic or proposition, break up the material into digestible chunks, so they become separate paragraphs that address distinct topics. Lead your reader from one paragraph to the next by adding effective transitions.

4. Within each paragraph, have you expressed your ideas in a logical and effective sequence? When a paragraph confuses but nothing is wrong with its length or the wording of individual sentences, the paragraph usually lacks *internal coherence*. That happens when ideas within the paragraph are presented in a sequence

---

[2] An example in your Civil Procedure casebook is *Pennoyer v. Neff*, 95 U.S. 714 (1878).

that makes it hard for the reader to understand how they fit together to prove the proposition or illuminate the topic.

§ 21.5   How to Test Your Sentences for Effectiveness

Just as paragraphs build documents, sentences build paragraphs. All of the characteristics of an effective paragraph depend upon the internal structure and sequence of the sentence components. Sentences usually do not become fully effective until the polishing stage. But at the first draft and rewriting stage, ask yourself the following questions.

1. Does the sentence deliver the subject and verb to the reader as soon as possible? The verb holds a sentence together by connecting its words to an idea. In fact, a sentence is usually incomprehensible until the reader finds both the subject and the verb. The longer it takes the reader to find both, the harder your reader must work.

For example, try reading this sentence:

The defendant's use of email spam to solicit contributions to a fake charitable organization purportedly engaged in disaster relief and his use of the contributions to buy a vacation home for himself constitute fraud.

A sentence like this cannot be understood in a single reading because it is "front-loaded." A frustrated reader searches for the verb ("constitute") and finds it nearly at the end of the sentence, after plowing through a 32-word compound subject ("The defendant's use of email spam to solicit contributions to a fake charitable organization purportedly engaged in disaster relief *and* his use of the contributions to buy a vacation home for himself"). Once the reader locates the verb, she must read the sentence again to understand it—because everything that came before the verb made no sense the first time.

During first drafts, writers often ask themselves, "What shall I talk about next?" and then write down the answer. That answer becomes the subject of a sentence, no matter how unreadable the result. We all do this in first drafts, but in rewriting you should spot the problem and fix it.

You can fix a front-loaded sentence by reshuffling it to deliver the verb to the reader quickly:

The defendant committed fraud by using email spam to solicit contributions for a fake charitable organization purportedly engaged in disaster relief, and by using the contributions to buy a vacation home for himself.

Or you can break up the sentence into two or more shorter sentences:

> <u>The defendant committed fraud</u>. He used email spam to solicit contributions for a fake charitable organization purportedly engaged in disaster relief, and he used the contributions to buy a vacation home for himself.

2. Have you put the verb near the subject, and the object near the verb? Many readers get lost in a sentence when something has been inserted between the subject and the verb.

> The Wabash Garage Orchestra, <u>even though it includes 32 musicians, some with cellos or other large instruments</u>, played the Philip Glass Violin Concerto while sitting in trees in Fabian Smedley's back yard.

The same problem occurs when words interrupt the reader between the verb and its object. To help your reader, move the interrupting clause or phrase to the end of the sentence (or to the beginning), leaving the subject and verb (or the verb and its object) relatively close together.

phrase or clause moved to end	The Wabash Garage Orchestra played the Philip Glass Violin Concerto while sitting in trees in Fabian Smedley's back yard, <u>even though the orchestra includes 32 musicians, some with cellos or other large instruments</u>.
phrase or clause moved to beginning	<u>Even though the Wabash Garage Orchestra includes 32 musicians, some with cellos or other large instruments</u>, they played the Philip Glass Violin Concerto while sitting in trees in Fabian Smedley's back yard.

3. Have you put the most complex and detailed part of the sentence at the end? To understand a sentence, a reader must figure out its structure. Readers do this quickly and subconsciously. When they cannot figure out the structure easily, they have to read the sentence again—or they lose interest, ignore the sentence, and read on without ever learning what the offending sentence meant.

Compare these examples:

complex part at beginning	<u>Because the defendant's website is interactive and allows a person in any state to order a catalog, send a message to the defendant, and purchase beer or wine by typing in credit card and other information</u>, the court held that it has jurisdiction over the defendant.

complex part in middle	The court held <u>that because the defendant's website is interactive and allows a person in any state to order a catalog, send a message to the defendant, and purchase beer or wine by typing in credit card and other information,</u> the court has jurisdiction over the defendant.
complex part at end	The court held that it has jurisdiction over the defendant <u>because the defendant's website is interactive and allows a person in any state to order a catalog, send a message to the defendant, and purchase beer or wine by typing in credit card and other information.</u>

Most readers find the third example the easiest to read because the first thing they see is a subject, verb, and object ("The court held that it had jurisdiction over the defendant"). Once they understand the basic sentence structure, the complex part at the end makes more sense.

4. Have you put what you want to emphasize at the beginning or at the end of the sentence? The beginning or end of a sentence is more obvious than the middle. Some writers call them *stress positions*. Sometimes, the end is more obvious just because that is the last thing the reader reads before going on to something else. And sometimes the beginning is more obvious—for example, if the sentence is the first one in a paragraph. If you want a theme or idea to resonate in the reader's mind, take advantage of the stress position in a sentence and put that information there.

5. When a sentence compares two ideas, have you used the most effective structure and wording? Some sentence structures show contrast better than others. For example:

> The Supreme Court has held that a defendant waives an objection by not making it at trial, <u>but</u> the Court has also held that, even without an objection, a conviction should be reversed when a prosecutor's conduct was as inflammatory as it was here.

The word *but* buried in the middle of a long sentence only weakly alerts the reader that one idea (waiver by failing to object) is knocked down by another (but not if the prosecutor's conduct is inflammatory). Everybody writes this kind of sentence in rough drafts, but you should recognize and cure it during rewriting.

> <u>Although</u> the Supreme Court has held that a defendant waives an objection by not making it at trial, the Court has also held that a conviction should be reversed, even without an objection, when a prosecutor's conduct was as inflammatory as it was here.

Although signals the reader from the beginning that the first clause will turn out not to matter. Contrast can also be effectively shown when *but* appears at the beginning of a sentence:

> The Supreme Court has held that a defendant waives an objection by not making it at trial. But the Court has also held that a conviction should be reversed, even without an objection, when a prosecutor's conduct was as inflammatory as it was here.

No rule of grammar forbids occasionally starting a sentence with *but* or *and*. But avoid overdoing it.

6. Is the subject of the sentence doing something concrete? Does the sentence use a verb in the active voice? If not, do you have a good reason for using passive voice? A sentence is easier to understand if it uses concrete words to paint a picture full of active imagery. First, figure out who is (or was, or will be) doing something. Make whoever or whatever that is the subject of the sentence. Then choose a verb in the active voice that expresses the subject's action or conduct.

When you choose a verb in the active voice, it describes what the subject is doing or has done ("Maguire *sued* Schultz"). But a verb in the passive voice makes the subject of the sentence the receiver or victim of the action ("Schultz *was sued by* Maguire"). Here are two more examples:

| **active** | The student missed the deadline. |
| **passive** | The deadline was missed by the student. |

In the active voice example, the *student* is the subject, who acted by missing the deadline. In the passive voice example, the deadline—an inanimate abstraction—is the subject of the sentence. And the reader must wait until the end of the sentence to find out who missed it.

The passive voice can be vague, weak, wordy—and just plain boring. For that reason, write most sentences in the active voice. But sometimes passive voice works better. For example, passive verbs may be more effective when you do not know who acted, when the identity of the actor is unimportant, or when you want to deemphasize the actor's identity. For example, compare these:

| **active** | The Department of Public Welfare has wrongfully terminated Ms. Blitzstein's aid-to-dependent-family benefits fourteen times in the last six years. |
| **passive** | Ms. Blitzstein's aid-to-dependent-family benefits have been wrongfully terminated fourteen times in the last six years. |

Depending on the context, the passive sentence might not be vague. Here, the reader might know that the Department is the only agency capable of terminating aid-to-dependent-family benefits. And to some readers, the passive sentence may be stronger and more interesting. To a judge who is asked to issue an order to stop this nonsense, the passive would be stronger because it emphasizes the outcome in a way the judge might find more appealing. Generally, a judge is more likely to sympathize with the victim of a faceless bureaucracy (the passive example) than condemn a named government agency for acting maliciously or incompetently (the active example).

7. Have you avoided using forms of the verb *to be*? *To be* verbs include *is*, *are*, *was*, *were*, and some other forms that occur less often. In law, people do things to other people and to ideas and objects, which are best described by concrete verbs that help the reader *see* the action. Variations on the verb *to be* fail to bring the story to life for the reader. Even worse, when a form of *to be* is used in combination with the word *there*, the resulting sentence is weak, wordy, and devoid of imagery.

Legal writing creates temptations to use *there is* and its variations (*there are*, *there were*). Editing them out usually creates stronger and tighter wording. For example:

weak	There is a possibility of action in the near future by the EPA to remove these pesticides from the market.
much better	The EPA might soon prohibit the sale of these pesticides.
weak	There are four reasons why the plaintiff will not recover.
much better	The plaintiff will not recover for four reasons.

In the "weak" examples, the reader can barely tell who has done what to whom because the weak verb and lofty tone obscure action. The subjects and verbs do not stand out and take charge. In the "much better" examples, the reader immediately knows what is happening without reading the same words twice.

Overusing the verb *to be* and its variations creates problems. They can effectively describe a condition or status ("the defendant is guilty"), and they work well to signal a declaratory rule ("the sentence for first-degree murder is forty years without parole"). But in other situations they obscure action.

Early drafts often include sentences like the weak examples above, but rewriting should produce final drafts that more closely resemble the much better ones. While rewriting, look for sentences like the weak ones. Figure out what is *really* going on (who is doing what?). Use your word processor's "find" function to locate each of the four most common forms of the verb *to be*—*is*, *are*, *was*, and *were*. Then search for each instance of *there* used in combination with one of these verbs. Each time you find one, ask yourself whether you can rewrite the sentence using an active verb to bring the action to life. We bet you can.

8. Have you used concrete verbs that communicate *exactly* what the reader needs to know? Help the reader by choosing concrete verbs that clearly communicate your meaning. Here are some examples of vague verbs that frequently fail to meet the reader's needs because they raise more questions than they answer:

Apply. "The Freedom of Information Act *applies* to this document." Does that mean the document must be published in the *Federal Register*? Or does it mean that the document must be given to anyone who asks for a copy? Or that the document must be made available to the public for photocopying, but not at government expense? Or does it give the government permission to refuse to do any of these things? Replace *applies* with a verb that communicates exactly what the Act does.

Deal with. "The court *dealt with* common law larceny." What exactly did the court do to larceny? Did the court define that term? Define only one of the elements? Clarify the difference between larceny and false pretenses? Decide that the legislature impliedly abolished the crime of larceny when it enacted a theft statute? Delete *dealt with* and insert a verb that tells exactly what the court actually did.

Indicate. "The defendant *indicated* that he was interested in buying hashish." How did he do that? By nodding affirmatively when asked if that was his desire? By asking, "Is hashish sold in this neighborhood?" By saying, "I want to buy some hash"? The law might treat each of these possibilities differently, and the reader needs to know exactly what happened.

Involve. "Section 452(a) *involves* the Rule Against Perpetuities." That sentence says only that § 452(a) has some connection with the Rule Against Perpetuities. Has § 452(a) codified the Rule? Modified it? Abolished it? Use a verb that specifies exactly what § 452(a) and the Rule Against Perpetuities have to do with each other.

Say or Said. "The court *said* that the defendant's conduct was unconscionable." Courts hold, conclude, or reason. The reader expects you to analyze the law and explain what it *means*. To do that, use a specific word that communicates exactly what the court *did*, not just what it said. Courts *say* things only in dicta. On the other hand, a judge writing a concurrence or dissent does not act for the court, and therefore can accurately be described as having *said* things. For clarity, when you use the word *say*, specify the context: "The court said in dicta," or "Justice McGillicuddy said in dissent."

Do not use the word *say* to refer to words found in a statute: "Section 243(a) says the plaintiff is not entitled to exemplary damages." Statutes are called Acts because the legislature does something by enacting them. Statutes *provide*, *create*, *abolish*, *prohibit*, *penalize*, *define*, and more. Whether you are analyzing case law, statutes, or some other legal authority, use specific and concrete verbs that explain what the law *means and does*, not just what it says.

9. Have you broken up sentences that are too long or too complicated for the reader to understand easily the first time? Express the sentence's ideas in fewer words, or split the sentence into two or more shorter sentences. Or do both. Legal ideas and concepts are difficult for a writer to communicate clearly, and even more difficult for the reader to comprehend. Long, convoluted sentences that try to impress by doing too much in fact do just the opposite. They fail to persuade because the reader gives up in frustration.

You have reached the benchmark for excellent legal writing when your reader understands each step of your analysis *effortlessly*. Use short sentences occasionally to give your reader a break.

10. Have you violated any of these guidelines *only* when you have a very good reason? Writing is creative work, and when you have a good reason, go ahead and break the rules. To test whether your reason is a good one, try to articulate for yourself exactly what it is. Your teacher might ask you to explain it.

> ### Exercise 21-A. Probative and Descriptive Paragraphs

Write two paragraphs—one descriptive and the other probative—about the first month or two of law school.

1. Descriptive paragraph. Summarize what happened during your first month or two of law school. Describe some of the things you saw, heard, read, and wrote. Do not try to prove any belief you might have about the first month or two of law school. Just describe your experiences without characterizing them.

2. Probative paragraph. State a proposition about the first month or two of law school that you might use to persuade a friend who is considering whether to apply for admission. After the proposition sentence that characterizes your experience, continue by explaining the reasons for your characterization to prove the proposition.

For example, the opening sentence of this paragraph might read, "The first month or two of law school is hard," or "puzzling," or "exciting," or "cruel," or "challenging," or any other characterization you choose. Then add "because," and complete the proposition sentence by listing and explaining the most important facts that led to your characterization. Then finish the paragraph by proving the proposition.

| Exercise 21-B. Editing for Effective Sentence Structure |

Each of the following sentences was written by a first-year law student. First, identify the structural problem or problems with each sentence. Then rewrite each sentence to resolve the problems and to make its meaning clear to the reader.

1. New York Civil Rights Law § 51 says that the commercial use of any person's name or likeness, used for an advertisement or to profit by selling, without having first obtained written consent, may sue for damages.

2. Although Ms. Roland is a person who was injured by the nonconsensual use of her picture for advertising and trade purposes by Online Images, Inc. and the incidental use of her photograph by the New York State Division was unlawful.

3. The question presented in this case is whether or not a minor who has entered into a cellphone contract in the State of Ohio can disaffirm said contract, taking into consideration whether the cellphone could, given the exception for necessities, be considered "necessary" and, assuming a disaffirmance was allowed, if there were time restrictions to which a minor would be subject.

4. Exemplary damages are allowed when it is found that a company or person used an image knowing that they do not have consent.

5. There is no cause of action for a plaintiff for invasion of privacy just because they are cast in a "false light."

6. Online Images, Inc. knew it did not possess written consent of Ms. Roland for the use of her photograph, thus satisfying the requirement for the jury to consider an award for exemplary damages.

7. The element of knowing use is usually a question for the jury once it has been found that compensatory damages are warranted.

8. The enactment of § 51 was immediately preceded by a lawsuit in which a young woman could not recover damages when a company nonconsensually used her photograph in a national advertising campaign because New York did not have a common law or statutory right of privacy.

22 Effective Style: Clarity, Vividness, Conciseness, and Precision

In first drafts, style is usually pretty awful. Most writers achieve effective style only through rewriting and polishing, as they look for opportunities to make the earlier draft more vivid, clear, and concise. This chapter explains why all three are so important in legal writing, and how to achieve those characteristics in yours.

§ 22.1 Clarity and Vividness

> If the reader thinks something you wrote is unclear, then it is, by definition.
> —*Deirdre N. McCloskey*

Unclear writing can make it hard or impossible for your reader to agree with you. Even if a reader—with effort—could figure out what you mean, readers in the legal profession usually cannot give you that effort. They do not have the time. If your writing lacks clarity, a disappointed senior lawyer may return your memo to you and ask you to rewrite it, which may damage your credibility. Or a judge may rule against your client because the judge cannot understand your arguments.

Deliver your legal analysis in writing that is so clear that your reader can understand it *effortlessly*. Unfortunately, many students arrive in law school without a solid instinct for effective style because much of what you were assigned to read in college lacks clarity and vividness. And in some subjects, students are encouraged to write obscure prose that is inherently difficult for the reader to comprehend. Law is different.

In the comic strip, Calvin (the boy) foresees being rewarded for writing papers using dense prose. Hobbes (the tiger) is already suffering the same frustration a legal reader feels when confronting unclear legal writing. In the legal profession, successful lawyers understand that *clear writing* is their stock in trade rather than the abstract prose characteristic of some other academic fields.

Vividness goes a step further than clarity. Clear writing communicates a *message*. Adding vividness—by creating a vivid image in the reader's mind using descriptive, concrete words—can make the message memorable and convincing. Vividness is not always necessary in legal writing. Most of the time clarity is enough. But add vividness to your writing when you see an opportunity so your message resonates in the reader's mind.

Flowery, important-sounding words almost always make your writing less clear and vivid than simple and straightforward ones. For example, do not write *utilized* instead of the simple, straightforward word *used*. Many first-year students try to imitate the "legalese" they read in their casebooks, often drawn from older cases written at a time when it was fashionable for lawyers to write that way. But opinions are edited and printed in casebooks for what they tell you about the law, not to show you how to write. Verbosity, obscurity, arcaneness, and disorganization that were tolerated generations ago are now considered unacceptable because they make the reader's job harder. If you adopt that writing style, you fail to *communicate* like a modern lawyer.

Similarly, judges repeatedly say they want clear, concise writing in legal briefs. In one experiment, some appellate judges and their law clerks were asked to assess the persuasiveness of contorted writing in "legalese." Others were asked to evaluate the same material rewritten in "plain English." They considered the original legalese version "substantively weaker and less persuasive than the plain English versions."[1] And

---

[1] Robert W. Benson & Joan B. Kessler, *Legalese v. Plain English: An Empirical Study of Persuasion and Credibility in Appellate Brief Writing*, 20 Loy. L.A. L. Rev. 301, 301 (1987).

the judges and law clerks assumed that the lawyers who wrote the plain English versions worked in higher-prestige jobs.[2]

§ 22.2   Conciseness

> The present letter is a very long one simply because I had no time to make it shorter.
>
> —*Pascal*

First drafts are usually too wordy. In later drafts, you can tighten up the writing by finding ways to say the same thing in fewer words so your reader can understand your message more quickly and easily. Later drafts might naturally expand with new *ideas* because the process of rewriting helps you see what was missing from earlier drafts. Rewriting for conciseness helps make room for these new ideas.

Compare the following two versions of the same sentence. The facts—though not the words—come from *Sherwood v. Walker*,[3] a classic mutual-mistake-of-fact case discussed in many Contracts casebooks.

verbose	It is important to note that, at the time when the parties entered into the agreement of purchase and sale, neither of them had knowledge of the cow's pregnant condition.
concise	When the parties agreed to the sale, neither knew the cow was pregnant.

How did the verbose first draft become the tight rewrite? Look at the following revisions:

Verbose Original		Concise Rewrite
It is important to note that	⟶	[deleted]
at the time when	⟶	when
entered into the agreement of purchase and sale	⟶	agreed to the sale
neither of them	⟶	neither
had knowledge of	⟶	knew
the cow's pregnant condition	⟶	the cow was pregnant

But do not edit out meaning. In the example above, it would be a mistake to eliminate so many words that a reader would not understand that the cow was

---

[2] *Id.* at 301-02.
[3] 33 N.W. 919 (Mich. 1887).

pregnant when sold, and that neither the buyer nor the seller then knew about the pregnancy.

§ 22.3   How to Test Your Writing for Effective Style

While rewriting, ask yourself the following questions.

1. Is everything crystal clear for the reader? Sometimes a phrase or a sentence will seem clear in a first draft. But when you read it again while rewriting, you are not so sure. You have an advantage the reader lacks: You know what you meant to say. Put yourself in the position of your reader. Will the meaning be clear to that person? Try to read your draft like the supervisor who will read your office memo or the judge who will read your motion memo or brief.

It will be easier to read your writing from the perspective of your reader if you allow some time to pass before going back to your draft. A day or two doing something else will help you return to the draft refreshed. Try to read quickly like a busy person and skeptically like someone who must make a decision. Is everything clear? If not, fix the problem.

2. Have you used transitions to show relationships between ideas? Transitional words can help lead the reader through ideas by specifying their relationships with one another, and by identifying ideas that are most important or compelling. Section 21.3 explained the use of transitions to connect one paragraph to the next. They can be used in a similar way to help the reader see connections between sentences. The Transitions table shows how transitions can be used.

You can use transition words or phrases at the beginning of a paragraph (§ 21.3), at the beginning of a sentence, or inside a sentence. Choose the spot that best makes the point without confusing the reader.

Some words work better than others at showing causation. For example, *because* is usually clearer than *since*, *as*, or *so*. *Since* is generally understood to refer to the passage of time ("no new Harry Potter book has been published *since* 2007"). Both *as* and *so* are generally used for other purposes, such as joining contemporaneous events ("the muggles gasped as Harry flew past on his Nimbus 2000") or emphasizing abundance ("they were so astonished that . . .").

3. Have you replaced unnecessarily complicated verbs with simple ones? When you have a choice, use shorter phrases and simpler words to replace unnecessarily complex verb forms. Use concrete action verbs rather than abstractions and nominalizations (verbs that are turned into nouns, such as "agreement" rather than "agree"). See the Simplifying Verbs table.

Transitions		
Purpose	**Examples**	
to introduce new or supplemental material	additionally and besides furthermore	in addition (to) in fact moreover

to explain how ideas relate to one another	after
	afterward
	at the same time
	before
	finally
	on these facts
	specifically
	in fact
		not only . . . , but
		also
		under these
		   circumstances
		first, . . . second, . . .
		   third, . . . (when
		   listing reasons)

to point out similarities	analogously similarly	
to introduce an inference or explain a cause-and-effect relationship	accordingly as a result because consequently	for that reason therefore thus
to point out differences, inconsistency, or lack of causation	although but conversely despite even if even though however	in contrast in spite of instead of nevertheless on the contrary on the other hand
when introducing examples	for example for instance such as	
to explain time relationships	later previously	then next

Simplifying Verbs	
Delete	**Replace with**
entered into an agreement	agreed
gave consideration to	considered
had knowledge of	knew
was aware of	knew
is able to	can
is binding on	binds
made a determination	determined
made allegations of	alleged
made a motion for	moved for
made the argument	argued
made the assumption	assumed
took into consideration	considered

A similar problem that can obscure meaning is turning common nouns and adjectives into abstract verbs. For example, the word *impact* is a noun, but it is sometimes used as an abstract verb rather than the more concrete action words *change* or *alter*. In the comic strip above, Calvin has a habit of "verbing" words, and Hobbes points out that turning nouns into verbs can impede understanding. For clarity, use nouns to refer to *things* and verbs to describe concrete *action*. Nominalizing verbs and "verbing" nouns both create unnecessary barriers between you and your reader.

4. Have you streamlined unnecessarily wordy phrases? For example:

Streamlining Phrases	
Delete	**Replace with**
because of the fact that	because
for the purpose of	to
for the reason that	because
in the case of	in
in the event that	if
in the situation where	where (or when)
subsequent to	after
with regard to	regarding
with the exception of	except

5. Have you deleted throat-clearing phrases (also known as "long windups")? Phrases like the ones below waste words, divert the reader from your real message, and introduce a shade of doubt and an impression of insecurity. They may be acceptable in first drafts to help you get your thoughts onto the page. But in rewriting, delete them.

It is significant that . . .
The defendant submits that . . .
It is important to note that . . .
It could be argued that . . .
It is clear that . . .

6. Have you used lists connected with transitions to express coordinated ideas? When you discuss several ideas together, lead the reader forcefully by making that clear, perhaps through some sort of textual list introduced by a roadmap sentence. For example: "The court rejected that position for four reasons . . . ," followed by sentences or paragraphs that begin with transitions to show how they connect to the roadmap ("First, ... Second, ..." and so on).

7. In a series or list, have you used parallel construction, making sure that every item in the list uses consistent grammatical structure? Readers are instantly confused by sentence structures that lack internal consistency.

For example, when introducing a series of offenses or claims, use a gerund to introduce each one. The sentence below is grammatically incorrect. Compare the underlined words.

Martha Stewart was convicted of <u>obstructing</u> justice, <u>making</u> false statements to government investigators, and <u>because she conspired</u> with her broker to commit various crimes.

You can see the structural problems more easily when the sentence is tabulated vertically:

Martha Stewart was convicted of
- <u>obstructing</u> justice,
- <u>making</u> false statements to government investigators, and
- <u>because she conspired</u> with her broker to commit various crimes.

Parallel construction requires you to structure each item in a list using the same grammatical form as the others to establish a predictable pattern for the reader. Failing to do that distracts the reader because she expects sentences and paragraphs to follow internally consistent structure. Martha Stewart's list of offenses is not internally parallel. While the first and second items begin with gerund phrases ("*obstructing* justice" and "*making* false statements"), the third item is a dependent clause (beginning with "because") followed by a subject ("she") and a verb ("conspired").

If you frustrate the reader's expectations by using inconsistent grammar forms, she will have to read the sentence two or three times to be sure she understands its message. In the example above, correct the problem by revising the third item in the list to begin with a gerund form like the others:

Martha Stewart was convicted of <u>obstructing</u> justice, <u>making</u> false statements to government investigators, and <u>conspiring</u> with her broker to commit various crimes.

191

8. Have you correctly structured the words that introduce a list so that each item in the list makes sense when read alone with the introductory words? Be sure each item in a list can be read independently from the others along with the words used to introduce the list. Test each item in the list by temporarily ignoring the other listed items to see whether the sentence works when you leap straight from the introductory words to the item you are testing.

In the incorrect example above, the second item satisfies the test: "Martha Stewart was convicted of . . . <u>making</u> false statements to government investigators . . . ." But the third item on the list fails the test: "Martha Stewart was convicted of . . . <u>because she conspired</u> with her broker to commit various crimes." If any item on a list fails this grammar test, your sentence lacks proper parallel structure and needs to be rewritten.

9. Have you used legal terms of art only when appropriate? When a term of art communicates an idea peculiar to the law, use that term. It conveys the idea precisely, and often it makes long and convoluted explanations unnecessary. For example, do not write "The court issued an order *telling the defendants to stop* building the highway." Instead, use precise wording: "The court issued an order *enjoining the defendants* from building the highway."

But use a legal term of art *only* when necessary to convey its exact legal meaning. If you use a term of art unnecessarily, perhaps because it sounds lawyer-like, your reader might assume you have misunderstood either the legal term or the law itself.

10. Have you edited out legalese? Notwithstanding grievous misconceptions of what is ubiquitously known to be fit and proper, said lawyer noises, by instrumentalities undisclosed herein, have been entirely expurgated, expunged, and otherwise eliminated from this textbook, both heretofore and hereinafter. (*Translation:* That stuff has been banished from this book.)

The most influential memos and briefs are written in real English.

just fine	Elvis has left the building.
bad	Elvis has departed from the premises.
worse	It would be accurate to say that Elvis has departed from the premises.

Some lawyerly wording conveys genuine meaning, and some does not.

meaningful	Uncontroverted evidence shows that Elvis has left the building.
meaningless	Elvis has clearly and unequivocally left the building.

Why is the phrase "clearly and unequivocally" meaningless? Elvis has either left the building or he has not. Writing something like "clearly and unequivocally" pounds the table without adding meaning. But "uncontroverted evidence" says that some evidence shows that Elvis has left, and no other evidence shows that he has not—which makes it easy for a court to decide that he has gone. We would expect to read in the next sentence about the two dozen witnesses who can testify that they saw Elvis walk through the stage door, step into a stretch limo, and disappear into the night.

It can take some time to learn how to distinguish between legalese and true terms of art (see question 9 above). When you come across a word or phrase used exclusively by lawyers, ask yourself the following questions:

- Is it part of a rule of law you have read in a case or a statute—for example, an element of a legal test?
- Is it the name of a concept that is part of the law, including the policies or the reasoning behind a legal rule?

If either answer is "yes," you probably have a legal term of art, although legalese does appear in some statutes and older cases. If both answers are "no," you probably have legalese (although it might be a term of art). These questions will not produce completely accurate answers every time, but they increase the odds of correctly categorizing a word or phrase.

Do not use legalese. But do use genuine terms of art when necessary to convey your meaning precisely.

11. Have you properly placed modifiers next to the specific words they modify to clarify your meaning? When people talk in conversation, their modifiers sometimes wander all over sentences, regardless of what those words are intended to modify. But in formal writing, more precision is required to avoid confusing the reader. For example, each of these sentences means something different:

- The police are authorized to arrest *only* the person named in the warrant.
  [They are not authorized to arrest anyone else.]
- The police are authorized *only* to arrest the person named in the warrant.
  [They are not authorized to deport her or do anything else except arrest.]
- *Only* the police are authorized to arrest the person named in the warrant.
  [No one else, including a civilian, is authorized to arrest her.]

To help your reader understand your meaning, place a modifier—in this example, the word *only*—as close as possible to the word or term it modifies.

12. Have you carefully selected words that communicate your meaning precisely? Clear writing depends on careful word choice to achieve precision. Review the list of troublesome words in § 21.5 question 8, and § 22.4. Use your word processor's search function to find them in your document, and edit carefully to ensure that the words accurately convey your intended meaning. Run spell-check for commonly misspelled words like *judgment*. Read carefully to be sure you have correctly used words like *argue* and *overrule* in the proper context.

13. Have you used gender-neutral wording whenever appropriate? The English language has traditionally used the masculine pronouns *he*, *his*, and *him* to refer generally to people of either sex. English lacks a gender-neutral singular pronoun that means any person regardless of gender.[4] In formal legal writing, do not use masculine pronouns when you intend to refer to persons of either gender because you might offend the reader. For example, the following sentence would be wrong because it uses the masculine pronoun "his" to refer to lawyers in general:

To calendar a motion, an attorney must file *his* motion papers with the clerk.

Here are some solutions:

replace the pronoun	To calendar a motion, an attorney must file <u>the</u> motion papers with the clerk.
make the actor plural	To calendar motions, <u>attorneys</u> must file their moving papers with the clerk.
eliminate the actor	A motion is calendared by filing the motion papers with the clerk.

Choose the solution that fits your goal. Here, the last solution is the most concise one. But if you want to warn lawyers who carelessly forget to file their moving papers, that point is lost if the sentence uses passive voice and does not mention lawyers at all.

14. Have you punctuated correctly? Correct punctuation is not decoration. It is essential because proper punctuation makes writing clear and easy to understand. Many readers will question your analytical ability if you fail to observe accepted rules of punctuation.

Before law school, you might have been able to get by without learning the rules of punctuation. But in legal writing, poor punctuation can miscommunicate meaning. In one case, a client lost a million dollars over a misplaced comma.[5] You would not want it to be *your* misplaced or missing comma.

---

[4] Some advocates have proposed new gender-neutral pronouns to address the void in the English language, such as *ze* (meaning he or she) and *hir* (meaning his or her). Eve Shapiro, Gender Circuits: Bodies and Identities in a Technological Age 73-74 (2010). But these should not be used in legal documents.

[5] *See* Ian Austen, *The Comma That Costs 1 Million Dollars (Canadian)*, N.Y. Times, Oct. 25, 2006.

§ 22.4 Precision and Word Choice

Clarity and conciseness require precision in word choice. Lawyers communicate precisely by carefully selecting words that convey the intended meaning. Until you become familiar with legal vocabulary, you may have trouble knowing how to use certain terms correctly. A few of them are especially troublesome for first-year law students.

And/or. This is both awkward and inherently ambiguous. Never write it, no matter how often you may have seen it elsewhere. *And* and *or* have different meanings and are not interchangeable. *And* is conjunctive (all elements must be satisfied), while *or* is disjunctive (a single element can be met in alternative ways, or alternative elements may satisfy a test). Do not make the reader guess which meaning you intend. Instead, select the word you mean and structure your sentence accordingly:

ambiguous   Under Rule 11, sanctions can be imposed on the attorney and/or the client.

Can the court impose sanctions on one or the other, but not both? Or can the court impose sanctions only on both? If the court imposes sanctions on one, must it also sanction the other? Because the writer used "and/or," we cannot know the answers to these questions.

much better   Under Rule 11, sanctions can be imposed on the attorney, the client, or both.

This sentence tells us unambiguously that a court can impose sanctions on either the lawyer or the client. The court can also impose sanctions on both, but need not do so.

Argue. Lawyers *argue*; courts do not. An argument is intended to persuade others. You *argue* when you lack the power to decide, and you try to persuade others who have that power. A court may decide, hold, find, rule, conclude, or determine. Although an individual judge might argue in a dissenting opinion that the majority incorrectly decided the case, the court's majority opinion decides and does not argue. Use the term *argue* only to describe what the lawyers for the parties say, or what individual judges say in dissenting or concurring opinions.

Guilty, not guilty, and innocent. The word *guilty* applies only to criminal prosecutions. A guilty defendant has been convicted of committing a crime. Despite what you may have heard in the media, criminal defendants do not plead "innocent," and juries never find them "innocent." *Not guilty* and *innocent* do not mean the same thing. *Innocent* means the defendant did not commit the crime. *Not guilty* means the prosecution did not prove beyond a reasonable doubt that the defendant committed the crime. If the prosecution fails to meet this burden of proof, the defendant is acquitted, even if he actually committed the crime.

Judgment. A judgment is a document a trial court issues to decide a dispute. By convention, lawyers always spell *judgment* with only one *e*—judgment—even if nonlawyers sometimes spell it "judgement."

Liable and guilty. In a civil case, a losing defendant might be held *liable* to the plaintiff for money damages. Some civil cases do not involve liability but may result in other remedies such as an injunction, a judgment partitioning land, or a child custody order. A defendant in a civil lawsuit might be *liable* to the plaintiff but is never *guilty*. And *liability* never refers to a penalty or sentence imposed when a criminal defendant is found guilty.

Overrule and reverse. An appellate court *reverses* when it determines that the lower court decided the same case incorrectly. When an appellate court reverses, it may remand the case for another trial, vacate the trial court's judgment, or do something else to set aside what the trial court has done.

In contrast, an appellate court may *overrule* its own precedent case (or a case issued by a lower appellate court in the same jurisdiction) when it decides the precedent is no longer good law. Do not use *overrule* to describe what an appellate court might do if a trial court's decision is challenged on appeal. In a trial setting, *overrule* sometimes has a different meaning. When a trial judge denies a lawyer's objection to evidence, the objection is *overruled* by the court.

The. Occasionally a lawyer will omit *the* before words like *plaintiff*, *defendant*, *appellant*, and *appellee* while capitalizing those words. This practice was once common but is now in decline. You have probably read older opinions in casebooks that refer to the parties this way.

Your writing will seem less artificial if you write *the* wherever it would normally appear in everyday English. For example,

avoid   Defendant is entitled to summary judgment unless Plaintiff presents enough evidence to create a genuine issue of material fact.

better   The defendant is entitled to summary judgment unless the plaintiff presents enough evidence to create a genuine issue of material fact.

A trial brief might properly be titled, "Memorandum of Law in Support of Defendant's Motion for Summary Judgment." But in the body of the brief write, "The defendant is entitled to summary judgment because the plaintiff has offered insufficient evidence to create a genuine issue of material fact."

§ 22.5   Our Style and Yours

If you notice clarity, vividness, or conciseness in our writing, it might be worth emulating whatever we did to achieve that—*if* doing so would work well in the assignment you are working on. (That is a big *if*.)

But in memos and briefs, the informal style of this book is *not* appropriate. A textbook's audience is students, who often learn more easily when the material is explained in a friendly tone. But the writing you submit to senior lawyers and judges should be formal in tone and style. For example, our own memos and briefs never contain contractions (two words merged with an apostrophe). They might be appropriate to use occasionally in an informal letter to a client, but they have no place in formal documents. For similar reasons, in our memos and briefs you would see far fewer dashes and italics than you see in this book. In a formal document, an occasional dash or italicized word or phrase might help make a point, but they should be used sparingly.

Here are some guidelines for office memos, motion memos, appellate briefs, and other formal documents:

- *contractions:* never
- *italics:* rarely (and only when truly helpful for emphasis)
- *dashes:* infrequently (and only when grammatically correct)

Exercise 22-A. Style, Sentences, and Rewriting

In each passage, identify the problems with sentence structure, clarity, and conciseness. Then rewrite the passage.

1. Facebook is being used more frequently by people in their twenties and thirties, which means that teenagers are being marketed to less.

2. Because the defendant made statements to the effect that the plaintiff was not able to have knowledge of the actual date of Michael Jackson's birth, the plaintiff brought suit against the defendant with allegations of defamation. The defendant made a motion for summary judgment and made the argument that the court should give consideration to the plaintiff's admission, in an earlier lawsuit, that he lacked knowledge of Michael Jackson's date of birth. After making a determination that the plaintiff had previously made an admission that he lacked knowledge of Michael Jackson's date of birth, the court made entry of judgment for the defendant and made provision for the defendant to obtain recovery of costs.

3. On the ground that the client's video is a violation of YouTube's user agreement, which makes prohibited material that is "unlawful, obscene, defamatory, libelous,

threatening, pornographic, harassing, hateful, racially or ethnically offensive, or encourages conduct that would be considered a criminal offense, give rise to civil liability, violate any law, or is otherwise inappropriate," YouTube's management effectuated a removal of the video from the website, and the client would like to know whether she has a cause of action against YouTube.

4. Jones was employed as a bouncer at Smith's nightclub. His job was to screen the people who were in line outside, admitting only those whose coolness was obvious. ("Coolness" and "cool" are business terms with specific meanings that are understood throughout the nightclub industry.) There were three reasons why Jones was fired by Smith. First, the people he admitted to the nightclub were not cool. Second, the people he left on the sidewalk were cool. Third, he was not liked by Smith.

23 Citing and Quoting Authority

Lawyers constantly analyze legal authority. Because legal readers are innately skeptical, lawyers use various methods of *attribution* to show convincingly that legal authority supports their arguments. Your reader will find your writing more persuasive when you demonstrate by careful attribution that the law supports your analysis.

§ 23.1   When and Why to Cite Authority

Cite authority in two instances:

1. to identify an authority that effectively supports something you say, or
2. to identify the source of words you directly quote from the authority.

Lawyers follow unique citation rules, unlike any you may have learned in college or used in other professional fields. A legal reader needs very specific information about each authority you cite to support your legal analysis. To meet those needs, essential information for each authority must be expressed precisely and succinctly in "citation language" that the law-trained reader can quickly skim and understand. A properly constructed citation conveys a large amount of information in a very small space.

Think of legal citation format as a professional code you must learn in order to communicate efficiently with other legal professionals. If your citation form is faulty, readers quickly notice. A lawyer who uses faulty citation form fails to meet the expectations of the legal reader, who can lose confidence in the quality of the legal writer's work in other ways.

How do you learn this specialized code? Your legal writing teacher has probably assigned one of two legal citation reference books that cover the conventional rules of legal citation—the *ALWD Guide to Legal Citation* and the *Bluebook*. Both address the same citation issues and produce identical citations.[1] Lawyers and judges routinely refer to one or more of these citation guides in their work, and they expect you to do the same when you communicate with them in writing.

In your legal writing course, you will learn the citation format used in office memos and briefs. Slightly different citation formats are used in scholarly writing, such as legal treatises and law review articles, which generally cite legal authority in footnotes. The *ALWD Guide to Legal Citation* is organized so that each separate rule covers citation formats for both professional and scholarly writing. The general rules apply to professional legal writing, and specially flagged subrules address variations required for scholarly legal writing. The *Bluebook* is primarily organized as a citation reference for scholarly writing, with separate Bluepages that show variations necessary for professional legal writing, including office memos and briefs. Because the rules printed in the *Bluebook*'s white pages are designed for scholarly writing in law reviews and treatises, they might not be appropriate for memos and briefs.

Do not imitate the citation forms you see in judicial opinions. Most are not consistent with the citation rules you will learn in your legal writing course. The reason is that many courts and publishers follow their own unique citation rules that are inconsistent with the rules in the *ALWD Guide* and the *Bluebook*. And many citation rules have changed over the years, so citations in older cases and law review articles may be in a format no longer considered acceptable.

From a citation in a legal document, a reader expects to learn where the authority can be found, and for a court opinion which court decided it, the date of the decision, and some other basic facts affecting the authority's value. These are communicated through a specialized citation code consisting of words, abbreviations, and numbers that convey a precise meaning to the legal reader when they are expressed in a particular order, properly capitalized, and properly punctuated.

This chapter explains some general principles of citation. For details, see the specific citation reference your teacher has assigned.

---

[1] The verb "bluebooking" does *not* mean using the *Bluebook* instead of the *ALWD Guide to Legal Citation*. When a senior lawyer asks whether you have "bluebooked your citations," she just wants to make sure your cites are in proper form. Which citation guide you use for that purpose does not matter because lawyers and judges cannot tell the difference between a citation created using the *ALWD Guide* and one using the *Bluebook*. The verb "bluebooking" is an example of using a commonly known brand name (like "Kleenex" or "Xerox") as a synonym for a type of product (like tissue or photocopy machines). Similarly, you may be asked whether you have "shepardized" your cases when a lawyer or judge wants to know whether you have checked to make sure your cases have not been reversed or overruled. It makes no difference whether you use Westlaw's Key Cite or Lexis's Shepard's to update your authorities. The results are nearly always the same. Notice that "bluebook" and "shepardize" are abstract verbs, each formed from the proper names of legal references—the *Bluebook* and *Shepard's* respectively. See § 22.3, question 3 ("verbing weirds language").

§ 23.2 Rules Governing All Citations

Legal readers expect to see a citation for *every* statement in a legal memo or brief that recites, explains, or illustrates a legal rule. Your readers are skeptical, and they rely on citations to your legal authority to gain confidence in your legal analysis and arguments.

When you first read a judicial opinion or a legal memo, you may be surprised how often you see legal citations. At first, the writing may seem choppy because legal citations interrupt the flow of the writing. But to lawyers and judges who read your writing, those citations are essential. They demonstrate, in the context of your legal analysis, how well your argument is supported with legal authority and how convincing those authorities will be to the decision maker. When writing each sentence in your Discussion or Argument, *assume that your reader will not believe what you say.* Then find a good legal authority to cite in support of your statement to convince the skeptical reader that you are right.

Full citations and short-form citations. Any legal authority can be cited using a full citation or a short-form citation. Short-form citations may take different forms depending on the circumstances. For example:

full citation	*Apple Computer, Inc. v. Microsoft Corp.*, 513 U.S. 1184 (1995).
short-form citation	*Apple Computer, Inc.*, 513 U.S. at 1199.
short-form citation	*Id.* at 1199.

Statutes and other kinds of legal authorities also have full citation formats and short-form citation formats, which are explained in detail in your citation guide.

Use a full citation when you mention a legal authority for the first time in your memo or brief. At any later point in the same document, use one of the short-form citations when citing the same authority. Use *id.* only when the same authority appears alone (without any other authorities) in the immediately preceding citation.

Citation sentences and clauses. A *citation sentence* includes one or more citations and nothing else, ending with a period. A *citation clause* is a citation that supports only part of a *textual sentence*, separated from the rest of the text with commas. A textual sentence is made up of words like the sentence you are reading now. An *embedded citation* is a citation used as a part of speech within the textual sentence itself.

citation sentence	*Apple Computer, Inc. v. Microsoft Corp.*, 513 U.S. 1184, 1199 (1995).

citation clause	The Supreme Court held in favor of the plaintiff, *Apple Computer v. Microsoft Corp.*, 513 U.S. 1184 (1995), and the trial court entered judgment for Apple on remand.
embedded citation	In *Apple Computer v. Microsoft Corp.*, 513 U.S. 1184, 1199 (1995), the Supreme Court held . . . .

Citation placement. When a cited authority supports an entire textual sentence, place the citation in a separate citation sentence immediately after the textual sentence:

> A defamation defendant enjoys an absolute privilege for expressions of mere opinion. *Gertz v. Robert Welch, Inc.*, 418 U.S. 323, 339-40 (1974).

When an authority supports only part of a textual sentence, you can insert the citation directly into your sentence as a citation clause, setting off the citation clause from the rest of the sentence with commas. For example, the following textual sentence includes two citations:

> A defamation defendant enjoys an absolute privilege for expressions of mere opinion, *Gertz v. Robert Welch, Inc.*, 418 U.S. 323, 339-40 (1974), and whether a statement expresses a fact or opinion is a question of law to be determined by the court and not the jury, *Info. Control Corp. v. Genesis One Computer Corp.*, 611 F.2d 781, 783 (9th Cir. 1980).

While the sentence above is technically correct, it is hard to read because of citation clutter. When reading it, you probably found it hard to climb over the full citation to *Gertz* so you could get to the rest of the sentence. For that reason, avoid writing sentences with citation clauses. Instead, when a citation supports only part of a textual sentence, try breaking up the sentence into two shorter ones, so you can use a citation sentence to support each one in turn:

> A defamation defendant enjoys an absolute privilege for expressions of mere opinion. *Gertz v. Robert Welch, Inc.*, 418 U.S. 323, 339-40 (1974). Whether a statement expresses fact or opinion is a question of law to be determined by the court and not the jury. *Info. Control Corp. v. Genesis One Computer Corp.*, 611 F.2d 781, 783 (9th Cir. 1980).

Readers usually have no problem when a single citation clause appears in a textual sentence. But readers can be distracted when a full citation appears inside a textual sentence, or when a writer includes too many citation clauses in a single textual sentence.

Pinpoint citations. A pinpoint citation directs a reader to the specific page in a case, treatise, or law review article that supports the statement in the writer's memo or brief. In this example, the pinpoint directs the reader to page 1201 in a case that begins on page 1184:

Apple Computer, Inc. v. Microsoft Corp., 513 U.S. 1184, 1201 (1995).

Most citations to cases, law review articles, or treatises require pinpoint citations to convince your reader that you have specific support in the legal authority for the statements in your memo or brief. When you refer to only part of an opinion, a reader often needs to know which specific pages you have in mind. Very few opinions are too short to need pinpoint citations.

Other kinds of legal authority also require pinpoint citations to the smallest subsection or subdivision that supports your statement. For example, if a defendant has been accused of violating a federal statute, do not cite the statute just by its popular name, title, or section number. Almost every statute is subdivided into subsections (and sometimes subparagraphs), usually designated with letters or numbers in parentheses. Cite to the smallest subdivision relevant to the statement for which you are citing the authority to help your reader focus her attention on that part of the statute.

Pinpoint citations are essential when quoting from authority. For *every* direct quotation from a legal authority, you must include a pinpoint citation so your reader can check its accuracy against the original source.

Judges and law clerks become annoyed with lawyers who omit pinpoint citations from cited legal authorities. A judge reading your brief expects you to back up your reasoning with specific citations to legal authority, including pinpoint citations. If you do not, you are effectively shifting that workload to the judge or the judge's law clerk, with an implied message that your time is more important than theirs.

String citations. A string citation is a list of authorities, all cited for the same purpose. If you have found eight cases, all holding that a minor in your state can void a contract for lack of legal capacity, you might be tempted to use all eight cases in one string citation to impress your reader that you have found them all. But usually that would be a mistake because your reader relies on you to filter out all but the *best* cases to cite.

The ideal case would be issued by the highest court in the controlling jurisdiction, and it would settle the law definitively on whether a minor can void a contract. It would explain the rule's policy and how the rule applies to facts like yours. If one of the eight cases you have found does *all* that, cite that one case alone, explain it thoroughly for your reader, and ignore all the others. But much more often, you might have to use more than one case to convince the reader that the law is well settled and to show how the rule works. Rather than cite several cases without much explanation, cite the few cases that will really matter to your reader, and explain them thoroughly.

In rare situations, a string citation can be helpful. For example, assume your state has no common law rule on an issue, and your state's courts could adopt either the majority rule from other states or the minority rule. You might use one or two string citations in your brief to show which states have adopted the majority rule and which ones have adopted the minority rule. But also explain a few cases illustrating the majority rule and a few others illustrating the minority rule to show how each one works. A string citation hardly ever does an effective job by itself, and most lawyers and judges are not impressed by lengthy string citations. They usually skip over them.

Explanatory parentheticals. Two types of parentheticals appear in legal citations. One is an integral part of the citation itself, such as the parenthetical reference in a case citation to the court and year. The other type is an *explanatory parenthetical* that provides information about the legal authority. That same information could be given outside the citation. But to save space, legal writers sometimes compress that information into a parenthetical phrase immediately following the citation itself.

Some kinds of explanatory parentheticals denote something important about the authority itself. For example, you *must* add a parenthetical to show when you are citing to a dissenting or concurring opinion rather than the majority opinion. But you can also add a parenthetical to show that a decision was unanimous:

> *Riley v. California*, 134 S. Ct. 2473 (2014) (unanimous).

Most legal writers use explanatory parentheticals when a full discussion of a case is not necessary. This kind of explanatory parenthetical generally begins with a gerund form of a verb, such as "holding" or "reversing." For example,

> *Riley v. California*, 134 S. Ct. 2473, 2485 (2014) (holding that police officer must generally secure warrant before searching contents of cellphone incident to warrantless arrest).

But avoid going overboard trying to express the substance of an authority in an explanatory parenthetical when the authority is important to your legal analysis. Compare the following example to the one above:

> *Carey v. Population Servs. Int'l*, 431 U.S. 678, 691-99 (1977) (holding that state statute prohibiting distribution of nonprescription contraceptives to persons under 16 years old is unconstitutional because sexual activity may not be constitutionally deterred by increasing its hazards).

This explanatory parenthetical is complex, awkward, and hard to read. And it oversimplifies and inevitably misrepresents the material in order to pack it into the form of an explanatory parenthetical.

If the authority is complicated and important to the issue in your memo or brief, explain it in your text and then cite the authority. Use explanatory parentheticals only for simple information that is not an important part of your discussion or argument. Do not rely on explanatory parentheticals to avoid the hard work of explaining complicated and important authority. And if you are citing a case simply to support a well-established legal rule, an explanatory parenthetical should be omitted entirely because it would not help the reader.

Typeface. Citations in memos and briefs use two typefaces, roman and italics. In a citation clause or sentence, both case names and signals appear in italics. So do specialized citation terms like *id.*, *supra*, *infra*, and other terms specified by your citation guide.

Other typefaces, such as large-and-small caps, are used only in scholarly legal writing to designate certain kinds of legal authority. You may see them in the footnotes of law review articles as you research the issues for your legal writing assignments. But other typefaces are not used in memos or briefs written by practicing lawyers or in judicial opinions.

If you use the *Bluebook*, be careful when using the examples in the Bluepages. Before computers were in common use, writers used underlining for emphasis because typewriters could not produce italics. The examples in the blue pages at the front of the *Bluebook* allow the use of underlining, even though computers are now used for virtually all legal writing. You can easily use your computer for italics, which look more professional than underlining in legal writing.

Section and paragraph symbols. In a citation, generally use a section symbol (§) and not the word *section*. Some citations to cases and treatises require a paragraph symbol (¶), which should be used instead of the word *paragraph*. Add a space between either symbol and the number that follows it. But when you begin a textual sentence with a reference to a section or paragraph, use the words and not the symbols ("Section 2-201 provides . . . .").

While you will not find the "§ " or "¶ "symbols on your keyboard, legal readers expect to see them in your writing. You can insert these symbols into your document using your word processing software. In most versions of Word or WordPerfect, click on "Insert," and then click on "Symbol." Find the § or ¶ symbol in the pop-up dialog box. Click on the symbol, and then click on "Insert." The symbol will then appear in your text at the location of your cursor.

Signals. Sometimes your purpose in citing an authority can be communicated most efficiently by using a *citation signal*. In legal writing, a signal is an italicized code word or abbreviation that introduces the citation and conveys a particular meaning about how the legal authority supports the statement that precedes the citation. Examples are *See*, *Accord*, and *Contra*. No signal is used when the authority you cite directly supports the statement that immediately precedes it, or when the authority identifies the source of a direct quotation or a legal rule. Your citation guide explains each signal and how to use it in more detail.

Signals can help compress information and clarify relationships among authorities cited in law review footnotes and in other kinds of scholarly writing, including the seminar papers you might write in the second or third year of law school. But in memos and briefs, use signals sparingly when truly necessary or helpful to reduce space. A person who must make a decision based in part on your writing needs to know not only what an authority stands for, but also exactly how the authority is relevant to the issue to be decided. Generally your own discussion of the authorities does that much better than signals can.

As you gain experience with legal writing, you will become more comfortable with using signals, and you will learn how to use them to communicate nuances about how legal authorities support your analysis. Just remember that they are part of a sophisticated code used by legal writers to communicate a lot of information as concisely as possible. During your first year of law school, it is more important to learn how to explain your legal reasoning in words. But citing legal authority properly and accurately with appropriate signals is an essential component of a convincing memo or brief.

§ 23.3   Quoting Effectively

Quoting legal authority can be useful occasionally. But if you are not careful, quotations can consume your writing. This section explains when (and when not) to use a direct quotation and how to satisfy the format requirements for quoting.

§ 23.3.1   When to Quote

Quotations help when they express *exactly* the idea you want to communicate to your reader. And the citation after a direct quote tells your reader that the idea has authority behind it. Especially when your issue would be resolved by interpreting certain words, quote those words. With statutory issues, for example, quote the most essential words in the statute.

There is less reason to quote from a case. The language of a case resolves the issues in that case, but it might not directly apply to facts in a different case. In some instances, using phrases or words from a case may be the best way to communicate the case's meaning. Your reader does not always need to know factual details from the precedent case that are irrelevant to the current problem. But be careful not to misrepresent the holding of a case by taking words out of their factual context.

§ 23.3.2 Quote Sparingly or Not at All

Quotations can eat up large chunks of your writing and your reader's attention. When that happens, many readers will simply refuse to read them. Your reader needs and expects your own analysis of the legal authorities and how they apply to the unique facts of your case.

Quoting from authorities is not legal analysis. Writers who over-quote fail to do the heavy lifting of weaving those authorities together to show how they resolve a specific legal problem.

When you do quote, keep it limited to small, *essential* passages. Edit out words that do not apply or details that are not meaningful in the context of your case. For example, although a statute or a case might set out the test that governs your facts, some of the elements might not be in dispute in your case. You can summarize or note the elements not in dispute, and then emphasize the contested ones by directly quoting those parts of the test. To illustrate, if a criminal defendant's only argument is that she lacked purposeful intent, the other elements of the crime are much less important. The only part of the statute worth quoting might be the part that requires purposeful intent for conviction.

Accuracy in quoting is absolutely essential. When you directly quote, check every word and every punctuation mark against the original to be sure you have not inadvertently misquoted the authority. And be very careful when you edit a quote. Make sure that your edited version accurately reflects the relevant meaning of the original. Sloppy editing will cost you credibility with your reader and will invoke the ire of a judge who expects quotations in a legal brief to be *precisely accurate*.

Block quotations are especially troublesome. A block quote is a long quotation (50 words or more) separated from the rest of your text, indented on both the left and right sides, and single-spaced. Busy readers will often skim or refuse to read large block quotations because they know from experience that only a few of the quoted words will really matter, and it may take too much effort to find them. The more block quotes you use, the more quickly a reader will refuse to read any of them.[2] Judges and supervising attorneys expect you to find the essential words, isolate them, and concisely paraphrase the rest. When you throw many block quotations at a reader, you are asking the reader to do some of your work.

On rare occasions, quoting an extended passage from a source of law helps the reader. But that is seldom true. Experienced and effective writers quote less often, and their quotes tend to be shorter.

---

[2] *See* Interview by Bryan Garner with Judge Alex Kozinski, Circuit Judge, U.S. Court of Appeals for the Ninth Circuit, *On Overquoting*, http://www.lawprose.org/interviews/judges-lawyers-writers-on-writing.php?vid= kozinski&vidtitle=Hon._Alex_Kozinski_On_Overquoting (last visited Nov. 15, 2014).

§ 23.3.3   The Mechanics of Quoting

Readers look not only at the content of what you quote, but also at how you follow the format rules for quotations. The *ALWD Guide to Legal Citation* and the *Bluebook* both set out rules governing the format of quotations. Here are the most essential requirements:

Quotation marks. Enclose any words directly quoted from your source in double quotation marks. If the quoted material includes an internal quotation from another source, you must retain those quotation marks, but change them to *single* quotation marks within the double quotation marks surrounding the entire direct quotation. Your citation identifying the source of the quotation must include a parenthetical citing the source of the internal quotation. Check your citation guide for detailed instructions.

Block quotations. Both the *ALWD Guide to Legal Citation* and the *Bluebook* require placing quotations of 50 words or more in block-quote form. A block quote is single-spaced and indented one tab on both the right and left margins. It does not begin or end with quotation marks. Blocking a passage tells the reader that it is a quote. If the block quote has internal quotations, retain the double quotation marks inside the block quote. Its citation should include a parenthetical identifying the source of the internal quotation.

The citation identifying the source of the quotation does not appear inside the quotation block. Instead, it belongs at the beginning of the *next line of your text following the block quote*, which will generally be double-spaced. The "wrong" example below is incorrect for two reasons. What are they?

right   The Seventh Circuit has explained the law's treatment of ligers:

> As its name suggests, a "liger" is a cross between a male lion and a female tiger. Ligers do not occur naturally, so all known ligers are in captivity. They apparently are a source of fascination in popular culture. *E.g.*, *Napoleon Dynamite* (Paramount Pictures, 2004) ("It's pretty much my favorite animal. It's like a lion and a tiger mixed . . . bred for its skills in magic.") As interspecies hybrids, ligers are not protected under U.S. wildlife laws.

United States v. Kapp, 419 F.3d 666, 670 n.1 (7th Cir. 2005). Nor do the wildlife laws protect basilisks, boggarts, dementors, or phoenix birds.

wrong   The Seventh Circuit has explained the law's treatment of ligers:

> "As its name suggests, a 'liger' is a cross between a male lion and a female tiger. Ligers do not occur naturally, so all known ligers are in captivity. They apparently are a source of fascination in popular culture. *E.g.*, *Napoleon Dynamite* (Paramount Pictures, 2004) ('It's pretty much my favorite animal. It's like a lion and a tiger mixed . . . bred for its skills in magic.') As interspecies hybrids,

ligers are not protected under U.S. wildlife laws." *United States v. Kapp*, 419 F.3d 666, 670 n.1 (7th Cir. 2005).

Nor do the wildlife laws protect basilisks, boggarts, dementors, or phoenix birds.

Alterations and omissions. When omitting words from the original, show the omission by inserting an ellipsis. In legal writing, an ellipsis is three dots, each separated by spaces, and with a space before and after each of the dots in the ellipsis: ^.^.^.^ (the carets illustrate where the spaces go). When you omit the last words of a sentence, place *four* periods, separated by spaces, at the end of the sentence—three for the ellipsis and one to end the sentence. But never include an ellipsis if you are omitting words from the *beginning* of a quoted sentence.

When you incorporate a quoted clause into a sentence of your own composition, do not place an ellipsis at the beginning or the end of the quotation unless the quotation, standing alone, is a complete sentence. Incorporating a quoted clause into a sentence of your own suggests to the reader that you have probably omitted something at the beginning or the end, so the ellipsis would be redundant. On the other hand, if the quoted material you have included in your sentence is complete enough to stand on its own as a sentence, include an ellipsis at the end if necessary to show that you have omitted part of the original sentence.

Use square brackets—[ ]—to enclose any alteration you make inside the quotation marks, including changing a lowercase letter into a capital letter (or vice versa). Do not use parentheses for this purpose. Parentheses and brackets convey different messages to the reader, and you cannot substitute one for the other.

If you add or delete italics from the original source, or if you omit citations from a quotation, note that change in a parenthetical following the citation, like this:

To obtain the names of a defamation defendant's confidential sources, a plaintiff must prove that she or he has "*independently* attempted to obtain the information elsewhere and has been unsuccessful." *Silkwood v. Kerr-McGee Corp.*, 563 F.2d 433, 438 (10th Cir. 1977) (emphasis added).

Introducing a quotation. If you use your own words followed by *that* to introduce a quotation beginning with a capitalized word, change the capital letter to a bracketed lower case letter, unless the capital letter denotes a proper name. And do not include a comma after "that." For example:

right   The court held that "[n]ot so long ago, in a studio far, far away from the policymakers in Washington, D.C., George Lucas conceived of an imaginary galaxy," but his trademark is not infringed when politicians refer to a proposed missile defense system as Star Wars. *Lucasfilm Ltd. v. High Frontier*, 622 F. Supp. 931, 932, 935 (D.D.C. 1985).

wrong   The court held <u>that "Not</u> so long ago, ..."

wrong   The court held <u>that,</u> "Not so long ago, ..."

An alternative way to introduce a quotation is to use a short but complete independent clause followed by a comma, such as "The court held, . . ." (without the word "that"). Using that method, when the quotation itself is a complete sentence, retain the original capitalization at the beginning of the quotation. For example:

right   The court held, "<u>Not</u> so long ago, in a studio far, far away from the policymakers in Washington, D.C., George Lucas conceived of an imaginary galaxy," but his trademark is not infringed when politicians refer to a proposed missile defense system as Star Wars. *Lucasfilm Ltd. v. High Frontier*, 622 F. Supp. 931, 932, 935 (D.D.C. 1985).

wrong   The court held, "[n]ot so long ago . . . ."

wrong   The court held <u>that,</u> "<u>Not</u> so long ago, ..."

§ 23.3.4   How to Test Your Quotations for Effectiveness

While rewriting, ask yourself the following questions.

1. Have you quoted and cited every time you use the words of others? The words of others must have quotation marks around them and a citation to the source. If not, you have plagiarized from your source, even if you did it out of sloppiness without intending to deceive your reader.

2. Have you quoted sparingly, and only the essential words? Most legal readers dislike overquoting. Avoid using lengthy block quotations, which many readers skip over entirely. Generally speaking, quoted words should appear in your work *only* when they fit into one of the following categories:

- words that must be interpreted to resolve the legal issue;
- words that communicate the thinking of a court, legislature, or expert in the field with remarkable economy or clarity; or
- words that eloquently and succinctly express an important idea.

The most convincing descriptions of authority are written almost entirely in your own words, with very few and very short quotations.

4. Have you followed the mechanical rules for direct and internal quotations? Although the rules are summarized in this chapter, check the details in the sections of the *ALWD Guide to Legal Citation* or the *Bluebook* that explain the formatting, capitalization, and punctuation rules for quotations.

5. Have you introduced each quotation with a grammatically correct lead-in, using proper capitalization and punctuation? Does your quotation make sense when read in context with your introductory clause? Follow proper formatting rules using correct capitalization and punctuation to introduce your direct quotations. If you need to alter the capitalization of the original to fit your context, use brackets to show the reader how your quotation differs from the original source.

Structure your quotation so it forms a grammatically complete and accurate sentence when read together with your introduction. If you need to edit the quotation to make it fit the context of your memo or brief, use ellipses or brackets to make the necessary alterations. Do not force your reader to mentally edit your quotation, which will require re-reading your work two or three times to make sense of it.

6. Have you placed quotation marks exactly where they belong? The most common problems are (1) omitting the closing quotation marks (the reader wonders, "Where does this quote end?"); (2) omitting the opening quotation marks ("Where does this quote begin?"); and (3) forgetting to change double quotation marks in the original source to single quotation marks when you have an internal quotation within a quote (except in block quotes, when the original double quotation marks must be retained for internal quotes).

7. Have you used proper punctuation at the end of your direct quotation? Periods and commas at the end of quoted sentences or clauses *always* belong *inside* the quotation marks closing the quote. If the original quotation is a question, the question mark also belongs inside the closing quotation mark. But if you use a quotation in a sentence you have structured as a question, the question mark belongs *outside* the closing quotation mark. And if you have structured your quotation in a sentence that calls for a semicolon following the quotation, it belongs *outside* the closing quotation mark.

8. Have you quoted accurately? Suppose you see language in a case that you want to quote. You type it into your draft, but—without realizing it at the time—some of the words you type are different from those in the case. *Do not allow yourself to rewrite the original source unconsciously while quoting from it.* The only way to prevent this is to carefully proofread, word for word, with the original source in front of you. It is always wrong—and inexcusable—to misrepresent the original source you are quoting. Your responsibility as a professional is to pay careful attention to prevent that from happening, and to proofread carefully to be absolutely sure your quote is accurate.

Exercise 23-A. Citation Clauses and Citation Sentences

In each of the following passages, determine whether each citation sentence, citation clause, or embedded citation is correctly placed. If it is incorrect, explain why. Then rewrite each passage to improve the citation placement for accuracy and readability. (Do not be concerned with the citation format.)

1. In *Morris v. Frudenfeld*, 185 Cal. Rptr. 76 (Ct. App. 1982), the California Court of Appeals agreed with a Michigan court holding that in wrongful birth cases, a mother should not be forced to mitigate damages by terminating the pregnancy or giving a child up for adoption. *See id.* at 80 (citing *Troppi v. Scarf*, 187 N.W.2d 511, 520 (Mich. Ct. App. 1971)).

2. In *Rideau v. Louisiana*, 373 U.S. 723 (1963), the Supreme Court reversed the conviction of a defendant whose staged, highly emotional confession had been filmed with the cooperation of local police and later broadcast on television for three days while he was awaiting trial, saying "[a]ny subsequent court proceedings in a community so pervasively exposed to such a spectacle could be but a hollow formality." *Id.* at 726.

3. Recognition of the right of privacy is comparatively recent. It was unknown to the common law. *Reed v. Real Detective Publ'g Co.*, 162 P.2d 133, 138 (Ariz. 1945). It was first discussed in an essay published in a law journal in 1860, but it never gained prominence until the article written by former U.S. Supreme Court Justice Brandeis, in collaboration with Frank Warren, was published in the *Harvard Law Review*. *Melvin v. Reid*, 297 P. 91, 91 (Cal. Dist. Ct. App. 1931).

4. While it is generally true "that abuse of discretion is the proper standard of review of a district court's evidentiary rulings," *Gen. Elec. Co. v. Joiner*, 522 U.S. 136, 141 (1997), matters of a more substantive nature are also reviewed under that standard. *See Cooper Indus., Inc. v. Leatherman Tool Group, Inc.*, 532 U.S. 424, 433 (2001) (noting that a federal district court decision upholding a state jury award of punitive damages is properly reviewed for abuse of discretion absent constitutional issue).

5. Both the trial court and the Appellate Division rejected the plain view exception and concluded that no other exception to the warrant requirement validated the search. We disagree and conclude that the plain view exception articulated by this Court in *State v. Bruzzese*, 463 A.2d 320 (N.J. 1983), which relied on *Texas v. Brown*, 460 U.S. 730

(1983) and *Coolidge v. New Hampshire,* 403 U.S. 443 (1971), controls this case. Because we believe the facts require a reversal based on the plain view exception, "it is not necessary for us to unburden ourselves of a definitive treatise" on either the search incident to an arrest exception or abandonment. *State v. Hill,* 557 A.2d at 324.

Exercise 23-B. Citation Placement

In the following passage from a first-year law student's office memo, put a star in each location that requires a citation, including a short-form citation. Be prepared to discuss your reasoning for each location where you think a citation is necessary or preferable.

I. **Plaintiff's wrongful life claim may not survive a motion to dismiss because the court will likely interpret the parents' choice to carry the fetus to term as the proximate cause of Gabriel's life.**

The analysis of Gabriel's wrongful life complaint focuses on the four elements of medical malpractice because the California Supreme Court has implicitly adopted the position that wrongful life is a specific form of medical malpractice. The California Supreme Court has held that a defendant may be liable for failure to diagnose a child's hereditary condition if it prevented the child's parents from making an informed decision about conceiving a second child. Subsequent cases continue to be bound by these parameters.

A. *The defendants owed a duty to Gabriel to administer the genetic tests properly so his parents could make an informed decision to conceive.*

"'[W]rongful life' [cases] are essentially actions for malpractice based on negligent genetic counseling and testing." The defendant's duty is to provide accurate genetic information so the parents can make an informed choice. For example, in one case, the defendants failed to properly test a child's hearing, causing the parents to conceive a second child without relevant information about their hereditary ailments. Furthermore, the court held that medical laboratories have a duty to administer genetic testing with care, so prospective parents can learn about a child's potential hereditary problems.

Here, the defendants' duty was simply to administer the genetic test competently so Gabriel's parents could make an informed decision whether or not to proceed with the implantation. Gabriel's parents proceeded with the implantation based on the defendants' faulty preconception information. They would not have conceived had they known that the embryo was male and would suffer from a life-threatening congenital disorder limited to male offspring. However, the court may view the post-conception information Gabriel's parents received about his condition as adequate; therefore, no duty was breached. But this view fails to account for a healthcare provider's duty not only to give post-conception information accurately, but also to give preconception information accurately.

Based on these facts, the defendants' duty was to give Gabriel's parents accurate information about the embryo's gender so they could make an informed decision in their future child's best interests. This failure to relay accurate information at the appropriate time establishes that the defendants breached their professional duty, and no subsequent actions can eliminate this duty.

B. *Gabriel's parents' choice to proceed with the pregnancy may be construed as an intervening act of proximate cause, thereby exonerating the defendants from liability.*

Establishing proximate cause is Gabriel's biggest challenge. On its face, cause in fact appears to be well defined in Gabriel's complaint. The complaint alleges that the defendants' negligent acts or omissions caused Gabriel's birth with full-blown Fabry's disease. These negligent acts included a breakdown in the testing and relaying of vital information to his parents; but for these acts, his parents would have chosen not to conceive him. The remaining question is whether the court will find that the defendants' negligent acts caused Gabriel's birth, or whether it will find that the negligent acts merely caused his conception.

Although no authority is on point, it is likely the court will find that the defendants' negligent acts were the cause of Gabriel's conception and not the cause of his birth (the resulting injury). In dictum, the California Court of Appeals stated,

> If a case arose where, despite due care by the medical profession in transmitting the necessary warnings, parents made a conscious choice to proceed with a pregnancy, with

full knowledge that a seriously impaired infant would be born, that conscious choice would provide an intervening act of proximate cause to preclude liability insofar as defendants other than the parents were concerned.

In the absence of any specific statute or holding addressing this particular situation, the court may give substantial weight to this dictum. The complaint discloses that the defendants informed Gabriel's parents of his condition early in the second trimester. This act may be viewed as sufficiently meeting the duty of due care. The defendants provided the relevant information needed for Gabriel's parents to make an informed choice whether to terminate the pregnancy at the defendants' expense. The Court may conclude that the parents' choice to proceed with the pregnancy was the intervening proximate cause of Gabriel's birth, consequently relieving the defendants of any liability.

Sound public policy is the best counterargument to the court's dictum. In *Morris v. Frudenfeld*, the California Court of Appeals agreed with a Michigan court's holding that in wrongful birth cases, a mother should not be forced to mitigate damages by having an abortion or giving a child up for adoption. Although those courts addressed wrongful birth damages, the logic is still applicable to proximate cause in a wrongful life context. No person should be forced to make a Hobson's choice because of another's negligence.

Exercise 23-C. Quoting the First Amendment

You are writing a memorandum involving the Freedom of the Press Clause of the U.S. Constitution's First Amendment. You intend to quote the words that the court must interpret. The entire First Amendment reads as follows:

> Congress shall make no law respecting an establishment of religion, or prohibiting the free exercise thereof; or abridging the freedom of speech, or of the press; or the right of the people peaceably to assemble, and to petition the government for a redress of grievances.

Write a properly punctuated sentence for your memo that accurately quotes the relevant words from the Amendment, without including more than your reader needs. Include a properly formatted pinpoint citation.

Exercise 23-D. Quoting Cases

Select a case you have read recently in any of your casebook classes. Write a one-sentence summary of the rule expressed in that case using the following four different formats. Be sure to use proper punctuation for each sentence, and include a properly formatted pinpoint citation.

1. A sentence that quotes an entire sentence from the case.
2. A sentence that quotes a phrase from the case.
3. A sentence that quotes only one word from the case.
4. A sentence that paraphrases information from the case.

Which sentence was the easiest to write? Which sentence would make the rule easiest to understand for your reader?

Part 6

Informal Analytical Writing

24 Advising and Counseling the Client

All clients expect counseling and advice. For the most part, lawyers do that in conversation, either in a meeting or over the telephone. But a significant portion is done in writing, typically in a client letter or an email.

This chapter explains advice and counseling as concepts. Chapter 25 explains how to communicate your analysis to a client in a letter. And Chapter 26 explains how to use email when communicating your analysis to clients and to other lawyers in your office.

Advice is explaining to a client how the law treats the client's situation. *Counseling* is guiding a client through the process of making a decision. Lawyers often use the words *advice* and *counseling* interchangeably, as synonyms. That is fine in the everyday practice of law. But to help you learn how to advise and counsel in writing, we will distinguish between the two concepts.

§ 24.1 Advice and Counseling

A client tells you many facts, shows you a contract she has signed, and asks, "Do I have to sell my fishing boat to Spano? What happens if I don't?" You read the contract carefully and check the law. Then you tell the client yes, she is legally obligated to sell her boat to Spano, and if she does not, she will have to pay damages. You explain how a court would calculate the damages.

"O.K. I'll sell it to him," she says. "I just wanted to know if I can get out of this deal." "You can't get out of it," you say. You have provided only advice. The client wanted to know how the law treats her situation, and you explained it. Many lawyers do this at least a dozen times in a week.

After hearing your advice, a client will typically decide to do or not to do something. For example, your client decided to sell the boat. But this was not a complicated decision. Once the client understood that she had no grounds to escape the contract, she felt she had only one option.

Counseling includes advice, but it is much more. Advice becomes counseling when the client struggles to make a complicated decision. The lawyer counsels by developing different options, evaluating them, explaining to the client the strengths and weaknesses of each option, and helping the client choose the one that will most effectively accomplish the client's goals.

Effective advice and counseling combine empathy and detachment. Empathy helps you understand the client's goals and needs. Detachment helps you see the problem as it really is.

§ 24.2   The Role of Writing in Advice and Counseling

Advice. Most advice is communicated orally, in the lawyer's office or over the telephone. Sometimes it is a good idea to follow up in writing, either in a client letter (Chapter 25) or by email (Chapter 26). A letter or email is helpful when your analysis is so complicated that a client might not understand it from conversation alone. The client can read, contemplate, and read again as needed.

Counseling. The first part of counseling is preparation. A lawyer identifies the client's goals; develops options—potential solutions—that, to varying degrees, might accomplish those goals; and evaluates each option for its advantages and disadvantages. This usually involves legal research and factual investigation.

The second part is a conversation with the client in which the lawyer explains the options, asks the client to choose one of them, and answers the client's questions until the client understands enough decide among them. Often this becomes brainstorming. The client might mention insights that had not occurred to the lawyer, and the lawyer and client might then talk about ways to improve the options.

Communicating with the client in writing can be useful during counseling. For example, a lawyer might explain the options briefly over the telephone and schedule a meeting at which the lawyer and client can discuss them. Between the phone call and the meeting, the lawyer might send a letter or email explaining each option's details so the client can think about them before the meeting.

§ 24.3   Who Decides What

Legally, the client defines the goals of the representation. The lawyer decides what the ABA Model Rules of Professional Conduct call "technical, legal, and tactical issues,"[1] such as where to sue, what theory of the case to rely on, what evidence to submit and witnesses to call, and what arguments to make. The case law allows a lawyer to make those litigation decisions alone, without consulting the client or even over the client's objections. But if you do such a thing, the case law will not stop the client from firing you and telling every other potential client never to hire you.

In other respects, however, the Model Rules require not only that a lawyer "abide by a client's decisions concerning the objectives of representation [but also] consult with the client as to the means by which they are to be pursued."[2] And the Model Rules suggest that the lawyer should defer to the client when technical and tactical decisions raise "such questions as the expense to be incurred and concern for third persons who might be adversely affected."[3]

§ 24.4 Predicting

Both advice and counseling require you to predict what will happen to the client. How can you possibly assure a client that you know with 100% certainty what the future will bring? You cannot be that certain, but the client needs your prediction anyway. It might help to remember that every day billions of dollars are invested, lent, or otherwise committed based on predictions about whether customers will like a product or hate it, or whether stock prices or interest rates will rise or fall. Many of those predictions turn out to be wrong. The earth will not swallow you up if a prediction you make turns out to be inaccurate. But lawyers whose predictions are right most of the time gain the loyalty and respect of their clients.

Out of fear of being wrong, you might want to hedge. One form of hedging—waffling—makes your advice less useful to a client, who must make a decision and needs the most accurate prediction you can make. From the client's point of view, if you waffle, you are not really predicting.

A different form of hedging—adding qualifications or conditions—makes your prediction *more* realistic because qualifications and conditions identify variables that might change your prediction. For more on this, see Chapter 16.

Often you will have to predict without complete knowledge of the facts or the law. Some facts might not become available to you until later (or never). And some parts of the law are unsettled, such as when courts have not yet filled a gap (see § 8.4). When you predict, you should identify for the client not only what you know, but also what you do *not* know. And when you identify something you do not know, tell the client exactly how it would influence your prediction.

---

[1] MODEL RULES OF PROF'L CONDUCT R. 1.2(a) cmt. 2 (2013).
[2] *Id.* R. 1.2(a).
[3] *Id.* R. 1.2 cmt. 2.

Your predictions should be frank and objective. If you have bad news, the client needs to know it. Hiding bad news does neither the client nor you a favor, and it risks the kind of misunderstanding that can turn into an ethics complaint or a malpractice action.

Step back from what you are doing and test the result of your reasoning for realism. If your result would strike the judicial mind as unrealistic and unreasonable, a court will reject your reasoning no matter how sound it seems to you.

Karl Llewellyn had the leading role in creating Articles 1 and 2 of the Uniform Commercial Code. He wrote that law as practicing lawyers know it is "[w]hat officials," including judges, "do about disputes"[4]—and not what statutes and cases say they should do. He also wrote that " 'rights' which cannot be realized are worse than useless; they are traps of delay, expense, and heartache."[5] Your client might appear to have rights under a literal reading of a statute, but if judges will find ways to rule otherwise, you will not help your client by counseling with false optimism. Your client needs a realistic prediction of what the court will actually do.

---

[4] KARL N. LLEWELLYN, THE BRAMBLE BUSH 3 (1930).
[5] *Id.* at 9.

25 Client Letters

§ 25.1 Why and How Lawyers Write Client Advice Letters

In advising and counseling clients, lawyers use letters and email when they need to communicate in writing. This chapter explains client letters. Chapter 26 explains email.

Client letters are midway between a conversation with the client and an office memo. They record the essence of what you would say to the client in a meeting in your office. And often they summarize an office memo. A sample client letter appears in Appendix B.

The tone of a client letter should be professionally precise and supportive. In choosing a tone, ask yourself these questions: What does the situation call for? What would this client want from a professional? What are you comfortable with in terms of your own style? And how do you want to present yourself to clients?

The second question—what this client would want from a professional—may be the most complex. Consider the client's level of sophistication (education, occupation, experience with lawyers). And consider the client's feelings. Is the client experiencing anxiety, grief, or anger? Even in positive situations, such as buying property, happiness can be mixed with anxiety. Or is this transaction pure business from the client's point of view? It probably is if the client is an organization or a business person, if the client considers the transaction or dispute to be routine, or if the client has a lot of experience with lawyers.

§ 25.2   Client Letter Format

A typical structure is set out below. If the letter is complex, you might use headings to break some of it up. But adapt the wording in the headings to the client and the situation. Contractions ("don't," "won't") are fine in a client letter, but not in a memo or brief.

1. The beginning formalities. These include the letterhead, which is already printed on your law office stationery; the date; the client's name and address; and the salutation ("Dear Ms. Lopez:"—always with a colon, never a comma).

2. One or two opening paragraphs, stating the problem about which the client has sought your help and a brief summary of your conclusion. This corresponds to the issue and brief answer in an office memo. If you have bad news, this is where the client learns that it is bad. Think long and hard about the words you use to convey that bad news. Reading words on a page can be a cold experience for the client.

3. One or more paragraphs reviewing the key facts on which your conclusions are based. You might think it wastes words to summarize the client's own facts, but there are several good reasons for doing so.

First, if you have misunderstood any of the facts and the client knows better, the client can correct you. Many lawyers add a sentence asking the client to do that ("If I have described any of the facts inaccurately, please call me").

Second, a fact recitation limits your conclusions to the facts recited, and that can be important if the facts change. A tenant who does not have a claim against the landlord for a filthy lobby might have one next week if the lobby ceiling caves in.

Third, you might have learned recently of some facts the client does not yet know about. If so, describe the newly found facts in ways that tell the client they are new ("Since we last spoke, I have discovered that the 1986 deed was never properly recorded in the county clerk's office").

And finally, a fact recitation is a professional transition into discussion of the law itself.

4. The advice, which can be structured in either of two ways. If the client wants to know how the law treats a certain situation—"Would I win a lawsuit against the airline?" or "Would my company violate the law if we were to import this product?"—you predict how a court would rule, or you explain the client's or other people's rights and obligations.

But if the client must make a decision, you counsel in the letter by suggesting the options from which the client can choose and, for each option, explaining the factors that might make it attractive or unattractive. List the options and explain their *advantages, costs, risks, and chances of success.* When you estimate risks and chances of success, you are making predictions. Costs are not limited to money. The cost of suing includes not only legal fees and other litigation expenses, but also the time and energy the client would have to invest in the lawsuit and the stress many litigants suffer while the suit is in progress.

Be especially careful about the words you use to communicate your degree of confidence in your prediction. When you write that "we have a reasonably good chance of winning at trial," you might mean that you believe the client will probably win, although the risk of loss is significant. But many clients would read those words to mean that victory is nearly assured. It is only human for a client who has suffered a wrong to assume that forces of justice will correct it. Vagueness on your part can imply unjustified optimism. Find ordinary, everyday words that the client will understand exactly as you mean them.

If the news truly is bad, do not cushion it so much that the client will not appreciate it. Do not say, "our chances in litigation are problematic," if you really mean, "we would probably lose if the other side sues."

A good client letter can be understood by a layperson in one reading. It takes much work on your part to accomplish that. Use as little lawyer talk as possible. If a legal term of art has a good equivalent in ordinary English, use the equivalent even if it does not convey 100% of the meaning of the term of art. Eighty percent is good enough, unless the missing 20% is relevant to the client's situation. If you do use a term of art, define it.

When you translate lawyer talk into ordinary English, do so respectfully. This is not just good communication. It is also good business. Clients often feel uncomfortable with a stereotyped lawyer who speaks in legalese. But they can like and trust a genuine human being who does a good job of being their lawyer.

Write simply, but do not oversimplify. If the law is unclear, point that out and explain why it is unclear ("courts disagree with each other on what the statute means"). Discuss authority only if it is central to the issue, such as a recent case that changes everything you have told the client in the past.

Reciting the law can be cold and confusing ("in this state, tax must be paid by the property owner on each lien against real property recorded in the county clerk's office"). But describing the law's effect on the client is warm, and it often eliminates the need to recite the law ("if you refinance the mortgage on your home, you will have to pay $1,250 in mortgage tax").

Unlike a supervising lawyer or a judge, your client assumes that you know the law, which means that you need not recite rules of law or cite and explain authority as thoroughly as you would in a memo or a brief. But you do have to know what you are talking about. Nobody is perfect at predicting. But if you are wrong because you do not understand the law, you will lose clients and learn a lot about the details of malpractice law.

Organize the material in any way that will help the client understand it. Sometimes clients are confused by the CREAC formula described in Chapters 17 through 20.

You are not writing for the skeptical supervising lawyer or judge to whom everything must be proved. You are writing for a layperson who trusts your judgment and assumes you know the law, but who probably will not understand a detailed and thorough explanation.

5. One or two closure paragraphs. Sum up in two or three sentences. Specify what can or should be done next, who should do it, and when it should be done. If the client needs to make a decision, set the stage. Invite the client to telephone you, or if extended conversation might be needed, suggest that the client make an appointment to see you. On the other hand, if the advice is negative ("although your competitors behaved badly, they did nothing illegal"), closure might be limited to an offer to answer questions if the client would like to call.

6. Closing formalities. These are your signatures above your typed name and under a closing like "Sincerely yours," or whatever words are customary in your office. Most readers never notice the closing or care about it, unless you say something completely inappropriate.

26 Professional Email

It is not so much that technology has imposed
itself on lawyers, as that changes in the demands
of law practice have required new solutions. . . .
The challenge for lawyers is managing mountains
of data while still protecting clients and their confidences.

—*Robert J. Ambrogi, Attorney, author of LawSites blog*

§ 26.1   How Technology Has Changed the Nature of Law Practice

Not so long ago, law offices used telephones and typewriters exclusively for communication. Lawyers dictated letters into Dictaphone machines, and secretaries transcribed the recordings into formal letters typed on law firm letterhead. Lawyers wrote memos and briefs the same way. Or they handwrote them on yellow pads for secretaries to type on typewriters. Changing a sentence would require retyping an entire page. In the late 1980s, most law students still typed their legal writing assignments on typewriters, or they paid typists by the page to convert handwritten drafts into typed manuscripts.

Most law students today have never known a time without computers and high-speed internet access. But many lawyers and judges began practicing law long before the internet age began. Until recently, the ABA Model Rules of Professional Conduct assumed that lawyers use regular mail for written correspondence and traditional methods of communication with clients. Some of the informal ways you have used email in the past are not permitted in law practice.

You will need to develop new skills for using email[1] for professional purposes.

---

[1] Both *email* and *e-mail* are correct spellings, and it does not matter which you use, as long as you spell the word consistently.

This chapter introduces you to the ways many lawyers communicate with one another and with clients by email, and the rules of professional conduct that require lawyers to use special care when communicating electronically.

§ 26.2 Email Professionalism

You *will* be judged by your emails.

—*Heather Canning*

This is a story, a very sad tale
Of intrigue, romance and electronic mail
A dangerous form of information
And the perils of instant gratification . . .
After opposing counsel had acted like jerks
Joe got [an email] from his law partner at work
He meant to make changes, cut and paste
But sent it off in his efficient haste
Well he tried to delete, he tried to get back the note
But the letter had flown and that was all she wrote
The message was polite with professional class
But the subject line still said, "What an ass."
So don't push send
Don't push send
There are things that you can never quite amend
I tell myself again and again
Don't push send.

—*Carrie Newcomer, Don't Push Send*

While email is a marvel of convenience, it can be dangerous. Even though an email communication is generally less formal than an office memo or client letter, it is still a professional communication. It should be written in a professional tone using precise language. Think of it as an abbreviated office memo or client letter. Imagine the possible readers of your email message, who may include the client, the client's family, another lawyer, or even the judge. Many lawyers caution against writing anything in an email message that you would not want to have attached as an exhibit in a case pending before a judge. Anything you put in an email message may eventually be part of the public record in a court file.

Because of the informal nature of email, a careless lawyer might not take the time to revise and edit carefully, which can lead to embarrassment, damaged credibility, or worse. The wording and tone of an email message can sometimes sound more harsh than another kind of written communication. In one recent case, for example, a lawyer who sent an angry email to opposing counsel late one night was chastised by the court for engaging in unprofessional conduct.[2] As a precaution, a lawyer might ask another lawyer in the same firm to do a "snark check" of a draft email message before finalizing and sending it.

The casual, informal tone you use for email messages to friends and family is not suitable for email communications with your client, any more than it would be for an email memo to your supervising lawyer. Emoticons, abbreviations, colloquialisms, slang, and other kinds of informality you might use in a text message are *never* appropriate in a professional email to a client. Like formal client letters, your email correspondence will be read over and over by your client, who will form an impression of your legal work based on the care you take to communicate professionally.

Proofread your emails carefully for spelling and punctuation errors. The informal nature of email makes it easy to send messages before carefully reviewing them for readability, tone, and proper grammar. Some lawyers compose email messages in a word processing program, which allows them to use formatting, spell-check, and other reviewing tools, and then copy and paste the final product into an email message.

Except for very short messages without sensitive information, do not send professional email messages from your smartphone. And never send a text message to a client. It is too easy to break many of the rules in this chapter.

If you intend to attach a document to your email message, be absolutely certain that the attachment is the correct version—not an earlier draft. And do not forget to attach the document you identify in the body of your email message. Avoid the embarrassment of sending an immediate follow-up message ("Here's the attachment I mentioned in my earlier email"), or even worse, receiving an annoyed response asking for the attachment you failed to include the first time. Finally, be careful about the title of the attached document, which will appear in your transmittal email. One lawyer told us about an email attachment she received with the following document title: "Antitrust Caselaw for Asshole 05_04_13." Imagine how your recipient would feel about reading that document attached to your email sending the case law she requested from you.

Finally, beware of "Reply all." Some email systems are programmed by default to send email replies to everyone who received the initial email message. For example, in 2014, a prosecutor in Georgia was suspended without pay for three days after inadvertently sending a disrespectful email reply to a message informing her that

---

[2] *Alexander Interactive Inc. v. Adorama, Inc.*, No. 12-CV-6608, 2014 WL 4058705, at *2 (S.D.N.Y. Aug. 14, 2014). The court held that the attorney's unprofessional email message prejudiced the administration of justice. "It is not any single phrase in the email that stood to substantially impair future cooperation between counsel but the overall tone, context and content. The communication was abusive litigation conduct violating an established norm of professional conduct and, thus, it was conduct undertaken in bad faith." *Id.*

a primary defense witness was too ill from cancer to be available for trial.[3] A good practice is to always update the subject line of a reply email message before sending it. That step will not only help your recipient better understand the issue you are addressing, but it will also remind you to double-check the email addresses of everybody who will receive your reply.

All of this means you must check *everything* before you hit "Send." Do not let the pressure of time cause you to make a painful mistake. Always be courteous and respectful in all your communications, including emails. If you draft an email message while angry, tired, or anxious, the tone of the message will sound much more stern to the recipient than you might think.

If time allows, wait to send the message until you have had a good night's sleep, and then review it carefully the next morning. If time does not allow you that luxury, take a long, careful look at everything in your email memo, including the "To" box and the subject line, to be sure every detail is exactly correct. Proofread your email by reading it aloud to yourself or to a fellow lawyer in your firm to catch and correct any errors. Then—and only then—can you safely hit "Send."

§ 26.3   Why and How Lawyers Write Email to Clients

> Technology has changed the way I practice in almost every way imaginable. . . . My presentations to clients, judges and juries are almost exclusively electronic. I communicate with my clients mostly through email. I can't remember the last time I sent a letter to a client.
>
> —*Darren E. Nadel*

§ 26.3.1   Email and Client Letters

A lawyer has a professional responsibility to keep a client "reasonably informed about the status" of the client's case and to promptly respond to a client's "reasonable requests for information."[4] Failing to keep in contact with clients is one of the most common reasons for ethical complaints and malpractice lawsuits against lawyers. Before email communication became common in law practice, lawyers kept their clients informed by telephone, by writing letters updating them about the status of the case, or by meeting with them in person. Writing a client letter typically requires a significant amount of a lawyer's time. But client letters are the best method for

---

[3] Debra Cassens Weiss, *Mistaken "Reply All" Email Leads to Suspension Without Pay for Prosecutor* (July 14, 2014), http://www.abajournal.com/news/article/mistaken_reply_all_email_leads_to_suspension_without_pay_for_prosecutor (last visited Nov. 15, 2014).
[4] Model Rules of Prof'l Conduct R. 1.4(a)(3), (4) (2013).

explaining detailed analysis to a client in writing. If something would be difficult for a client to understand, put it in a letter—not in email.

Email is essential in communicating with clients. But reserve email for routine matters such as notifying a client about a judge's decision on a discovery motion and summarizing material that you will later explain in detail during a telephone conversation or face-to-face meeting.

§ 26.3.2 Client Confidentiality

The ethics rules for communicating with clients using email are still evolving. We must explain not only what the rules are now, but also what they are likely to be in the near future.

While email is a time-saving convenience, using email to communicate with clients raises challenging issues about keeping client information confidential. Model Rule of Professional Conduct 1.6(a) provides, "A lawyer shall not reveal information relating to the representation of a client unless the client gives informed consent, the disclosure is impliedly authorized in order to carry out the representation[,] or the disclosure is permitted" by an exception to the rule. If you use email to contact clients about a legal matter, how can you be sure the information remains confidential? The answers are not yet entirely clear.

In 1999, the American Bar Association issued an opinion concluding that the use of email to communicate with clients generally does not violate client confidentiality rules.[5] The authors of the opinion reasoned that email communication offers reasonable privacy from a technological and legal standpoint. For that reason, lawyers are not required to use encrypted[6] email to protect client confidentiality. However, the opinion cautioned lawyers to consult with clients regarding the risks of inadvertent disclosure and to follow their clients' instructions on how to communicate confidential information.

A more recent ABA ethics opinion cautions lawyers to appropriately advise the client if circumstances create a significant risk that if communicated by email, others might be able to get access to information the client wants to keep confidential.[7] For example, if a client uses an employer's computer or email account to read and

---

[5] ABA Standing Comm. on Ethics & Prof'l Responsibility, Formal Op. 99-413 (1999).
[6] Microsoft explains encryption this way:

> Encrypting an email message in Microsoft Outlook protects the privacy of the message by converting it from readable plain text into scrambled cipher text. Only the recipient who has the private key that matches the public key used to encrypt the message can decipher the message for reading. Any recipient without the corresponding private key sees garbled text.

http://office.microsoft.com/en-us/outlook-help/encrypt-email-messages-HP010355559.aspx (last visited Nov. 15, 2014). Other email systems might work slightly differently.
[7] ABA Standing Comm. on Ethics & Prof'l Responsibility, Formal Op. 11-459 (2011).

respond to your email messages about her pending case, the client's employer may have the right to access that information without the client's consent.

Many lawyers try to avoid inadvertent disclosures to unauthorized parties by adding labels to email messages, such as "CONFIDENTIAL—ATTORNEY-CLIENT PRIVILEGE." Most law firms also include a standard confidentiality notice at the foot of every email message. While many variations exist, the following paragraph is one example:

> The information contained in this transmission, including attachments, is privileged and confidential information intended for the use of the individual or entity named above or XYZ Law Firm. If the reader is not the intended recipient or an authorized representative of the intended recipient, you are hereby notified that any review, dissemination, distribution, or copying of this information is strictly prohibited. If you have received this transmission in error, do not read it. Please immediately reply to the sender (admin@xyzlawfirm.com) that you have received this communication in error and then delete this transmission and its attachments. Thank you.

Recent developments in the ethical standards for lawyers raise serious doubts about whether either method of cautioning unintended recipients is enough. In particular, the ABA has concluded that a third party, such as your client's employer, who obtains access to an email communication between you and your client is *not* required to notify you or delete the message, unless the third party was an "unintended recipient" to whom you or your client inadvertently directed the message.[8]

In 2012, the ABA amended several Model Rules to address lawyers' professional obligations with respect to email and other developing technology. The most important change was in Rule 1.6, which now requires lawyers to "make *reasonable efforts* to prevent the inadvertent or unauthorized disclosure of, or unauthorized access to, information" relating to client representation.[9] How do you know if you have satisfied the "reasonable efforts" requirement under the new rule? The commentary to Rule 1.6 sets out a factors test that includes the following:

- sensitivity of the information
- likelihood of disclosure without taking additional safeguards (such as encryption)
- cost of undertaking additional safeguards
- difficulty of implementing additional safeguards
- effect of additional safeguards on the ability to represent clients.[10]

---

[8] ABA Standing Comm. on Ethics & Prof'l Responsibility, Formal Op. 11-460 (2011).
[9] MODEL RULES OF PROF'L CONDUCT R. 1.6(c) & cmt. 16 (2013) (emphasis added).
[10] *Id.* R. 1.6 cmt. 16.

Nevertheless, the rule specifically provides that "[a] client may require the lawyer to implement special security measures . . . or may give informed consent to forgo security measures that would otherwise be required by [the] Rule."[11] In other words, you have the responsibility to advise your client about the risks of disclosing confidential information when using email, including alternatives that may offer greater security against interception or unintended disclosure.

Other state and federal laws may require lawyers to take even more precautions when emailing clients.[12] For example, the ethics committee of the California bar issued a 2010 opinion suggesting that encrypting email may be a reasonable step if the client information is highly sensitive.[13]

By including a warning label or boilerplate paragraph about confidentiality, you put unintended recipients on notice that the email contains private information. But that may not be sufficient to comply with current ethical rules. If a lawyer receives a misdirected message, the Model Rules require the lawyer only to *notify* the sender.[14] They do not require an unintended recipient to do anything more, and state law controls whether a lawyer has any additional obligations, such as returning or deleting the message.[15] And the Model Rules govern only *lawyers* who receive this kind of confidential information, not other people.

Even if you include confidentiality notices in your client emails, never use unencrypted email to communicate sensitive or confidential information. It is too easy for you or the client to misdirect an email communication to someone else. If you inadvertently send client information by email to someone who is not entitled to have it, you violate your professional responsibility to maintain client confidentiality. And if your client misdirects the message, he may waive the attorney-client privilege—a rule of evidence law that prevents a trial court from admitting communications between a lawyer and client into evidence. But a client can waive the privilege by not treating the information as confidential. For example, if a client tells everyone in the neighborhood bar what he told his lawyer earlier in the day, the client has waived the privilege. The same thing can happen if your client misdirects a confidential email, even accidentally.

Moreover, your client may inadvertently waive the attorney-client privilege simply by using a computer to receive or transmit sensitive information. If the client's employer, business partners, or family members can access the computer system, the privilege may not apply at all.[16]

---

[11] *Id.*

[12] *Id.*

[13] State Bar of Cal. Standing Comm. on Prof'l Responsibility & and Conduct, Formal Op. 2010-179, at 4 (2010), http://ethics.calbar.ca.gov/LinkClick.aspx?fileticket=wmqECiHp7h4%3d&tabid=837 (last visited Nov. 15, 2014).

[14] MODEL RULES OF PROF'L CONDUCT R. 4.4(b) & cmt. 2 (2013).

[15] *Id.*

[16] ABA Standing Comm. on Ethics & Prof'l Responsibility, Formal Op. 11-459.

Beyond concerns about confidentiality, consider the context in which a client will read the email message you send. She probably will be busy reading a multitude of other emails before she reads yours. If the information could cause her anxiety or raise immediate questions, another method of communication would be better. For example, you might send a brief email explaining that an important development requires you to consult with her, and ask that she contact your office to schedule a meeting.

Whenever you correspond with a client, keep your communications professional in appearance and tone. Use an appropriate salutation ("Dear Ms. Woodbridge:" or "Dear Jane,") and a suitable closing ("Best regards, [Your Name]"). Always include your signature block along with your phone number so your client can easily reach you with questions.

§ 26.3.3   A Sample Client Email

To: Darrell and Latesha Worthington
From: Emilia Orosco
Subject: Potential lawsuit against Slugger Field
Date: August 22, 2015

Dear Darrell and Latesha,

We believe you would probably win a lawsuit against Slugger Field for your daughter's injuries.

Please call my secretary to schedule an appointment so we can talk about what to do next. In this email, I'll describe briefly the key issues so you can be thinking about them before we meet.

At trial, we would have to prove that Slugger Field had a duty to protect Sophie while she was on its property. We can prove that because Slugger Field advertised the event she was attending, essentially inviting her into the ballpark. If the Field knew or should have known of dangers there, it at least had a duty to warn her about them. The National Weather Service had issued an alert that could be heard through the weather radio in the ballpark manager's office. The ballpark has covered areas where Sophie would have been protected from lightning if the management had warned spectators that a lightning storm would arrive soon.

The Field might defend by arguing that weather is an inherent risk of baseball and that spectators at a ball game assume those risks. The Field would probably lose this argument. Sophie assumed the risk of being hit by a foul ball—not by lightning.

We should talk about something lawyers call comparative negligence. Although you will probably win the lawsuit, there is a possibility that a court might award less money than we would hope. This is a complex issue and difficult to summarize accurately in an email. When we meet, we can talk it over in detail.

I look forward to hearing from you.

Best regards,

Emilia Orosco
Attorney at Law
1189 Arapaho Street
Trail Ridge Mesa, CO 34500
123-456-7890

NOTICE: The information contained in this transmission, including attachments, is privileged and confidential information intended for the use of the recipient to whom it is addressed. If you are not the intended recipient or an authorized representative of the intended recipient, this is notice that reading, distributing, or copying this information is prohibited by law. If you have received this transmission in error, do not read it. Please immediately reply to the sender (admin@xyzlawfirm.com) that you have received this communication in error and then please delete this transmission and its attachments. Thank you.

§ 26.4 Why and How Lawyers Write Email Memos to Other Lawyers

An email memo resembles a very short office memo. Sometimes an email memo may be appropriate if a supervising lawyer needs your legal analysis sooner and more concisely than you could accomplish in a formal office memo. An email memo will be written and read under unusual time pressure for both you and your supervising lawyer. But your supervisor's time is much more valuable and costly to the client than your own time as a recently hired lawyer. For that reason, take enough time to prepare an email memo so your supervisor's time is used most efficiently.

Because of the special characteristics of email technology, most memos transmitted by email use a more flexible format than the traditional office memo. But that does not mean you should devote any less time to preparing, rewriting, polishing, and proofreading your work product. Keep your email communications with other lawyers as professional as possible within your time constraints, and *always* proofread your work carefully before hitting "send."

§ 26.4.1 Email Memo Format

Traditional office memo format has developed by custom over the years. Although specific preferences vary from one practice setting to the next, most lawyers generally agree on how an office memo should be structured. But email memos are a relatively recent development in law practice, and little consensus exists about how to format them. An email memo might be structured somewhat like an office memo, or it might follow an entirely different format.[17]

An email memo should follow a flexible format depending on the circumstances and your time constraints. What works in one situation might not work in another. On Monday, a lawyer might send an email memo to the firm's litigating partner concerning a proposed jury instruction. On Friday, the same lawyer might send an email memo to the same partner explaining the law concerning a discovery demand in a different case. These email memos might be structured in entirely different ways because the problems they address are different.

Similarly, some legal questions call for narrow, straightforward answers, and a less formal email may better meet the needs of the supervising lawyer. But a more complex and debatable issue may require comprehensive legal analysis not suitable for an email memo. In that instance, a lawyer may write a more formally structured office memo and send it as an attachment to a short transmittal email.

The following format is one way you might structure an informal email memo to another lawyer.

Address line. Be sure your email message is directed to the intended recipient. You have probably experienced an incomplete email suddenly disappearing into cyberspace, seemingly beyond your control. Once sent, email messages cannot be retrieved. To avoid this problem, many lawyers wait to fill in the address line until the email memo is complete, including rewriting, polishing, and proofreading. That way if you inadvertently hit the "send" button, the draft email will go nowhere.

Also, use care with email systems that automatically populate the address line after you type the first two or three characters. Your email system may automatically enter the address of one of your regular contacts who should not receive the information in your memo. Before completing your email, double-check the addresses following "To:" so your email goes where you want it to go.

Subject line. Specify clearly and concisely what your email memo is about. Your message will appear with many others in your supervisor's inbox. To make it stand out, your subject line should clearly and succinctly identify the case and the issue your email memo addresses.

---

[17] *See* Kristen Konrad Robbins-Tiscione, *From Snail Mail to E-Mail: The Traditional Legal Memorandum in the Twenty-First Century,* 58 J. LEGAL EDUC. 32, 43–44 (2008).

Some law firms require lawyers to include very specific information in the subject line, such as the client's name, the case number, and a detailed reference to the content ("West v. South, No. 15-cv-123, Dr. Expert's Deposition Summary"). That way a busy lawyer can easily search through her email correspondence to find the message you sent several days earlier about the matter she is working on now. Think carefully about how useful the information in the subject line will be to a lawyer who may receive hundreds of email messages each day.

Issue. In the first sentence of your email message, explain briefly why you are sending the memo to your supervising lawyer, including the issue it answers. For example:

> You asked whether we are required to answer Interrogatory No. 6 in the Plaintiff's second set of interrogatories.

If you prefer, you can use a heading to draw the reader's attention to the issue, and structure it as a question:

> **Issue:**
>
> Are we required to answer Interrogatory No. 6 in the Plaintiff's second set of interrogatories?

Answer. Next, in one or two sentences, briefly state your answer in a way that directly responds to the issue, along with the essential reasons supporting your answer. If you have included a heading for the Issue, also include a heading like "Answer" or "Brief Answer" here:

> **Answer:**
>
> No, because Interrogatory No. 6 seeks material that the attorney-client privilege protects from disclosure.

Alternative format. Instead of writing a separate issue and answer as shown above, you might combine them into one or two sentences following the first sentence that explains your reason for sending the memo:

> We are not required to answer Interrogatory No. 6 in the Plaintiff's second set of interrogatories because it seeks material that the attorney-client privilege protects from disclosure.

Facts. Recite only the facts that are *essential* to your legal analysis. If you are preparing an informal email memo, your supervising lawyer has probably asked you a narrow question. If your supervisor needs a quick answer by email, she most likely already knows the facts in general because she is working right now on the case. In your email memo, the only facts that matter are the ones directly relevant to the specific issue and your analysis.

Analysis. Concisely but completely explain why your answer is correct, citing the legal rule and supporting legal authority as necessary. Follow one of the abbreviated versions of the CREAC formula (Chapter 18). Determine the level of rule explanation that will satisfy your supervisor's needs for both a speedy answer and sufficient confidence that your answer is correct. If a comprehensive analysis is needed, an email message might not be adequate for your reader's needs. Instead, you can prepare a formal office memo using the conventional, more structured format and attach it to a transmittal email.

Finding the right balance to meet your reader's competing needs will become easier with experience. If you are not sure, err on the side of including more explanation within the timeframe available.

Conclusion. If your analysis is brief, you probably do not need a separate conclusion. But be sure your analysis is complete enough to clearly support the answer you gave at the beginning of your email memo. Do not leave your reader wondering how your analysis supports your answer. Close the loop so your reader can follow your legal analysis to your predicted conclusion.

§ 26.4.2   Typography and Document Design

While email memos are less formal than traditional office memos, they should still look professional in format and design. Depending on your email system, you may have a choice of fonts, type sizes, colors, underlining, and other typography features. If so, use the typography options that your law office prefers in its day-to-day internal email correspondence. Your supervising lawyer may have a preference so your email memo is easy to read.

In an email, headings do not center well. Instead of centering, place internal memo headings along the left margin, or indent them five spaces from the left margin. Indenting makes the headings more obvious to your reader. Headings should be in bold type if your email system will support bold. If not, put the headings entirely in capital letters for emphasis.

Unlike the indented paragraphs in a printed document, the first line of a paragraph in an email generally begins at the left margin. If you format your paragraphs that way, be sure to add a space between paragraphs so your reader can easily see each step in your analysis. Paragraph structure is no less important in an email memo than in a formal document.

§ 26.4.3   A Sample Email Memo

To: Emilia Orosco
From: Peter Reiser
Subject: Slugger Field probably has no affirmative defense (Sophie Worthington)
Date: August 18, 2015

Slugger Field probably has no affirmative defense to the Worthingtons' premises liability claim.

While no Colorado case is directly on point, the court is unlikely to hold that lightning is an inherent risk of baseball, as the Colorado Baseball Spectator Safety Act would require for the ballpark to avoid all liability.

The ballpark also cannot argue that the danger of inclement weather was open and obvious because the Colorado Supreme Court has specifically held that the Premises Liability Act abrogates that common law defense. But the family's damages might be limited by the doctrine of comparative negligence, which was not abrogated by the Act.

Yesterday I explained by email that the Worthingtons have a claim because Sophie was an invitee as defined by the Premises Liability Act.

If you wish, I can write an office memo analyzing the statutes and case law in detail on all the issues we have discussed.

Inherent risks of baseball

The Baseball Spectator Safety Act limits Slugger Field's liability for injuries that are "inherent risks" of watching baseball. The Act does not define "inherent risk." Colorado courts have never held that baseball spectators bear the risk of being struck by lightning in a ballpark. Courts and statutes in other states limit the meaning of "inherent risks" to those a spectator might expect from the sport itself, such as injury from a foul ball or a broken baseball bat.

For example, the Missouri Supreme Court recently declined to hold that a spectator's serious eye injury was an inherent risk of baseball when the team's mascot used an airgun to shoot hotdogs into the stands. *Coomer v. Kansas City Royals Baseball Corp.*, 2014 WL 2861763, at **7-9 (Mo. June 24, 2014). Weather risks are more attenuated from baseball than the actions of an employee such as a mascot. But even the mascot's behavior was not considered a risk inherent in the sport. Baseball can be played without mascots and hotdogs, but it cannot be played without bats and balls.

Open and obvious danger

Even if Sophie saw the storm approaching, Slugger Field has no open and obvious danger defense. The Colorado Supreme Court has held that the Premises Liability

Act abolished the common law open and obvious danger doctrine. *Vigil v. Franklin*, 103 P.3d 327, 332 (Colo. 2004).

Although Slugger Field cannot avoid liability entirely, it might be able to mitigate damages by asserting comparative negligence. The Colorado Supreme Court has held that the Act does not abrogate comparative negligence, which was not recognized at common law and is not an affirmative defense to a negligence or premises liability claim. *Union Pac. R. Co. v. Martin*, 209 P.3d 185, 190 (Colo. 2009). Comparative negligence instead simply allocates proportionate liability among the parties and others whose negligence contributed to the injury. *Id.*

Sophie may have been somewhat negligent because her friend noticed the approaching storm and called Sophie's attention to the warning signs in the sky. Sophie could have moved to a covered area of Slugger Field until the storm passed.

On the other hand, a jury might consider the fact that Sophie was 16 years old at the time of her injuries, and therefore was not in the same position as an adult to fully appreciate the safety risk posed by the weather. In fact, she was attending a youth tournament, and most of the people in the ballpark were probably teenagers. We can explore that in discovery.

Exercise 26-A. Critiquing Email Messages to Clients

Critique each of the following email messages sent by a junior associate to a client. Is the content of the message suitable for email correspondence? Is the tone appropriate? Is the length of the message suitable to meet the client's needs? Imagine you are the client who has received each message. How would you react to the writer? How would you rewrite each message to improve it?

1. To: Ms. Client
   From: Your Attorney
   Subject: Your (Almost) Ex-husband's Latest Stunt

   Hey there, Suzy. Did you get my letter about your husband's settlement offer? He wants custody of the two kidlets, but he's willing to let you keep the house and one of the cars if you want. He says no deal to your alimony demand, and he won't budge on that one. :-(Let me know.

   _____

2. To: Ms. Client
   From: Your Attorney
   Subject: Request for Settlement Conference

PRIVILEGED AND CONFIDENTIAL

Dear Ms. Client:

Thank you for meeting with me last week. I hope you are resting well at home after your long hospital stay following your bicycle accident.

The lawyer for the defendant's insurer contacted me today to initiate settlement discussions. Are you available to set up a conference sometime next week? Please give me a call at your convenience so we can arrange a time that works for everyone.

If I am not personally available when you call, please let my administrative assistant know when you might be able to meet with the insurer's legal counsel.

Very truly yours,

Sam Attorney

---

3. To: Ms. Client
     From: Your Attorney
     Subject: Re: Question about my case [Auto-response]

I receive approximately 75-100 emails per day. It is often impossible for me to respond the same day or within a week to the emails I receive. As such, please review the following disclaimer:

If you are an attorney:
Please note that due to the volume of emails, I cannot accept service or notice via email and if your recent communication is an attempt at such, please call my office immediately to notify my staff of your communication. (123) 456-7890.

If you are a current client:
If you are in need of a response in a quick manner, please call my office and let my staff know that you have an urgent request. If they are able to assist you they will, if it is something that requires my attention, they will contact me and notify me of your concern. We strive to respond promptly to our clients; however, we do so in a "triage" format where emergencies, time sensitive matters, and court matters are addressed first. We appreciate your understanding and patience in your acknowledgement of this protocol. You may always call the office and have a telephone conference call scheduled to discuss your concerns, if you are unable to wait for a response.

If you are a potential client:
Please note that unless you have retained our firm by signing a fee agreement and/ or paying a retainer, I am not able to give legal advice and will likely not be able to

respond to your email questions. You are more than welcome to call the office and schedule an appointment.[18]

---

4. To: Ms. Client
     From: Your Attorney
     Subject: **URGENT:** Your case

We have a problem. Please give me a call.

---

5. To: Ms. Client
     From: Your Attorney
     Subject: Your inquiry about alternatives to litigation

You inquired whether alternative dispute resolution mechanisms might be acceptable for utilization in lieu of litigation to resolve your legal dispute with your liability insurance carrier regarding coverage of the casualty recently sustained on your real property by a licensee. Please be advised that your liability insurance policy provides for mandatory binding arbitration of any legal disputes arising under the coverage or exclusion provisions of your policy. Fundamentally, that is your sole and exclusive alternative at this point in the litigation. If you have additional questions or concerns about the content of this communication, please do not refrain from exercising your right to contact me telephonically.

---

[18] We thank Jay Fleischman, Attorney and author of *LegalPracticePro*, http://www.legalpracticepro.com, for providing this email example.

Part 7

The Shift to Persuasion

27 What Persuades a Court?

What could you write to persuade a judge to give you what you are asking for? What persuades?

§ 27.1 A Compelling Theory and Theme Persuade

A *theory* is a way of looking at the controversy that makes your client the winner. A *theme* is a sentence or two or even just a phrase that summarizes the theory. You are already familiar with theories and themes in a commercial sense. Think of the businesses or products to which you are loyal. Each of them has been marketed with a theory and theme—sometimes implied rather than stated openly—that has persuaded you to spend money. Here are a few examples:

- Uber—moving people: tap a button, get picked up in minutes
- Amazon—stop driving to stores: just click, and it's delivered to you
- jetBlue—fly on an airline that's fun

In law, a persuasive theory is a view of the facts and law—intertwined together—that *justifies* a decision in your favor and that *motivates* a court to render that decision. A persuasive theory

1. relies on the supportive facts;
2. explains why the adverse facts should not prevent a decision in your favor;
3. has a solid basis in law and overcomes your adversary's interpretation of the law;
4. appeals to a judge's sense of fairness and good policy; and
5. can be summarized in one or two sentences, or captured in a vivid image, that a judge can easily remember.

Unfocused writing can make a judge feel as though she is drowning in detail without a clear idea how all the detail adds up to a coherent view of the case. Judges complain about lawyers who write that way. A judge needs a clearly stated theory and a motion memo or brief sharply focused on proving that theory.

§ 27.2   A Compelling Story Persuades

The client's story makes the theory *come alive*. Although we live in a scientific world where logic is expected to explain everything, we think in stories. Stories grab our attention and engage our imagination.

You probably know this from your own experience. Suppose you are in an audience. Someone is speaking from a podium in the front of the room. For half an hour, that person talks about the logical connection between the Heisenberg uncertainty principle and the invention of chocolate. Your eyelids grow heavy, and you contemplate sleep. Then the speaker stops talking about logic. To illustrate some point, he tells about a family of ducks who start crossing a busy highway at rush hour—the mother at the head of a line of ducklings, the father who-knows-where. Brakes are screeching. Officer O'Leary is rushing up, waving his arms in the air.

Suddenly you are sitting upright on the edge of your seat. Why are you listening differently now? It cannot be that chocolate has bored you. Instead, the story's tension has gripped you. Never mind about Heisenberg and his uncertainty. Will the cars hit the ducklings? Will all that slamming of brakes cause a huge chain collision, followed by drivers standing on the pavement and swearing at each other? Will Officer O'Leary be able to prevent all this?

All good stories have tension. The stories lawyers tell courts have tension because they involve conflict. When we start to hear or read a story like that—and if the story is told well—we naturally start asking questions like these: Who is the good person? Who is the bad person? What bad thing did the bad person do? How did it affect the good person? (We are worried.) What happens next? How will the story end?

Every lawsuit has a story. You have been reading them in the casebooks in other courses. Actually, every lawsuit has at least two stories, one for each side. The one you read in the court's opinion is the winning story. Sometimes you read the losing story in a dissenting opinion.

How do we know judges are persuaded by stories? The judges say so in the opinions they write. They tell us, by the way they explain the case's facts, *how* they have been influenced by a story. For example, here are the first three paragraphs of *BMW v. Gore*,[1] a U.S. Supreme Court case:

> The Due Process Clause of the Fourteenth Amendment prohibits a State from imposing a "grossly excessive" punishment on a tortfeasor. The wrongdoing involved in this case was the decision by a national distributor of automobiles not to

---

[1] 517 U.S. 559 (1995) (citations omitted).

advise its dealers, and hence their customers, of predelivery damage to new cars when the cost of repair amounted to less than 3 percent of the car's suggested retail price. The question presented is whether a $2 million punitive damages award to the purchaser of one of these cars exceeds the constitutional limit.

In January 1990, Dr. Ira Gore, Jr. (respondent), purchased a black BMW sports sedan for $40,750.88 from an authorized BMW dealer in Birmingham, Alabama. After driving the car for approximately nine months, and without noticing any flaws in its appearance, Dr. Gore took the car to "Slick Finish," an independent detailer, to make it look "snazzier than it normally would appear." Mr. Slick, the proprietor, detected evidence that the car had been repainted. Convinced that he had been cheated, Dr. Gore brought suit against petitioner BMW of North America (BMW), the American distributor of BMW automobiles. Dr. Gore alleged, *inter alia*, that the failure to disclose that the car had been repainted constituted suppression of a material fact. The complaint prayed for $500,000 in compensatory and punitive damages, and costs.

At trial, BMW acknowledged that it had adopted a nationwide policy in 1983 concerning cars that were damaged in the course of manufacture or transportation. If the cost of repairing the damage exceeded 3 percent of the car's suggested retail price, the car was placed in company service for a period of time and then sold as used. If the repair cost did not exceed 3 percent of the suggested retail price, however, the car was sold as new without advising the dealer that any repairs had been made. Because the $601.37 cost of repainting Dr. Gore's car was only about 1.5 percent of its suggested retail price, BMW did not disclose the damage or repair to the Birmingham dealer.

Dr. Gore is going to lose this appeal. We know it already. Here are the clues from the way the court tells the story:

- Dr. Gore drove the car for nine months without noticing that it had been damaged and repaired. Only a specialist noticed it.
- He paid about $40,750 to buy the car.
- The pre-purchase damage was so minor that the repair cost BMW only about $600.
- Dr. Gore sued for $500,000 in compensatory damages and was awarded $2 million in punitive damages.

The amounts claimed are so disproportionate to Dr. Gore's loss that he seems greedy, and the damages seem irrational. This is BMW's story. The Court adopted it and tells us so before even beginning to analyze the law.

But Dr. Gore has a different story, which the Court rejected. We know about it only because a dissenting justice told the story in the following words near the beginning of her dissent:

> Dr. Gore's experience was not unprecedented among customers who bought BMW vehicles sold as flawless and brand-new. In addition to his own encounter, Gore showed . . . that on 983 other occasions . . . , BMW had shipped new vehicles to

dealers without disclosing paint repairs costing at least $300, [and] at least 14 of the repainted vehicles . . . were sold as new and undamaged to consumers in Alabama.[2]

Which story do you find more persuasive?

§ 27.3   Compelling Arguments Persuade

Arguments provide the logical reasons to accept a writer's theory. They are based on interpretation of statutes and judicial precedent as well as public policy. In all your courses, you have been immersed in arguments since you started law school.

§ 27.4   How Arguments and Stories Work Together

Suppose you are asked to believe the following:[3] *A farmer in India can earn dramatically more income simply by owning a basic mobile phone capable of no more than voice calls and text messages.*

Assume that you are a government official with a budget. You are besieged by people and organizations asking you to spend money on projects they consider important. For every request you approve, you will have to turn down a hundred more. You must decide whether to spend several million dollars to subsidize construction of rural cellular transmitting towers and to get cell phones into the hands of Indian farmers and the rural merchants who buy food from them.

A logical argument in support of this plan appears in the left column. Read it and decide whether it persuades you and, if so, how deeply you are persuaded ("this might work," "it probably will work," or "it absolutely will work!").

Then read the stories in the right column.

A Logical Argument	**Two Stories**
In economics, a market is any system in which buyers and sellers can transact	Suraj Chopra is a farmer in a small village some distance from New Delhi. He lives

---

[2] *Id.* at 608 (Ginsburg, J., dissenting).
[3] *See* The World Bank Group, *Poverty Headcount Ratio at $2 a Day (PPP) (% of Population)*, THE WORLD BANK, http://data.worldbank.org/indicator/SI.POV.2DAY/countries/IN?display=graph (last visited Nov. 15, 2014); India Ministry of Home Affairs, *2011 Census Data*, OFFICE OF THE REGISTRAR GEN. & CENSUS COMM'R, http://censusindia.gov.in/Census_And_You/literacy_and_level_of_education.aspx (last visited Nov. 15, 2014); *60% of Rural India Lives on Less Than Rs 35 a Day*, THE ECONOMIC TIMES (India), May 4, 2012 http://articles.economictimes.indiatimes.com/2012-05-04/news/31559329_1_rural-areas-mpce-nsso-survey; Kevin Sullivan, *For India's Traditional Fishermen, Cellphones Deliver a Sea Change*, WASH. POST, Oct. 15, 2006, http://www.washingtonpost.com/wp-dyn/content/article/2006/10/14/AR2006101400342.html; Kevin Sullivan, *Cell Phone Turns Out To Be Grocer's Best Buy*, WASH. POST, Oct. 14, 2006, http://www.washingtonpost.com/wp-dyn/content/article/2006/10/13/AR2006101301043.html.

business with each other. In an efficient market, all information is available to everybody so that each buyer or seller can make rational decisions. If all information is available to everybody, each person gets the most value out of the market, and waste is minimized.

But developing countries are plagued by inefficient markets, where people do not have access to the information they need, and where buyers and sellers have a hard time even finding each other. These inefficiencies are one of the greatest burdens that developing countries must overcome to achieve widespread prosperity.

More than two-thirds of the people of India live on income of less than $2 a day, according to the World Bank. The situation is worse in rural areas, where three-fifths of the population survives on little more than half a dollar a day, according to Indian government statistics.

The smallest and cheapest medium for transmitting information instantly is a cell phone. It is cheaper than a laptop and does not require telephone wiring or wifi infrastructure. It does require cellular transmitting towers, which have been built in urban areas where cell phone users are concentrated. Too few towers are in the less populated countryside where almost 70% of Indians live.

A cell phone does not require any education. The adult literacy rate in India is about 65%. But a person who cannot read or write can place voice calls on a cell phone.

Although the U.S. cost of buying a cell phone and paying the monthly bills would consume much more than an average Indian worker's entire income,

with his family in a two-room hut with a dirt floor and no running water. He can see no way to improve that situation.

Sometimes a rural merchant will buy some of what Chopra grows and transport it in an unrefrigerated truck to a wholesale market in New Delhi. But a significant amount of Chopra's crop never leaves his village. In a hot climate, produce must be harvested as it ripens and taken to market fast before it spoils.

He has no phone of any kind. No cell tower is nearby, and his village, like many in India, was never wired for landlines. He has no way of contacting the outside world when he needs to.

Devi Datt Joshi sells fruit and vegetables from a three-wheeled cart on the streets of New Delhi. He has no store and no refrigerator. Before dawn each day, he goes to a fruit and vegetable wholesale market and buys as much as he thinks he can sell that day. This is the same market where a rural merchant might take produce grown by Suraj Chopra.

Joshi's pre-dawn decision of how much to purchase is crucial to whether he will make any money that day and how hard he will have to work to make it. Without refrigeration in the Indian heat, if he buys more than he can sell, he will have to throw away most of the excess because it will spoil by the following day. If he buys too little, he will lose sales and risk losing frustrated customers to other sellers.

Making this kind of gamble, Joshi used to earn an average of $3 a day for more than twelve hours of work. Everything changed when he got a cell phone. Now customers call him the night before to place their orders. He knows how much costs in India are lower. Cell phone air time charges in India are a fraction of what U.S. consumers pay.

"One element of poverty is the lack of information," according to C.K. Prahalad, a professor in the business school at the University of Michigan, who has studied how cell phones can help people escape poverty. "The cell phone gives poor people as much information as the middleman."

Therefore, if farmers in India have cell phones, their incomes can grow significantly. The food distribution chain from farmers to city populations can become more efficient, with less food spoilage. And that can lower food prices for consumers in all income groups.

to buy, and they can depend on him to supply what they need.

"The mobile phone has more than doubled my profits," Joshi told an American newspaper reporter. He now earns $8 a day for about eight hours of work. He still gets up before dawn, but his work day ends before lunch. He has hired an assistant and put his children into better schools. And the food he buys rarely goes to waste.

Meanwhile Suraj Chopra, the farmer, sometimes sees his crops go to waste because, without a phone, he cannot contact a merchant when his crops are ready to sell. And a merchant cannot quickly and easily contact him when the merchant is ready to buy.

Again, you are the government official with a budget. Suppose you hear the stories *without* hearing the logical argument. The stories make you interested, even excited, about the idea. But you do not yet have confidence that this is a good use of money from your limited budget. Then you hear the logical argument, which gives you the confidence you did not have before. *The stories provided motivation, and the argument finished the job by justifying with logic.*

The story and the logical argument complement each other. Neither alone would be sufficient. A story touches us and motivates us to act. A logical argument explains why the story is valid and provides a justification that a decision maker can rely on to explain the decision to someone else. Persuading thus requires a good story *and* an argument that *work together*.

§ 27.5   Overcoming Your Weaknesses Persuades

Which cases and statutes favor your adversary? Which facts work to your adversary's advantage? What are your adversary's strongest arguments? And what will your adversary say to contradict your arguments? The answers to these questions identify your weaknesses.

Hiding from these problems will not make them slink away in the night. You must confront and defeat them. "Be truthful in exposing . . . the difficulties in your case," an appellate judge has written. "Tell us what they are and how you expect to deal with them."[4] If you fail to mention your weaknesses, and if you fail to explain why they do not undermine your case, the court probably will hold them against you. Acknowledging your challenges can preserve your reader's trust in you.

§ 27.6   Solving Judges' Problems Persuades

Make it easy for the judge to rule in your favor.

Imagine an office with a desk, a side table, and bookshelves. On the desk and side table, many files are piled up. Each file is very thick and represents a motion or appeal the judge must decide. The judge behind the desk has a huge docket of cases. To decide each of them, the judge must read what the lawyers have submitted—page after page after page of reading—and for most judges there are too few hours in the day to read all that.

Most writing read by judges has a high word-to-meaning ratio: Many words are used to express a given amount of meaning. If *your* writing has a low word-to-meaning ratio—no wasted words, every word carrying weight—your work will be more persuasive simply because for the judge it solves a problem instead of creating one. You may have spent days writing a motion memo or brief, but the judge needs to be able to read it—and *completely understand it*—in minutes. To persuade, you will spend more time writing so the judge can spend less time reading.

Think about the other problems a judge might have with your memo or brief, and solve them too so that the judge finds your writing a pleasure. For example, the font should be easy to read, and the headings should look like genuine headings (and not like part of the text). A visually inviting document is more likely to be read with care. See Appendix E on document design.

§ 27.7   Professionalism Persuades

Professionalism generates trust. Judges respect lawyers who hold themselves to high professional standards. One mark of professionalism is to produce memos and briefs that are sharply focused on the issue, carefully reasoned, thoroughly researched, precisely written, and diligently proofread, with careful attention to details.

---

[4] Roger J. Miner, *Twenty-five "Dos" for Appellate Brief Writers*, 3 Scribes J. Leg. Writing 19, 24 (1992).

Writing a Motion Memorandum

28

§ 28.1 Persuasive Writing in Trial Courts

A *motion* is a formal request, usually in writing, asking the court to issue an *order*. A lawyer who wants the court to issue an order favorable for her client *files a motion* or *moves* for an order.[1] Whenever a court makes a decision, it takes action by issuing a written order.

An order usually requires one of the parties to do something. Some orders, called *injunctions*, might prohibit a party from doing something. Many court orders take the form of *final judgments* that conclude the litigation. As a general rule, only final judgments may be appealed.

Most motions are filed in trial courts, but occasionally a lawyer files a motion in an appellate court. Often motions are filed before trial (*pretrial motions*), asking the court to make a decision on some or all of the disputed issues or to admit or exclude certain kinds of evidence. Other motions are filed after the trial concludes (*post-trial motions*). Still others are filed while a trial is ongoing, such as a motion asking the court to give a particular instruction to the jury or to declare a mistrial.

If you file a pretrial motion for summary judgment, for example, you are asking the court to grant summary judgment in your client's favor without going to trial. With your motion, you will submit a supporting memorandum arguing why the court should grant summary judgment to your client. The title of the document might be "Memorandum in Support of Motion for Summary Judgment." When you file your motion

---

[1] A lawyer does not "motion for an order." Lawyers, like everybody else, "motion" by making physical gestures, such as waving or pointing at something. And a lawyer does not "move the court for an order." In that phrase and others like it, "the court" is understood and need not be stated.

and memorandum, court rules require you to file an identical copy with your adversary's lawyer, who will most likely file a response with the court (and send a copy to you) titled "Memorandum in Opposition to Motion for Summary Judgment." In that document, your opponent will argue that the action you want the court to take should not be granted.

Similar documents submitted to the trial court might be called *trial memoranda* or sometimes *trial briefs*. They all refer to the same thing—a written request for the court to act (or not act), supported by an argument explaining why (or why not).

Once your adversary has time to file a response in opposition to your motion, the trial court will read both sides' memoranda and decide whether to grant or deny your motion. Some courts give lawyers an opportunity to orally argue the motion before they make a decision, but many do not, especially federal courts. You cannot count on your oral argument to persuade the judge to rule for your client on a motion. The court will most likely make a decision based solely or primarily on your written arguments in the motion memo.

The judge (and the judge's law clerk) may look at a motion memo more than once. The judge may read some of it in preparation for a hearing or oral argument on the motion (if time allows), a second time just before deciding the motion, and a third time while writing the court's order or opinion. You cannot assume that a motion memo will be read from front to back, or even at one sitting.

And you cannot assume that a long motion memo will be read in its entirety. Most trial judges are overwhelmed by their workload and have very little time—perhaps fifteen minutes or less—to read your motion and supporting memo. If you do not make your point quickly and persuasively, you risk losing your audience.

§ 28.2   Motion Memorandum Format

The format of a motion memo is often more flexible than the format for an office memo or appellate brief. Few court rules govern the content of motion memos, and customs among lawyers differ from one jurisdiction to another. A typical motion memo might include these parts:

1. a heading identifying the court
2. a case caption, case or docket number, and document title
3. a Preliminary Statement, sometimes called an Introduction
4. a Statement of Facts, sometimes called a Statement of the Case
5. an Argument, divided by headings
6. a Conclusion
7. a closing and signature block
8. a Certificate of Service

For an example of one typical format, see the motion memo in Appendix C. You might want to put a sticky note or a bookmark there now to help you easily move back and forth in the book while reading this chapter. Appendix C illustrates much of what this chapter explains.

Heading. The full name of the court that will decide the motion appears at the top center of the first page, usually in all-caps or bold type.

Caption. The case caption identifies the parties to the case by name, including their procedural designations (plaintiff, defendant, etc.). In a criminal case, the prosecution is called *State*, *Commonwealth*, *People*, or *United States*, depending on the jurisdiction, and no procedural designation follows any of those terms in the caption. (The prosecution is not a *plaintiff*.) In a civil case, place a comma after the name of the first party and again after that party's designation (usually *Plaintiff*). In both criminal and civil cases, add a comma after the second party's name, and place a period after that party's designation (usually *Defendant*).

Case Number. On the right half of the page, directly across from the case caption, the trial court's *case number* or *docket number* appears. This number is assigned to each case by the clerk of court when the complaint is filed, initiating the litigation. Accuracy is essential because the clerk relies on this number to properly file your motion with the rest of the documents in the case. Copy the number exactly as it appears on previous documents filed in the same case.

Document Title. The document title identifies the type of motion or memorandum and its purpose. For example, a motion memo supporting a motion to dismiss a complaint might be titled "Memorandum in Support of Defendant's Motion to Dismiss."

Generally, the title of the document appears just below the caption, centered on the page, as shown in Appendix C. Some courts prefer the title of the document to appear just below the case number directly to the right of the case caption. Consult local court rules and follow the preference of the court that will decide the motion.

Preliminary Statement. The purpose of the Preliminary Statement is to tell the judge why the matter has come before the court and to identify the type of decision to be made. Sometimes known as the Introduction, the Preliminary Statement briefly sets out the case's procedural posture; identifies the parties (by name and relationship, to the extent necessary); explains the nature of the litigation; and describes the motion before the court and the relief it seeks. If it can be done concisely, the Preliminary Statement might also summarize the parties' contentions, emphasizing the writer's theory supporting the motion. The whole Preliminary Statement might be shorter than a half page.

For example, a Preliminary Statement might begin this way:

> This motion seeks an order preliminarily enjoining the defendant from marketing its Thimble Camera, which fits over the end of the photographer's finger. The defendant's product infringes nineteen separate patents held by the plaintiff. This memorandum explains how the plaintiff will prove its patent infringement claims and why the defendant has no defense to them.

The next few sentences will identify each of the parties by name and supply other details to help the court understand why a decision is needed at this stage of the case. It might seem illogical to summarize the reason for filing the motion before introducing the parties, but the judge will want to know the reason for the motion before reading the rest of the details. The two sentences in the example above will quickly get a judge's attention.

Statement of Facts. The Statement of Facts corresponds to the Facts in an office memo, but there are differences in substance and in drafting technique. Often a motion brings the case before the trial judge for the first time, so a concise summary of the facts is essential. Chapters 29 through 31 explain how to write a Statement of Facts in a trial or appellate brief. In a motion memo, include only the facts that are relevant to your theory supporting the action you want the court to take. Do not make legal arguments in the Statement of Facts, and do not include references or citations to the law.

Argument. The Argument corresponds to the Discussion in an office memorandum, but once again the goal is to *persuade* the reader as well as to clearly explain the law and show how it applies to the facts. The Argument is the largest section of your motion memo because it presents your legal analysis, supported by citations to legal authority. It is divided up by point headings and subheadings. Chapters 32 through 34 explain how to write an Argument in a motion memo or appellate brief.

Conclusion. In a motion memo, the Conclusion reminds the judge what you want the court to do, together with a quick summary of your supporting legal theory. The Conclusion does not include citations to legal authority and should not be longer than one reasonably sized paragraph.

A Conclusion will not persuade if it is cut to the bone. Compare the following examples:

Example A

CONCLUSION

> For all these reasons, this Court should preliminarily enjoin the defendant from marketing its Thimble Camera.

Example B

CONCLUSION

In the three weeks Thimble Cameras have been on the market, the defendant has sold 170,000 of them. Each one infringes nineteen patents held by the plaintiff, nearly ruining sales of the plaintiff's cameras. To preserve the status quo and prevent irreparable harm that would drive the plaintiff out of business, this Court should issue a preliminary injunction barring the defendant from selling its Thimble Cameras pending the outcome of trial.

The second example does a much better job by concisely reminding the court not only what specific action the motion requests (a preliminary injunction) but also why the court should grant it (to prevent irreparable harm to the plaintiff's business pending trial).

Closing and signature. Following the Conclusion, add the closing phrase "Respectfully submitted," followed by your signature, typed name, mailing address, phone number, and email address. Some courts also require your bar license number to show you are licensed to practice law in that jurisdiction. The closing, signature, and signature block are *left*-justified, but they appear on the *right* side of the page, just below the Conclusion.

Court rules uniformly require attorneys to sign motion memos and other documents filed with the court.[2] Your signature certifies that you have carried out your professional responsibility to assure the court that the legal arguments are well-supported by existing law (or a good-faith argument for changing or developing the law), and that the facts asserted have evidentiary support.[3] A court clerk will refuse to accept an unsigned document.

Certificate of Service. When you file a brief or other document with a court, court rules require you to simultaneously serve an identical copy on the lawyer for the opposing party, either in person or by mail. Your professional duty is to share with your adversary any communication you give the court, whether written or oral.[4] In turn, your adversary will do the same, in fairness to both parties.

The Certificate of Service concisely demonstrates how and when you have served the motion or brief on the other parties. It must include the title of the document, the name and address of each lawyer who has been served, together with the exact date and method of service. Most courts provide a standard format to use for the Certificate

---

[2] *E.g.*, Fed. R. Civ. P. 11(a).
[3] Fed. R. Civ. P. 11(b)(2), (3).
[4] *See* Model Rules of Prof'l Conduct R. 3.5(b) (2013) (generally prohibiting *ex parte* communications with the court).

of Service, which must be signed by the person who certifies to the accuracy of its representations. Courts will not accept a motion memo or brief for filing without a properly completed and signed Certificate of Service.

While motion memos (as well as appellate briefs) always require Certificates of Service in practice, your legal writing teacher might or might not require you to include one with your assigned brief. Follow your teacher's preference.

§ 28.3   Writing the Memorandum

Lawyers differ regarding the sequence they follow for drafting parts of a motion memo. Most lawyers modify the order somewhat from document to document because a practice that works well in one instance might not work well in another.

Many lawyers start with the Statement of Facts. Telling a story in a persuasive way can be a productive beginning to help the writer develop the Argument. Other lawyers write the Argument first because that helps them better understand which facts to include. Some lawyers write the Argument and Statement of the Facts simultaneously. Still others outline the Statement of the Facts while writing the Argument.

Sometimes the Argument takes shape more easily by drafting the point headings and subheadings first, serving as a rough outline. Or a lawyer may begin by writing a rough draft of the Argument, waiting to see how it flows before crafting persuasive point headings and subheadings. The Conclusion is usually done last because it summarizes the key points in your legal argument.

There is no one "right" place to start writing, and it helps to remain flexible. Write the parts of the motion memo in whatever order works best for you. But save time to rewrite the motion memo so all of the parts form a cohesive whole before submitting it to the court.

§ 28.4   Handling the Procedural Posture

Because most of your law school courses focus on the substantive law of Torts, Contracts, Property, and Criminal Law, you might view legal issues primarily from the standpoint of whether your client will win or lose on the merits of the case. But judges consider legal issues in terms of their *procedural posture*—the procedural step, usually a motion, that places an issue before the court.

Each type of motion is governed by procedural rules that dictate how the motion is to be decided. If you move for summary judgment, for example, your motion will be granted only if you satisfy the legal test for summary judgment. The elements of the test for summary judgment are (1) whether the case raises a genuine dispute regarding a fact that is material to the outcome, and (2) whether the plaintiff is entitled to judgment as a matter of law.[5] Your arguments in your motion memo should be designed to satisfy that legal test. The procedural posture also determines how you discuss the facts.

§ 28.4.1 Types of Trial Motions

Trial motions fall into four categories:

1. motions that challenge the quality of allegations in an adversary's pleading;
2. motions that otherwise challenge how the litigation began;
3. motions that challenge the quality and sufficiency of a party's evidence; and
4. case management motions.

Motions that challenge the quality of a party's allegations. Before answering a plaintiff's complaint in a civil action, a defendant can file a motion to dismiss it for failing to state a claim on which the court can grant relief. You might have studied this procedural step already in Civil Procedure.[6] Because this kind of motion tests only the sufficiency of the complaint's allegations (and no evidence has yet been offered to prove them), the "facts" for purposes of this kind of motion are limited to those allegations. The motion is filed so early in the case that no one yet knows which (if any) of those alleged facts will be disputed by the defendant or proved by the plaintiff.

So in this kind of motion, the question is *not* whether either party has proved the allegations, or even whether they can or will be proved eventually at trial. Instead, the court will assume, *only for purposes of deciding the motion*, that the facts alleged in the complaint can be proved at trial. The court will then decide whether those facts, *even if true*, would support a claim for relief recognized by the law. If not, the court will dismiss the complaint, bringing the case to an early end, unless the plaintiff files an amended complaint with different alleged facts that, if true, will support a claim for relief.

Because no evidence has yet been submitted at this early stage of the case, lawyers do not describe the "facts" alleged in the pleadings as events that *actually happened*. Until a court receives evidence later, it has no idea whether the alleged "facts" truly happened. The lawyers arguing the motion describe the "facts" purely as *allegations*:

> Although the plaintiff has alleged that the defendant struck him from behind with a stick, he has not alleged that the defendant intended to cause him injury.

---

[5] Fed. R. Civ. P. 56.
[6] *See* Fed. R. Civ. P. 12(b)(6).

In this kind of motion, it would be wrong to write the following:

> Although the defendant <u>struck</u> the plaintiff from behind with a stick, the defendant <u>did not intend</u> to cause him injury.

The judge or jury will find out much later—after evidence has been produced—whether the defendant *in fact* struck the plaintiff or *in fact* intended to cause injury.

Motions that otherwise challenge how the litigation began. A defendant might move to dismiss the plaintiff's complaint for other reasons than failure to state a claim: for example, that the court lacks subject matter jurisdiction, or that it lacks personal jurisdiction over the defendant, or that venue is improper, or that the summons did not include all the information required, or that it was improperly served, or that somebody who should have been made a party has not been. As you may have learned already in Civil Procedure, any of these reasons can be enough to support a defendant's pretrial motion to dismiss.[7]

Arguments for or against these motions need not be limited to the contents of the complaint. For example, if the defendant asserts that the summons was improperly served, the court might hold a hearing on the motion so the process server and the defendant can each testify about how the summons was delivered.

Motions that challenge the quality and sufficiency of a party's evidence. These include:

- pretrial motions for summary judgment;[8]
- trial motions for judgment as a matter of law, or for a directed verdict (in a jury trial);[9] and
- post-trial motions for judgment as a matter of law, or for judgment notwithstanding the verdict (in a jury trial).[10]

All of these motions require the court to decide whether a party has carried its *burden of production* at that procedural stage, which is not the same as the burden of proof. A party who has the burden of producing evidence must produce enough to create a *genuine* dispute (not a manufactured one) about a legally relevant fact—a factual issue to be resolved by the jury or the judge in deciding the case.

Each of these motions is decided according to the same logic. The motion should be granted if (1) there is no genuine issue of material fact because the party with the

---

[7] *See* FED. R. CIV. P. 12(b).
[8] *See* FED. R. CIV. P. 56.
[9] FED. R. CIV. P. 50(a).
[10] FED. R. CIV. P. 50(b).

burden of production at that stage of the case has failed to carry it, *and* (2) the moving party is entitled to a favorable judgment under the applicable law. The first element of the test considers how much evidence has been offered on the fact question and whether the fact is relevant to the legal issue. The second element of the test applies the substantive law to the case. For example, if you represent the defendant and file a pretrial motion for summary judgment in a negligence case, the second part of the summary judgment test asks whether the plaintiff has failed to produce evidence to support any element of her negligence claim.

Case management motions. These motions help move the case along toward trial. Examples are motions for preliminary injunctions, discovery motions, motions in limine to limit the evidence admissible at trial, and suppression motions in criminal cases. Motions can be filed by either party to simplify the issues for trial or to govern the trial process. For example, if two co-defendants are prosecuted for bank robbery, the one who allegedly drove the getaway car may file a motion for a separate trial.

§ 28.4.2 Researching the Law Governing the Procedural Posture

First, identify the procedural posture. What kind of motion has been filed? What has the court been asked to do?

Next, find the *procedural* law that tells the court *how* to decide the motion. You are looking for—

- the test for granting the motion, such as:

Summary judgment is appropriate if there is no genuine issue of material fact and if the moving party is entitled to judgment as a matter of law.

- procedural rules on how to evaluate the record when deciding the motion, such as:

In deciding a motion for summary judgment, the court views the evidence in the light most favorable to the party opposing the motion.

You might find what you are looking for in court rules or statutes. Often, both the test and the procedural rules for deciding the motion are explained in court opinions deciding that kind of motion, just after the fact summary and before the legal analysis begins. This is typical of what you might find:

Summary judgment is appropriate "if the pleadings, depositions, answers to interrogatories, and admissions on file, together with the affidavits, if any, show that there is no genuine issue as to any material fact and that the moving party is entitled to judgment as a matter of law." Fed. R. Civ. P. 56(c); *see also Celotex Corp. v. Catrett*, 477 U.S. 317, 322-23 (1986). "The moving party bears the initial burden of showing the absence of a genuine issue of material fact." *Plant v. Morton Int'l, Inc.*, 212 F.3d 929, 934 (6th Cir. 2000). Once the movant has satisfied its burden, the nonmoving party must produce evidence showing that a genuine issue remains. *Id.*[11]

This paragraph is quoted from a federal court of appeals case. Because of the hierarchy of authority (Chapter 8), the court first cites the mandatory primary authority for the test (Rule 56(c)). But the Supreme Court case cited next provides the ultimate judicial interpretation of that test (*Celotex*). In your motion, cite the legal authorities that will best help the court identify and explain the test that it will apply in its written opinion deciding the motion.

§ 28.4.3 Writing Within the Procedural Posture

Because the procedural posture and the rules governing it control the way the judge will make the decision, your motion must show the judge how to decide it within those procedural rules. How can you do that in writing?

First, remember that in deciding a motion, the core rule is *not* the rule of substantive law that provides your client with rights, obligations, or remedies. The core rule is the one defining the procedural test for that particular kind of motion.

But several procedural tests for motions include one element that incorporates the substantive legal standard for the case as a whole. For example, in the summary judgment test quoted in § 28.4.2, the second element requires the moving party (usually the defendant) to demonstrate that it is entitled to *judgment as a matter of law*. Similarly, the test that applies to a motion for preliminary injunction has an element requiring the moving party to demonstrate that it is likely to *succeed on the merits* of the case at trial. In these motions, the court makes a procedural decision on the motion, but one element of that test for deciding the motion requires the court to consider the underlying substantive law.

Second, using CREAC, organize the Argument section of your motion memo based on the procedural test that applies to that particular motion. If the overall procedural test incorporates the substantive law, begin by organizing one CREAC structure for the procedural test, and then organize the substantive element of the test as a sub-rule. (See Chapter 19.)

Finally, do not go overboard in citing legal authority for the procedural test. Most judges know the procedural tests by heart because they routinely decide these kinds of motions. While you must identify the controlling procedural test and cite the

---

[11] *In re Rodriguez*, 487 F.3d 1001, 1007 (6th Cir. 2007).

mandatory law that governs, a conclusory explanation is usually sufficient. The court will expect you to write a paragraph or two that the judge can use, with only minor edits, in its opinion deciding the motion in your client's favor.

Exercise 28-A. Writing Parts of a Motion Memorandum

Part 1. Write a Preliminary Statement for a pretrial motion memorandum asking the court to grant summary judgment for your client, who is the manager of a retail store that sells e-cigarettes, pipes, and tobacco products. Your client has been sued by a customer for false imprisonment after the customer was caught shoplifting an e-cig starter kit from a store display. Your client has presented deposition transcripts and other documentary evidence to support each element of the shopkeepers' privilege (see § 3.1).

Part 2. Write a persuasive Conclusion and the Closing for the motion memo you began in Part 1. Include your signature and signature block.

Part 8

Telling the Client's Story

The Statement of the Case in a Motion Memo or Appellate Brief

§ 29.1 How a Statement of the Case Persuades

> It may sound paradoxical, but most contentions of law are won or lost on the facts.
>
> —*Justice Robert H. Jackson*

In a persuasive memorandum or brief, the judge learns about the facts in the Statement of the Case (also called a Statement of Facts or just Facts). In the Statement, you must include every fact that you mention elsewhere in your memo or brief. You must also include in the Statement all facts on which your adversary relies. This is the one place in the document where all the legally significant facts can be seen together in the context of your client's story. And you lose credibility if you omit unfavorable facts.

In the Statement, do not argue, analyze law, draw factual inferences, or even characterize the facts. It is called a *Statement* of the Case because the facts are *stated* there and analyzed elsewhere. Inferences and characterizations of facts belong in the Argument. But you may report the inferences witnesses drew and the characterizations they made while testifying.

If you cannot argue in a Statement of the Case, how can you persuade there? Persuade by *telling the story in a way that emphasizes facts that support your theory, while saying nothing that the adversary could reasonably claim to be inaccurate*.

Consider the two examples below. Assume that the plaintiffs are suing a backcountry hiking guide for negligence after the guide led them into disaster. (Citations to the record have been deleted.)

Version A

On July 2, the plaintiffs asked in Stove Pipe Springs whether a back-country guide might be available to lead them through certain parts of Death Valley. After some discussion, they hired the defendant to take them on a full-day hike.

When they started out the next day, the defendant carried a compass and map. Each plaintiff carried sunglasses, a large-brim hat, and a quart of water.

A climatologist testified about the climate in Death Valley. Occasionally, winter temperatures fall below freezing, but there is no water to freeze. Spring and fall temperatures approximate summer temperatures elsewhere. July is the hottest month, with an average high of about 116° and an average low of about 87°. The highest temperature ever recorded in Death Valley was 134°. Average annual rainfall is about 1½ inches, and precipitation falls on only eight days in an average year.

Version B

The climate in Death Valley is one of the hottest and driest known. The highest temperature recorded each summer reaches at least 120° and in many years at least 125°. The highest temperature recorded in Death Valley—134°—is also the highest recorded anywhere on earth.[1] Rainfall is only 1½ inches per year, the lowest in the Western Hemisphere, and in a few years no rain falls at all.

In the summer sun in Death Valley, a person can lose, on average, about four gallons of perspiration per day. After losing about two gallons, that person can become delirious and die of dehydration if the lost water is not quickly replaced.

The defendant advertised that he was a professional and experienced backcountry guide. Relying on the advertisement, the plaintiffs hired him. He then took them into Death Valley for a full-day hike in July with one quart of water each.

After reading Version B, you can believe that this hike was madness and that the guide was responsible for it. But in early drafts, many beginners instinctively produce a Statement more like Version A, which tells the story but not in a compelling way. How does Version B persuade?

First, in Version B the writer selected the few facts that would illustrate the theory: You can lose four gallons of water a day in such a place. After losing two gallons, you can become delirious, and if the water is not replaced, your life will be in danger. This was a full-day hike. The plaintiffs had a quart of water each. The defendant claimed to be a professional and experienced guide. As each of these facts is added to the story, the logic of the theory unfolds.

Second, Version B is free of factual clutter—marginal facts, such as temperatures in other months, that obscure critical information. It focuses instead on the facts crucial to the persuasive story.

---

[1] *See supra* Chapter 21, n.1.

Finally, Version B provides the kind of vivid details that make a theory come alive—the delirium, for example.

But Version B appears to be nothing more than a description of the relevant facts. An adversary cannot reasonably challenge anything in it as untrue. Each fact is objectively verifiable in the record. And—most importantly—the writer never expressed any inferences from the evidence. *You drew all the inferences yourself.*

Sometimes a reader can think, "I can't tell whether this Statement was written by the plaintiff's lawyer or by the defendant's." That confusion is the surest sign that the Statement fails to persuade. Is it true of either of the Death Valley excerpts? If so, which one?

§ 29.2   The Record

The record might include any or all of the following:

- the pleadings
- evidence in the form of testimony, affidavits, and exhibits
- prior court orders, judicial opinions in the same case, and the judgment below in an appeal

A Statement of the Case can describe *only* the facts that are in the record. Other facts must be ignored, a process called *limiting the Statement to the record*. But you can point to the *absence* from the record of a particular allegation or piece of evidence—for example, "no witness identified the defendant"—if the absence shows that the opposing party has failed to satisfy a relevant legal test or burden of production.

In the Statement, describe the facts in terms of the type of record where they can be found. If the record includes testimony, explain how the witnesses testified. But if the "facts" are allegations in a pleading,[2] do not describe those allegations as events that actually happened. Section 28.4.1 explains how to describe this kind of record and why.

For every fact you mention, courts require you to cite a specific page or paragraph in the record—not only when you recite the fact in the Statement of the Case, but also when you analyze it in the Argument.[3] This provides an easy method for the court to check the accuracy of what you say. Court rules aside, cites to the record have a persuasive effect of their own. Careful cites give the reader confidence that every fact on which you rely is fully supported in the record. Spotty or missing cites arouse a court's skepticism. Both the *ALWD Guide to Legal Citation* and the *Bluebook* explain

---

[2] Allegations are most often at issue when the pleading is challenged in a motion to dismiss for failure to state a claim. *See* FED. R. CIV. P. 12(b)(6).

[3] *See, e.g.,* FED. R. APP. P. 28(a)(6), (c).

how to cite to the record. In the *ALWD Guide*, see Rule 25. In the *Bluebook*, look in the index for "record" or "records."

§ 29.3   Fact Ethics

It is unethical for a lawyer to "knowingly . . . make a false statement of fact . . . to a tribunal."[4] Even if it were not unethical, misrepresenting the facts never fools a court and hurts only the misrepresenting lawyer and that lawyer's client. Misrepresentations are quickly spotted by opposing lawyers, and once a misrepresentation is pointed out to a court, the entire motion memo or brief will be treated with deep suspicion. And afterward the court will mistrust the misrepresenting lawyer. You and your clients cannot afford to lose a court's trust.

---

[4] MODEL RULES OF PROF'L CONDUCT R. 3.3(a)(1) (2013).

30 Developing a Persuasive Story

> When I was an attorney . . . , I realized after much trial
> and error that in a courtroom whoever tells the best story wins.
>
> —*John Quincy Adams (fictionally) in the movie* Amistad

§ 30.1 The Power of Stories

Robert McKee[1] has taught many of the best screenwriters in Hollywood how to write stories. So many screenwriters are in his debt that he was actually portrayed in that role in the movie *Adaptation*. Nicholas Cage plays a screenwriter who consults McKee about writer's block.

McKee also teaches business people how to persuade by telling stories. In a typical business situation, a young start-up company has developed a valuable idea, such as a drug that will prevent heart attacks, and the company needs investment bankers to lend money or buy stock so the company can finish the job and put the drug on the market. This situation resembles the one lawyers face when asking a court for relief: A person who wants something (a lawyer or a company's executives) tries to persuade a decision maker (a judge or an investment banker) who has very rational criteria for making the decision (legal rules or the math that would predict whether an investment will make a profit).

If the company's chief executive officer meets with the investment bankers and makes only a logical presentation with Powerpoint slides, based on statistics and sales projections, the "bankers would nod politely and stifle yawns while thinking of all the

---

[1] The quotes from McKee and the material about him are from Bronwyn Fryer, *Storytelling that Moves People: A Conversation with Screenwriting Coach Robert McKee*, HARV. BUS. REV., June 2003, at 51.

271

other companies better positioned" to bring this drug to market. But suppose the CEO tells a compelling story about how the company overcame obstacles to develop the drug, get it patented, and get regulatory approval, and now must overcome one final hurdle—financing—to bring the drug to market. That causes "great suspense" and the possibility that "the story might not have a happy ending. The CEO has the bankers on the edges of their seats, and he says 'We won the race, we got the patent, we're poised to go public and save a quarter-million lives a year.' And the bankers just throw money at him."

Why? Nothing should be more rational than finance. If the numbers on the spreadsheets and Powerpoint slides show that this project will produce a profit without too much risk, the bankers should invest in it. But they will not invest unless they have been captured by the story. If you challenge McKee on this, he will say, "I know the storytelling method works, because after I consulted with a dozen corporations whose principals told exciting stories to Wall Street, they all got their money."

§ 30.2   How Stories Persuade

In a law school classroom, making the best logical argument is everything. That is as it should be. Legal argumentation is difficult to master, and legal education devotes a lot of effort to teaching students how to argue.

But in the real world, when you make purely logical arguments to decision makers like judges, as McKee points out, "they are arguing with you in their heads"—because logic and argument naturally arouse skepticism—and "if you do persuade them, you've done so only on an intellectual basis. That's not good enough because people are not inspired to act by reason alone." A story, he says, persuades "by uniting an idea with an emotion."

A story also persuades by letting the reader decide—on her own—to agree with you *before* you have asked her to agree. In an argument, you start by telling the reader what you want her to believe, and then you set out the steps of logic to prove that position. With a story, you tell what happened. If you develop a good story and if you tell it well, the reader's decision *comes from her* while reading the story, and she is therefore more committed to it. She is motivated to act for two reasons. First, she saw the point before you told her what it was. (If you tell her the point during the story, it is no longer a story. It is an argument.) And second, stories move us in ways that logic cannot.

Some litigation stories can be told only to juries. Those stories have too much emotion, and if you were to tell those stories to judges, they would feel that you have insulted their sense of professionalism. A story told to a judge can succeed only by simultaneously addressing both the legal issues and the judge's basic human sense of right and wrong.

§ 30.3 Building the Story—Generally

In a Statement of the Case, the story should

1. "ignite action"—motivate by making a judge care enough to act
2. "communicate who you are"—actually, communicate who your side is by defining your client and supporting witnesses favorably
3. communicate who the other side is by unfavorably defining the opposing party or the harmful witnesses or some combination of them
4. "neutralize bad news" by explaining why facts that at first seem bad for your case should not be held against you (more about this in Chapter 31).[2]

These are the four goals in storytelling.

Most stories have a simple, three-part structure:

1. The story starts in a state of equilibrium. Things might not be wonderful, but they are at least okay.

2. Bad things happen to disrupt the equilibrium. If you represent the plaintiff or the prosecution, the disruption is whatever the defendant did wrong. If you represent the defendant, the disruption is the wrongful lawsuit or prosecution itself, which puts the defendant under stress and at risk.

3. The protagonist struggles to restore equilibrium. Unless you are the prosecutor in a criminal case, the protagonist is probably your client. Because prosecutors have no client, they often cast the crime victim as a protagonist. If you represent a plaintiff, equilibrium could be restored by a judgment awarding your client an injunction or damages. If you represent the prosecution, equilibrium could be restored by convicting and sentencing the defendant. If you represent the defendant in either kind of case, equilibrium could be restored by dismissing the lawsuit or prosecution and freeing the defendant from the unjust burden of being an involuntary litigant in fear of losing.

Next time you watch a movie, ask yourself whether the plot in the movie has this structure—equilibrium, disruption, struggle to restore equilibrium. Most do. Sometimes you will tell your client's story in exactly this sequence, and sometimes you will tell it differently.

This structure also works when the issue is not who should win in the end, but instead some smaller part of the litigation. For example, if you represent a party

---

[2] The quotes are from STEPHEN DENNING, SQUIRREL INC.: A FABLE OF LEADERSHIP THROUGH STORYTELLING 44, 47 (2004). See also Stephen Denning, *The Springboard: How Storytelling Ignites Action in Knowledge-Era Organizations* (2001).

resisting discovery before trial in a civil case, the equilibrium is your client's possessing private information that your client reasonably wants to keep secret. Disruption is the other side's demand for this information through interrogatories or a deposition. The struggle to restore equilibrium is your attempt to persuade the judge to grant a protective order that would prevent discovery of this information.

The judge is a hidden character in the third phase of the story, the struggle to restore equilibrium. Will the plaintiff win an injunction? Will the defendant win a dismissal? Will the party resisting discovery win a protective order? That is all up to the judge. If you build a good story and tell it well, the judge should *want* to restore equilibrium.

Once you have determined the inner structure of the story, the most important components are characters and imagery.

§ 30.4   Characters

Character cannot be described. You cannot say, "My client is a really nice person, extremely conscientious and responsible." Nobody will believe you. You have to imply character by reciting things your client has or has not done. You will do the same, if you can, with witnesses and with other parties.

> Take, for example, a rear-end collision that caused a lot of soft-tissue and nerve damage to the driver. At first glance, it seemed like a routine personal injury case. The at-fault driver was a business woman coming home from work who had been talking on her cell phone when the accident occurred. What really established her character was the fact that she continued talking during the accident and for another five minutes afterward [which defined her] as callous.[3]

§ 30.5   Imagery

If you want to win a case, paint the Judge a picture *and keep it simple.*
                                                                —*John W. Davis*

Imagery has a powerful effect in stories.

A truck runs off the highway, through a farmer's fence, and into the farmer's cow. The truck driver's insurance company wants to pay as little as possible for this cow, and the farmer, of course, wants more.

---

[3] Joel ben Izzy, *Character Development*, L.A. DAILY J., Oct. 26, 1999, at 8.

The insurance company's lawyer will tell a story in which the cow is "a unit of livestock" or "a farm asset," as though the issue is how much money the farmer should get to replace a machine-like object that consumes grass as fuel to produce milk and an occasional calf. This story will focus on numbers from the farmer's books that show the productivity of this object, its acquisition costs, depreciation, useful life remaining at the time of its destruction, etc. The insurance company's lawyer will use this story because the numbers show the cow to be an unexceptional object.

The farmer's lawyer looks for a different story to tell. "Tell me about the cow," she asks the farmer. "That wasn't just any cow," replies the farmer.

> That was Bessie! She was the only Guernsey cow left in this county. She didn't give that thin milk you get out of a Holstein that people buy in the grocery store. She gave the thickest, most flavorful milk you ever tasted. We didn't sell it to the dairy. They wouldn't pay a decent price for it anyway because dairies care about quantity, not quality. We drank it ourselves and made the best butter and cheese out of it. And Guernseys are smaller cows. They're friendly, like pets, and Bessie was part of our family.

Imagery you can "see" in your mind creates the persuasive weight of each of these stories. The farmer's lawyer wants us to see a big pair of eyes in a Guernsey head nudging the farmer with affection—a loss to the farmer's family that exceeds the loss of a grass-to-milk machine. The insurance company's lawyer, on the other hand, wants us to see the farmer's balance sheet, where a certain item of livestock is carried as an asset valued at a certain number of dollars.

If you develop an eye for revealing detail, your stories will much more quickly come to life as vivid and compelling. Vividness not only helps the reader remember the story, but it makes the story more believable. Imagery makes a story real.

Word choice is critical. The right words help the judge see the image.

§ 30.6 Finding the Story

Facts are not the story. They are the raw materials for the story.

A client sits in your office, describing in detail a problem that the client wants you to solve. The facts are these details. The client is not telling you a persuasive story. Clients usually do not know how to do that. They hire lawyers to do it for them. The client can tell you only facts—"I got this letter in the mail," "Smith told me the company was going bankrupt," "I can't pay my bills." In a law school writing assignment, you might get these details as part of your assignment.

Regardless of how you get the facts, they are not yet a story. The story is *hidden* in the facts. You have to find it there. Look for the equilibrium, the disruption, and the struggle to restore equilibrium. Look for details that reveal character. Look for details that lend themselves to persuasive imagery. Assemble these into a story that fulfills the four purposes of storytelling—to motivate the judge to act, to communicate who your client and witnesses are, to communicate who the other side and its witnesses are, and to neutralize the unfavorable facts.

Try telling the story to a friend or relative whose intelligence and judgment you respect and who does not know the case you are working on. Telling the story orally helps you refine it and test it out before you start writing it. *Saying* it helps you understand it and how to improve it. Then ask how your friend or relative feels about the story. Does it motivate? Do the characters seem realistic? And so on.

§ 30.7   Two Last Questions

You have discovered the story. Now step back and ask yourself two questions.

First, can you summarize the essence of it *persuasively* in one or two sentences? If you can do that, those sentences are your theme (see § 27.1). If not, either the story is too complicated or you have not identified the core facts. If the story is too complicated, your reader will get lost. If you do not know the core facts, you will not be able to focus on them when you tell the story. You will need to focus on them at the very beginning of the Statement of the Case. The Statement of the Case should begin with a paragraph that summarizes these very facts (see Chapter 31).

Second, will the judge care? If not, the story will not work because it fails to motivate.

31 Telling the Story Persuasively

§ 31.1 Selecting Facts to Tell the Story

Selecting the facts is a four-step process.

Step 1: Identify the facts that show how the relevant legal tests have or have not been satisfied. Make a list of the facts that show either how you have satisfied the governing legal tests or how your adversary has not. Some lawyers do this by making an elements-facts-witness/evidence chart. For example, you might make the chart on the next page if you represent the plaintiff and must show that you have satisfied the test for negligence concerning an auto accident witnessed by two pedestrians, Smith and Jones, both of whom corroborate the plaintiff's story (π = plaintiff; Δ = defendant).

The chart helps you see what the dispute is all about. The elements of duty, injury, and proximate causation are easily satisfied. The real issue is breach. Three witnesses say the defendant ran the stop sign, and one says the defendant did not. The chart helps you realize that your factual theory should be that the two disinterested witnesses (Smith and Jones), as well as the plaintiff, testified that the defendant ran the stop sign, and that only the defendant testified that he stopped before entering the intersection. Why is that a good theory? The plaintiff and defendant testified consistently with their own interests. But Smith and Jones are credible because they are disinterested.

Elements, Facts, Witnesses/Evidence Chart			
Elements	Satisfied?	Facts	Witnesses/Evidence
1. duty owed by Δ to π	yes	π driving on street that has no stoplight or stop sign—Δ driving on cross street with stop sign	testimony of π, Δ, Smith, and Jones
2. Δ's breach of that duty	probably yes	Δ drove through stop sign without stopping	testimony of π, Smith, and Jones—contradicted only by Δ
3. injury to π	yes	π's medical injuries and damage to π's car	testimony of π, doctor, paramedic, mechanic, Smith, and Jones; x-rays and photos
4. proximately caused by Δ's breach	yes (if Δ breached)	the front of Δ's car hit the side of π's car	testimony of police officer, mechanic, π, Smith, and Jones; photos of damaged cars

When you write the Statement of the Case, include everything in the Facts column together with the supporting proof from the Witnesses/Evidence column. For example, find the duty element in the chart. Look at the facts that satisfy that element and the witnesses who testified to those facts. Now you know what to say in the Statement of the Case concerning that element:

> All the witnesses, including the defendant, testified that the intersection did not have a traffic light; that the plaintiff entered the intersection from the north on State Street, where there was no stop sign; and that the defendant entered from the east on Maple Lane, where a stop sign required him to stop.

In the Statement, you will *not* mention the duty element or say it was satisfied. That is legal analysis, which you will do in the Argument. In the Statement, you will only mention the substantiating facts and whatever proved them.

The defendant's lawyer might make her own version of this chart to identify the facts and proof she will need to mention in the Statement.

If several tests are involved, you might make a chart for each test. For example, suppose the defendant in the auto accident case has pleaded the affirmative defense of comparative negligence. Now two tests are in the case. The plaintiff must prove that the defendant was negligent. And the defendant must prove that the plaintiff was comparatively negligent. The facts relevant to each test can be identified by making a chart for that test.

Step 2: Identify additional facts that help tell your client's story persuasively. Include facts that accomplish the storytelling goals explained in § 30.3, such as facts that communicate who your client and witnesses are, as well as similar facts about the other side. Who is an innocent victim, who is predatory, who is careless, and so forth? Only by understanding what each fact *reveals* about people and events can you tell the client's story in a compelling way. Also include facts that a reader would need to understand the story, facts that hold the story together.

Step 3: Identify facts that hurt your case and facts on which your adversary will rely. If you do not include unfavorable facts, your Statement of the Case will lack credibility. Treat an unfavorable fact as an opportunity rather than a threat. If you include the unfavorable fact, you can try to neutralize it. The next section in this chapter explains how (see question 6 there). If you do not include the unfavorable fact in your Statement, you cannot neutralize it—and it really will be a threat.

Step 4: Eliminate factual clutter. Too much information distracts from the story. Identify a witness by name only if the reader really needs to know. In the example above, the names of Smith and Jones are needed because they testify to so many different things, and because their testimony is crucial to the disputed element. But the doctor, paramedic, mechanic, and police officer can each be identified by their role instead ("the emergency room doctor who treated the plaintiff testified that . . .").

Specify dates, times, and places only if they are essential to the story or your theory. Specifics about them can be seductively concrete while you are writing. But to a reader they can also obscure what really happened. It is not necessary to say that the witnesses agree that the accident occurred at 1:25 p.m., that an ambulance arrived at 1:40, that at 1:53 the ambulance delivered the plaintiff to the emergency room at Highview Memorial Hospital, or that at 1:55 a doctor there began to treat the plaintiff. Just say, "Thirty minutes after the accident, the plaintiff was treated by a hospital emergency room physician." Unless the hospital is being sued or its identity is otherwise significant, naming it gets in the way of telling the story. The exact times also get in the way.

§ 31.2 How to Test a Statement of the Case for Persuasiveness

While rewriting, ask yourself the following questions.

1. Have you correctly decided which facts to include in the Statement? See the first section of this chapter.

2. Have you chosen a method of organization that tells the story persuasively? Set out the facts in a sequence that persuades and can easily be understood. Sometimes the most effective sequence is chronological. But more often, a topical organization works better because you can use the way you organize the facts to imply the logical relationships between them. In some cases, you might try a topical organization that breaks into a chronological narrative where it is important for the reader to understand the sequence in which events happened. If the Statement is long, you can add headings to break it up and to show how you have organized it.

3. Have you started with a punch? Begin the Statement with a short passage—one or two paragraphs—summarizing your most compelling facts and perhaps neutralizing the most unfavorable facts so that the judge understands the heart of your theory. This functions as an introduction to the story, although you might not call it that. For example:

> The defendant drove through a stop sign and into the plaintiff's car, putting him in the hospital for a week and disabling him from working for seven months. Every witness except the defendant testified that he entered the intersection without stopping. Although the plaintiff was driving an uninsured car with an expired registration, there was no evidence that these infractions caused the accident or contributed to the plaintiff's injuries.

Then, in the rest of the Statement, tell the story—describing in detail the facts you summarized at the beginning.

The opening passage is the most important part of the Statement. If written well, it puts the judge in a receptive frame of mind, tells the judge what facts to look for later, and creates a lasting impression. The opening passage is also one of the hardest parts of the Statement to write. But the extra time and effort are worth it. Never begin the Statement with neutral facts or unimportant facts. You can include the most unfavorable facts to neutralize them (as in the last sentence of the example above), but the introductory paragraphs are not always the best place to do this.

4. Have you reflected your theory throughout the Statement? Tightly focus the Statement on facts that advance your theory. If the Statement wanders aimlessly through the facts, the reader will not grasp your theory and may not even understand the story. Throughout the Statement, the reader should be aware of whom you represent from the way you tell the story. If the reader wonders about that, even for a paragraph or two, your Statement probably is unpersuasive. Every word should be selected to make the theory more clear. If you focus the Statement in this way, it can be surprisingly short.

5. Have you emphasized favorable facts? You can do that through organization. Readers tend to be most attentive at the beginning, least attentive in the middle, and attentive to a middling degree at the end. You can also describe the most favorable facts in detail while omitting marginal facts that would cloud the picture you want the reader to see. If a favorable fact is undisputed, you can point that out:

> Every witness, including the defendant, testified that the stop sign could easily be seen by a driver in the defendant's position. (T. at 14, 35, 62, 68, 97, 132.)

You can also point to things that are missing from the record, if that helps you:

> No evidence suggested an emergency or other situation that might have justified disregarding a stop sign.

6. Have you neutralized unfavorable facts? The most effective method is to juxtapose an unfavorable fact with one or more favorable facts that show why the unfavorable fact should not hurt you. Juxtaposition is placing two things side by side. Effective juxtapositions often use "although" or "even though" contrasts. For example:

> Although the plaintiff was driving an uninsured car with an expired registration, there was no evidence that these infractions caused the accident or contributed to the plaintiff's injuries.

An unfavorable fact cannot be neutralized by tucking it away in an obscure part of the Statement. Hiding it will not make it go away.

7. Have you humanized your client? Be careful about how you refer to the parties. You could write "the plaintiff" and "the defendant" in a civil case or, in a criminal case, "the defendant" and "the State" (or "the People," "the Government," or "the Commonwealth"). More still can be conveyed by using some generic factual designation related to the issues: "the buyer" and "the seller" in a commercial dispute or "the employer" and "the employee" in a discrimination case. All those are clear enough for a reader to understand.

But how you refer to the parties can also have a persuasive effect. Many lawyers try to humanize their clients by referring to them by name while depersonalizing the opposing party ("the insurance company" or "the university"). Sometimes that works, and sometimes it does not. If the parties are both people, for example, it can be confusing and look unfair to call one party "Ms. Falco" and the other "the defendant."

In an appellate brief, a reader will be confused if you refer to the parties continually as "appellant" and "appellee." These designations identify only who lost in the court below. In many appellate courts, you are not allowed to use these designations inside a brief, although they appear on the cover page.[1]

Exercise 31-A. Storytelling

Using a case you have read in another course, develop the facts of the case into a story. Do not change or embellish the facts. Stay strictly faithful to the *substance* of what you read in the case. But develop a story that would move a listener or reader to feel or think that one party or the other should win. Use the techniques described in this chapter and in Chapter 30. Then tell the story to another student and ask that student to suggest improvements.

Exercise 31-B. Factual Inferences

You work at the local prosecutor's office and need to determine whether to charge a defendant with a basic crime (battery) or an aggravated version of that crime (domestic battery). Domestic battery is punished more severely. A local resident, Victor Tyne, was punched in the face by A.A. Bragenkrantz, who is the boyfriend of Victor's cousin, Anna Canelli. You already know you can charge battery. Can you also charge domestic battery, which would require Bragenkrantz to be one of Tyne's "household members"?

Bragenkrantz and Canelli stayed overnight at Tyne's house every Sunday through Thursday during the summer so they could attend summer classes at the university. Bragenkrantz and Canelli slept on a fold-out futon in Tyne's spare bedroom. They each kept clothing in a drawer of a dresser in the spare bedroom. Bragenkrantz had registered for summer classes using Tyne's address as his home address in order to qualify for in-state tuition. Bragenkrantz and Canelli spent their weekends at Canelli's parents' home, about two hours' drive away. Bragenkrantz has kept most of his possessions in a storage locker since his recent divorce.

Create a diagram like the one below to determine whether Bragenkrantz is a member of Tyne's household. Put your diagram on a piece of paper, and leave space so you can add horizontal rows as you identify facts. Add facts from the paragraphs above this one if relevant inferences can be drawn from them. If a fact tends to show Bragenkrantz *was* a household member, add the inference you draw from that fact in the column on the far left. If a fact tends to show he *was not* a household member, add your inference in the column on the far right. If the fact could go either way, add inferences in both columns. (To help you get started, we have inserted a fact that could go either way.)

---

[1] *See, e.g.*, Fed. R. App. P. 28(d), 32(a)(2)(E).

Facts and Inferences				
Inference?	Fact tending to show he **was a** household member	Facts that could go **either way**	Fact tending to show he **was not** a household member	Inference?
clothes indicate a permanent connection to the household	—	clothes in the drawer	—	not many clothes—so this is probably not his household
(add additional horizontal rows as needed)				

If the clothes in the drawer tended to show *only* that Bragenkrantz was a member of the household, the inference on the left would appear in the diagram, and no inference would appear on the right. If, on the other hand, the clothes tended to show only that he was *not* a household member, the only inference would be on the right. Both inferences appear here because the clothes can be used to support each of them.

Part 9

Making the Client's Arguments

32 The Argument in a Motion Memo or Appellate Brief

§ 32.1 Arguments

Monty Python's Flying Circus was a British comedy group that created television shows and movies. In their Argument Clinic sketch, a man walks into an office and announces that he would like a good argument. A second man, sitting at a desk, contradicts everything the first man says. After several minutes of this, the first man complains that what is happening is not an argument. "Yes it is," replies the man at the desk.

"An argument isn't just contradiction," says the first man. "*An argument is a connected series of statements intended to establish a proposition.*"

"No it isn't," contradicts the man at the desk. Things go downhill from there.

In a motion memo or appellate brief, an argument—a connected series of statements intended to establish a proposition—is expressed in the Argument section of the document. An Argument section can contain several arguments. Often, you need to establish several propositions. For example, you might need to show that

- the words of a controlling statute support your position,
- the courts have interpreted that statute consistently with its wording, and
- the court's interpretation is consistent with the reasons the legislature enacted the statute (the legislative purpose and the policy behind the statute).

Each of these propositions must be supported by its own argument or arguments. Sometimes it takes several arguments to prove a proposition.

Writing the Argument is a process of (1) identifying the propositions you must prove, (2) developing persuasive arguments to support each of them, and (3) finding the words to articulate those arguments.

§ 32.2   Understanding the Judicial Audience

Ask yourself, "What will make the court *want* to agree with me?"

Proving that you are right is not enough. Before starting law school, most of us have already had a fair amount of experience justifying our own beliefs. But that is not the same as getting inside another person's thinking and persuading that person to *want* to do something. To motivate, we need to learn not only a new argument style, but also a new process of creating arguments. That is because the process of justifying our own position is different from *the process of persuading others to agree with us.* Here is how one student began to learn the difference:

> [In a college course, Kathleen wrote a paper on the] question "Is American Sign language (ASL) a 'foreign language' for purposes of meeting the university's foreign language requirement?" Kathleen had taken two years of ASL at a community college. When she transferred to a four-year college, the chair of the foreign languages department at her new college would not allow her ASL proficiency to count for the foreign language requirement. ASL isn't a "language," the chair said summarily. "It's not equivalent to learning French, German, or Japanese."[1]

Is this really why the department chair rejects Kathleen's request? If it is, Kathleen will be able to change his mind if she can prove that ASL is a real language, equivalent to French, German, or Japanese. But it might be only a rationalization for his decision—a statement he can use to justify saying no. If it is only his rationalization, then his motivation—the true cause of the refusal—remains hidden. If he is rationalizing, he might not even be aware of his own motives. In a moment we will see whether what he has stated is a rationalization or his true motivation.

Kathleen was not satisfied with what the department chair had said, and in a different college course she decided to write a paper on this issue.

> While doing research, she focused almost entirely on subject matter, searching for what linguists, brain neurologists, cognitive psychologists, and sociologists had said about the language of deaf people. Immersed in her subject matter, she was [not] concerned with her audience, whom she thought of primarily as her classmates and the professor [who taught the class in which she was writing the paper. They] were friendly to her views and interested in her experiences with the deaf community. She wrote a well-documented paper, citing several scholarly articles that made a

---

[1] The quotes in this section are from John D. Ramage & John C. Bean, WRITING ARGUMENTS: A RHETORIC WITH READINGS 10-11 (4th ed., 1998).

good case to her classmates (and the professor) that ASL was indeed a distinct language.

Proud of the big red A the professor had placed on her paper, Kathleen returned to the chair of the foreign language department with a new request to count ASL for her language requirement. The chair read her paper, congratulated her on her good writing, but said her argument was not persuasive. He disagreed with several of the linguists she cited and with the general definition of "language" that her paper assumed. He then gave her some additional (and to her fuzzy) reasons that the college would not accept ASL as a foreign language.

Now Kathleen has addressed the concerns the department chair expressed before. But rather than agree with her argument, he nitpicks it and offers new reasons that he had not mentioned before. Something else—which he has not specified—must be motivating him. Because Kathleen has not discovered the real cause of his refusal, she inadvertently made an argument that only challenged his rationalizations instead of one that addressed his true motivations.

What has happened to Kathleen is a common experience when *an advocate justifies a position rather than trying to influence the person making the decision*. The decision maker ignores ideas that made perfect sense to Kathleen and everybody else—except the decision maker. It makes no difference whether that person is a college administrator (as here) or a judge.

To persuade, figure out how a judge would react to the issues. Proving you are right and persuading the judge sound like the same thing, but they are not. Think about the person you are trying to persuade and what would matter to *that person*.

It would be easy for Kathleen to dismiss the chair of the foreign language department as a numskull, but for two reasons she cannot and should not. First, she cannot get around the fact that, like a judge, he has the power of decision. The only way she can get her ASL work to count for the foreign language requirement is to *change his mind*.

Second, he might have sincere concerns that deserve to be addressed. Does Kathleen know what they might be? At this point, she does not. Imagining only a friendly audience, she had not considered how a skeptical audience might react. But that audience—the department chair—has the power to decide. The skeptical audience may seem frustrating, but if we want action, we have to *concentrate* on that audience.

How can Kathleen find out what the department chair's concerns might be? How can she address them?

Spurred by what she considered the chair's too-easy dismissal of her argument, Kathleen . . . once again immersed herself in research, but this time it focused not on subject matter (whether ASL is a distinct language) but on audience[, the department chair]. She researched the history of the foreign language requirement at her college and discovered some of the politics behind it (an old foreign language requirement had been dropped in the 1970's and reinstituted in the 1990's, partly—a math professor told her—to boost enrollments in foreign language courses). She also interviewed foreign language teachers to find out what they knew and didn't know about ASL. She discovered that many teachers [inaccurately] thought ASL was "easy to learn," so that accepting ASL would allow students . . . to avoid the rigors of a real foreign language class. Additionally, she learned that foreign language teachers valued immersing students in a foreign culture; in fact, the foreign language requirement was part of her college's effort to create a multicultural curriculum.

Now Kathleen has begun to understand what's *really* going on. She has gained insights into what the department chair is worried about, and she can write arguments that might genuinely influence him.

This new understanding of her target audience helped Kathleen totally reconceptualize her argument. She condensed and abridged her original paper. . . . She added sections showing the difficulty of learning ASL (to counter her audience's belief that learning ASL was easy), and literature (to show how ASL met the goals of multiculturalism), and showing that the number of transfer students with ASL credits would be negligibly small (to allay fears that accepting ASL would threaten enrollments in language classes). She ended her argument with an appeal to her college's public emphasis (declared boldly in its mission statement) on eradicating social injustice and reaching out to the oppressed. She described the isolation of deaf people in a world where almost no hearing people learn ASL and argued that the deaf community on her campus could be integrated more fully into campus life if more students could "talk" with them [in their own language]. Thus, the ideas included in her new argument, the reasons selected, the evidence used, the arrangement and tone all were determined by her primary focus on persuasion.

This second paper was good lawyering. She got inside the decision maker's thinking and showed him that what he cared about would actually benefit from doing what she wanted.

Judges tend to be skeptical, but they know less about your case than you do. *Audience sense* is a writer's ability to understand a reader. How do judges think?

Judges are *skeptical*. They will not believe a proposition until you have proved it. Their job requires that frame of mind. You earn a favorable decision only by proving—with persuasive arguments and good storytelling—that your client deserves it.

Judges *know less about your case than you do*. In most courts, judges are generalists rather than specialists. Although they know a great deal about rules of procedure (which they use constantly), they usually know much less about individual rules of substantive law (which come up less often). Thus, you will often know more than the judge does about the *details* of the substantive law governing your case.

Judges want you to *teach* them your case. Think of an Argument as a *manual on how to make a particular decision.* If you show the court how the decision should be made, laying out all the steps of logic, you stand a much better chance of winning. If done in a respectful tone, this is not as presumptuous as you might think. A good Argument shows the court how to write the judicial opinion that justifies a decision in your favor.

Truly persuasive writing speaks to each reader directly. How can you do that if you will meet judges for the first time when you appear in court for oral argument—*after* you have written and submitted your trial court memo or appellate brief?

An experienced lawyer has usually developed an instinct for how judges generally make decisions and view their responsibilities. And to some extent, the lawyer can research an individual judge by reading the judge's past opinions and talking to other lawyers who have appeared before the judge in past cases.

As a student, you might write to an imagined judge. Think of someone whose intelligence, wisdom, and judgment you deeply respect. Write to persuade this person, as though she or he were a judge with the power to decide for or against your client. Do that in your first draft. In later drafts, continue to write to this person. Rework your writing to improve its capacity to persuade your imagined judge and to satisfy the professional standards expected in your legal writing course.

§ 32.3 How to Test Your Arguments for Effectiveness

While rewriting, ask yourself the following questions.

1. Have you tried to persuade the court rather than just prove that you are right? See Kathleen's story earlier in this chapter. Judges have the difficult responsibility to decide. To them, a lawyer who does not help can seem like Calvin (the boy in the comic strip), who takes positions without worrying about others' needs.

2. Have you focused on what is most likely to persuade, and have you summarized or cut out the rest? On its website, the North Dakota Supreme Court warns that judges "don't like to have to look for the pony."[2] A boy opens the door to his bedroom and finds it filled from floor to ceiling with manure. With a shout of joy, he gets a shovel and starts cleaning out the room. Asked why he is so happy, the boy exclaims, "With all that manure, there must be a pony in there somewhere!" Your most persuasive arguments may be *somewhere* in your writing. But unlike the boy, judges do not have time to dig around until they can find them.

Start by asking the question asked earlier in this chapter—"What will make the court want to agree with me?" Focus on your strongest contentions. Develop them fully. Leave out the weak ones. That creates a document that is more compact but explores more deeply the ideas that will most influence the court.

You might be tempted to throw in every good thing you can think of about your side of the case and every bad thing about your adversary's side. But do not hide the pony. Include only contentions that have a reasonable chance to persuade.

3. Have you organized persuasively? First, present the issues on which you are most likely to win. Within each issue, make your strongest arguments first, and use your best authority first.

Early impressions tend to color how later material is read, and, like most people, a judge might read most carefully at the beginning. In addition, because judges are so busy, they expect the strongest material first. If they find themselves reading weak material early, they assume that nothing better follows and might stop reading altogether. Sometimes, however, the logic of the dispute requires that the strongest material be delayed to avoid confusing the court. Some arguments are simply hard to understand unless preceded by less punchy material. In these situations, weigh your need for clarity against your need to show merit from the start.

In the Argument, the CREAC formula can be varied for persuasive reasons. For example, lawyers sometimes summarize the most compelling facts for a given issue before stating the rule. Normally, the CREAC formula puts the facts almost entirely in rule application (see Chapter 17). But if the most compelling facts are summarized before the rule, a judge can read the legal analysis in a frame of mind aroused by the story. Those same compelling facts would appear again in rule application to show how they combine with the rule to produce the conclusion.

---

[2] http://www.ndcourts.gov/_court/filing/tips.htm (Appellate Practice Tips).

4. Does your discussion of each issue begin with a roadmap briefly summarizing your argument? Insert the roadmap at the beginning of your analysis of the issue. For example,

> The defendant is subject to the jurisdiction of this state. Courts in other states have generally held that a defendant who maintains an interactive website is subject to the jurisdiction of any state where residents can access the website and interact with it. The defendant maintains a website that meets this test. The plaintiff, a resident of this state, ordered a $15,000 motorcycle and paid for it with a credit card—all through the defendant's website.

This paragraph lays out a roadmap, showing the reader that in the following pages you will prove each of these propositions. To find where you prove a particular proposition, a reader can look at your point headings and subheadings (Chapter 33), which should reflect what you promise in the roadmap.

5. Have you given the court a precise statement of the rule or rules on which the case turns? In an appellate court, a judge may ask, "Counselor, what rule would you have us enforce?" The judge may be wondering how—if you win—the court should word the rule component of the CREAC formula when it writes the opinion. If the court will be making law, it wants to know exactly what rule you want it to adopt, and exactly how to phrase that rule for maximum clarity. In your brief, state the rule in the words that most precisely express it.

6. Have you handled authority well? Use the hierarchy of authority (Chapter 8) to choose the best authority. Focus on the cases and statutes that really matter. A judge does not have time to read an exhaustive explanation of every case you found. But if you cite and explain too little, the judge will not be persuaded. How do you steer a middle course between underciting and overciting and between underexplaining and overexplaining?

Predict the amount of citation and explanation a skeptical but busy judge would need. Then carefully study the available authorities. Place in a "major authority" category those that will probably *influence* the court and in a "peripheral" category those that are merely related to the issue. If you had to make the judge's decision, which authorities would be most likely to have an effect on you (including those adverse to your position)? The potentially influential authorities are the ones you must discuss. Peripheral authorities can be discarded unless they would fill holes in your argument not settled by the major authorities.

With case law, choose the few cases that most clearly make your argument. Concentrate on them and explain them thoroughly. Use other cases to settle odds and ends related to the issue. For a given issue, do not be afraid to spend 75% of your words on a few cases (for example, three) and 25% on the other cases (for example, ten). Taking a judge deeply into a compelling precedent can be very persuasive. Two, three, or four cases, thoroughly explained, can fill a judge with confidence in your argument. Thirty cases, each with no more than a sentence of explanation each, are background noise.

Your goal is to give the court confidence that you are right without trying the court's patience.

7. Have you made persuasive policy arguments? Have you explained the benefits of a decision in your favor and the harm that would result from a decision in your adversary's favor? Explain how the parties have been affected by the dispute, how they would be affected by the relief you seek, or how in some other way what you seek is fundamentally fair. And go further to show that what you want will produce the best result in future cases as well, remembering that the decision could become precedent. If a court must choose between competing rules, for example, explain how the rule you urge is better than others. If you win, the decision will stand for that rule. Lawyers often introduce policy-based arguments with wording like the following:

> This court should reject the rule urged by the defendant because it would cause . . . .

> Automobile rental companies [or some other category of litigants] should bear the risk of loss because . . . .

> Not only is the order requested by the plaintiff not sanctioned by this state's case law, but such an order would also violate public policy because . . . .

To learn how to make policy arguments in appellate briefs, see Chapter 38.

8. Have you attacked your adversary's authority and arguments? Hiding from your weaknesses and your adversary's strengths does not work. Your odds of winning are greatly increased if you confront them openly and boldly. Is a statute or case inconsistent with your argument in a troubling way? Adverse authority will not go away just because you ignore it. The court will know about it, and if you fail to argue against it, the court may assume that you have no defense to it.

If the adverse authority is a statute, show that the provision was not intended to govern the controversy, or that it was intended to govern it but without harm to your client. Use the canons of statutory interpretation explained in Chapter 9.

If the adverse authority is precedent, distinguish it or use other techniques explained in Chapter 10. If none of those techniques will work, you might need to attack the precedent head-on, challenging its validity on the ground that it is poorly reasoned or that changes in society or in public policy have made it unworkable. But in general, do not ask a court to overrule mandatory authority if you can win through distinguishing, reconciling, or some other skill of precedent analysis. Judges simply prefer distinguishing and reconciling precedent to overruling it.

Make your own arguments first. You will win more readily if the court's dominant impression is that you deserve to win, rather than that your adversary deserves to lose. A defensive tone can undermine an otherwise worthwhile argument. And your theory will be more easily understood if you argue it before you attack opposing arguments.

How much should you emphasize an attack on an adverse argument or authority? Give it as much emphasis as necessary to convince the judge not to rule against you. Little treatment is necessary if the point is minor and if the argument or authority is easily refuted. Say more if the point is significant or if your counteranalysis is complex.

Students sometimes have difficulty writing the transition and thesis sentences that introduce attacks on opposing arguments. Begin your counterargument in the very sentence in which you introduce the other side's argument:

> The plaintiff misconstrues § 401(d)(1). Four other circuits have already decided that § 401(d)(1) provides only for compensatory damages and not, as the plaintiff contends, for punitive damages as well. *[Follow with an analysis of the circuit cases.]*

Argue affirmatively and not defensively. These are much weaker than the example above:

> The plaintiff has argued that § 401(d)(1) provides for punitive damages, but . . . .

> The plaintiff might argue that § 401(d)(1) provides for punitive damages, but . . . .

A dependent clause can be useful in thesis and transition sentences:

> Although the House Judiciary Committee report notes that its bill would have provided for punitive damages, § 401(d)(1) more closely tracks the bill drafted in the Senate Judiciary Committee. Both that committee's report and the conference committee report flatly state that § 401(d)(1) does not provide for punitive damages.

9. Will a judge be able to understand your Argument quickly and easily? Think about the judge's limited time and heavy caseload. Have you written the Argument so that a busy judge will not have to struggle to understand what you are trying to say?

§ 32.4 Argumentation Ethics and Professionalism

The law of professional ethics—which in nearly all states includes the Model Rules of Professional Conduct—places limits on what you are permitted to do in argument.

First, and most importantly, you may not "knowingly . . . make a false statement of fact or law" to a court.[3] Imagine what courts would be like if lawyers were free to lie to judges.

Second, a lawyer must inform a court of "legal authority in the *controlling jurisdiction* known to the lawyer to be *directly adverse* to the position of the [lawyer's] client and not disclosed by opposing counsel."[4] Imagine what courts would be like if lawyers were free to hide the law from judges. But you can inform the court of the adverse authority and at the same time try to neutralize it. To learn how, see question 8 in the preceding section.

Third, you may not advance a "frivolous" theory or argument, although you may make a "good faith argument for an extension, modification or reversal of existing law."[5] In a legal system like ours, where "the law is not always clear and never is static," the rules of ethics permit a lawyer to advance theories and arguments that take advantage "of the law's ambiguities and potential for change."[6] But a frivolous theory or argument—one that stands little chance of being adopted by a court—is unfair to courts and to opposing parties because it wastes their time, effort, and resources.

---

[3] Model Rules of Prof'l Conduct R. 3.3(a)(1) (2013).
[4] *Id.* R. 3.3(a)(2) (emphasis added).
[5] *Id.* 3.1. See also Rule 11 of the Federal Rules of Civil Procedure and Rule 38 of the Federal Rules of Appellate Procedure. Both are printed in the rules supplement used in most Civil Procedure courses.
[6] Model Rules of Prof'l Conduct R. 3.1 cmt 1.

33 Point Headings and Subheadings

Megan McCallister: You're not at all worried that something
might happen to Kevin?
Buzz McCallister: No, for three reasons:
A. I'm not that lucky,
2. We have smoke detectors, and
D. We live on the most boring street in the United
States of America.

—Home Alone

§ 33.1 What Point Headings Do

Somebody hands you a book or some other publication, says "Read this," and then walks away without explanation. How do you know what you are reading?

Imagine a book without a title, chapter names, section divisions, or headings. It is just a sea of words from the first page to the end. How would you navigate a book like that? How would you know what topic comes next? Topics need labels to help the reader figure out how to navigate through the sea of words.

Written legal arguments need a similar structure. Point headings and subheadings in a legal argument are short guides to readers about what they can expect to read next. More importantly, they structure and strengthen your Argument.

In persuasive writing, a *point* is an independent unit within your Argument. Your reader will be better able to understand a lengthy Argument if it is divided into logical parts. Each point represents an alternative way your client can win the Argument, assuming the court agrees with that point.

For example, suppose your client is sued for breach of contract and wants to escape the contractual obligation. You might argue two alternative points: first, that the contract is void for lack of mental capacity, and second, that the contract is unenforceable for lack of consideration. Either point would persuade the court that your client should win the breach of contract claim. If the court disagrees with one point but agrees with the other, your client still wins.

An alternative way to use points (or subheadings under one main point) is to enumerate the elements of a claim your client must prove to win—for example, each element of a criminal offense the prosecutor must prove to establish the defendant's guilt. The point heading might be a general statement that the prosecution has established each required element of the offense, and subheadings would address each of the specific elements that must be established beyond a reasonable doubt.

Strike a balance between too many and too few points. Too many separate points can make it challenging for a reader to connect the points into an integrated whole. On the other hand, collapsing a complex argument into just one point can make your reader work too hard to sort out each step of the argument. Effective point headings unpack the argument into its logical parts that add up to support the overall legal conclusion you seek for your client.

Crafting point headings can be a good way to check for an effective structure for your Argument. If two point headings resemble each other too closely, you might really have just one point to make. And if a point heading seems impossibly complicated or difficult to understand, you might be attempting to cover too much at once. Consider dividing the single point heading into two or more point headings or subheadings.

Effective point headings help persuade your reader. The point heading plants an idea in the reader's mind that you hope the reader will embrace as her own after reading that section of your Argument. Avoid overstating the point. Strive for *forceful reasonableness*—somewhere between neutral, which does nothing for your client, and too aggressive, which could harm your credibility with the court. Taking the middle ground demonstrates why the judge should have confidence that your Argument is not only legally correct, but also achieves a just result.

§ 33.2 What Each Point Heading Should Include

An effective point heading is a *complete declaratory sentence* that includes each of the following components:

- the conclusion you want the court to draw, or the ruling you want the court to make
- a reference to the relevant legal rule or legal issue
- the essential fact or facts showing why the legal issue should be resolved for your client

A declaratory sentence is a *statement*, not a question. A point heading is not the same as an issue statement or a question presented, which are structured as questions. Think of each point heading as the Conclusion at the beginning of the CREAC formula you follow to write the supporting legal argument for that point heading.

First, identify the legal conclusion you want the court to reach, or the specific ruling you want for your client.

For example, a point heading that refers to the client's desired *legal conclusion* might look like this:

> The Complaint Is Legally Insufficient Because It Fails to Allege Any Facts That Could Be Construed as an Offer.

The legal conclusion you want the court to reach for your client is a holding that the complaint is insufficient.

In the alternative, your point heading can refer to the *specific ruling* you want the court to make, like this:

> The Court Should Dismiss the Complaint Because It Fails to Allege Any Facts That Could Be Construed as an Offer.

This alternative specifically refers the court to the procedural posture (a pending motion to dismiss the claim) and suggests the specific action you want the court to take.

Each of these point headings could be followed by identical legal arguments. The only difference is that the first specifically asks the court to draw a legal conclusion (the complaint is legally insufficient to support a breach of contract action) and implies the result the writer wants from the court (dismissal of the complaint), while the second specifically asks for the desired result (dismissal) and implies the desired legal conclusion (the complaint is legally insufficient).

Second, be sure your point heading identifies the legal rule or issue you need the court to resolve. In the example above, the point headings allude to the legal issue by referring to an offer as an essential element in contract formation. Identifying the relevant legal rule or issue resembles the analysis you use to find the applicable legal rule when reading a case for your other classes.

Third, include the essential fact or facts that support the conclusion or result you seek. Finding those facts resembles identifying determinative facts in a judicial opinion. What specific facts make your client's case unique or especially difficult to decide? What facts make your client a winner in this part of your Argument? In the example above, the point heading relates the essential facts by noting the *absence* of allegations in the complaint that are necessary for an enforceable contract.

Do not go too far in defining the action you want the court to take in one point heading. Sometimes a single point heading can appropriately ask for all the relief your client desires. If this section of your Argument, standing alone, justifies granting or denying a motion, or justifies reversing a trial court decision, go ahead and ask for that result. For example, if you represent a criminal defendant charged with burglary, you can win an acquittal if you defeat just one element of the criminal offense. A single point heading might challenge the sufficiency of the evidence to prove that your client had the intent to commit a felony before breaking and entering a dwelling. Because specific intent to commit a felony is an essential element of the offense, your client can win if you defeat just that one element of the prosecution's case.

But often the point you are working on will be just one of several building blocks in your Argument and would not be enough on its own for your client to win the entire motion or appeal. For that kind of argument, a single point heading would not be suitable.

§ 33.3   Subheadings

As explained above, you can often make your Argument more clear for the reader by subdividing it with subheadings. Each subheading identifies one step in logic necessary to support the main point heading. Under each subheading, develop the reasons to support that logical step in reaching the legal conclusion or result you have identified in the point heading.

For example, assume you want to convince the court that your client deserves compensatory damages after a law student smashed into the back end of her client's brand new Lexus after a drinking binge following his first set of final exams. Your main point heading would refer to your client's negligence claim (rule of law), provide the facts leading up to the collision (essential facts) and state that your client seeks an award of compensatory damages (result sought).

You would then craft four subheadings, each addressing one element of negligence and the key facts supporting a favorable result on each element: (1) the law student owed a duty of care to your client; (2) the law student breached that duty by carelessly smashing into your client's car; (3) the collision was the cause-in-fact and proximate cause of her harm; and (4) she sustained property damage to her car. If the court agrees with you on every subheading, those elements add up to the legal conclusion you want.

None of the subheadings *standing alone* will result in a winning claim for your client because negligence requires a finding in her favor on *all four* elements. For that reason, the main point heading focuses on the overall negligence claim for compensatory damages. Each subheading demonstrates how she can meet every essential element of that claim, adding up to a winning case for compensatory damages for the defendant's negligence.

But avoid going overboard with subheadings. Too many subheadings, with only two or three paragraphs under each one, can result in a choppy, ineffective Argument that fails to persuade.

§ 33.4 Organizing Your Point Headings and Subheadings

Organize your point headings and subheadings in traditional outline format, using Roman numerals for main point headings, capital letters for subheadings, and Arabic numbers (if necessary) for sub-subheadings. The sample appellate brief in Appendix D shows how to enumerate and properly indent your point headings and subheadings. Be sure your headings are worded, punctuated, and indented *identically* in the body of your brief as well as your table of contents. The following diagram shows how to designate and organize your headings:

I. **Point heading** . . . .
   A. *Subheading* . . . .
   B. *Subheading* . . . .
      1. Sub-subheading . . . .
      2. Sub-subheading . . . .
   C. *Subheading* . . . .
II. **Point heading** . . . .
III. **Point heading** . . . .
   A. *Subheading* . . . .
   B. *Subheading* . . . .

The emphasis (bold or italics) and indentation differ for each level of heading, which helps the reader follow each division and subdivision of your argument. In your table of contents, the headings reveal the overall structure and organization of your Argument for your reader's benefit—and they present the most persuasive first impression to the court.

§ 33.5 How to Test Your Point Headings for Effectiveness

While rewriting, ask yourself the following questions:

1. Do your headings and subheadings lay out a complete, logically sequenced, and persuasive outline of your Argument? Many judges read the point headings *before reading any other part* of a memo or brief. In an appellate brief, a judge generally reads them all at once because they form an outline of your Argument printed in the table of contents. In a motion memo, a judge often reads the headings first by leafing through the Argument section. Well-crafted point headings and subheadings introduce and outline your legal theory of the case. Your goal is to persuade the judge to rule in your client's favor by the time the judge finishes reading *only* your Argument headings. The rest of your Argument should reinforce that conclusion.

Some lawyers draft the headings before writing the full Argument. Others write the headings and the supporting Argument at the same time. Once you compile the headings and subheadings in the table of contents of an appellate brief, you may discover ways to redraft them to fill in gaps or resolve inconsistencies that are not apparent when the headings are scattered around in the Argument. Even in a motion memo without a table of contents, you may find it helpful to copy and paste your headings into a separate document (without the supporting argument) so you can check them for effectiveness. Chances are the court will read your headings first, even if they are not compiled in a separate table of contents. Take every opportunity to persuade the court by redrafting and polishing your headings to summarize your Argument step by step.

2. Do you have an appropriate number of point headings and subheadings—neither too many nor too few? Too many headings overwhelm the reader with complexity and interrupt the flow of your Argument. Too few weaken your Argument by insufficiently breaking down your legal reasoning and by failing to accurately outline your Argument. Use subheadings to subdivide the argument when a point heading requires separate logical steps in reasoning to persuade the court to reach the result you seek.

3. Is each heading or subheading a single sentence that a reader can immediately understand? Readers simply ignore headings that are too long or dense. Because an effective point heading includes a request for relief, a reference to the legal rule or issue, and at least one essential fact, a single heading can easily become unreadable. Edit your headings to convey the point as clearly and concisely as possible. A single heading cannot fully develop the argument. Instead, it summarizes the essence of the argument and introduces what comes next: the supporting rule explanation and detailed rule application. If too long, a heading discourages your audience from reading further. Effective point headings are short, complete, and case-specific, priming your reader for persuasion.

4. Does each point heading identify the legal conclusion or judicial decision you want? Point headings should not leave the judge wondering what you want the court to do next. Each point heading *must* clearly state your client's desired result or legal conclusion for that part of your Argument. Because subheadings divide up the argument supporting and reinforcing each point heading, they do not need to restate the relief or conclusion you seek.

5. Does each point heading allude to the relevant legal rule? A point heading need not state the legal rule completely. Often it is enough to allude to the legal concept involved. But be specific. For example, assume your brief or motion memo challenges whether the parties entered into an enforceable contract, and this part addresses whether an offer was ever made. Your point heading should use the more specific word "offer" rather than a broader term like "contract formation," which could include other legal concepts like "acceptance" and "meeting of the minds."

6. Does each point heading include at least one essential fact? Beginning legal writers often make the mistake of writing point headings that simply restate the applicable legal rule. An effective point heading isolates the key facts that *persuade* the court to reach the desired legal conclusion *in this unique case*. The court may agree with your statement of the applicable legal rule, but that alone is not sufficient to persuade the court to rule in your client's favor. The law is what it is, but facts persuade. Identify the persuasive facts favoring your client's position, and deliver them on a silver platter to the court by clearly and concisely integrating them with the relevant legal rule in the point headings. They must show the court how the legal rule applies to the determinative facts to support the legal conclusion you seek.

7. Are your headings appropriately numbered and subdivided? Use Roman numerals, letters, and numbers as you would in a formal outline. Under a point heading, never use just one subheading. Remember that subheadings *divide* the argument on that point to show each of its supporting logical steps, which implies more than one step in the legal reasoning. If you find yourself with just one subheading under a point heading, look again at the legal rule and reconsider whether you need any subheadings. If you have trouble coming up with at least two subheadings, try to figure out whether it helps your reader to subdivide that section. Avoid subdividing the flow of your argument without good reason.

8. Are your headings appropriately typeset? Traditionally, lawyers used ALL CAPITAL LETTERS for point headings. The reason is that all-caps were the only method available to add emphasis to headings when typewriters were state-of-the-art for preparing legal briefs. Even in the computer age, some lawyers still use all-caps to make their point headings stand out on the page. Many others use **bold type** instead of all-caps.[1] Similarly, subheadings were once underlined because typewriters were not capable of adding any other kind of emphasis. Today, most lawyers use either *italics* or underlining (but never both) for subheadings.

In subheadings, and in headings that are not all-capped, many legal writers capitalize the first letter of each significant word, as you would in the title of a book or law journal article. Some capitalize only the first word of the sentence. Always single-space point headings so they stand out on the page. For more on the persuasive aspects of document design, see Appendix E.

---

[1] *See* Ruth Anne Robbins, *Painting with Print: Incorporating Concepts of Typographic and Layout Design into the Text of Legal Writing Documents*, 2 J. ALWD 108, 115-16 (2004) (making the case that the use of all-caps in brief headings slows down reading speed).

Exercise 33-A. Evaluating Point Headings

The U.S. Supreme Court ruled in *Riley v. California*[2] that as a general rule, police officers may not search the digital contents of an arrestee's cell phone without first securing a search warrant. Point headings from the petitioner's and respondent's Supreme Court briefs are reprinted below as they appeared in each brief's table of contents.

Critique each set of point headings in light of the tips you have read in this chapter. How could the brief writers have improved them? Did the writers make the right choices in balancing completeness against brevity? If you had been on the Court when the case was decided, which side of the case would you have found more persuasive based *solely* on the point headings and subheadings? Which party's headings are easier to read? Explain your answers.

Petitioner's Brief:

I. The Search Of The Digital Contents Of Petitioner's Smart Phone Exceeded The Bounds Of A Legitimate Search Incident To Arrest.
   A. The Search Was Unnecessary To Serve Any Legitimate Governmental Interest.
      1. Digital Data Does Not Threaten Officer Safety.
      2. Once Seized, It Is Unnecessary To Search A Smart Phone Without A Warrant To Preserve Evidence.
   B. The Degree of Intrusiveness Of The Search Of Petitioner's Phone Rendered The Search Unreasonable.
      1. Smart Phones Hold Extraordinary Amounts Of Sensitive Personal Information.
      2. Smart Phones Hold Information That Implicates First Amendment Concerns.
   C. Limiting Searches Of Smart Phones To Situations In Which Officers Believe Such Phones Contain Evidence Of The Crime Of Arrest Would Not Solve The Constitutional Problems Inherent In Such Searches.
II. The Search Of Petitioner's Phone At The Stationhouse Was Too Remote From His Arrest To Qualify As A Search Incident To Arrest.

---

[2] 134 S. Ct. 2473 (2014). The petitioner's opening brief is available on Westlaw at 2014 WL 844599. The respondent's brief is available at 2014 WL 1348466.

Respondent's Brief:

I. Under existing law, the police were entitled to search photos and videos on petitioner's phone as an incident to his lawful arrest.
   A. The law has long allowed police to search objects found on the person of an individual who is lawfully arrested.
   B. Cases addressing searches of the area of an arrest have not questioned the categorical rule applicable to the arrestee's person and effects.
   C. The evidence at issue here was properly obtained under any standard.
      1. The photos and videos were found in searches of an object recovered from petitioner's person during his arrest.
      2. The searches here were reasonably related to the crime of arrest.
      3. A cell phone such as petitioner's presents safety, identification, and evidentiary issues at least as powerful as those relating to other items routinely seized and searched incident to arrest.
         a. Safety and identification
         b. Preservation of evidence
II. The technological advances that petitioner highlights do not warrant the adoption of special rules for cell phones in this case.
   A. The information taken from petitioner's phone is not fundamentally different from that found in other searches incident to arrest.
   B. The circumstances of this case suggest no basis for specially limiting cell phone searches incident to arrests.

Exercise 33-B. Creating a Point Heading

Part 1. For a motion memo or brief that your teacher has assigned, select one point you have written about or will be writing about. Before writing the heading for that point, identify words or phrases for each entry in the following chart:

_____

Relief or conclusion requested

_____

Relevant legal rule or issue

_____

Essential determinative fact(s)

Part 2. Now combine these words and phrases in several alternative configurations to see which produces the most effective point heading.

Part 3. Write persuasive subheadings as needed to subdivide the argument into the logical steps in reasoning the court must follow to grant the requested relief or to reach the desired legal conclusion.

Exercise 33-C. Revising Point Headings

The point headings below were drafted by first-year law students based upon the following facts and legal issues. First, revise each point heading for completeness to be sure it includes all necessary components. Second, revise the headings for persuasiveness. Finally, edit them for clarity and conciseness.

Facts: A California Highway Patrol officer spotted Megan Goering driving her copper red 2007 Mazda Miata just outside the city limits of Los Angeles. While driving, Ms. Goering was wearing Google Glass, an eyeglass-like device that allows a wearer to view a small video display in the upper-right corner of her field of vision. After the officer stopped her car, he asked Ms. Goering whether she was viewing a video display while driving. She responded that she was, but only to follow directions to her ultimate destination using the Google Maps website. Her Miata convertible does not have an installed GPS navigation system. The officer cited her for violating the following statute. Should the court dismiss the charge?

California Vehicle Code § 27602

(a) A person shall not drive a motor vehicle if a television receiver, a video monitor, or a television or video screen, or any other similar means of visually displaying a television broadcast or video signal that produces entertainment or business applications, is operating and is located in the motor vehicle at a point forward of the back of the driver's seat, or is operating and the monitor, screen, or display is visible to the driver while driving the motor vehicle.

(b) Subdivision (a) does not apply to the following equipment when installed in a vehicle:

(1) A vehicle information display.

(2) A global positioning display.

(3) A mapping display.

(4) A visual display used to enhance or supplement the driver's view forward, behind, or to the sides of a motor vehicle for the purpose of maneuvering the vehicle.

(5) A television receiver, video monitor, television or video screen, or any other similar means of visually displaying a television broadcast or video signal, if that equipment satisfies one of the following requirements:

(A) The equipment has an interlock device that, when the motor vehicle is driven, disables the equipment for all uses except as a visual display as described in paragraphs (1) to (4), inclusive.

(B) The equipment is designed, operated, and configured in a manner that prevents the driver of the motor vehicle from viewing the television broadcast or video signal while operating the vehicle in a safe and reasonable manner.

. . . .

Student A (representing the defendant)

I. The court should dismiss the count alleging a violation of California Vehicle Code § 27602 because the defendant was using Google Glass as a mapping display, which is one of the exceptions within the statute.

Student B (representing the state)

I. The court should deny the defendant's motion to dismiss the traffic citation because the product used by the defendant, Google Glass, is a means of visually displaying a television broadcast or video signal, which is prohibited by the traffic statute.

II. The court should deny the defendant's motion to dismiss the traffic citation because the Google Glass product was being operated at the time of the traffic stop and was located at a point forward of the back of the driver's seat.

III. The court should deny the defendant's motion to dismiss the traffic citation because the Google Glass product was not installed in the vehicle while the defendant was using the mapping display.

Student C (representing the defendant)

I. The court should grant the Motion to Dismiss because the defendant did not violate California Vehicle Code § 27602, which states:

> A person shall not drive a motor vehicle if a television receiver, a video monitor, or a television or video screen, or any other similar means of visually displaying a television broadcast or video signal that produces entertainment or business applications, is operating and is located in the motor vehicle at a point forward of the back of the driver's seat, or is operating and the monitor, screen, or display is visible to the driver while driving the motor vehicle.

Student D (representing the State)

I. The California court should deny defendant driver's Motion to Dismiss because she violated a California traffic statute by viewing a monitor or video display while driving.

    A. The court should deny defendant driver's Motion to Dismiss because the visual display that her use of Google Glass provided was at a point forward of the back of the driver's seat.

    B. The court should deny defendant driver's Motion to Dismiss because her use of Google Glass provided a display visible to defendant driver while she was operating her motor vehicle.

    C. The court should deny defendant driver's Motion to Dismiss because the visual display that Google Glass provided her was not one that has been installed in her vehicle.

Part 10

Appellate Briefs and Oral Argument

34 Appellate Practice

§ 34.1 Introduction to Appeals

A *judgment* (or, in equity, a *decree*) is the document through which a court terminates a lawsuit and determines the parties' rights and obligations. The judgment might award damages to one party or grant an injunction to the other. An *order*, on the other hand, is a court's command during the lawsuit that something be done or not be done while the litigation is still in progress. Usually an appeal is from a judgment, although sometimes it is from an order.

The appellate process performs two functions. One is correcting errors made by trial courts. The other is making new law and clarifying existing law through the precedents created by appellate decisions. A lower appellate court tends to view its job largely as error correction, although it necessarily engages in some law formation and clarification because appellate decisions are precedents. Higher appellate courts, on the other hand, generally view their work primarily as making and clarifying law.

The party who appeals is the *appellant* or the *petitioner*, and the opposing party is the *appellee* or *respondent*, depending on local court rules and the type of appeal. Before writing a brief, check the court's rules for the terms appropriate to your type of appeal. If you cannot find the answer, see how the court referred to parties in a reported case that *procedurally* resembles your own.

§ 34.2 The Roles of the Brief and the Oral Argument

The brief and oral argument perform different functions. Each is crucial, but in a different way.

In a brief, you can tell the client's story and make the client's arguments in persuasive detail. A successful brief not only persuades the judge that your client should win, but it can also be used as a manual explaining to the judge how to make the decision and how to justify it in an opinion. A judge may use the brief when preparing for oral argument, deciding whether to reverse or affirm, preparing for the conference with other judges, and writing the opinion.

The oral argument can do two things better than the brief: First, in oral argument you can more immediately motivate the court by focusing on the most important ideas—the few facts, rules, and policies that most make your case compelling. Second, in oral argument you can try to discover, through the bench's questions, each judge's doubts. And, on the spot, you can explain exactly why those doubts should not prevent a ruling in your favor. Oral argument, in fact, is your only opportunity to learn directly from the judges the problems they have with your arguments.

But oral argument also has a significant disadvantage: It lasts only a few minutes, and memories of it can fade. The brief, on the other hand, has permanence. It is always among the judge's working materials, and it "speaks from the time it is filed and continues through oral argument, conference, and opinion writing."[1]

There is another important difference between the brief and oral argument. Detail is communicated best in writing, which can be studied. But the spontaneity of conversation during oral argument encourages dialogue and lends itself to the broad sweep of underlying ideas.

§ 34.3   How Judges Read Appellate Briefs

In a single month, an appellate judge might hear oral arguments and confer with colleagues on several dozen appeals. For each appeal, the judge will read at least two briefs or, in multiparty cases or public-interest cases, perhaps a half-dozen briefs or more, together with portions of the record. The judge will write majority opinions in a proportion of the appeals. On a five-judge court, for example, each judge will write one-fifth of the majority opinions. In addition, the judge may write several concurring or dissenting opinions. The judge will also read opinions drafted by other judges and at times will write memoranda to colleagues suggesting changes in those opinions. And the judge will spend a fair amount of time reading some of the cases and statutes cited in all these briefs and draft opinions.

With all this work, the typical appellate judge would find it a luxury to spend as much as an hour reading the average brief. The time available is often no more than half an hour. That is why briefs, although sometimes lengthy, must be written carefully to persuade with the least possible time and effort from the reader.

---

[1] Herbert Funk Goodrich, *A Case on Appeal—A Judge's View* (1952), *reprinted in* A CASE ON APPEAL 10-11 (Joint Comm. on Continuing Legal Educ. of A.L.I. & A.B.A., 4th ed. 1967).

How does a judge read a brief? The answer may vary considerably from judge to judge, but the following is not unusual:

> Usually I first read both parties' statements of the questions presented; then I read the appellant's statement of the general nature of the controversy. Then I look at his outline of argument to see what points he makes. Then I look at the appellee's outline of argument to see what he is going to do in reply. . . . Then I read the appellant's statement of the facts and the appellee's statement. Thereafter I examine the two briefs one point at a time, first the appellant's and then the appellee's, on the first point; then both briefs on the second point, etc. If the point is an obvious one, or if one side or the other seems to be wholly without strength on it, I do not spend too much time on that point in my first study. On the really contested points I study both sides, read the cases, and, if facts are critical check the record references.[2]

Other judges might read the parts of a brief in a different sequence—perhaps reading the point headings before anything else—and a given judge might vary the sequence from case to case. But several things are true regardless of the judge's work habits.

First, you write for several different readers. Depending on the court, an appeal might be decided by a bench of from three to nine judges. Briefs are also read by law clerks or research attorneys who assist the judges by studying the briefs and recommending decisions.

Second, briefs—like memos—are not necessarily read from beginning to end at a single sitting. They are read in chunks, at different times, depending on the needs of the reader. You probably read an appliance or automobile owner's manual in pretty much the same way, and a good brief is a manual for making a decision.

Finally, a brief is read for different reasons at different times, depending on who is reading and when. The judges will read or at least scan it in preparation for oral argument. Afterward, they will read the brief again to decide how to vote. One judge will be assigned to write the court's opinion, and that judge will reread various portions of the brief several times, looking for the detail needed to justify and explain the decision. And all along the way, the judges will be assisted by law clerks who check the details of the brief while the judges focus on the broader principles. Each segment of the brief must be written to satisfy all of these purposes.

---

[2] E. Barrett Prettyman, *Some Observations Concerning Appellate Advocacy*, 39 Va. L. Rev. 285, 296 (1953).

35 Writing the Appellate Brief

§ 35.1 Appellate Brief Format

Although rules on format differ from court to court, the required structure commonly includes the following. Some courts require additional material, such as a statement specifying how the court acquired jurisdiction over the appeal in question.

1. a cover page
2. a Table of Contents (sometimes called an Index)
3. a Table of Authorities
4. the words of a constitutional provision, statute, administrative regulation, or court rule—if the appeal rests on interpreting those words
5. a Preliminary Statement (also called Proceedings Below or Nature of the Proceedings)
6. a Question Presented or Questions Presented (also called Statement of the Issues)
7. a Statement of the Case
8. a Summary of Argument
9. an Argument, broken up with point headings and subheadings
10. a Conclusion

See the brief in Appendix D.

The **cover page** includes the caption, followed by the document's title—such as "BRIEF FOR APPELLANT"—and the name, address, and telephone number of the lawyer submitting the brief. The caption includes the name of the appellate court, the appellate court's docket number, and the names of the parties and their procedural designations (appellant, appellee, etc.) in the appellate court. The cover page does not have a page number.

The **Table of Contents** begins on the page after the cover page. It lists all of the components of the brief (except the cover page and the Table of Contents itself); reproduces the point headings and subheadings from the Argument; and sets out the page number on which each component, point, or subpoint begins.

The **Table of Authorities** appears on the first page after the Table of Contents. It lists the cases, statutes, and other authorities cited in the Argument together with every page number in the brief where each listed authority is cited.

The **Constitutional Provisions, Statutes, Regulations, and Court Rules Involved** specifies any enacted law crucial to the appeal and quotes the section at issue. A provision is crucial to the appeal if the parties disagree about its meaning and *if the court cannot dispose of the appeal without resolving the disagreement*. A court rule that merely provides for the type of motion made below is not critical to the appeal unless the parties disagree about the rule's meaning and the appellate court has been asked to resolve the disagreement. Phrase the heading of this section of the brief to fit its content. If the First Amendment—and nothing else—is at issue, the heading would read "Constitutional Provision Involved" with no mention of statutes, regulations, or court rules.

The **Preliminary Statement** briefly sets out the appeal's procedural posture by explaining who the parties are, listing the relevant procedural events, and describing the judgment or order appealed from. (If a party is a government or a large, well-known organization, you need not explain who that party is.) The Preliminary Statement can also describe the reasoning of the court below and identify the grounds on which that court's judgment or order is challenged on appeal. The Preliminary Statement should tell the court why the appeal is before it and specify the type of decision you want the court to make. That can usually be done in less than a page. Many lawyers add a paragraph summarizing their own arguments.

This portion of the brief goes by different names in different courts. If it is not titled "Preliminary Statement," the heading might read "Proceedings Below," "Nature of the Proceedings," or the like. In some courts, the Preliminary Statement is called the "Statement of the Case" (and the client's story is told elsewhere in the brief in a "Statement of Facts").

A persuasive **Question Presented** is explained in Chapter 37.

The **Statement of the Case** is explained in Chapters 29 through 31.

A **Summary of the Argument** is what its name implies. The point headings and subheadings, as they appear in the Table of Contents, *outline* the Argument. The Summary, on the other hand, *condenses* the Argument into a few paragraphs—perhaps one paragraph per issue—with more explanation than will fit into headings. The Summary should not merely repeat the point headings, and it should not include citations to legal authority.

The **Argument** is explained in Chapters 32 and 33.

Although some lawyers use the **Conclusion** to reargue and resummarize the theory of the appeal, it is better to limit the conclusion to a one- or two-sentence reiteration of the relief you want together with the ground on which that relief would be based. For example:

> For all the foregoing reasons, the Circuit Court's order dismissing the complaint should be affirmed because the complaint does not state a cause of action.

The primary purpose of the Conclusion is to remind the judges exactly what you want them to do.

Every court has rules governing the contents of briefs and other submitted documents. The rules are designed to make briefs easier for judges to use, and judges understandably become exasperated when the rules are ignored. Egregious violations of court rules can result in the court's striking the brief, in financial penalties imposed on the lawyer, and even in dismissal of the appeal.

§ 35.2 Three Brief-Writing Suggestions

1. Start writing before you finish the research. "I can't start writing yet," you might say. "I haven't found *all* the cases." But waiting until you find all the cases can feed procrastination. Until you start writing, you cannot know for sure what kind of cases you should be looking for.

Certainly in the beginning you must cast a wide net in researching. But at some point researching like a vacuum cleaner becomes inefficient. Starting to write helps you identify that point because writing and thinking are inseparable. The act of writing will help you focus on what really matters to the arguments you must make and thus show you where you need more authority.

Start writing as soon as you have enough research to know roughly what your theory will be. When you go back into research after doing some writing, you can focus on what you really need. Research will take less time and effort if you know what you are looking for.

2. Start practicing oral argument before you finish writing the brief. It might seem illogical to spend time on oral argument when you are up against a deadline with the brief. But many students discover that when they *talk* about a complicated subject, they say surprisingly interesting and perceptive things—and come to valuable insights—because talking helps them understand more deeply. Many people learn not just by reading and listening, but also by talking and doing. The best reason for practicing oral argument early is to help you write a better brief.

Suppose you disregard this advice. You submit your final draft brief, rest for a few days, and then start developing an oral argument. As you practice, you come up with some terrific wording and wish you could put it in the brief—but by then it is too late.

3. Think of brief-writing as a collection of small tasks—rather than as one huge task. A huge task can be intimidating and cause procrastination. But a collection of smaller tasks can be done one by one.

"The secret to good brief writing is to write small pieces."[1] You have not been given one big assignment. You have been given several smaller ones: a Question Presented, a Statement of the Case, and so on. You can write all these things separately—as separate word processing files, if you prefer—and then stitch them together into a single document. Even the Argument can become two or more smaller jobs. If you have two points, writing each of them is a separate task. But be careful to coordinate all these smaller tasks so that the resulting brief is coherent and internally consistent.

§ 35.3   What Part of the Brief to Write First

Just as a judge does not read a brief from beginning to end, neither does a lawyer write it that way. The Table of Contents and Table of Authorities are always done last (see the last section in this chapter for why). The order in which the other parts are written differs from lawyer to lawyer and from appeal to appeal because one lawyer's work habits are not necessarily effective for someone else, and because an effective lawyer adapts to the individual task at hand. Eventually, you will settle into a range of work habits that work for you. Your first brief is an opportunity to begin to understand yourself in that way.

To help you start, consider two very different methods of writing a brief.

Sequence in Which a First Draft Might Be Written	
Model I	**Model II**
1. point headings	1. Questions Presented
2. Argument	2. Statement of the Case
3. Statement of the Case	3. point headings
4. Questions Presented	4. Argument
5. rest of brief	5. rest of brief

A lawyer who uses Model I writes point headings and subheadings first as a way of outlining the Argument. This lawyer might draft the Statement of the Case after

---

[1] John T. Gaubatz & Taylor Mattis, The Moot Court Book: A Student Guide to Appellate Advocacy 41 (3d ed. 1994).

writing the Argument on the ground that writing the Argument reveals which facts have the most legal significance. The Questions Presented would be written afterward because the lawyer identifies the most essential facts—the ones recited in the Questions—while working out the Argument and the Statement of the Case.

But a lawyer using Model II would begin the first draft by writing the Questions Presented in the belief that the other parts of the brief will be more focused if the issues are first precisely defined. A lawyer who uses this model writes the Statement of the Case next, using it to work out the details of the theory of the appeal (which the Model I lawyer does while writing the Argument). Both lawyers draft the point headings before the Argument because the Argument is easier to write in segments (which the headings create).

A lawyer with flexible work habits might use Model I in an appeal with difficult and complex legal issues and authority and Model II in a more fact-sensitive appeal. Some lawyers write the Question Presented and the Statement of the Case (and sometimes even the Argument) simultaneously.

§ 35.4   The Last Step: Creating the Table of Contents and the Table of Authorities

Why you should create the Tables last. For pagination purposes, a brief is broken down into two parts. The two Tables (sometimes called the "front matter") are paginated in lowercase roman numerals ("i," "ii," "iii," and so on). The rest of the brief (the "body") is paginated separately in arabic numbers, beginning with "1," on the first page immediately following the Tables.

This might seem odd. But it has a very practical purpose. Because the Tables must include page references to the body, *any* change in the body—even a change of only a few words—can alter the page breaks and require changes in the Tables. And because you cannot know how many pages the Tables will occupy until you are ready to print them, the body must begin on page 1. The only efficient solution is to use two separate paginations: lowercase roman numbers for the Tables and arabic numbers for the body. (The same thing is done for the same reasons in your textbooks, including this one. Look at the pages *preceding* Chapter 1.)

What the Table of Authorities should look like. Although the Table of Contents is easy to visualize and put together, the Table of Authorities is more complicated. In the Table of Authorities, list a complete cite for every authority, with an asterisk to the left of those authorities that form the core of your theory. In a footnote, identify those citations as "authorities chiefly relied on" or similar words to the same effect.

The Table of Authorities is broken down into at least three sections headed "Cases," "Statutes," and "Other Authorities." List cases in alphabetical order. If constitutional provisions, court rules, administrative regulations, or legislative histories are cited in the brief, you can add one or more extra sections for them. Regulations, court rules, and legislative histories might be grouped under one heading. Sometimes legislative histories are included with statutes instead. Some lawyers include constitutional provisions with statutes. Others put them in a separate section. The heading should reflect where they are. "Other Authorities" is reserved for secondary authorities, such as restatements, treatises, and law review articles (which are listed there in that order).

36 Handling Standards of Review

[T]here are some words with legal meaning that you simply cannot avoid. Take "standard of review." . . . To the judge, it is everything.

—*Deanell Reece Tacha, former Chief Judge,
U.S. Court of Appeals for the Tenth Circuit*

If the appellant satisfies the standard of appellate review, the appellant wins. And if the appellee prevents the appellant from doing that, the appellee becomes the winner.

Appellate judges cannot reverse a lower court merely because they disagree with the decision. They can reverse only when the relevant *standard of review* lets them do so. Even if an appellate court thinks the trial court was wrong, the applicable standard of review is the procedural rule that controls the ultimate decision whether to affirm or reverse.

Think about the implications if appellate courts did not apply standards of review. If lower court decisions were reversed whenever appellate courts disagreed with them, few legal disputes would be resolved in a timely fashion. Appellate courts would be glutted with cases awaiting review. Standards of review have been developed by appellate courts as a means of controlling the number and nature of appeals. The standards reflect the principle that parties are not entitled to a *perfect* trial but only a *fair* one.[1]

Under certain standards of review, an appellate court will affirm even if it would not have reached the same decision the lower court did. Appellate judges respect the crucial role of the trial judge and jury in weighing the evidence admitted at trial and the credibility of witnesses. An appellate court has available for review only a "cold" printed transcript of the trial testimony, but the trial judge observed the witnesses and experienced the trial first hand.

Appellate judges become frustrated and annoyed when lawyers write briefs and make arguments as though standards of review do not matter. Identifying the correct

---

[1] "'[A] defendant is entitled to a fair trial but not a perfect one,' for there are no perfect trials." *Brown v. United States*, 411 U.S. 223, 231-32 (1973) (citations omitted).

standard of review is sometimes the most important step in predicting the outcome of an appeal. It specifies the minimum threshold the appellant must reach in persuading the appellate court to set aside or reverse the lower court's decision.

§ 36.1   The Four Main Standards of Review

The *type* of ruling below determines the standard of review on appeal. Appellate courts apply various standards of review depending on the *degree of deference* they give that type of ruling. The standard of review depends on the nature of the issue (law or fact) and who made the decision challenged on appeal (the trial judge, the jury, or an administrative agency).

The four most important standards of review follow, listed in order from the least to the most deferential:

1. *de novo* review for issues of law decided by a state or federal court
2. *clearly erroneous* review for issues of fact decided by a trial judge in federal courts and some state courts
3. *substantial evidence* review for issues of fact decided by some state trial courts, and for issues of fact decided by federal agencies after formal hearings, and
4. *abuse of discretion* review for issues within a trial judge's discretion

Where do standards of review come from? Most are developed by the appellate courts as a matter of procedural common law, but a few are specified in court rules or statutes. For example, the clearly erroneous standard of appellate review, which applies to a federal trial judge's finding on an issue of fact in a bench trial, is required by the Federal Rules of Civil Procedure.[2] A *bench trial* is a trial without a jury in which the trial judge not only decides issues of law, but also makes findings of fact. All standards of review are based on *policy decisions* about which decision maker is in the best position to correctly resolve the dispute underlying the issue challenged on appeal.

How do you determine the standard of review for your appellate brief assignment? You can generally find the appropriate standard of review by researching cases in your jurisdiction that have resolved similar issues based on the same procedural posture. Most appellate court decisions include one or two sentences clearly identifying the standard of review before turning to the legal analysis based on the specific facts of that case.

De novo review—issues of law. A trial court decides an *issue of law* when it interprets the law or decides what the law is. For example, when a trial judge instructs

---

[2] *See* FED. R. CIV. P. 52(a)(6).

the jury at the end of a trial, the judge explains the elements of the legal rules the jury must follow in reaching a verdict. In determining which instructions to give the jury, the judge decides pure issues of law. If the jury instruction accurately states the relevant law, the trial judge has not committed an error. But if the jury instruction incorrectly states the law, or if the instruction gives the jury the wrong legal rule for that case, the judge has erroneously decided an issue of law.

If the losing party appeals, the appellate court asks whether it would have interpreted the law in the same way the trial court did. *De novo* is the label the appellate courts generally use when describing this standard of review. In Latin, it means to do "from the beginning" or "as though new." Some appellate courts use other phrases, such as *plenary review* or *independent review*—they mean the same thing. If the trial court applied the wrong legal rule or interpreted the law incorrectly, the appellate court is likely to apply *de novo* review and reverse the decision.

When you receive an appellate brief assignment, look first for *the type of issue* the trial court decided that the losing party has challenged on appeal. If the issue is one of the following, you almost always have an issue of law that triggers *de novo* appellate review:[3]

- an order dismissing a complaint or other pleading
- an order granting summary judgment
- an order granting a directed verdict (or in federal courts, judgment as a matter of law)
- a jury instruction
- an order granting judgment notwithstanding the verdict (or in federal courts, judgment as a matter of law)
- an order denying any of the above

Other trial court decisions may resolve issues of law, but these are the most common.[4]

A *de novo* standard of review is neutral, like a pane of glass through which light passes without distortion. It is the only standard of review that gives no deference whatsoever to the trial court's decision. The reason is that appellate judges consider themselves just as capable as trial judges at interpreting the law or determining what the law is in any particular case. An appellate court might do an even better job deciding a pure issue of law than the trial judge because at least three judges (and sometimes more) decide a case on appeal. And the appellate court has much more time for research and reflection because very few legal issues decided by the trial court in a single dispute are eventually challenged on appeal.

As compared to *de novo* review, the other standards (described below) are more like filters and lenses that modify the image on appeal because they give more or less deference to the trial court's decision. When an appellate court defers to the trial

---

[3] Some issues of law, such as trial court rulings on the admissibility of evidence, invoke more deferential standards of review.

[4] Law school appellate brief assignments often (but not always) involve *de novo* standards of review.

court, the reviewing court is less likely to reverse, even if the trial court was wrong. In effect, the appellate court gives the trial court the benefit of the doubt by beginning with a presumption (which may be weak or strong) that the lower court was right. In those instances, it takes a good deal of persuasion for the appellant to overcome the presumption of deference in order to win reversal.

Clearly erroneous review—issues of fact (federal bench trials). An issue of fact is a question about what actually happened between the parties. For example, was the defendant's gun loaded or unloaded at the time of the crime? Who was more believable: the witness who testified that the accused loaded the gun with bullets just before the crime, or the witness who testified that the accused emptied the gun of bullets then? When fact issues are decided by a trial court judge in a bench trial or in a pretrial motion, the appellate court reviews challenged findings for *clear error.*[5]

A pretrial motion asks the judge to make a procedural decision *before the trial begins.* For example, assume that a criminal defendant seeks to keep his confession from being admitted into evidence during the upcoming jury trial. If the defendant claims that he confessed to the alleged crime only because a police officer threatened to beat him up, the trial judge would have to decide before trial whether the police did that or not—a fact issue. In that case, the trial judge would be making a pretrial finding of fact (whether or not the police coerced the confession) leading to a legal decision (whether the confession is admissible into evidence).

When identifying the applicable standard of review, do not confuse a fact issue with a legal issue. For instance, suppose the defendant claims that before his confession, the police officer bragged about being such a good amateur boxer that he almost qualified for the United States boxing team at the last Olympics. Whether the police officer bragged about his boxing ability is an *issue of fact.* Assuming the officer did brag, whether that conduct influenced the defendant to confess is also an *issue of fact.* But even if the officer's bragging *did* lead the defendant to confess, whether the officer's conduct violated the defendant's legal rights by coercing the confession is an *issue of law.*

issue of fact:	Did the police officer brag about his boxing prowess in the defendant's presence before he confessed?
issue of fact:	Did the officer's bragging about his boxing prowess cause the defendant to confess out of fear that the officer might beat him up?
issue of law:	Does that kind of police coercion of a confession violate the defendant's Fifth Amendment right against self-incrimination?

---

[5] *See* Fed. R. Civ. P. 52(a)(6).

Unless the trial court's pretrial findings of fact were *clearly erroneous* (not just mistaken), the appellate court will not reverse. It will not be enough that the trial court may have been wrong. A deeper level of error is required for reversal.

When reviewing for clear error, courts sometimes say that they will reverse only if they "are left with a definite and firm conviction that a mistake has been made."[6] The Seventh Circuit has put it more bluntly: "To be clearly erroneous, a decision must strike us as more than just maybe or probably wrong; it must . . . strike us as wrong with the force of a five-week-old, unrefrigerated dead fish."[7] Other courts use less colorful language to express the same idea. However expressed, clear error is a very difficult standard for an appellant to satisfy.

Substantial evidence review—issues of fact (state trial courts and state or federal administrative agencies). In most state appellate courts, the substantial evidence standard of review applies when determining whether sufficient evidence was presented to support the trial court's final judgment or order. For example, assume a trial court decides that a defendant was in custody when interrogated without receiving a *Miranda* warning, and that he gave an incriminating testimonial statement to the police. If the trial court grants the defendant's motion to suppress the statement based in part on the finding that he was in custody at the time of questioning, the appellate court will decide on appeal whether the trial court's decision was supported by substantial evidence. If it was, the court will affirm the suppression order.[8]

The substantial evidence standard is also applied when a state or federal appellate court reviews a finding of fact by an administrative agency, especially when the finding is made following a formal hearing on the record.[9]

Under this standard, appellate review is limited to a determination of whether there was any substantial evidence, contradicted or uncontradicted, that supports the finding. Substantial evidence is not the same as "any" evidence; the reviewing court's focus is on the quality of the evidence, not the quantity. Very little evidence may still qualify as "substantial" if it is competent and compelling, while lots of extremely weak evidence might not be considered "substantial."[10]

Most appellate courts consider the substantial evidence standard of review even more difficult for an appellant to meet than the clear error standard. As long as the

---

[6] *United States v. Brown*, 156 F.3d 813, 816 (8th Cir. 1998) (citation omitted).

[7] *Parts & Elec. Motors, Inc. v. Sterling Elec., Inc.*, 866 F.2d 228, 233 (7th Cir. 1988).

[8] *See State v. Banks*, 2 N.E.3d 71, 77 (Ind. Ct. App. 2014) ("In reviewing a trial court's motion to suppress, we determine whether the record discloses 'substantial evidence of probative value that supports the trial court's decision.'" (citations omitted)).

[9] *E.g.*, Harry T. Edwards & Linda A. Elliott, Federal Courts Standards of Review 175-77 (2007); Michael E. Tigar & Jane B. Tigar, 4C N.Y. Prac., Com. Litig. in N.Y. State Courts § 102:21 (3d ed. 2013) ("In a case that rests, in part, on factual assessments made by an agency or government body, once the court has concluded that the findings are rational or supported by *substantial evidence*, its authority to review the facts is at an end." (emphasis added)).

[10] *E.g.*, Eileen C. Moore & Michael Paul Thomas, Cal. Civ. Prac. Procedure § 41:5 (2014) (citations omitted).

appellate court can find *some* substantial evidence in the trial court record that supports the determination of fact by the lower court or agency, the appellate court will affirm the challenged finding.

Abuse of discretion review—discretionary issues. Many issues involving procedure or routine decisions about the admissibility of evidence are within the trial judge's discretion. The policy reason for granting broad deference on such decisions is to respect the challenging role of the trial judge, who must decide a multitude of procedural and evidentiary issues on the spot each day. Here is a typical appellate court formulation of what that level of discretion means in practice:

> [W]hen we say that a decision is discretionary, . . . we do not mean that the district court may do whatever pleases it. The phrase means instead that the court has *a range of choice, and that its decision will not be disturbed [on appeal] as long as it stays within that range* and is not influenced by any mistake of law. An abuse of discretion, on the other hand, can occur . . . when a relevant factor that should have been given significant weight is not considered; when an irrelevant or improper factor is considered and given significant weight; and when all proper factors . . . are considered, but the court, in weighing those factors, commits a clear error of judgment.[11]

The most important part of the abuse-of-discretion standard is that the court has a range of choice. As long as the trial judge reaches a decision within the permissible range of choice, the decision will be affirmed on appeal. But how do you know what that range is? Reading your jurisdiction's case law addressing the same issue in a similar fact setting will help you discover the acceptable range of discretion.

The abuse-of-discretion standard is the most deferential to the trial court. Appellate courts reason that the trial judge is closer to the problem and probably has a better view about how to solve it. Accordingly, this standard generally applies to decisions about admissibility of evidence, discovery disputes, and matters of courtroom management. When the abuse of discretion standard applies, a party who challenges that decision on appeal will have a very high burden of persuasion to convince an appellate court to reverse.

Combination standards of review. Occasionally you will come across a trial court's conclusion of law that is subject to more than one standard of appellate review. For example, one federal circuit applies a different standard of review to each portion of a trial court's holding that laches bars a claim:

> Our standard of review on the laches issue has various components. We review factual findings such as length of delay and prejudice under the clearly erroneous

---

[11] *Kern v. TXO Prod. Corp.*, 738 F.2d 968, 970 (8th Cir. 1984) (emphasis added).

standard; we review the district court's balancing of the equities for abuse of discretion; and our review of legal precepts applied by the district court in determining that the delay was excusable is plenary [*de novo*].[12]

Suppose a plaintiff moves for a preliminary injunction alleging that the defendant is infringing the plaintiff's trademark by selling a new beverage product called Blue Bull. (A preliminary injunction is a court's command to a party to do or not do certain things before trial.)

Some appellate courts will divide up the various issues this way:

issue of fact: Is the defendant selling a beverage product called Blue Bull?

issue of law: What rules of trademark law govern this dispute?

discretionary issue: Is a preliminary injunction an appropriate remedy in this situation?

An appellate court will review the trial court's fact finding for clear error, its articulation of the applicable trademark law *de novo*, and the discretionary decision to grant or deny a preliminary injunction for abuse of discretion.

Mixed issues of law and fact. Appellate courts often decide mixed questions of fact and law. In this instance, the issue of fact cannot be readily separated from the issue of law. For example,

issue of fact: What events occurred that led to the dispute?

issue of law: What is the governing legal test?

mixed issue: How does the legal test apply to these facts?

It is difficult to generalize about how appellate courts handle mixed issues of law and fact. Sometimes a court will apply a *de novo* standard to a mixed question; at other times a court will separate the decision into its factual and legal components and apply the relevant standard of review to each part. Still other courts apply the standard of review that governs the predominant aspect of the mixed issue: *de novo* if the dispute primarily involves a legal issue, or clearly erroneous if the fact issues are more significant to the dispute.

If you have a mixed issue of law and fact, find case law on issues like the one in your assignment. Read carefully to see how the courts in your jurisdiction analyze the issue. Then apply a similar analysis to the issue in your assignment. If the case law gives you a

---

[12] *Bermuda Express, N.V. v. M/V LITSA*, 872 F.2d 554, 557 (3d Cir. 1989) (citation omitted).

reasonable choice among various standards of review, select the one that most favors your client's position, and be prepared to defend it by citing to appropriate legal authorities.

§ 36.2 How to Determine Which Standard of Review Governs Your Issue

Suppose the trial court determined the facts, interpreted the applicable law, and granted a discretionary remedy to one of the parties. Suppose also that the losing party appeals, but challenges only the trial court's interpretation of law. The other issues decided by the trial court are not challenged on appeal.

Look at the issue the appellate court must decide. In this example, the appellant has challenged *only* the trial court's decision of law. The fact and discretionary issues have not been preserved for appeal and therefore are not before the appellate court. Sometimes an appellate court does not clearly identify the kind of issue it is addressing. But any time the court *interprets a legal rule*, whether based on common law precedent, a statute, a court rule, or an administrative regulation, that is an issue of law, which is reviewed *de novo*.

Look also at how the analogous case law in your jurisdiction discusses your issue. When an appellate court mentions the standard of review in a decision, it usually does so right after reciting the facts and just before beginning the legal analysis. Find cases that tell you not only what the standard is, but also what it means and how it works. Standards of review are usually found in case law, although they might partially be addressed in court rules or statutes.

Here is an example of language you will find in an appellate court opinion that identifies the applicable standard of review:

> We review de novo the district court's dismissal of a complaint for failure to state a claim under Rule 12(b)(6). In reviewing such a motion, we accept all material allegations of fact as true and construe the complaint in a light most favorable to the non-moving party. We have consistently emphasized, however, that "conclusory allegations of law and unwarranted inferences" will not defeat an otherwise proper motion to dismiss.[13]

From this opinion, we learn that the standard of review is *de novo*. The court explains how the standard works in reviewing the trial court's decision by describing the procedural standard the lower court should have applied to the motion to dismiss the complaint for failure to state a claim. Here, the appellate court will consider

---

[13] *Vasquez v. L.A. Cnty.*, 487 F.3d 1246, 1249 (9th Cir. 2007) (citations omitted).

de novo whether the trial court properly applied that procedural standard to the motion, without giving any deference to the trial court's reasoning or its legal conclusion.

§ 36.3 How to Use Standards of Review in an Appellate Brief

In federal appeals, the appellant's argument "must contain . . . for each issue, a concise statement of the applicable standard of review."[14] The appellee's brief can omit the standard of review "unless the appellee is dissatisfied with appellant's statement."[15] State appellate courts generally have similar rules that require briefs to include the standard of review.

When you tell the court the standard of review, it often helps to explain the procedural posture of the case as decided by the trial court and the procedural test that governed below. If it can be done succinctly, tell the court how the standard of review justifies reversal (if you represent the appellant) or how it justifies affirmance (if you represent the appellee).

For example, assume that the trial court granted summary judgment to Blue Bull, the defendant in the trademark infringement case discussed in § 36.1. The following paragraph might appear in the appellant's brief:

> Plaintiff Red Bull appeals from summary judgment, which is reviewed *de novo* in this court. [Citation.] Summary judgment should be granted only if no genuine issue of material fact remains to be resolved and the moving party is entitled to judgment as a matter of law. Fed. R. Civ. P. 56(a). In this case, Defendant Blue Bull should not have been granted summary judgment because it was not entitled to judgment as a matter of law.

This passage tells us that the standard of review is *de novo*. The appellant will argue that the trial court granted summary judgment in error because the second element of the conjunctive test was not satisfied. In the paragraphs that follow, the writer will have to explain thoroughly why the appellee was not entitled to judgment as a matter of law. (It does not matter whether a genuine issue of fact remains because the appellant did not raise that argument in the appeal.)

Explain your standard of review at or near the beginning of the Argument for each issue. Some appellate courts require a separate section of the brief that identifies the standard of review for each issue raised on appeal. Follow the court rules for the appellate court in which you are filing your brief.

---

[14] Fed. R. App. P. 28(a)(8)(B).
[15] Fed. R. App. P. 28(b).

Concisely identify the issue raised on appeal. Next, set out the relevant standard of review for that issue, citing mandatory authority for your jurisdiction. If you have more than one issue, each with a different standard of review, the standard for each one should be set out shortly after the point heading for that issue. After you identify the relevant standard of review, give a concise rule explanation. A conclusory rule explanation (see § 18.6) is usually sufficient because appellate courts are generally familiar with the applicable standards of review. Finally, explain how the standard of review supports a ruling in your client's favor on appeal.

§ 36.3.1   Integrating the Standard of Review into the Argument

The standard of review "must become an integral part of the argument."[16] For example, if you represent the appellant and the standard of review is *de novo*, your client is in a favorable position on appeal because the reviewing court will give no deference to the trial court's decision. Weave the standard of review into your Argument to remind the court that it can reverse if it disagrees with the trial court's decision. If you represent the appellee, however, a *de novo* standard raises the risk of reversal on appeal. That is because the *de novo* standard does not give you the benefit of a presumption that the trial court's decision should be affirmed.

If the standard of review is more deferential to the trial court—clear error, substantial evidence, or abuse of discretion—argue your client's position in terms of the standard. For example, if you are appealing a decision committed to the trial court's discretion, show exactly how the trial court abused its discretion. As the appellant, you have a difficult task to convince the appellate court that the trial court's decision was too wide of the permissible range of choices. But if you represent the appellee, you have an easier task. Using the more deferential standard of review, show the appellate court that the trial court's decision was well within the range of permissible choices. When you are the appellee and you have a deferential standard of review, weave it into your Argument at every opportunity.

If you are unsure about how to do any of these things, take a look at several appellate opinions in the same jurisdiction that apply the same standard of review in cases involving similar procedural postures. Look for a definition of the standard, and try to learn its relationship to other procedural rules. And get a feel for the appellate court's expectations about how the standard should be used. Use what you learn to guide you in writing a persuasive standard of review section for your appellate brief.

---

[16] W. Wendell Hall, *Standards of Appellate Review in Civil Appeals*, 21 St. Mary's L.J. 865, 868 (1990).

§ 36.3.2 Integrating the Standard of Review into the Point Headings

Chapter 33 explains how to write point headings in motion memos and briefs. Now that you understand the value of standards of review to an appellate court, you can make the point headings in your appellate briefs even more persuasive.

If you have a favorable standard of review, work it into your point headings. For example, assume you are appealing a trial court's jury instruction defining the burden of proof in a fraud case. You might write a point heading like this one:

> Under *de novo* review, this Court should reverse because the trial court failed to properly instruct the jury that the plaintiff had the burden of proving each element of fraud by clear and convincing evidence.

But if you represent the appellee, you would not want to emphasize that the *de novo* standard applies. That standard favors the appellant because it gives no deference to the trial court's decision. As the lawyer for the appellee, you would give your client no advantage by emphasizing the *de novo* standard because you want to defend the trial court's decision against reversal. So you might write a point heading like this one:

> This Court should affirm because the trial court properly instructed the jury on each element of the fraud claim that the defendant deliberately misled the plaintiff about the true cost of the flat-screen television.

But what if a deferential standard applies? The more deference a standard of review gives to the trial court's decision, the more favorable that standard of review will be for the appellee, who wants the appellate court to affirm. So if you represent the appellant, you would avoid emphasizing the standard of review in your point heading:

> This Court should reverse because the jury's guilty verdict necessarily relied on two eyewitnesses whose testimony was unreliable, and the trial court erred by excluding expert testimony on the deficiencies of eyewitness testimony.

The appellee, however, would have the advantage of a favorable standard of review because it gives great deference to the trial court's evidence ruling. In the same case, the appellee's point heading might look something like this:

> This Court should affirm because the trial court's ruling excluding expert testimony was not an abuse of the trial court's broad discretion, and the jury was capable of evaluating the credibility of the eyewitnesses based on its common sense experience.

Use the same process when other standards of review apply. First identify the standard of review for each issue, and decide whether the standard favors your client's position on appeal. If it does, take advantage of its power to persuade by integrating it into your Argument point headings. If you have two or more issues on appeal, the relevant standard may differ for each one. In your point headings, integrate those that help make your argument more persuasive, whether you represent the appellant or the appellee.

Exercise 36-A. Identifying Standards of Review

For each of the following issues, identify the standard of appellate review: *de novo*, **clearly erroneous**, **substantial evidence**, or **abuse of discretion**.

1. A trial court ruling that the State of Nebraska recognizes a common law cause of action for intentional infliction of emotional distress.

2. In a bench trial, a finding by a federal court that the defendant passed counterfeit $20 bills.

3. A state trial court judgment entered on a jury verdict finding a defendant guilty of burglary.

4. An order denying the defendant's discovery request.

5. An evidentiary order excluding the statement made by defendant truck driver just after colliding with a bicycle.

6. A jury instruction explaining how to decide whether the manager of a golf course breached a legal duty to warn golfers about the risk of lightning.

7. A trial court's order granting a motion for summary judgment in a legal malpractice claim.

8. A federal agency's decision after a formal hearing determining that an applicant for social security disability benefits was not "disabled."

37 Questions Presented

§ 37.1 The Purpose of a Question Presented

An effective Question Presented does two things. First, it *identifies the legal question* the court is being asked to resolve. Second, it *persuades* by framing the legal question in the context of your client's most determinative facts that support your theory.

If the Question Presented defines the legal issue too objectively, it fails to perform the function of persuasiveness. But if it frames the case-specific facts too strenuously in your client's favor, the Question Presented fails to credibly articulate the legal question. The solution is to persuade the court through juxtaposition and careful word choice, just as you do in a Statement of the Case—but much more concisely.

A Question Presented combines

- the legal issue or question to be resolved,
- a reference to the legal test or concept that governs the result, and
- the most important determinative facts.

The "question presented" by the situation includes not only the legal issue, but also a reference to the governing legal test or concept and the key determinative facts. Asking "Is a manufacturer liable to a purchaser?" is a question, but it is not a *Question Presented* that includes each of the three necessary components. An effective Question Presented provides the essential legal and factual context for the question that the decision maker must resolve. And it puts the parts together in a way that immediately persuades the decision maker to rule in your client's favor based on the key facts relevant to the legal issue.

§ 37.2   Two Generally Effective Formats

Both of the formats explained in this section do a good job satisfying the criteria in § 37.6 of this chapter. But in some briefs, one format will work better than the other. Choose the one that better reflects your approach to the case.

The Verb/Concept/Facts format. Here is an example:

Question Presented	Is the manufacturer of an electronic keyboard liable to a purchaser for violating an implied warranty of fitness for a particular purpose, when the keyboard exploded in the purchaser's hands the first time it was plugged in?
inquiry	is an electronic keyboard manufacturer liable to a purchaser?
legal concept	implied warranty of fitness for a particular purpose
facts	keyboard exploded in purchaser's hands when first plugged in

Start with a verb and subject that help make your case:

Is the manufacturer of an electronic keyboard liable . . . ?

Does a manufacturer violate a duty to the purchaser . . . ?

Can the purchaser of an electronic keyboard recover . . . ?

Here, the subjects are the manufacturer in the first and second examples and the purchaser in the third example. The verbs are underlined to show you how to combine them with the subjects.

After beginning the Question Presented this way, add the legal concept—here the implied warranty. Then attach the most determinative facts in a *when* clause.

The Under/Does/When format. This format works particularly well when your reader needs to know what jurisdiction's law applies to the case. To structure a Question Presented this way, begin with the word *under*. Then specify the jurisdiction whose law governs the issue, together with a reference to the general nature of the legal rule:

Under § 51 of the New York Civil Rights Law, ...

Under federal copyright law, ...

Next, add the word *does* and introduce the basic inquiry and the legal issue or concept:

> . . . does a professional model have a cause of action for invasion of privacy against an online vendor . . . .

> . . . does a music composer have a copyright claim against iTunes . . . .

Finally, add the word *when* and list the most determinative facts:

> . . . when the defendant advertised the plaintiff's photograph for sale on its website without her consent?

> . . . when iTunes sold the composer's recordings without paying her a royalty?

Once all the parts are put together, the Under/Does/When format results in an effective Question Presented:

> Under § 51 of the New York Civil Rights Law, does a professional model have a cause of action for invasion of privacy against an online vendor when the defendant advertised the plaintiff's photograph for sale on its website without her consent?

> Under federal copyright law, does a music composer have a copyright claim against iTunes when it sold the composer's recordings without paying her a royalty?

§ 37.3   Incorporating Determinative Facts

With either of the formats explained in § 37.2, facts that do not naturally fit into the phrasing of the Question Presented can be listed at the end, introduced by *when*.[1] For example, the keyboard manufacturer's lawyer might have written the following Question Presented:

> Is the manufacturer of an electronic keyboard absolved of liability under an implied warranty of fitness for a particular purpose, when a purchaser bought the disassembled keyboard pieces from a street vendor and attempted to reassemble them himself, even though the keyboard case was engraved with the words, "Do Not Open or Attempt to Repair This Product"?

The list of determinative facts should appear at the end of the Question Presented because the factual details make sense only after the reader knows the basic inquiry and the governing legal concept.

---

[1] Although the word *where* has traditionally been used to introduce a list of determinative facts in a Question Presented, fewer lawyers use it today, and the current trend is to use *when*. Use *where* only when an employer or teacher requires it.

In comparison, the following examples are much more difficult to understand because the determinative facts are not placed at the end:

facts at the beginning   If a purchaser bought a disassembled electronic keyboard from a street vendor and attempted to reassemble it himself, even though the words "Do Not Open or Attempt to Repair This Product" were engraved on the keyboard case, is the manufacturer absolved of liability under an implied warranty of fitness for a particular purpose?

facts in the middle   Is the manufacturer of an electronic keyboard, which was bought from a street vendor by a purchaser who attempted to reassemble it himself even though the words "Do Not Open or Attempt to Repair This Product" were engraved on the keyboard case, absolved of liability under an implied warranty of fitness for a particular purpose?

Your reader will find it much easier to understand your Questions Presented when the detailed facts appear at the end.

§ 37.4   Formats to Use Only in Certain Situations

The Whether/Concept/Facts format.   This format begins with the word *whether*.

Whether the manufacturer of an electronic keyboard is absolved of liability under an implied warranty of fitness for a particular purpose, when a purchaser bought the disassembled keyboard pieces from a street vendor and attempted to reassemble them himself, even though the keyboard case was engraved with the words, "Do Not Open or Attempt to Repair This Product."

This is not a complete sentence. The word *whether* has turned it into a dependent clause. And it does not ask a question. A true question would be a complete sentence built on a question-asking verb, ending with a question mark. A true question invites an answer. In comparison, a *whether* Question Presented is often harder to read and can seem artificial. The formats explained in § 37.2 are more concrete and easier to understand because they look like questions written in ordinary English.

The Whether/Concept/Facts format, however, is traditionally used in some courts. Many lawyers use it based on custom. Use it yourself only when an employer or teacher requires it.

The Narrative Paragraph format. In some cases, a reader would drown in a series of *when* clauses in a Question Presented because even the most essential facts are so complicated that they cannot be reduced to a short list. In extraordinarily complicated appeals—when the trial went on for weeks preceded by many motions and hundreds of pages of pleadings—lawyers sometimes use a format that begins with a separate narrative paragraph giving the determinative facts, followed by an inquiry and the governing legal concept. Here are the ingredients:

[Paragraph stating the essential facts common to most or all issues]

[First Issue, including an inquiry and a reference to the legal concept]

[Second Issue, if applicable, stated the same way]

[Third Issue, if applicable, stated the same way]

This format almost never works well in a first-year appellate advocacy assignment, although rarely it might be effective in an upper-level appellate brief competition or a third-year appellate clinic. In a first-year assignment, do not use this format as an easy fix when your list of determinative facts is long and complicated. Instead, choose one of the formats in § 37.2. Try to compress your list of essential facts. Then revise your wording to make it as concise as possible.

§ 37.5   How to Write a Question Presented

Drafting a Question Presented can be one of the most difficult tasks in legal writing. An effective Question Presented conveys a great deal of useful information to the reader in relatively few words. Many drafts might be needed to prepare one that persuasively communicates the necessary information in a way that is readable and concise.

Start by outlining your raw materials. Write out the inquiry and the reference to the governing legal test or concept. Separately list the facts that are most essential for resolving the legal issue. Then experiment with the formats in § 37.2 to work out a concise wording of the facts, merging them into the inquiry. In later drafts, make sure your Question Presented satisfies the criteria discussed in § 37.6.

Many lawyers write the Question Presented after writing a first draft of the rest of the brief. After carefully analyzing the relevant law and applying it to the client's facts, a writer fully understands the essential determinative facts that will best persuade the reader. Sometimes, however, you might be able to write the Question Presented earlier. But if you do, remain flexible about rewriting it after you have completed the rest of the brief to be sure it reflects the key facts on which your Argument relies.

§ 37.6 How to Test Your Questions Presented for Effectiveness

While rewriting, ask yourself the numbered questions that appear later in this section.

Assume that a stockbroker grew tired of his work and decided to do something more creative. He persuaded a gourmet bakery to take him on as an apprentice baker. The bakery has perfected a secret method of adding a citrus flavor to its croissants, which have become a trendy food for that reason. The bakery requires its employees to sign a three-year covenant not to compete with the bakery anywhere in the two urban counties in Arizona, an otherwise rural state. After a short time, the stockbroker quit working for the bakery and formed his own company to sell gourmet baked goods in one of the state's two urban counties. His former employer has sued to enforce the covenant by securing an injunction.

In Arizona, a covenant not to compete is enforceable if the prohibition is "reasonably limited" in duration and geographic area, and if its provisions are (1) "reasonably necessary for protection of the employer's business," (2) "not unreasonably restrictive" of the employee's rights, and (3) not inconsistent with public policy.[2]

The lawyers might draft these Questions Presented:

for the employer

Under Arizona common law, should the court enjoin a successful former stockbroker who entered the baking business from violating a three-year covenant not to compete with his former bakery employer, when the plaintiff trained him as a baker, the defendant had access to a secret recipe for the plaintiff's most popular product, and the defendant has established the only competing business within a two-county market for specialized gourmet baked goods?

for the apprentice baker

Under Arizona common law, is it inequitable for the Court to enjoin an apprentice baker from working "in any baking capacity" for as long as three years, in a geographic area that encompasses three-quarters of the state's population, when the plaintiff's only realistic fear of potential injury is that the apprentice baker might use a single croissant recipe in his own baked goods business?

---

[2] *Am. Credit Bureau, Inc. v. Carter*, 462 P.2d 838, 840 (Ariz. Ct. App. 1969).

These Questions Presented are referenced in some of the following paragraphs.

1. Have you kept conclusions of law or fact out of your Question Presented? In the following Question Presented, the "facts" are not really facts at all. They are *conclusions of law*, which the writer must prove later in the Argument section of the brief. This Question Presented asks whether the defendant should be enjoined assuming *the applicable legal test has been satisfied*:

> Should a defendant apprentice baker be enjoined from violating a covenant not to compete if the covenant is reasonably limited in duration and geographic area, its prohibitions are reasonably necessary to protect the former employer's business, it does not unreasonably restrict the former employee's rights, and it does not violate public policy?

Of course the answer to this question will always be yes. If a plaintiff can satisfy the test for an injunction, a court will grant the injunction. But that is not the issue the court must decide. The issue is *whether* that legal test has been satisfied based on the determinative facts. Conclusions of law and conclusory factual inferences— such as "the covenant is reasonably limited in duration and geographic area"—cannot be posited as though they are undisputed facts and legal conclusions. You must prove each of those conclusions and inferences in the Argument section of the brief.

If you find legal or factual conclusions in your Question Presented, edit them out and replace them with the determinative facts that will support those conclusions. For example, which *facts* support the conclusion that the covenant's restraints on the apprentice baker are reasonably necessary to protect the former employer's bakery business? Those *facts* belong in the Question Presented. The Argument will show why those facts support the inference or the legal conclusion you want for your client.

2. Is each fact in your Question Presented undeniably true and stated in a way that your adversary cannot reasonably dispute? A Question Presented persuades only if based on undeniable facts. Look at the two Questions Presented near the beginning of this section. Each persuades in part by listing facts that the opposing lawyer cannot refute or disclaim. Moreover, neither side has argued that the other side's strongest facts are wrong or inaccurate.

The apprentice baker's lawyer must concede that his client has established a competing baked goods company. But in doing so, his Question Presented diminishes the unfavorable fact's importance by suggesting that the former employer will suffer only insignificant injury ("the apprentice might use a single croissant recipe"). The former employer's lawyer cannot dispute that most of Arizona's population is concentrated in the two counties subject to the covenant. But while conceding that fact, she demonstrates why it makes sense to enforce the covenant in that area ("a two-county market for specialized gourmet baked goods").

As in your Statement of the Case (Chapter 31), careful juxtaposition is the key to neutralizing unfavorable facts.

3. Will a judge be able to understand your Question Presented without reading it twice? List only essential facts, and omit details. Use concise wording without sacrificing clarity.

Striking the right balance of clarity and conciseness is not easy. Consider this example:

> Under Arizona common law, should this court enjoin the violation of a covenant not to compete that applies only to the baking industry and includes a prohibition on competition that lasts three years, when the defendant baking apprentice previously made a substantial income as a stockbroker and continues to derive passive income as a partner in a brokerage house; the plaintiff bakery trained him as a baker, and he has no other instruction or experience in the field; the defendant had access to the plaintiff bakery's secret recipe for a unique croissant embodying citrus flavors; the defendant has set himself up in business as the plaintiff bakery's only competitor in this field; and the parties compete in a specialized gourmet baked goods market that extends over two adjacent counties, each including a major city?

Can you understand this Question Presented in one reading? Can you tell immediately what facts are important? Compare it—phrase by phrase—with the former employer's Question Presented near the beginning of this section. There is no difference in meaning. The only difference is that the example immediately above adds unnecessary details and uses too many words to say the same thing. It takes much rewriting to make a Question Presented both concise and understandable.

4. Will the judge readily understand who the parties are and their relationship to one another? It is often more clear and concise to refer to the parties with meaningful generic phrases—such as "the former employer," "the bakery apprentice," and so forth—rather than by each party's proper name. Using procedural references like "appellant" and "appellee" can confuse the reader.[3] In some cases, even referring to the "plaintiff" and the "defendant" might obscure the parties' roles in the controversy. However, in a criminal case, it is rarely confusing to refer to the prosecution as the "state" or "government" and the other party as the "defendant."

Although a busy judge can be confused when briefs refer to the parties only by their proper names ("Jack Jones" rather than "the plaintiff"), it is sometimes tactically wise to "personalize" your client as long as the context clarifies who is who. For

---

[3] Federal appellate courts discourage lawyers from referring to the parties as "appellant" and "appellee" in their briefs. *See* Fed. R. App. P. 28(d).

example, if you represent the defendant in a criminal case, you can gently remind the court that your client is a human being by referring to "Ms. Woodbridge" rather than the more abstract term "the defendant."

5. Does your Question Presented clearly define what the court must decide? Many judges read the Question Presented *before* they read any other part of the brief. For that reason, do not assume in the Question Presented that the reader already knows the parties and the facts.

> Should the court enjoin violation of a covenant not to compete when the defendant is a successful stockbroker who was trained entirely by the plaintiff, had access to the plaintiff's secret croissant recipe, and has now set himself up in business as the plaintiff's only competitor?

If you had not already read about the facts at the beginning of this section, this Question Presented would not make much sense. Did the plaintiff train the defendant to be a *stockbroker*? Does the plaintiff want to enjoin competition *in the stock brokerage industry*? What does a croissant recipe have to do with any of this? When writing your Question Presented, remember that the judge most likely has not yet read the Statement of the Case and certainly has not yet read the Argument. A Question Presented that confuses the reader cannot persuade.

6. Do you have the right number of Questions Presented? Write a Question Presented for each primary issue on appeal—but not more than that. The bakery example has many specific issues—whether the covenant not to compete unreasonably limits the former employee's baking career options in duration and geography, whether it limits his options more than reasonably necessary to protect the former employer, and so on. But these are really sub-issues under one big, comprehensive issue: whether the court should enforce the covenant not to compete.

In the example below, the bakery's lawyer has carved up that one big, comprehensive issue into three Questions Presented, none of which includes all of the determinative facts:

I. Did the trial court properly enjoin the violation of a covenant not to compete, which was limited to a three-year period in a two-county area?
II. Did the trial court properly enjoin the violation of a covenant not to compete when the enjoined former employee had access to the plaintiff's secret croissant recipe and has now set himself up as the plaintiff's only competitor?
III. Did the trial court properly enjoin the violation of a covenant not to compete when the former employee was a successful stockbroker and does not depend on baking for his livelihood?

Too many Questions Presented defeat their purpose because they diffuse the reader's attention away from the big picture.

7. Does the Question Presented communicate the determinative facts using vivid, concrete imagery? Engage your reader's attention by painting a visual image with the words you select to frame the legal issue. Use active verbs and descriptive terms to bring the story to life. Avoid nominalizations, which obscure meaning. For example, compare the following two Questions Presented. Which is the more engaging and interesting? If you were a judge reading hundreds of pages a day, which would you prefer to read? Which is more persuasive?

Example A   Can a celebrity singer and songwriter recover damages from the corporate manufacturer of a newly purchased electronic keyboard for breach of implied warranty, when the celebrity sustained disfiguring personal injuries while performing onstage to a sellout crowd after the keyboard suddenly exploded in his hands the first time it was plugged in?

Example B   Has the manufacturer of a new electronic keyboard breached the implied warranty of fitness for a particular purpose when the purchaser was injured when the keyboard failed to operate properly the first time it was plugged in?

8. Is your Question Presented written to persuade by eliciting an affirmative answer? A persuasive Question Presented causes a skeptical judge to think, "This lawyer has the winning side," or at least, "On these facts, I don't want to rule against this lawyer." The Question Presented should overcome a judge's natural tendency to ask, "So what?" or "Is this really so bad that I should use the power of the court to interfere?"

Draft the Question Presented in a positive tone to invite the answer you seek. The answer you want is always "yes." For example, if you represent the bakery that seeks an injunction, write the Question Presented to suggest that the court should grant the injunction, as in the example above in criterion number 5. If you represent the apprentice baker, write the Question Presented to suggest just the opposite, weaving in the determinative facts:

> Should the court deny an injunction to enforce a covenant not to compete when an apprentice baker, who learned the trade while employed by the plaintiff, has elected to establish his own baked goods business in another densely populated county, and when the plaintiff bakery has no other competition in the baked goods market in two adjacent counties?

An effective Question Presented helps the reader see the determinative facts from your client's perspective, even before beginning to read your version of the Statement of the Case. As you refine your Argument, it is well worth your time to rewrite and edit your Question Presented to maximize its power to persuade.

Exercise 37-A. Questions Presented and Google Glass

The following Questions Presented were drafted by first-year law students based on the hypothetical facts in Exercise 33-C.

Part 1. Critique each Question Presented below. Does each include all necessary parts? If not, which parts are missing? Is each Question Presented clear and concise? Does it appropriately identify the parties and their relationship using generic but meaningful descriptive references? Is it written to invite an affirmative answer in favor of the party the writer represents?

1. Did the officer misapply California Vehicle Code § 27602 when he found out that Ms. Goering was using Google Glass for turn-by-turn directions to her destination?

2. Should the Court refuse to grant a motion to dismiss a California traffic citation that prohibits visual display screens in the front of vehicle, when the driver was viewing turn-by-turn directions through a transparent screen located in the right eye of a product known as "Google Glass"?

3. Under California law, was the Highway Patrol officer correct in issuing Ms. Goering a citation for using Google Glass while driving because of the increased risk to safety that this use posed?

4. Should this Court deny a traffic violator's motion to dismiss when the traffic violator knowingly and admittedly used a device that is unsafe to use when driving, and which California law prohibits using when driving?

5. Does a driver violate California Vehicle Code § 27602 for viewing only a transparent, thumbnail-size, hands-free, turn-by-turn navigation screen within her peripheral vision while driving?

6. Has the operator of a motor vehicle violated the California law banning the use of a television receiver, video monitor, or a television or video screen when the operator was using a wearable device that projects a display that is visible while she is driving?

7. Did the State of California correctly charge defendant driver with violating a California statute that prohibits persons from driving a motor vehicle with a television display device in front of the driver's seat, when the defendant drove her vehicle while using a transparent visual display device disguised as glasses?

Part 2. Now rewrite each Question Presented above, incorporating determinative facts from the summary on page 302.

38 Making Policy Arguments

§ 38.1 Why Policy Is Especially Important in an Appeal

When a court enforces a rule of law, it tries to do so in a way that accomplishes the policy behind the rule. In any court—trial or appellate—your odds of winning increase if you can show that the decision you want would achieve important public policy goals.

A substantial part of an appellate court's work is clarifying ambiguous law and making new law. The higher up you go in the appellate system, the more that is true. Clarifying the law and making new law are virtually the only things the U.S. Supreme Court does. When a court makes law in this way, it tries to do so consistently with policies that are already accepted in the law (or should be).

When you appear before a court in a law-making case, judges will naturally ask questions like this: What rule of law would a decision in your favor stand for (remembering that it would become binding precedent)? In what words would that rule be most accurately expressed? If the court does as you request, how would the law in the future treat facts that are similar to—but not exactly the same as—yours? What would be the practical effects in the courts, in the economy, and in society as a whole? Why is the rule you advocate better than the one your adversary urges?

In your brief, make policy arguments that would answer these questions persuasively.

§ 38.2 Types of Policy Arguments

The following article will help you choose public policies and argue them.

Teaching Students to Make Effective Policy Arguments in Appellate Briefs
Ellie Margolis
9 Perspectives 73 (2001)

. . . While there are several different types of policy arguments, all policy arguments share the common attribute of advocating that a proposed legal rule [or a proposed interpretation of a statute or constitutional provision] will benefit society, or advance a particular social goal (or conversely, that the proposed rule [or interpretation] will cause harm and should not be adopted). . . . Thus, all policy arguments involve an assessment of how a proposed rule will function in the real world. . . .

A. *Judicial Administration Arguments*

. . . These are arguments about the practical administration of the rule by the courts. The goal at the heart of these arguments is a fair and efficient judicial system. . . .

The dual goals of fairness and efficiency are sometimes at odds, however. This tension gives rise to the first type of judicial administration argument, the "firm vs. flexible rule" argument. The argument for a firm rule is that a clear, specific standard will be easy for the court to administer, and therefore promote efficiency. A firm rule also promotes fairness by leaving little room for judicial discretion and leading to more consistent application, which makes it easier for [the public] to understand the rule and act accordingly [because of the] adoption of a clear, precise rule. The "flexible rule" argument, on the other hand, focuses more heavily on fairness. The argument for a flexible rule is that flexibility will allow the court to . . . take into account the individual circumstances of each case[, which would be] more responsive and fair . . . .

There are three other judicial administration arguments that focus primarily on efficiency. These can be made individually or combined with the firm/flexible rule arguments. The first is the "floodgates of litigation" argument.[*] This argument asserts that a proposed rule, if adopted, will inundate the court with lawsuits. . . .

The second of these arguments is the "slippery slope" argument [which] asserts that if the proposed rule is adopted, the court will not be able to prevent its application to a broader and broader set of cases. First it will be applied to one new circumstance, then another, leading the court to hear a whole range of cases it had never intended to entertain [—and may additionally] lead to a large number of frivolous claims. . . .

---

[*] [Author's footnote] This argument is much overused and used inappropriately. Over the years, I have seen many student briefs making "floodgate" arguments because the students knew they should make some kind of policy argument and this was the only one they could think of. While this argument still has value, it should be used selectively, and only where truly appropriate.

The final judicial administration argument asserts that a proposed rule, even if firm, is so complex that it will be impossible to administer efficiently[,] . . . making it difficult [for the public] to understand and comply with the law [and] undermin[ing] judicial efficiency by requiring a large number of judicial resources in order to resolve claims under the rule.

B. Normative Arguments

. . . Although there is a significant overlap between different types of normative arguments, they can be broken down into roughly three categories: moral arguments, social utility arguments, and corrective justice arguments. Normative arguments tend to appear more "political" in nature because, in today's complex society, there is rarely widespread social consensus on issues of morality or other social good. As a result, the goal of a normative policy is not always as obvious or easy to establish as the goal in a judicial administration argument.

Moral arguments generally take the form of asserting that a particular rule should be adopted because it is consistent with generally accepted standards of society. . . .

. . . Under [a social utility] argument, the advocate asserts that a proposed rule will serve a social good and benefit society, or conversely, that it will undermine a social value and harm society [—because it] either deters or encourages conduct that affects . . . public health, public safety, economic health, [or] national security. Social utility arguments are particularly useful in tort law cases. . . .

[A] corrective justice argument . . . centers on the goal of fairness and asserts that as between two innocents, the one that caused the damage should be responsible. . . . In common law cases of first impression, [when] the court is being asked to establish a new cause of action, [especially in torts,] corrective justice arguments could be very useful.

C. Institutional Competence Arguments

. . . These are arguments about which branch of government (generally the judiciary or the legislature) should address a particular issue. . . .

[Although a legislature is the primary creator of new law, u]nder the common law method, judges have the power to fill in gaps in the law and formulate new rules . . . creating the potential for arguments over whether an issue is better suited to the courts or the legislature.

An argument that an issue is better suited for the courts focuses on the nature of courts as institutions set up for resolving individual disputes . . . . The argument would emphasize the court's ability to [act on the facts before it when the legislature has not acted and to learn facts from] witnesses and make objective determinations of credibility. . . .

The argument that the legislature is better suited . . . asserts that the courts are not competent to resolve the issue because . . . the legislature [is better able] to reflect changes in public opinion, and to hold hearings and gather complex and varied facts that may not be relevant in the [narrow] context of litigation. . . .

D. Economic Arguments

. . . One form of economic argument focuses on the efficient allocation of resources. . . . For example, a rule might be desirable because it spreads loss over a large segment of the population. On the other hand, a defendant trying to avoid liability in a products liability suit might argue that the cost of such liability will be passed on to the public, ultimately punishing those the rule was designed to benefit.

Another form of economic argument asserts that a cost-benefit analysis dictates that a rule should be adopted. Under this analysis, the arguer must show that the economic benefits of a rule outweigh the costs of implementing it. . . . The key to a cost-benefits analysis is the determination of the factors going into the cost. In addition to obvious costs, such as the monetary costs of fixing a defective part, costs such as emotional damage can be factored in. . . .

A third type of economic policy argument is that the proposed rule will have a positive or negative effect on economic efficiency and affect the operation of the free-market economy[, asserting, for example,] that a proposed rule would either promote or inhibit competition . . . .

§ 38.3   How to Make a Policy Argument

Think carefully about the cases and statutes you have found in your research. What policies do they enunciate? When you write the brief, make policy arguments in three steps:

Step 1 Identify one or more public policies that a decision in your favor would further. Tell the court exactly which policy or policies should guide its decision.

Step 2 Persuade the court that the policy or policies you have identified are important. Your adversary will urge competing policies. Show that yours are more important. It is not enough just to say yours are worth more. Prove it with argument.

Step 3 Show exactly how a decision in your favor will further the policy or policies you have identified. Do not assume that the court will understand how. Explain it *specifically*.

Policy arguments are much stronger if supported by authority. If the policy you urge has already been recognized by the courts in other cases, cite and explain those cases. If the legislature has adopted the policy in enacting statutes that are not directly related to your case, cite those statutes and explain how they reflect the policy you are urging. If you have only a few cases or statutes, try to find secondary authority, such as treatises and law review articles, that explain policies that should govern your case.

You might also cite and explain nonlegal sources that show a genuine public need. For example, if you argue that the courts should adopt strict tort rules assigning liability for contamination with industrial chemicals, you can cite scientific studies showing the presence of toxic chemicals in the food or water supply.

When a court is asked to clarify the interpretation of a statute, the court is not free to attach to the statute any policy the court likes. Instead, the court must use the policy the legislature adopted when it enacted the statute. Sometimes that policy is expressed in the statute or the legislative history. If not, the court (with your assistance) must figure out what policy the legislature probably adopted.

When making a policy argument, use the terminology you find in the cases and statutes in preference to the terminology used in this chapter. You will be able to recognize a normative policy when you see one in a case or statute. But when you argue that policy to a court, refer to it in the way the cases or the statutes do. Or simply say in plain language what you mean: "This rule would be consistent with standards of behavior generally accepted throughout society. Specifically, ..." The terms "normative argument," "social utility argument," and "corrective justice argument" rarely appear in the case law, although many statutes and thousands of cases have adopted policies that can be categorized as normative, social utility, or corrective justice. Courts and law school teachers sometimes use different words to refer to the same policies. When writing for a court, use the wording that judges use.

Avoid telling a court that it is a less competent institution than a legislature. It would be more diplomatic to say that the legislature is "in a better position" to decide whether to adopt the rule of law urged by your adversary, or that the decision is a type that "should be reserved to" the legislature. Then show why.

39 Oral Argument

§ 39.1   Three Goals at Oral Argument

First, you want to engage the judges' attention by getting them *interested* in your case and *motivated* to rule in your favor. They will hear many other arguments on the same day, and they will read many other briefs in the week they read yours. You want to touch their natural desire to do the right thing.

Second, you want to focus the judges' attention on the *few aspects of your case that are most determinative*—the fundamental one or two issues, the most prominent facts in your story, and the most compelling policy considerations. Judges expect oral argument to help them find the heart of the dispute. Oral argument works best when it concentrates on a few important ideas, while details are best left to the briefs.

Third, you want *access to the judges' thinking.* You want to discover each of their doubts about your theory and any way in which they are confused about your case—so you can dispel their doubts and clear up their confusion. Listening to the judges' questions is the only way you can get access to their thinking. And the most effective thing you can do in oral argument is to answer their questions well. Usually when judges interrupt you with questions, they are not trying to debate with you. They are telling you what troubles them and asking you to help them make the decision. Thus, an experienced oral advocate goes into the courtroom *for the purpose of being interrupted.*

§ 39.2   Structure of an Oral Argument

You will (1) introduce yourself and the case, (2) summarize the client's story and identify the core issue or issues raised by the story, (3) make a legal argument, and (4) conclude.

If you represent the appellant, you will argue first. Begin by introducing your yourself and your client and identifying the decision below from which you have appealed. Here are two examples of effective openings:

example 1   Good morning, Your Honors. I am Sandy Amoros, representing Jodie Beeler, the appellant here and the plaintiff below. A jury verdict in her favor was overturned when the trial court granted the defendant's post-trial motion for judgment as a matter of law.

example 2   May it please the court, I am Sandy Amoros, representing Jodie Beeler. The jury returned a verdict in her favor, but the trial court granted the defendant's post-trial motion for judgment as a matter of law—a decision Ms. Beeler now asks you to reverse.

Next, summarize the story and identify the core issue or issues. If you will use the issues to introduce the story, identify the issues first. Otherwise, tell the story and identify the issues afterward as a bridge into your legal argument.

Focus on the most essential facts so the judges do not get lost in marginal details. Think carefully beforehand about how you will tell the story and what words you will use. One of the most successful Supreme Court advocates once said that "in an appellate court the statement of the facts is not merely a part of the argument, it is more often than not the argument itself. A case well stated is a case far more than half argued."[1] You must mention the facts that hurt you, but you can minimize their effect through juxtaposition, just as you did when you wrote the Statement of the Case. Some courts study the briefs carefully before argument, and they might consider a fact recitation to be a waste of time. In those courts, lawyers are discouraged—either informally or through court rules—from opening with the facts.

If you represent the appellee, your opening may be similar to the appellant's, except that you should explain how your positions differ from the appellant's. For example, rather than tell your version of the story, you might point out the ways in which the appellant has not given a full or accurate picture. Suppose a group of plaintiffs won a judgment against the owner of a dam that collapsed; the owner has appealed; and the owner's lawyer has opened oral argument by stressing that the plaintiffs had reason to know the dam had weakened. The plaintiffs' lawyer can respond like this:

The key fact is *not* that slowly rising waters in a creek could have alerted nearby residents that something might be wrong, but that the defendant's dam burst, sending a wall of water seven feet high down the valley where the plaintiffs lived. Slowly rising water cannot be considered a warning of that.

---

[1] John W. Davis, *The Argument of an Appeal*, 26 ABA J. 895, 896 (1940), *reprinted in* 3 J. App. Prac. & Process 745 (2001).

You can begin your legal argument with a statement of the rule or rules most essential to your position. If you are arguing two or more issues, you might have to do this separately for each issue. On each issue, your argument can resemble the CREAC structure. Persuade the judges that they should adopt and enforce the rule you urge, explain how the rule works, and apply it to your facts.

If you represent the appellee, listen carefully to the appellant's oral argument. When your turn comes, you will respond to the appellant's contentions. You may have anticipated most of them when you read the appellant's brief and when you planned your argument. But if the appellant surprises you during oral argument by saying something new that truly might hurt, you will need to find a way to neutralize it on the spot.

Appellate advocates distinguish between a "hot" bench, which erupts with questions, and a "cold" bench, which listens impassively. If the bench is hot, the judges may ask so many questions that you will be surprised to find that your time is about to run out, or already has. Your time is up when the presiding judge says, in a firm tone, "Thank you, counselor." Then conclude with *one short sentence* in which you specify the relief you seek ("Therefore, the judgment below should be affirmed. . . ."). If you are in the midst of answering a question when your time runs out, ask for permission to finish the answer. If your request is granted, finish quickly. If the judges continue to ask you questions after your time expires, answer them fully. The court has implicitly enlarged your time. If you finish your argument before your time expires, conclude anyway, pause to see whether you will be asked further questions, and if not, sit down. Whatever the situation, you can signal your intent to finish by using an introductory phrase such as "In conclusion, ..."

At the beginning of the argument, the appellant's lawyer sometimes reserves a minute or two for rebuttal by saying so after the introductory sentences. The time reserved is subtracted from the time allowed for the appellant's main argument. After the appellee has argued, the appellant can use the reserved time to reply. But a court considers rebuttal time wasted if an appellant uses it to reiterate arguments already made or to raise new arguments for the first time. If you reserve rebuttal time, use it only to correct significantly inaccurate or misleadingly incomplete statements made by the appellee, and preferably not more than one or two of those. If the appellee's misstatements are trivial, an appellant looks petty correcting them. If it turns out that there is no need for rebuttal, an appellant makes a confident impression by waiving it.

§ 39.3   Questions from the Bench

Listen carefully to the question and understand it before answering.
Answer the question when it is asked.
Don't evade.

If you don't know the answer to a question, say so.

If the premise of a question is wrong, politely say so.

If a Justice throws you a life preserver, don't bat it away.

Justices ask hypothetical questions because they are concerned about how the decision in your case may affect other cases. What are the limits of the principle you advocate?

—*North Dakota Supreme Court*
Appellate Practice Tips

Some questions are neutral requests for information. Some are challenges, asking you how you would overcome an adverse case or a policy contrary to your argument. Some are expressed as concerns: The judge asks how a particular problem in the case can be resolved. Some questions are openly friendly, asking you to focus on an aspect of your case that the judge believes to be particularly persuasive. And some questions are prompts, suggesting that whatever you are discussing at the time can be dispensed with in favor of something else the court cares about more. Some questions are asked because the answer is crucial to the judge's thinking. Others grow out of the spontaneity of the moment, and the answer may have little or no impact on the decision.

When you hear a question, listen to it carefully. Do not be afraid to pause for a moment to think before answering. Never interrupt a question. Try to figure out the question's purpose and exactly what is troubling the judge. Then craft your answer to satisfy the skepticism or curiosity implied by the question. In your answer, do not say too little or too much. Do not give a one-sentence reply to a question that a judge plainly considers to be the crux of the case. And do not spend three minutes resolving a straightforward request for simple information.

Make no assumptions about a judge's predispositions from the questions the judge asks. A neutral judge might ask challenging questions just to see whether your theory will hold up. A friendly judge might ask challenging questions to get you to argue matters that the judge believes might persuade others on the bench. And an adverse judge might ask friendly or neutral questions out of politeness and a sense of fairness.

Answer the question on the spot. Do not promise to get back to it later at a place in your outline where you had already planned to discuss the subject. Other questions might prevent you from getting that far, and your answer will be most persuasive immediately after the question is asked. Even if a question asks you to discuss an entire issue earlier than you had planned, do it and rearrange the order of your presentation to accommodate the judge's needs. Later, when you reach the spot where you had intended to discuss the issue, simply skip what you have already covered.

Answer the question you have been asked, not one you would rather have been asked. You can persuade only by facing the problems raised by the question and by showing the judge why those problems should not prevent a decision in your favor. In every fully litigated case, each side has points of weakness. If your side had none, your adversary would have given up long ago. When a judge has truly identified a point of weakness, face it and give a realistic counterargument. Here are three ways to begin:

example 1   I agree, Your Honor, that in your hypothetical the police would have had probable cause, but the facts of the hypothetical are not the facts of this case. For example . . . .

example 2   Yes, *Soares* did so hold, but later rulings of this court have impliedly undermined *Soares*. For example . . . .

example 3   Certainly, the record does reflect two isolated events that might be construed as evidence of good faith by the defendant, but the record also includes many, many events, stretching over several years, that show exactly the opposite. For example . . . .

During the answer, build a bridge to the rest of your argument. If you do this smoothly, it may be hard for a listener to tell where your answer has ended and your planned presentation has picked up again. Bridge-building helps you redirect the argument back to your theory of the appeal so you can show the court how your theory, as a coherent whole, satisfies each concern raised from the bench.

If you are asked a question you do not know how to answer, the best thing to say is exactly that. Judges know you are human, and, unless the point is a big one, you gain credibility by admitting that you cannot answer. Moreover, judges are skilled interrogators, and if you try to fake your way through an answer, they will realize what you are doing. If you knew the answer when you prepared but cannot remember it now, you might feel a little better saying something like "I'm sorry, Your Honor, but I do not recall." In real appeals (not in law school assignments), a lawyer might offer to file a supplemental brief or memorandum if the lawyer fears that the unanswered question might be crucial to the decision. Courts usually refuse these offers, which may suggest that the point is not critical after all.

If you are not sure you understand the question, signal that indirectly so the judge can correct you, if necessary:

If your Honor is asking about the possibility that the issue has not been preserved for review—and please correct me if I've misunderstood—trial counsel objected to the evidence and moved for . . . .

Or do it directly:

I'm sorry, Your Honor. Are you asking whether the order appealed from is final?

Except for the kinds of examples above, it is not a good idea to ask the judges questions.

In many legal writing courses, students are assigned to coauthor briefs, usually in teams of two, and to split the oral argument between them. If you are working with another student, you may be asked questions about material that your colleague intends to argue. Do not respond by saying that your colleague will answer the question. That can annoy judges because they expect you to know enough of the other student's material that you can give at least a summary answer. If you are arguing first, your colleague can elaborate on your summary later.

§ 39.4   Affect, Delivery, and Style

The most effective tone for presenting arguments has been called "respectful intellectual equality."[2]

> [I]f the lawyer approaches a court with . . . awe, perhaps verging on fear, he will not be able effectively to stand up to the court's questioning. . . . It is just as important, however, not to talk down to a court . . . . The only proper attitude is that of a respectful intellectual equality. The "respectful" part approximates the quantum and type of respect that a younger [person] should show when speaking to an older one . . . . Counsel must stand up to the judges quite as he would stand up to the senior members of his own firm. If he permits himself to be overawed . . . then he—and his case—are well on their way to being lost.[3]

Although the judges have the power to decide your case, their *need* to decide the case causes them to look to you for intellectual leadership.

What works best in this situation is not a speech, but a *conversation* in which you take the initiative, talking *with* the judges—not at them. It is an unusual kind of conversation, limited by the formalities of the occasion and by a focus on the decision the bench must make, but it is a conversation nonetheless. Try to create for yourself a *persuasive presence* that helps you reach and engage the bench.

Think of nervousness as a fact of life. Even the most experienced lawyer is nervous before making an oral argument. But that anxiety seems to disappear once the lawyer becomes engaged in the conversation. For beginners, the *moment of engagement*—when you are so caught up in the work that you forget to be nervous—might not come for several minutes into the argument. But with each succeeding performance, that moment will move closer and closer toward the opening, until eventually it coincides with the words "May it please the court" or "Good morning, Your Honors."

Look straight at the judges throughout the argument, preferably making eye contact. Look at your notes only to remind yourself of the next subject for discussion and,

---

[2] Frederick Bernays Wiener, *Oral Advocacy*, 62 HARV. L. REV. 56, 72-74 (1948).
[3] *Id.*

even then, get your eyes off your notes and back to the bench as fast as possible. Whenever you look away from the judges, their attention can wander to other thoughts, partially tuning you out. And judges can become impatient with lawyers who read their arguments to the court.[4]

Speak loudly enough that the judges do not have to strain to hear you. If you are soft-spoken by nature, breathe in deeply before you begin and exhale while speaking your first words. Do this again whenever your voice falters. Make your lungs do the work, not your throat muscles. You will be surprised at how well your voice can carry. But if you already have a powerful voice, do not get carried away. A loud voice can make the bench uncomfortable.

Use the tone and volume of your voice to emphasize the more important things you say. Pause before or after your most important remarks.

Communicate tenacity with what one judge has called "disciplined earnestness": "a communicated sense of conviction that pushes a case to the limits of its strength but not beyond," using "words and body language, facial expression and eye contact, to radiate a sense of conviction without making every point a life-and-death issue."[5]

Avoid multitudes of detail when discussing cases and statutes. Focus on the big ideas. If your case is built on a synthesis of authority, describe it generally ("the majority of jurisdictions," "the recent trend of cases in other states," "seven of the federal circuits," "this court has previously held"). If you must quote—as you might with a crucial statute or holding—limit yourself to the half-dozen or so essential words that the court must interpret. Concentrate on the few most determinative facts. But you can also mention along the way a few facts that most bring the story to life. Some facts have little legal significance but help the judges "see" the story and put the case into a realistic perspective.

Do not distract the court with restless or anxious movements. Stand up straight. Do not play with a pen, shuffle your papers around frequently, put your hands in your pockets, or sway forward and back. Limit your gestures to those that naturally punctuate your argument. A visually busy lawyer radiates nervousness, rather than the confidence needed to establish psychological leadership. Stand at the lectern throughout your argument. Do not stroll out from behind it unless you need to find something in your briefcase to answer a question. And try not to let that happen. Wear conservative clothing that communicates professionalism.

---

[4] *See* Sup. Ct. R. 28.1 ("Oral argument read from a prepared text is not favored"); Fed. R. App. P. 34(c) ("Counsel must not read at length from briefs, records, or authorities").
[5] Frank M. Coffin, The Ways of a Judge: Reflections from the Federal Appellate Bench 132 (1980).

§ 39.5   Formalities and Customs of the Courtroom

While a courtroom is in session, lawyers do not speak to each other. They speak only to the bench and—when the bench gives permission—to witnesses and juries. But because there are no witnesses or juries in appellate courts, you will speak only to the judges.

The dignity of the occasion will be demeaned if you speak in slang, in emotional rhetoric, or in terms that unnecessarily personalize the lawyers or judges. Even when discussing your adversary's arguments, refer to them as the party's, rather than as the lawyer's. There is a world of difference between "The plaintiff mistakenly relies . . ." and "Mr. Maggione mistakenly told you . . . ." Similarly, do not speak to the bench in flattering language. Judges are satisfied with respect. Obsequiousness makes them uncomfortable.

While your adversary argues, listen attentively and without facial expressions that could convey your opinion of what is transpiring. Write down whatever notes you will need to help you respond in your own argument (if you represent the appellee) or in rebuttal (if you represent the appellant). Do not interrupt your adversary's argument.

§ 39.6   Preparation for Oral Argument

Prepare two versions of the same presentation. One version would include the material that you *must* argue—the absolute core of your case. When delivered without interruption, it should fill no more than 30% or 35% of the time you are allowed. The other version would be an expanded development of the first. It would include the first version as well as supplemental material that makes the core of your case more persuasive. If delivered without interruption, it should fill about 80% or 90% of the available time. You will know within the first two or three minutes of the argument whether the bench is hot or cold. If it is hot, you can deliver the core presentation and try to work the supplemental material into your answers. If the bench is cold, you can deliver the expanded argument.

There are many ways to prepare notes to use at the lectern. After you have argued several times, you will figure out which type and style of notes work best for you. But the consensus of experienced advocates is that you are better off with the fewest notes possible because you need them only to remind yourself of the subjects you intend to cover as well as a few key phrases that you intend to use.

If you are well prepared, you will know your case so well that a single page on a legal-size pad might be sufficient. If, in preparing the argument, you come up with an excellent phrasing for a difficult concept, you might write down those few words to remind yourself to use them. Otherwise, your notes should be only a list of subjects to cover. You can outline both versions of your argument on a single page divided by a vertical line, the core version on one side of the vertical line and the expanded version on the other side. Or you could take two pads to the podium, one for each version. But try to use only the top page on a pad. If you go to the second page, you might have too many notes. Some advocates take to the lectern notecards with synopses of the record and the major relevant cases. You might or might not find that helpful. If you already know your case thoroughly, the cards might only get in your way.

Take the record and both briefs to the podium as well, in case you are asked about them.

Make a list of every weakness in your case and every question that you might ask if you were a judge. Prepare ways of overcoming the weaknesses and answering the questions. If you cannot imagine hard questions a judge might ask, study your adversary's brief and the precedents that are contrary to your position.

Try also to predict any concessions you might be asked to make. Figure out which concessions you cannot afford to give up and which you might have to make to protect the reasonableness of the rest of your case. If you need to think about this for the first time at the podium when a judge asks you a question, you could make a serious and costly mistake.

Practice making your argument to a person who will ask you tough questions but who knows little about your theory of the appeal. If the person mooting you knows too much about your theory, the experience will be unrealistic.

Finally, update your research the day before you argue. The time between submission of the brief and oral argument might equal up to a month in law school and perhaps several months in the practice of law. Check to see whether controlling statutes have been amended or repealed, whether any of the key cases has been overruled, and whether any of the recent precedents has been reversed or affirmed. It can be devastating to discover in the courtroom that some important texture of the law has changed.

Appendices

A

Sample Office Memorandum

MEMORANDUM

TO: Emilia Orosco
FROM: Peter Reiser
RE: Baseball park's potential liability to a minor spectator injured by lightning
         (Sophie Worthington)
DATE: August 20, 2015

ISSUES -presents

QUESTIONS PRESENTED

I. Under Colorado law, did a minor league baseball park breach a legal duty of care to a minor spectator who was struck by lightning while watching a youth baseball tournament, when ballpark personnel failed to warn her about an approaching thunderstorm and the danger of lightning?

II. Under Colorado statutes, does the baseball park have an affirmative defense to a premises liability claim, either on the ground that the danger of thunderstorms and lightning is an inherent risk of baseball, or that inclement weather is an open and obvious danger?

BRIEF ANSWERS

I. Probably yes. Under the Colorado Premises Liability Act, the baseball park owed a duty of reasonable care to baseball spectators, who qualify as invitees. The ballpark manager had access to weather monitoring equipment that would have informed him about the approaching storm in time to warn spectators to take cover. Although lightning was the immediate cause of the minor's injury, a court would probably find that the ballpark's failure to warn spectators was a contributing factor.

II. Probably not. The Colorado Baseball Spectator Safety Act provides a defense only for injuries to spectators that result from the inherent risks of baseball. Other courts have interpreted the term "inherent risk" to mean the risk that a baseball spectator might be injured by foul balls or baseball bats. Although the Colorado statute does not expressly define "inherent risk," the danger of lightning is probably not the kind of risk a court would consider inherent to the game of baseball. Further, the Colorado Premises Liability Act has superseded common law defenses, including the open and obvious danger defense. While the minor observed a thunderstorm approaching, she may not have had enough knowledge and experience to appreciate the risk of lightning.

STATEMENT OF FACTS

The parents of Sophie Worthington have asked whether the owners of a baseball park are liable for her injuries after lightning struck her while attending a youth baseball tournament.

1

The Rocky Mountain Sluggers are a minor league baseball team. This dispute involves the team's stadium, Slugger Field, which is located on the western slope of the Rocky Mountains at one of the highest elevations of any professional ballpark in North America. According to the National Lightning Safety Institute, lightning is the most frequent weather hazard affecting outdoor athletic events, and the risk of lightning strikes is greater at higher elevations.

Early in the morning of July 27, 2015, the National Weather Service issued a severe thunderstorm watch for an area surrounding Slugger Field and extending fifty miles from the ballpark in every direction. The weather cleared by mid-afternoon, and the thunderstorm watch expired. Slugger Field opened to the public at 4:30 p.m. for a youth baseball tournament, scheduled to begin at 5:30 p.m. The Sluggers had advertised the tournament to the public for several weeks on its website and in the local newspaper.

Sophie Worthington and a friend, both age sixteen, arrived at the ballpark around 4:45 p.m. About twenty minutes after the tournament started, the sky clouded over and light rain began to fall. Early in the game, Ms. Worthington's friend saw sheet lightning on the horizon to the west of the stadium. She nudged Ms. Worthington to catch her attention and then pointed to the western sky, where dark storm clouds were gathering. Ms. Worthington just shrugged and turned her attention back to the play on the field.

In the meantime, the ballpark manager was in his office, which was equipped with internet access and a National Weather Service emergency radio. At 5:45 p.m., the Weather Service issued a new severe thunderstorm weather advisory for the area just to the west of the ballpark. The warning urged extra precaution due to the high risk of lightning accompanying the storm.

Ms. Worthington and her friend were seated in the crowded general admission area near the right outfield. While the stadium roof extended over the reserved seat section, the metal bleachers in the general admission seating area were in the open air. At 5:50 p.m. it began to sprinkle, but the baseball tournament play continued. At 6:14 p.m., Ms. Worthington was struck by lightning, causing her to suffer severe and permanently disabling injuries.

DISCUSSION

In Colorado, premises liability claims are governed by the Colorado Premises Liability Act, Colo. Rev. Stat. § 13-21-115 (2013), which has been called a "comprehensive scheme for determining a landowner's liability to persons injured on his land." *S.W. v. Towers Boat Club, Inc.*, 315 P.3d 1257, 1259 (Colo. 2013). The statute in part codified the common law doctrine of premises liability, under which the duty owed by a landowner depends on the classification of the injured person. *See id.* This Discussion will first address Ms. Worthington's legal status as a visitor on the premises while watching the baseball tournament before turning to the question of liability.

I. The owner of the ballpark owed a duty of reasonable care to Ms. Worthington as an invitee, and it probably breached that duty by failing to warn spectators about the risk of lightning from the approaching thunderstorm.

In 1986, the Colorado Legislature enacted the Colorado Premises Liability Act, which superseded the state's common law doctrine of premises liability. Colo. Rev.

2

Stat. § 13-21-115 (amended 1990). After the original statute was ruled unconstitutional in *Gallegos v. Phipps,* 779 P.2d 856, 862 (Colo. 1989), the Legislature reenacted a substantially modified version in 1990, which reflects current law. *See S.W. v. Towers Boat Club, Inc.*, 315 P.3d at 1262. Colorado's highest court has held that the Act's "definition of landowner duty is complete and exclusive, fully abrogating landowner common law duty principles. [T]he plain language preempts prior common law theories of liability, and establishes the statute as the sole codification of landowner duties in tort." *Vigil v. Franklin*, 103 P.3d 327, 328 (Colo. 2004).

    A.   The Colorado Premises Liability Act re-established the traditional special relationships recognized at common law but altered the definitions of those traditional categories.

The traditional special relationships that dictate a landowner's duty in a premises liability case were abolished by the Colorado Supreme Court in 1971. *Mile High Fence Co. v. Radovich,* 489 P.2d 308, 312–13 (Colo. 1971). The Colorado Legislature later enacted the Colorado Premises Liability Act, Colo. Rev. Stat. § 13-21-115, which effectively reinstated the traditional premises liability analysis.

Under the Act, the status of the injured individual as an invitee, licensee, or trespasser determines the duty owed by the landowner. Colo. Rev. Stat. § 13-21-115(1.5(a)); *Larrieu v. Best Buy Stores, L.P.*, 303 P.3d 558, 561 & n.3 (Colo. 2013) (citing *Vigil v. Franklin*, 103 P.3d at 325–26). Section 1.5(d) articulates the legislature's purpose "[t]o create a legal climate which will promote private property rights and commercial enterprise and will foster the availability and affordability of insurance." § 13-21-115(1.5).(d); *Maes v. Lakeview Assocs., Ltd.*, 892 P.2d 375, 377 (Colo. Ct. App. 1994), *aff'd*, 907 P.2d 580 (Colo. 1995). By inference, this language suggests that the legislative intent was to ensure some degree of predictability by landowners and their insurers.

The classification of the injured person under the Premises Liability Act is an issue of law. *See* § 13-21-115(4); *Traynom v. Cinemark USA, Inc.*, 940 F. Supp. 2d 1339, 1353 (D. Colo. 2013) (citing *Vigil v. Franklin,* 103 P.3d at 328). However, issues of liability and damages are questions of fact. § 13-21-115(4). Therefore, to determine whether the ballpark owed a duty of care to Ms. Worthington and the nature of that duty, the first question is whether she was an invitee, a licensee, or a trespasser, as the Colorado statute defines those status categories.

    B.   Ms. Worthington qualifies as an invitee because she was at the ballpark for the parties' mutual benefit, in response to an express invitation to the general public advertising the youth baseball tournament.

The Colorado Premises Liability Act defines invitee as follows:

3

(5) As used in this section:

   (a) "Invitee" means a person who enters or remains on the land of another to transact business in which the parties are mutually interested or who enters or remains on such land in response to the landowner's express or implied representation that the public is requested, expected, or intended to enter or remain.

§ 13-21-115(5)(a).

The Colorado Court of Appeals has acknowledged that the Act's definition of "invitee" creates two subcategories that sometimes overlap: "(1) those present to transact business of mutual interest, and (2) public invitees." *Wycoff v. Grace Cmty. Church of Assemblies of God*, 251 P.3d 1260, 1267 (Colo. Ct. App. 2010). In *Wycoff*, for example, the court concluded that a seventeen-year-old patron who had attended a church-sponsored event was a business invitee because the church had arranged the location, facilities, meals, and lodging for participants, and it had encouraged the plaintiff's attendance by paying part of her admission cost. *Id.* But the patron was also a public invitee because she participated in response to an invitation the church had affirmatively extended to the public. *Id.* at 1268.

Here, a court is almost certain to classify Ms. Worthington as an invitee and not as a licensee or trespasser. She was in the ballpark to watch a baseball tournament, which the stadium had advertised to the public for several weeks on its website and in the local newspaper. Ms. Worthington and her friend paid the required admission fee in response to the stadium's express invitation to attend. Therefore, she entered the ballpark to transact business for the parties' mutual benefit. *See* § 13-21-115(5)(a).

Even if the court holds that attending a baseball tournament does not qualify as "transact[ing] business," Ms. Worthington still qualifies as a public invitee because she entered and remained in the ballpark at the stadium's express invitation. *See id.*

   C. *The ballpark owed Ms. Worthington, as an invitee, a duty of reasonable care to protect her from harm while on the premises, and it probably breached that duty by failing to warn spectators about the approaching thunderstorm and the risk of lightning.*

The Colorado Premises Liability Act specifies the duty of care a landowner owes its invitees: "[A]n invitee may recover for damages caused by the landowner's unreasonable failure to exercise reasonable care to protect against dangers of which he actually knew or should have known." Colo. Rev. Stat. § 13-21-115(3)(c)(I). As recently interpreted by the Colorado Supreme Court, the statutory duty of care does not apply solely to "activities and circumstances that are directly or inherently related to the land." *Larrieu*, 303 P.3d at 563. Rather, the duty extends to "conditions, activities, and circumstances on the property that the landowner is liable for in its legal capacity as a landowner." *Id.*; *see* § 13-21-115(2). The nature and scope of the landowner's duty to an invitee depends on the facts and circumstances of each case. *Larrieu*, 303 P.3d at 563.

4

In this case, Ms. Worthington's injury occurred while she was on the ballpark's property. While her injury was not a direct result of the activities on the field or the condition of the property itself, it was the result of "circumstances existing on the property." *Id.* The National Weather Service had issued a weather advisory for the area, urging extra caution because of the risk of lightning. The ballpark manager had access to an emergency weather radio and a computer while he was working in his office. Even if the ballpark manager did not actually know about the approaching storm and the risk of lightning, he should have known because he had the necessary means to learn about the imminent risk to the safety of baseball spectators. At the very least, the manager should have announced a warning over the ballpark's public address system to give spectators a reasonable opportunity to take cover, especially those seated in the general admission bleachers.

    D.   *By failing to warn spectators about the risk of lightning, the ballpark failed to meet its duty of reasonable care to protect Ms. Worthington and the other spectators from a dangerous condition about which the ballpark should have known.*

To recover damages in a premises liability claim, an invitee must show an *"unreasonable failure* to exercise reasonable care" to protect her from danger. Colo. Rev. Stat. § 13-21-115(3)(c)(I) (emphasis added). The Colorado Supreme Court has interpreted this language to be consistent with the common law duty of reasonable care: When a plaintiff establishes that a landowner failed to exercise reasonable care, the statute requires no additional showing that the landowner *unreasonably* failed to do so. *Lombard v. Colo. Outdoor Educ. Ctr., Inc.*, 187 P.3d 565, 575 & n.8 (Colo. 2008). In other words, "the failure to exercise reasonable care is by definition unreasonable." *Id.* at 575.

Whether the ballpark breached its duty of reasonable care to Ms. Worthington is a question of fact based on all the evidence. *Larrieu*, 303 P.3d at 563. Based on the preliminary facts, the stadium had weather forecasting capability on site, and a weather advisory had been issued that warned about the risk of lightning in the immediate vicinity. It is no defense that the ballpark manager lacked actual knowledge of the risk because constructive knowledge of danger is sufficient to support a claim under the plain language of the Act. *Lombard*, 187 P.3d at 571-72 (quoting § 13-21-115(3)(c)(I)). Therefore, the evidence is probably sufficient to present the issue of liability to the factfinder. *See Sall v. T's, Inc.*, 136 P.3d 471, 484 (Kan. 2006) (applying Kansas common law); *see also Maussner v. Atl. City Country Club, Inc.*, 691 A.2d 826, 835 (N.J. Super. Ct. App. Div. 1997) (applying New Jersey common law).

Under Colorado law, as in other states, the fact that an injury occurred as a direct result of a lightning strike does not preclude landowner liability. *Pearce v. Mountain States Tel. & Tel. Co.*, 173 P. 871, 873 (Colo. 1918) ("if lightning and defendant's negligence concurred as the efficient cause . . . , defendant would be liable, [if] the jury . . . find[s] that the negligence of defendant was an efficient cause, without which the injury would not have happened").

5

To support a claim under the Premises Liability Act, Ms. Worthington would need to rely on the ballpark manager's failure to actively monitor weather conditions about which he should have known, and his failure to warn spectators when the forecast suggested a serious risk of harm. The court is almost certain to conclude that she was an invitee, and the factfinder would probably find that the ballpark failed to comply with its duty of reasonable care.

II. The ballpark probably does not have an affirmative defense to Ms. Worthington's premises liability claim on the ground that injury from lightning is an inherent risk of baseball, or that the approaching inclement weather was an open and obvious danger.

The Colorado Premises Liability Act has been interpreted to supersede traditional common law defenses. *Vigil v. Franklin*, 103 P.3d at 327. However, the Colorado Supreme Court has more recently suggested that some common law defenses may survive. *See Lombard*, 187 P.3d at 574 ("the premises liability statute has abrogated certain common law claims and defenses in the premises liability context"). While Colorado's codification of premises liability generally supersedes common law claims and defenses, the Act does not supplant *statutory* defenses to premises liability. This section addresses the two most likely affirmative defenses the ballpark may assert to avoid liability.

A. The Colorado Baseball Spectator Safety Act does not provide a viable defense because the risk that a baseball spectator will be struck by lightning is not the sort of common, frequent, and expected risk that most courts consider inherent to baseball.

The ballpark owner is likely to rely on the Colorado Baseball Spectator Safety Act, Colo. Rev. Stat. § 13-21-120, which applies by its terms to professional baseball, including minor league baseball. *Id.* § 13-21-120(3)(b). Under the Act,

> [s]pectators of professional baseball games are presumed to have knowledge of and to assume the inherent risks of observing professional baseball games, insofar as those risks are obvious and necessary. These risks include, but are not limited to, injuries which result from being struck by a baseball or a baseball bat.

Id. § 13-21-120(4)(a). In general, the statute bars liability by baseball team owners and ballparks for spectator injuries "resulting from the inherent risks of attending a professional baseball game." *Id.* § 13-21-120(4)(b). If the ballpark asserts this defense, the specific issue is whether the risk of injury from inclement weather, including lightning, is an "inherent risk" of attending a baseball game. If so, the statute bars liability for Ms. Worthington's injuries.

6

The Baseball Spectator Safety Act codifies what some other courts have recognized as the "baseball rule," a specialized application of the implied primary assumption of risk defense. *E.g., Coomer v. Kansas City Royals Baseball Corp.*, 437 S.W.3d 184, 194–98 (Mo. 2014) (discussing history of the baseball rule and citing cases). Under the baseball rule, a plaintiff is barred from recovering for personal injuries suffered as a result of risks inherent to baseball. Even in jurisdictions that follow the rule, it does not apply unless the specific risk of injury is "common, frequent, and expected" during the sporting activity in question. *Teneyck v. Roller Hockey Colo., Ltd.*, 10 P.3d 707, 708 (Colo. Ct. App. 2000).

In Colorado, the Act bars liability only for injuries resulting from "the *inherent risks* of attendance at professional baseball games." *Id.* at 710 (dicta) (emphasis added). The policy reasons underlying the rule are to keep baseball ticket prices affordable by limiting liability for safety risks that are necessarily inherent in the game, such as the risk that a spectator will be hit by a foul ball or a thrown baseball bat. § 12-21-120(2) (statement of legislative purpose). Those kinds of risks qualify as inherent—meaning "common, frequent, and expected"—given the nature of baseball. In contrast to the risk of injury to a spectator from foul balls and thrown or broken baseball bats, a court would probably be reluctant to hold that the risk of being struck by lightning is an "inherent risk" of watching the game in a ballpark.

Most courts hold that whether a particular risk is inherent to baseball is a question of law for the court. *Coomer*, 437 S.W.3d at 200. No Colorado court has ever held that lightning or other life-threatening weather conditions are an inherent risk of watching baseball or other sporting activity. Other jurisdictions that have addressed the issue have generally applied the baseball rule narrowly. For example, the Missouri Supreme Court, one of the first to recognize the baseball rule, recently declined to hold that a spectator's serious eye injury was an inherent risk of baseball when the baseball team's mascot used an airgun to shoot hotdogs into the stands. *Coomer*, 437 S.W.3d at 203; *cf. Turner v. Mandalay Sports Entm't, LLC,* 180 P.3d 1172, 1176 (Nev. 2008) (adopting the "limited duty rule" but only to the extent of limiting ballpark's duty to protect spectators from foul balls within confines of ballpark).

As one court observed, "[t]he majority of jurisdictions to consider the [duty owed by stadium owners and operators to spectators struck by foul balls] have limited this duty by adopting some variation of the Baseball Rule." *Rountree v. Boise Baseball, LLC*, 296 P.3d 373, 377 (Idaho 2013). A few states, like Colorado, have adopted a variation of the rule by statute. *Id.* at 379 (citing, *e.g.*, Arizona, Colorado, New Jersey, and Illinois statutes). But some state supreme courts have recently rejected the baseball rule altogether. *E.g., id.* at 378 (declining to adopt baseball rule after reviewing authorities from several other states); *S. Shore Baseball, LLC v. DeJesus*, 11 N.E.2d 903, 909 (Ind. 2014) ("we are not convinced that any sport, even our national pastime, merits its own special rule of liability").

7

Although the Colorado statute does not expressly define "inherent risk," a court is likely to interpret the statute in light of the policy reasons for its enactment—to limit liability for injuries to spectators that a reasonable person would anticipate as an inherent risk of watching a live baseball game. *But cf. Pichardo v. N. Patchogue Medford Youth Athletic Assoc., Inc.*, 569 N.Y.S.2d 186, 187 (N.Y. App. Div. 1991) (holding that summer league baseball player who was struck by lightning assumed the risks inherent in continuing to play when thunder and lightning were readily apparent in the distance).

If Ms. Worthington alleges that the ballpark manager failed to make a reasonable, prudent effort to use the available weather monitoring equipment and the ballpark's speaker system to warn spectators of the approaching storm, the Colorado Baseball Spectator Safety Act probably will not protect the ballpark from liability. The court is unlikely to conclude as a matter of law that lightning injuries are an inherent risk of watching baseball. Even if it did, the ballpark probably cannot rely on the Act alone as a complete defense because the facts suggest that the risk could have been reduced or eliminated if the ballpark manager had warned spectators to take cover until the danger had passed.

B. *The ballpark most likely will not prevail if it argues that the risk of lightning was an open and obvious danger that a reasonable spectator would have heeded by taking cover.*

The ballpark may argue that the approaching thunderstorm was an open and obvious danger to spectators, and therefore the landowner owed no duty to protect Ms. Worthington from the risk of harm. However, this affirmative defense is unlikely to succeed because Colorado courts have rejected common law defenses in analogous cases.

In *Vigil*, 103 P.3d at 329-30, the Colorado Supreme Court acknowledged the power of the Legislature to abrogate or modify common law. In that case, a developmentally disabled individual dove into a shallow part of the defendant's swimming pool and sustained disabling injuries as a result. *Id.* The defendant landowners claimed that the danger was open and obvious, thus negating any duty of care they might have owed the plaintiff. *Id.* at 325. A majority of the court squarely held that "the common law open and obvious danger doctrine does not survive the enactment of Colorado's premises liability statute." *Id.* at 332; *see also Muniz v. Kmart Corp.*, No. CIVA 06CV00084WDMPAC, 2007 WL 1964069, at *3 (D. Colo. July 2, 2007) (observing that under *Vigil,* Colorado landowners can no longer rely on the open and obvious danger defense to premises liability claims).

While the ballpark cannot avoid liability entirely by arguing that the danger of lightning was open and obvious, it may be able to mitigate its liability for damages by asserting comparative negligence. The Colorado Supreme Court has clarified that the Colorado Premises Liability Act does not abrogate comparative negligence, which was not recognized at common law and is not an affirmative defense to a negligence or premises liability claim. *Union Pac. R. Co. v. Martin*, 209 P.3d 185, 190 (Colo. 2009). Comparative negligence instead simply allocates proportionate liability among the parties and others whose negligence contributed to the injury. *Id.*

8

The facts in this case suggest that Ms. Worthington may have been somewhat negligent because her friend noticed the approaching storm and called Ms. Worthington's attention to the warning signs in the sky. While Ms. Worthington responded with a nonchalant shrug, she was apparently aware of the approaching thunderstorm and could have taken steps to protect herself by moving to a covered area of the ballpark until the storm passed. On the other hand, a jury might consider the fact that Ms. Worthington was a minor at the time of her injuries, and therefore was not in the same position as an adult to fully appreciate the safety risk posed by the weather conditions. *See Lakeside Park Co. v. Wein*, 141 P.2d 171, 172 (Colo. 1943) (holding that a minor plaintiff is bound to exercise only the degree of care an ordinarily prudent child of similar age and like intelligence would exercise under similar circumstances); John W. Grund, *et al.*, 7 *Colo. Prac., Personal Injury Torts & Insurance* § 11:6 (3d ed. 2013).

CONCLUSION

Sophie Worthington most likely qualifies as an "invitee" as a matter of law. Therefore, the ballpark owed her a duty of reasonable care. In this case, the ballpark manager's office was equipped with an emergency weather radio and computer access, which the manager could have used to monitor weather conditions. A weather advisory had specifically warned about the risk of lightning nearly thirty minutes before lightning struck and injured Ms. Worthington. Although lightning was the direct cause of her injury, a jury would probably find that the ballpark's failure to warn her about the approaching storm was a contributing factor. Had the ballpark warned spectators about the risk, Ms. Worthington would have had time to take cover before lightning struck her.

The ballpark probably does not have an affirmative defense. First, the Colorado Baseball Spectator Safety Act limits the ballpark's liability only for injuries that are "inherent risks" of watching baseball. The Act does not define "inherent risk," and Colorado courts have never held that baseball spectators bear the risk of being struck by lightning in a ballpark. Courts and statutes in other states that recognize the baseball rule generally limit the term to risks that a baseball spectator might expect, such as being injured by a foul ball or a broken bat. A court is likely to interpret the Act consistent with persuasive authority from other states, as well as the policy reasons underlying the rule.

Second, the Colorado Premises Liability Act supersedes all common law defenses to premises liability claims, including the open and obvious danger defense. Therefore, even if the minor saw the storm approaching, the ballpark cannot assert the defense to bar her claim. At most, the ballpark may be able to limit its liability by asserting comparative negligence because Ms. Worthington failed to take cover when she saw the storm approaching.

9

B Sample Client Advice Letter

Orosco & Strombeck
Attorneys at Law
1189 Arapaho Street
Trail Ridge Mesa, CO 81643

August 22, 2015

Darrell and Latesha Worthington
4830 Gunnison Road
Trail Ridge Mesa, CO 81643

Re: Potential lawsuit against Slugger Field

Dear Mr. and Mrs. Worthington:

Thank you for meeting with me earlier this week. I hope Sophie is beginning to recover and feeling better each day. When we met, I promised that we would research the law relevant to Sophie's injuries.

We believe you would probably win a lawsuit against Slugger Field for Sophie's injuries. It's possible, however, that a court might award less money than we would hope.

Please call my secretary to schedule an appointment so we can talk about what to do next. In this letter, I'll briefly describe the key issues so you can be thinking about them before we meet.

The next few paragraphs describe the facts as I understand them. If I have misunderstood anything, please let me know soon because the law might treat this situation differently if the facts are different.

Early on the day Sophie was injured, the National Weather Service had issued a severe thunderstorm watch. She and a friend, both age 16, entered the ballpark in late afternoon to attend a youth baseball tournament. By then the thunderstorm watch had expired. Sophie and her friend sat in the outfield general admission area, which is not covered by the ballpark's roof.

At 5:45 p.m., the Weather Service issued a new severe thunderstorm weather advisory for the area just to the west of the ballpark. This advisory urged extra precautions due to the high risk of lightning accompanying the storm. It appears that the ballpark manager was then in his office, which was equipped with an internet-connected computer as well as a Weather Service emergency radio. The manager most likely has the weather radio in his office to alert him when a game might need to be rescheduled because of an impending storm. No announcement was made over the ballpark's public address system to inform spectators about the weather. Sophie and her friend did not know about the thunderstorm advisory.

1

About ten minutes before 6:00 p.m., it started to sprinkle. Baseball play continued on the field. Around 6:00, the sky clouded over and light rain began to fall. Sophie's friend pointed to sheet lightning on the horizon. Sophie saw this distant lightning and continued watching the baseball game. At 6:14 p.m., she was struck by lightning and sustained severe injuries.

Sophie was what the law calls an invitee of the ballpark. Slugger Field advertised the tournament and invited the public to attend. For that reason, the ballpark owners owed Sophie a duty of reasonable care to protect her from harm. In the words of the Colorado Premises Liability Act, "an invitee may recover for damages caused by the landowner's unreasonable failure to exercise reasonable care to protect against dangers of which he actually knew or should have known."

We believe that a jury would probably find that the owners breached that duty of care by not warning tournament spectators, including Sophie, about the Weather Service's thunderstorm advisory and the risk of lightning. Even if it turns out that the ballpark manager did not know about the lightning, he should have known because he had a weather radio and a computer in his office, and a thunderstorm watch had been issued earlier in the day. At the very least, the manager should have announced a warning over the ballpark's public address system to give spectators a reasonable opportunity to take cover, especially those, like Sophie, who were seated in the general admission bleachers, which are not under a roof.

A ballpark owner isn't legally responsible for injuries to spectators caused by an inherent risk of attending a baseball game, such as being hit by foul balls. Slugger Field might argue that weather is an inherent risk of baseball and that spectators at a ball game assume the risk of bad weather. But the Field will most likely lose this argument. Foul balls and thrown bats are inherent risks of watching baseball because the game can't be played without them. Sophie may have assumed the risk that she would be struck by a foul ball, but not by lightning.

When we next meet, we should also talk about a concept the law calls comparative negligence. Although you will probably win a lawsuit against the owners of Slugger Field, a court might award less money than would compensate Sophie fully for her injuries. Slugger Field might argue that Sophie should have been able to recognize the danger on her own and protect herself by moving to a covered part of the ballpark until the storm passed. Light rain had started to fall, and she observed lightning on the horizon a few minutes before lightning struck her.

On the other hand, a jury might decide that, at Sophie's age, she was not as able as an adult to understand fully the risk posed by the deteriorating weather. In fact, she was attending a youth tournament, and the adults in charge had not stopped the baseball game before she was struck by lightning. As far as she could tell, none of the adults in positions of authority were acting as though the weather was dangerous, and we would argue that a 16-year-old ought to be able to trust them.

The outcome of the comparative negligence issue is the most difficult one for us to predict because the law is less clear cut on that point than on other aspects of Sophie's

2

case. The results of a lawsuit might depend on facts that we can learn only if you decide to sue Slugger Field. Before a lawsuit is filed, the ballpark owners have no legal obligation to tell us what they know about what happened that night. But once a lawsuit begins, they must truthfully answer questions that we ask them. This is called discovery, which I'll explain when we meet.

We appreciate your confidence in our firm to represent Sophie's interests in this matter, and we will do our very best in seeking compensation from the owners of Slugger Field. When you and I next meet, you can decide on the next steps you would like us to take. My secretary, Julie Allen, can schedule an appointment when you call. We look forward to hearing from you.

Sincerely yours,

Emilia Orosco
Emilia Orosco

3

C Sample Motion Memorandum

IN THE UNITED STATES DISTRICT COURT
FOR THE CENTRAL DISTRICT OF TEXAS

Findlay Division

LURENE R. MCCRACKEN,

  Plaintiff,

   v.

UBER TECHNOLOGIES, INC.,

  Defendant.

Case No. 15-cv-5432-olr

MEMORANDUM IN SUPPORT OF DEFENDANT'S MOTION TO DISMISS

Defendant Uber Technologies, Inc. ("Uber") respectfully asks this Court to dismiss the complaint filed on September 28, 2015, by the plaintiff, Lurene R. McCracken, for failure to state a claim. Fed. R. Civ. P. 12(b)(6).

PRELIMINARY STATEMENT

The plaintiff's complaint seeks declaratory and injunctive relief, as well as attorney fees and litigation expenses, for an alleged violation of Title III of the Americans with Disabilities Act (ADA), specifically 42 U.S.C. §§ 12181-12189, and one of its implementing regulations, 49 C.F.R. § 37.29 (2014). For the reasons summarized below, the complaint fails to state a claim upon which relief can be granted, so no responsive pleading is required. *See* Fed. R. Civ. P. 12(a)(4).

First, Uber's smartphone application does not qualify as a "public accommodation" under 42 U.S.C. § 12182(a), the general statutory provision cited in the complaint. McCracken Complaint ¶ 2 (Sept. 28, 2015). Second, Uber's "vehicle-for-hire" service does not qualify as a "taxi service" within the meaning of 49 C.F.R. § 37.29, cited in ¶ 19 of the Complaint. At most, based on the plaintiff's allegations, Uber qualifies as a "demand responsive service," 42 U.S.C. § 12181(3), which is not required to purchase accessible automobiles for its contract drivers. *See* 49 C.F.R. § 37.103 (2014). Nor does anything in the statute or its implementing regulations require Uber to retrofit its drivers' automobiles to make them wheelchair accessible. *See* 42 U.S.C. § 12182(b)(2)(A)(iv) (2012). Therefore, the complaint fails to show that the plaintiff is entitled to any remedy under the ADA, injunctive or otherwise. *See* 42 U.S.C. § 12188(a) (2012).

1

STATEMENT OF FACTS

The following alleged facts are drawn from the complaint. The plaintiff, Lurene R. McCracken, resides in Findlay, Texas, and she has a disability. Complaint ¶ 7. Specifically, she has a mobility impairment and uses a wheelchair. Complaint ¶¶ 2, 7. Without stating what kind of wheelchair she uses, the complaint alleges that any vehicle in which she travels must be accessible to wheelchairs "for transportation needs and other accommodating services," such as storing her wheelchair. Complaint ¶¶ 2, 16.

Uber provides passenger vehicle transportation services in Findlay, Texas, and in other Texas locations. Complaint ¶¶ 12, 15. Uber customers use a smartphone application to locate, schedule, and pay for transportation services. Complaint ¶ 15. The customers contract with Uber on an as-needed basis to transport them to their desired locations, and the customer agrees to pay for the service, including safety fees and surcharges when applicable, using credit card data and a smart phone. Complaint ¶ 15.

The complaint alleges that Uber does not provide services to mobility-impaired consumers, Complaint ¶¶ 2, 17, and that it allows vehicles for hire to deny services to consumers who have disabilities, Complaint ¶ 2. The complaint also alleges that Uber does not provide training or guidance to drivers of vehicles-for-hire concerning "the needs of disabled consumers." Complaint ¶ 2. However, the complaint does not allege specific facts or circumstances showing that the plaintiff was ever personally denied services by either Uber or its drivers. Nor does the complaint allege that she is unable to use her smartphone to access Uber services. On the other hand, no facts are alleged to support a conclusion that the plaintiff is physically able to use Uber's transportation services.

The plaintiff's sole claim for injunctive and other relief alleges that Uber and its unnamed service providers "have failed to provide any mechanism . . . to serve mobility impaired individuals." Complaint ¶ 20.

ARGUMENT

Uber's Motion to Dismiss Should be Granted Because the Complaint Fails to State a Claim that Uber's Private Transportation Services Violate Title III of the Americans with Disabilities Act.

When deciding a motion to dismiss under Rule 12(b)(6), "'the central issue is whether, [considered] in the light most favorable to the plaintiff, the complaint states a valid claim for relief.'" *Doe v. MySpace, Inc.*, 528 F.3d 413, 418 (5th Cir. 2008) (quoting *Hughes v. The Tobacco Inst. Inc.*, 278 F.3d 417, 420 (5th Cir. 2001) (internal quotations omitted)). This Court is required to accept each factual allegation in the complaint as true, but a plaintiff must plead "'enough facts to state a claim to relief that is plausible on its face.'" *Id.* (quoting *Bell Atl. Corp. v. Twombly*, 550 U.S. 544, 570 (2007)). A complaint is plausible on its face only "when the plaintiff pleads factual content that allows the court to draw the reasonable inference that the defendant is liable for the misconduct alleged." *Ashcroft v. Iqbal*, 556 U.S. 662, 678 (2009) (quoting *Bell Atl. Corp. v. Twombly*, 550 U.S. at 556).

2

The complaint includes nonspecific allegations of fact and only vague references to the legal theory on which the allegations are based. Uber acknowledges that the Court must take the plaintiff's allegations as true in considering this motion to dismiss. *See Frame v. City of Arlington,* 657 F.3d 215, 222 (5th Cir. 2011). To avoid dismissal, however, the complaint must plead facts sufficient to state a plausible claim for relief. *Gentilello v. Rege*, 627 F.3d 540, 544 (5th Cir. 2010). "We do not accept as true conclusory allegations, unwarranted factual inferences, or legal conclusions." *Plotkin v. IP Axess Inc.*, 407 F.3d 690, 696 (5th Cir. 2005). "While legal conclusions can provide the framework of a complaint, they must be supported by factual allegations." *Iqbal*, 556 U.S. at 679; *see also Gentilello*, 627 F.3d at 544. For that reason, "a court considering a motion to dismiss can choose to begin by identifying pleadings that, because they are no more than conclusions, are not entitled to the assumption of truth." *Iqbal*, 556 U.S. at 679.

Disregarding the unsupported legal conclusions, the allegations of fact in the complaint fail to state a claim upon which this Court may grant relief under the ADA and its implementing regulations.

Part A below explains the pleading and proof required to succeed on the plaintiff's ADA claim. Part B addresses why the complaint fails to state a claim under Title III based on Uber's smartphone application. Part C explains why the complaint fails to state a claim based on the vehicles owned and operated by the drivers who contract with Uber to provide on-demand transportation. Part D discusses why the complaint fails to allege that removing any communication or transportation barriers, assuming they exist, is "readily achievable" as required to impose any obligation on Uber.

A. *To plead an ADA claim, the plaintiff would have to allege that Uber failed to remove structural communication barriers or transportation barriers and that removing the barriers is "readily achievable."*

The ADA is composed of separate titles, each prohibiting discrimination by three major categories of entities. Title I proscribes discrimination against individuals with disabilities in employment and hiring. 42 U.S.C. §§ 12111-12117. Title II, prohibiting discrimination in access to public services, is divided into two parts. Part A governs public services generally, 42 U.S.C. §§ 12131-12134, and Part B governs public transportation services, 42 U.S.C. §§ 12141-12150, 12161-12165. Finally, Title III prohibits discrimination in "public accommodations" as that term is defined in the Act. 42 U.S.C. §§ 12181-12189; *see id.* § 12181(9) (defining the term).

The complaint in this case does not allege discrimination in employment, to which Title I applies, or discrimination by a public entity, to which Title II applies. The plaintiff alleges only that Uber's "demand responsive system," as defined by § 12181, violates Title III, specifically § 12184(a). Complaint ¶¶ 14, 19.

Title III provides, "No individual shall be discriminated against on the basis of disability in the full and equal enjoyment of the goods, services, facilities, privileges, advantages, or accommodations of any *place of public accommodation* by any person who owns, leases (or leases to), or operates a *place of public accommodation*."

3

§ 12182(a) (emphasis added). The vague allegations in the complaint do not specify how Uber owns, leases, or operates any "place of public accommodation"; nor do they explain how Uber has violated the statute.

Section 12182(b)(2)(A)(iv) defines "discrimination" for purposes of the general prohibition in § 12182(a). The relevant language refers specifically to

> (iv) a failure to remove . . . transportation barriers in existing vehicles . . . used by an establishment for transporting individuals (not including barriers that can only be removed through the retrofitting of vehicles . . . by the installation of a hydraulic or other lift), where such removal is readily achievable.

§ 12182(b)(2)(A)(iv).

No facts in the complaint allege either that the plaintiff has been, or that she has reasonable grounds for believing that she is about to be, discriminated against based on her disability. *See* 42 U.S.C. § 12188(a)(1). Therefore, the complaint does not state a claim for remedies otherwise available under the Civil Rights Act of 1964, 42 U.S.C. § 2000a-3(a). *See* § 12188(a)(1). To be entitled to injunctive relief as authorized by the ADA, the plaintiff must establish a violation of either § 12182(b)(2)(A)(iv) (quoted above) or § 12183(a). *See* § 12188(a)(2) (basis for injunctive relief).

Section 12183(a) defines discrimination with respect to new construction and alterations to public accommodations and commercial facilities (other than elevators). That provision does not apply to Uber's transportation services, which are not provided through any fixed building or commercial facility that could be made accessible by architectural alteration or new construction.

Therefore, to state a plausible claim for injunctive relief under § 12188(b) for discrimination on the basis of disability, the complaint must allege sufficient facts to support a claim under § 12182(b)(2)(A)(iv). Specifically, the complaint must allege—

(1) that Uber failed to remove communication barriers that are structural in nature, or
(2) that Uber failed to remove transportation barriers—
    (a) in existing vehicles
    (b) used for transporting individuals,
    (c) except "barriers that can only be removed through the retrofitting of vehicles . . . by the installation of a hydraulic or other lift," and
(3) that removing the barriers is "readily achievable."

See § 12182(b)(2)(A)(iv).

B.   *The facts alleged in the complaint, even if true, do not show that Uber's smartphone application qualifies as either a "public accommodation" or a structural "communication barrier."*

The complaint fails to allege any facts that support plaintiff's apparent argument that Uber is a "place of public accommodation" for purposes of § 12182(a).

4

The ADA defines "public accommodation" by enumerating a detailed list of illustrations, as follows:

(1) Public accommodation

The following private entities are considered public accommodations for purposes of this subchapter, if the operations of such entities affect commerce—

(A) an inn, hotel, motel, or other *place* of lodging . . . ;
(B) a restaurant, bar, or other *establishment* serving food or drink;
(C) a motion picture house, theater, concert hall, stadium, or other *place* of exhibition or entertainment;
(D) an auditorium, convention center, lecture hall, or other *place* of public gathering;
(E) a bakery, grocery store, clothing store, hardware store, shopping center, or other sales or rental *establishment*;
(F) a laundromat, dry-cleaner, bank, barber shop, beauty shop, travel service, shoe repair service, funeral parlor, gas station, office of an accountant or lawyer, pharmacy, insurance office, professional office of a health care provider, hospital, or other service *establishment*;
(G) a terminal, depot, or other *station* used for specified public transportation;
(H) a museum, library, gallery, or other *place* of public display or collection;
(I) a park, zoo, amusement park, or other *place* of recreation;
(J) a nursery, elementary, secondary, undergraduate, or postgraduate private school, or other *place* of education;
(K) a day care center, senior citizen center, homeless shelter, food bank, adoption agency, or other social service center *establishment*; and
(L) a gymnasium, health spa, bowling alley, golf course, or other *place* of exercise or recreation.

42 U.S.C. § 12181(7) (emphasis added).

Based on the facts alleged in the complaint, Uber's smartphone application does not qualify as a "place of public accommodation." 42 U.S.C. § 12182(a). The smartphone application uses cellphone signals and internet service to communicate a prospective customer's needs for a vehicle to an Uber driver, who in turn confirms availability, timing, and price to the customer by sending a smartphone reply message. All of the examples listed in the statutory definition of "public accommodation" relate to *physical* places and establishments, not communication services without any connection to a physical structure, establishment, or other fixed place.

The plaintiff may rely on authorities from a few federal circuits that have interpreted "public accommodation" more expansively than the physical structures and places

5

enumerated in the definition itself. *E.g., Carparts Dist. Ctr., Inc. v. Auto. Wholesaler's Ass'n of New England, Inc.*, 37 F.3d 12, 20 (1st Cir. 1994) ("Neither Title III nor its implementing regulations make any mention of physical boundaries or physical entry.") But courts in other circuits have limited the term to physical structures and facilities based upon the examples enumerated in the statutory definition. *E.g., Nat'l Fed'n of the Blind v. Target Corp.*, 452 F. Supp. 2d 946, 952 & n.3 (N.D. Cal. 2006) ("Under Ninth Circuit law, a 'place of public accommodation,' within the meaning of Title III, is a physical place." (citing *Weyer v. Twentieth Century Fox Film Corp.*, 198 F.3d 1104, 1114 (9th Cir. 2000)). As the Eleventh Circuit has observed, "the purely legal question of the application of Title III to [such services as] Internet web sites is far from 'beyond any doubt.' In addressing the question, we would be wading into the thicket of a circuit split on this issue. Plainly, this is not an easy question." *Access Now, Inc. v. Sw. Airlines Co.*, 385 F.3d 1324, 1334 (11th Cir. 2004) (citations omitted).

The Fifth Circuit sides with those circuits that have interpreted the term narrowly, consistent with the plain language of the statutory definition. For example, in deciding that the ADA does not apply to insurance services, the Fifth Circuit has interpreted "Title III to prohibit an owner . . . of a *place of public accommodation* from denying the disabled access to the good or service and from interfering with the . . . full and equal enjoyment of the goods and services offered. But *the owner . . . need not modify or alter the goods and services that it offers* in order to avoid violating Title III." *McNeil v. Time Ins. Co.*, 205 F.3d 179, 188 (5th Cir. 2000) (emphasis added).

Applying this definition to the facts alleged here, no Fifth Circuit precedent supports an argument that Uber's smartphone application somehow violates the ADA. Even if it did, the Fifth Circuit has specifically held that the ADA does not require a covered place of public accommodation to modify its services in order to comply with Title III. *MacNeil*, 205 F.3d at 188. The complaint fails to state a claim that Uber's smartphone application violates Title III of the ADA.

C. *The facts alleged in the complaint do not show that Uber is a place of public accommodation or that it has failed to remove transportation barriers in existing vehicles, excluding any barriers that would require retrofitting vehicles by installing wheelchair lifts.*

The complaint quotes 49 U.S.C. § 12184(a), which governs "specified public transportation services provided by a private entity that is primarily engaged in the business of transporting people and whose operations affect commerce." The complaint assumes, without alleging any supporting facts, that Uber provides services within the scope of this statute. *See* 42 U.S.C. § 12181(10) (defining "specified public transportation" as "transportation by bus, rail, or any other conveyance (other than by aircraft) that provides the general public with general or special service (including charter service) on a regular and continuing basis"). Even if it does, the complaint does not allege that Uber is *primarily engaged* in that business. *See* § 12184(a).

With respect to vehicles operated by Uber's contract drivers, the complaint does not allege facts showing what, if any, *transportation barriers* that *existing vehicles* impose

6

or maintain. *See* § 12182(b)(2)(A)(iv). The complaint vaguely suggests only that Uber has "failed to provide any mechanism by which to serve mobility impaired individuals." Complaint ¶ 20.

Nor has plaintiff alleged facts addressing how any of the alleged transportation barriers can be removed without "retrofitting vehicles" by installing hydraulic or other lifts. *See* § 12182(b)(2)(A)(iv). The plain language of the statute makes clear that even if a transportation provider qualifies as a place of public accommodation, it is *not* required to retrofit existing vehicles with hydraulic or other kinds of lifts. *Id.* In fact, the complaint does not even specify what the plaintiff would have this Court order Uber to do to comply with what the ADA requires pertaining to transportation services. Complaint p. 5, Prayer ¶ b.

> D. *Even if the complaint did allege sufficient facts to show that Uber failed to remove communication or transportation barriers, the complaint does not allege that the removal of barriers is "readily achievable" as that term is defined in 42 U.S.C. § 12181(9).*

Even if this Court were to hold that the plaintiff has alleged a plausible claim that Uber is a place of public accommodation, and that the services Uber provides impose some kind of communication or transportation barrier, the complaint does not allege how removing those alleged barriers would be "readily achievable." § 12182(b)(2)(A)(iv).

The ADA defines "readily achievable" as follows, and sets out a factors test to determine whether a specific accommodation meets the standard:

> (9) Readily achievable
> The term "readily achievable" means *easily accomplishable and able to be carried out without much difficulty or expense.* In determining whether an action is readily achievable, factors to be considered include—
>
> > (A) the nature and cost of the action needed under this chapter;
> > (B) the overall financial resources of the facility or facilities involved in the action; the number of persons employed at such facility; the effect on expenses and resources, or the impact otherwise of such action upon the operation of the facility;
> > (C) the overall financial resources of the covered entity; the overall size of the business of a covered entity with respect to the number of its employees; the number, type, and location of its facilities; and
> > (D) the type of operation or operations of the covered entity, including the composition, structure, and functions of the workforce of such entity; the geographic separateness, administrative or fiscal relationship of the facility or facilities in question to the covered entity.

42 U.S.C. § 12181(9).

7

The U.S. Supreme Court has interpreted this definition to extend to other considerations than the cost of the modification. *Spector v. Norwegian Cruise Line Ltd.*, 545 U.S. 119, 135 (2005) ("use of the disjunctive—'easily accomplishable and able to be carried out without much difficulty or expense'—indicates that it extends to considerations in addition to cost" including "'the impact . . . upon the operation of the facility'"). For example, "a structural modification is not readily achievable within the meaning of § 12181(9) if it would pose a direct threat to the health or safety of others." *Spector*, 545 U.S. at 136.

In this case, the complaint does not allege that any action the plaintiff desires Uber to take would be "readily achievable." 42 U.S.C. § 12181(9). Nor does the complaint allege any facts relevant to any of the four factors listed in the applicable statute for making that determination. § 12181(9)(A)-(D).

Finally, as the statute itself makes clear, a transportation provider is *not* required to retrofit existing vehicles with hydraulic or other kinds of lifts. § 12182(b)(2)(A)(iv). The plaintiff's complaint has not addressed how any of the alleged unspecified barriers can be removed without "retrofitting vehicles" by installing hydraulic or other kinds of wheel-chair lifts to accommodate her mobility impairment. The complaint, in fact, fails to specify just what the plaintiff would have the court order Uber to do. Complaint at 5, Prayer ¶ b.

Next, the complaint alleges a violation of 49 C.F.R. § 37.29. Complaint ¶ 19. But the complaint quotes only one subpart of the regulation, taken out of context. The plaintiff has misinterpreted the regulation's plain language when read in its entirety. Moreover, § 37.29 does not even apply to Uber because it is not a "taxi service," a term that is not defined anywhere in the ADA or the implementing regulations. *See* 42 U.S.C. § 12111; *see also* 49 C.F.R. § 37.3 (listing definitions).

Title 49 C.F.R. § 37.29 reads as follows:

Private entities providing taxi service.

(a) Providers of taxi service are subject to the requirements of this part for private entities primarily engaged in the business of transporting people which provide demand responsive service.

(b) *Providers of taxi service are not required to purchase or lease accessible automobiles.* When a provider of taxi service purchases or leases a vehicle other than an automobile, the vehicle is required to be accessible unless the provider demonstrates equivalency as provided in § 37.105 of this part. *A provider of taxi service is not required to purchase vehicles other than auto-mobiles in order to have a number of accessible vehicles in its fleet.*

(c) Private entities providing taxi service shall not discriminate against individ-uals with disabilities by actions including, but not limited to, refusing to pro-vide service to individuals with disabilities who can use taxi vehicles, refusing to assist with the stowing of mobility devices, and charging higher fares or fees for carrying individuals with disabilities and their equipment than are charged to other persons.

49 C.F.R. § 37.29 (2014) (emphasis added).

8

Even if Uber were a "taxi service" (and it is not), the regulation specifically provides that a taxi service is *not* required to purchase automobiles that are accessible, and a taxi service is *not* required to purchase other vehicles to ensure that it has accessible vehicles in its fleet. 49 C.F.R. § 37.29(b). Moreover, the subsection of the regulation quoted in the complaint assumes that the person who seeks accommodations is someone "with disabilities *who can use taxi vehicles*." § 37.29(c). Nothing in the complaint alleges that the plaintiff "can use taxi vehicles."

The complaint contains at best only vague, nonspecific allegations, and it fails to specifically allege how the plaintiff has been a victim of discrimination by Uber or any of its contract drivers. Uber is not a taxi service, and the complaint does not allege any facts suggesting that it is. For that matter, the complaint does not even allege facts showing that Uber qualifies as a "specified transportation service" for purposes of 49 U.S.C. § 12184(a). Nor does the complaint allege that Uber is engaged primarily in the business of transporting people. *See* Title 49 C.F.R. § 37.103(a).

The complaint points to no statute or regulation that requires Uber to purchase wheelchair accessible vehicles for use by its drivers or otherwise alter its contract drivers' own vehicles to permit wheelchair access. In fact, the most pertinent regulation, even assuming it applies, is not cited in the plaintiff's complaint. *See* § 37.103. That regulation apples to "demand responsive systems," *id.*, defined to mean "any system of providing transportation of individuals by a vehicle, other than a system which is a fixed route system," 42 U.S.C. § 12181(3). An extensive discussion appears in Appendix D to Part 37, Title 49 C.F.R., which explains how to interpret Part 37, including the definition of "demand responsive systems."

And while the complaint fails to allege that Uber is primarily engaged in the business of transporting people, *see* 49 C.F.R. § 37.103(a), even the regulations applicable to those entities *do not* require them to purchase automobiles that are accessible to persons with disabilities:

> (c) Demand responsive systems. If the entity operates a demand responsive system, and purchases or leases a new vehicle *other than an automobile*, [or] a van with a seating capacity of less than eight persons (including the driver), it shall ensure that the vehicle is readily accessible to and usable by individuals with disabilities, including individuals who use wheelchairs, unless the system, when viewed in its entirety, meets the standard for equivalent service of § 37.105 of this part.

49 C.F.R. § 37.103(c) (emphasis added). Nothing in the complaint alleges that Uber or any of its drivers has purchased or leased a new vehicle other than an automobile, or a van with seating capacity of fewer than eight persons. Even if it did, the most pertinent regulation specifically *permits* demand responsive systems to acquire new automobiles that are not accessible. *See id.*

In summary, the complaint fails to state a plausible claim, supported by allegations of fact, that Uber has in any way violated the applicable provisions of Title III of the Americans with Disabilities Act.

9

CONCLUSION

The complaint does not allege facts, even if true, that support a claim for violation of any provision of the ADA applicable to Uber. Based on the allegations of the complaint, Uber at most qualifies as a private "demand responsive system" under Title III of the ADA because its customers use the Uber application on their smartphones to locate and pay for a driver and a vehicle to transport the customer to her desired location. As the complaint alleges, Uber operates a "vehicle-for-hire" service using private drivers, who own their own cars. Even assuming that Uber qualifies as a demand responsive system under the ADA, the complaint has identified nothing in the ADA or its implementing regulations that supports her claim that Uber has violated the law in any way.

For all of these reasons, Uber respectfully asks this Court to grant its motion to dismiss the plaintiff's complaint for failure to state a claim.

Respectfully submitted,

Dated: October 17, 2015

Jean Vander Meer
Jean Vander Meer
Texas Bar No. 00432
Shotton & Camilli, LLC
1224 Thalia Street
Findlay, TX 78315
Vandermeer.law@gmail.com
(234) 764-8921

CERTIFICATE OF SERVICE

I certify that on October 17, 2015, this Motion to Dismiss was served on counsel for plaintiff Lurene R. McCracken by depositing a copy in first-class mail, postage prepaid, addressed to:

Charles Gehringer
Law Offices of Gehringer & Bluege
115 Calliope Avenue
Findlay, TX 78315

Jean Vander Meer
Jean Vander Meer

10

D Sample Appellate Brief

In some ways, the format of this brief does not follow practices in the Seventh Circuit, where the appeal is set. Instead, the brief's format blends practices in many courts so that it is somewhat representative nationally.

In the UNITED STATES COURT OF APPEALS
for the SEVENTH CIRCUIT

Docket No. 2011—Civ.—141

AMOS KENDALL,
Appellant,
v.
GEORGE VEDITZ,
Appellee.

ON APPEAL FROM A JUDGMENT OF
THE UNITED STATES DISTRICT COURT
FOR THE SOUTHERN DISTRICT OF ILLINOIS

BRIEF FOR THE APPELLANT

Joanne Olson
Caroline Borden
Attorneys for the Appellant

TABLE OF CONTENTS

Page

i

TABLE OF AUTHORITIES

---

* Authorities chiefly relied on are marked with an asterisk.

Statutes, Regulations, Court Rules, and Legislative Histories

Secondary Authorities

iii

PROCEEDINGS BELOW

George Veditz, Appellee, is a former client of Amos Kendall, Appellant and a member of the Illinois bar. Veditz sued Kendall, alleging that Kendall failed to comply with Title III of the Americans with Disabilities Act and seeking an injunction and court-ordered mediation. (R. at 2, 11.) Kendall denied all the allegations in the complaint. (R. at 6.) Both parties waived their rights to a trial by jury. (R. at 11.)

Over Kendall's objection, the District Court ordered both parties to submit to mediation, but stayed the execution of the order pending appeal. (R. at 11.) Mr. Kendall has now appealed to this Court. (R. at 28, 29.)

QUESTION PRESENTED

Mediation is a form of alternative dispute resolution through which disputing parties, with the assistance of a mediator, try to resolve their dispute. It is a collaborative alternative to an adversarial trial. Because mediation is collaborative rather than adversarial, it succeeds when parties discuss their dispute together and work with each other to resolve it. In this lawsuit, Kendall objects to mediation and is convinced that it will fail. He believes that his rights can be protected only through a trial because he provided Veditz with a deaf-signing translator at a settlement conference and because he otherwise communicated with Veditz through typing on a laptop, which Veditz himself uses in his own job to communicate reliably. On these facts, did the District Court exceed its authority or abuse its discretion in ordering Kendall to mediate this lawsuit? Did the District Court err in determining that the accommodations provided by Kendall violate the Americans with Disabilities Act?

STATEMENT OF THE CASE

Amos Kendall, a seasoned attorney, is committed to providing clients with disabilities full and equal enjoyment of his legal services. His office is free from physical barriers, and he has represented many disabled clients. George Veditz, a client, has sued Kendall alleging that Kendall failed to provide a Signed Exact English (SEE) interpreter or a Computer Assisted Real Time Transcription (CART), even though Veditz did not request either of these accommodations.

Accommodations Provided to Veditz

While Kendall was representing Veditz in his divorce proceedings, Veditz became deaf due to viral meningitis. (R. at 13.) As a late-deafened adult, Veditz can communicate most accurately through writing, which he has known and used all his life. (R. at 14.) At work, he communicates through writing. (R. at 14.) Veditz has never had formal training in any signed language. (R. at 4.) After the loss of his hearing, he has attempted to teach himself how to sign and now has a small vocabulary of signs. (R. at 14.) Veditz can understand some Signed Exact English (SEE), which has a grammar structure identical to English, but he is not fluent in SEE. (R. at 14.) He has a difficult time

1

understanding American Sign Language (ASL), which uses its own unique grammar. (R. at 4.) While Computer Assisted Real Time Transcription (CART) is an efficient method of written communication for late-deafened adults, handwritten or typed exchanges are also effective. (R. at 19.)

Initially, Kendall and Veditz communicated in part through written exchanges via a laptop. (R. at 15.) Kendall typed so that Veditz could read on the laptop screen. (R. at 15.) Veditz communicated by speaking. (R. at 15.) They also used email. (R. at 15.) Veditz testified that although writing was not fast communication, he always understood what Kendall was telling him, and that he uses writing almost exclusively himself to communicate at work. (R. at 14-15.) Knowing that Veditz was learning signs, Kendall hired a sign language interpreter, Jane Fesenden, for the divorce settlement negotiations. (R. at 8.) Veditz did not ask Kendall to provide an interpreter or CART for the negotiation. (R. at 18, 24.)

The Divorce Negotiation

During the negotiation, Veditz told Fesenden he was unfamiliar with the grammar of ASL. (R. at 15.) Fesenden tried to use English grammar when signing to Veditz, but had to repeat herself and occasionally used ASL grammar. (R. at 16.) Regardless of the grammar Fesenden used, Veditz had trouble understanding her because he did not understand many of her signs. (R. at 16.) Privately during the negotiation, Veditz told Kendall that he could not understand much of what Fesenden was translating. (R. at 16.) After learning that, Kendall typed accurate summaries of what each person said during the negotiation for Veditz to read. (R. at 16, 23.) Veditz testified that the typed summaries of the negotiation were "a way to be sure" he was understanding things correctly. (R. at 16.) Kendall testified that with the typed summaries Veditz was able to participate in the settlement. (R. at 23.) Veditz did not tell Kendall in any other way that the communication was ineffective, and he did not ask for CART services at that time. (R. at 18.) Moreover, Veditz did not ask that the negotiation be adjourned, and he did not ask that it be reopened later. (R. at 18.) At the time of the negotiation, Veditz had never before used CART. (R. at 18.)

Adequacy of Accommodations Balanced Against Cost

Veditz alleged he was unable to fully participate in the negotiation and now needs continued legal counsel from Kendall to renegotiate the maintenance settlement. (R. at 2, 16.) Veditz also alleged that the communication obstacle would be remedied by the use of CART. (R. at 17.) From these allegations, Veditz claimed that Kendall did not make sufficient accommodations. (R. at 2.) Veditz testified that he wanted Kendall to use CART if he represents him in the future. (R. at 17.)

Kendall has tried but cannot find a certified SEE interpreter in southern Illinois (R. at 8.) Although CART is available, it costs $150 per hour, which Veditz wants Kendall to pay. (R. at 23.) Kendall bills only $100 per hour for his services. (R. at 23.) Kendall has made sure his office has no physical barriers that would hinder his many clients with movement disabilities. (R. at 8.) As far as Kendall knows, every other disabled client has been satisfied with Kendall's work and the disability accommodations that he has provided. (R. at 8.)

2

SUMMARY OF THE ARGUMENT

The finding that Veditz requested CART services is clearly erroneous because it is contradicted and unsupported by the evidence. Even if Veditz had requested CART services, Kendall was not required to provide CART because CART is unnecessary and unreasonable. CART is unnecessary because Kendall provided Veditz with Veditz's own best method of communication, written English in typed summaries. As a late-deafened adult, Veditz has communication needs that are unique, and unlike most deaf people, he communicates best with written English. Finally, Kendall does not have to provide CART, which would be an unreasonable accommodation. Providing CART would be an undue burden because Kendall would lose $50 for every hour he supplies CART.

The District Court abused its discretion by ordering mediation over Kendall's objection. Even if the District Court has the power to order mediation in some cases, it should not have done so here because mediation would be pointless. Because Kendall objects to it and believes that only a trial can protect his interests, mediation probably would not lead to a settlement.

ARGUMENT

I. Kendall Should Not Be Required, over His Objection, to Mediate a Case That He Could Reasonably Win at Trial.

Whether Veditz asked for CART services is a pure question of fact subject to the clearly erroneous standard of review. Fed. R. Civ. P. 52(a). A finding of fact is clearly erroneous if it leaves the court with "the definite and firm conviction that a mistake has been committed." *Anderson v. City of Bessemer City*, 470 U.S. 564, 573 (1984). The Court of Appeals does not have to accept the District Court's findings of fact if they are not supported by the evidence. *Campana Corp. v. Harrison*, 114 F.2d 400, 405 (7th Cir. 1940).

The remaining ADA questions are mixed questions of law and fact. Whether Kendall provided an appropriate auxiliary aid that ensures effective communication is a mixed question requiring the court to apply legal rules to undisputed facts. The last issue under the ADA claim, the undue burden defense, is also a mixed question requiring a court to interpret and apply the undue burden test to the facts of the case. In the Seventh Circuit, a mixed question of law and fact is reviewed *de novo* when "there is a need for uniformity" and "the issue is so important that there is a felt need to authorize second-guessing of" the District Court. *Cook v. City of Chicago*, 192 F.3d 693, 697 (7th Cir. 1999). Both are true here because the court below took the extraordinary step of ordering Kendall, over his objection, to take part in mediation, a process that works only when the parties participate voluntarily.

3

A. *Veditz Did Not Request CART and Therefore Cannot Win at Trial Concerning That Accommodation.*

Veditz failed to request CART. Even if Veditz had made such a request, CART is unnecessary and unreasonable given the cost, and Kendall still could not be required to modify his practice of providing deaf clients with interpreters and written exchanges, which are generally effective.

When providing auxiliary aids to disabled people, a business subject to the ADA should ask what auxiliary aid will work best, but the business is not obligated to provide the stated preference. *Majocha v. Turner*, 166 F. Supp. 2d 316, 321 (W.D. Pa. 2001). In *Majocha*, the court held that if a business provided an auxiliary aid that ensured effective communication, a disabled person could not insist on a different auxiliary aid. *Id.* at 323. A business is not obliged to change its practices in order to provide a more technologically advanced auxiliary aid so long as the aid in current use ensures effective communication. 28 C.F.R. pt. 36, App. B (2014) (Attorney General's Report).

If a business provides ineffective auxiliary aids, disabled people can request that the business change its practice of providing such aids, and the business is obligated to change the practice if the modification is requested, reasonable, and necessary. 42 U.S.C. § 12182(b)(2)(A)(ii) (2012); *Dudley v. Hannaford Bros. Co.*, 333 F.3d 299, 307 (1st Cir. 2003). In determining whether a modification is reasonable, courts balance the effectiveness of the modification against the cost of making the modification. *Fortyune v. Am. Multi-Cinema*, 364 F.3d 1075, 1083 (9th Cir. 2004). A modification is necessary if a disabled person would be unable to use the facilities, services, or goods without it. *See PGA Tour, Inc. v. Martin*, 532 U.S. 661, 682 (2001).

Here, the District Court found that Veditz had requested CART services and that Kendall failed to provide the requested service. (R. at 28.) At the time of the negotiation meeting, Veditz had never used CART. (R. at 18.) He admits that he never asked for CART services. (R. at 18.) If Veditz did not ask for the services, the only request that the court could find would be an implied one. But an implied request does not give a business enough notice to change its policy. An explicit request is necessary because without it the business may not know how or why to change its practices. The District Court erred because no evidence in the record supports the District Court's findings.

The District Court's finding that Veditz requested CART is not supported by any evidence in the record and should be reversed.

B. *Veditz Needed No Accommodation Because Kendall Provided Effective Communication.*

The District Court erred in finding that Kendall did not provide effective communication. The typed summaries Kendall provided resulted in effective communication during the negotiation settlement because Veditz was able to understand and participate in the negotiation settlement.

4

The evidentiary record does not support the District Court's conclusion that the communication provided by Kendall was ineffective. (R. at 13.) Veditz testified that the typed written communication *was* effective during the office meetings with Kendall. (R. at 13.) During the negotiations, Veditz had trouble understanding the interpreter, and he stopped the meeting, seeking to remedy this communication problem. (R. at 16.) He did not object after Kendall began typing summaries. (R. at 16.) If the typed summaries were ineffective, Veditz could have easily stopped the meeting a second time. From these uncontroverted facts, the most reasonable inference is that Veditz let the meeting continue because he understood and participated in the negotiations.

The District Court's decision that Kendall failed to provide effective communication is clearly erroneous and should be reversed because Kendall provided Veditz with written English, his best way of communicating.

C. Kendall Probably Will Not Be Enjoined to Provide CART Services Because the Cost Would Impose an Undue Burden.

A business need not provide disabled persons with auxiliary aids if doing so would be an undue burden. 42 U.S.C. § 12182(b)(2)(A)(iii) (2012). Providing an auxiliary aid would be an undue burden if it is overly expensive or difficult to provide. 28 C.F.R. §§ 36.104, 36.303 (2014). Because of their high costs, the District Court erred in finding that CART services were not an undue burden.

The case law provides examples of how to apply the factors listed in 28 C.F.R. § 36.104. *E.g., Roberts v. Kindercare Learning Ctrs., Inc.*, 86 F.3d 844 (8th Cir. 1996); *Mayberry v. Von Valtier*, 843 F. Supp. 1160 (S.D. Mich 1994). In *Mayberry*, the court determined that an auxiliary aid which costs $28 per hour would not be an undue burden for a doctor who charges $40 per hour. *Mayberry*, 843 F. Supp. at 1160. In *Roberts*, the court held that Kindercare did not have to provide a disabled person with a Personal Care Attendant when such an aid cost $200 per week and the cost of the child's weekly tuition was only $105. *Roberts*, 86 F.3d at 844.

The legislative history of the ADA provides the following example of the undue burden analysis, which balances the costs of the auxiliary aide against the resources of the business:

> A small day-care center might not be required to expend more than a nominal sum, such as that necessary to equip a telephone for use by a secretary with impaired hearing, but a large school district might be required to make available a teacher's aide to a blind applicant for a teaching job.

H.R. Rep. 101-485 pt. 2 (1990). In this example, it would be an undue burden for the small day care to provide an aide, but not for the large school. *Id.* Congress defined undue burden in this way because it was concerned about balancing the needs of disabled people with the high costs of accommodations. *Id.* at pt. 3; 136 Cong. Rec. S9686 (daily ed. July 13, 1990). The legislative history shows that Congress intended to eliminate discrimination against disabled people in "a clear, balanced and reasonable manner." H.R. Rep. 101-485 pt. 2.

5

Here, providing CART would result in an undue financial burden. This case is factually similar to *Roberts* and distinguishable from *Mayberry*. In *Mayberry*, the cost of providing an interpreter did not exceed the doctor's hourly charge, while in *Roberts*, the cost of providing a Personal Care Attendant did. The hourly cost of CART exceeds the amount of money that Kendall makes representing Veditz. (R. at 23.) If forced to provide CART, Kendall would lose money at a rate of $50 per hour. (R. at 23.)

Veditz claims that CART is not an undue burden because Kendall will have to provide CART only when the parties are communicating face-to-face, or during group meetings at which Veditz is present. (R. at 20.) The fact remains, however, that Kendall would still lose money. For every hour that Kendall provides CART, he would not be paid for that hour of work, and his next hour of regular work would be at half pay. Kendall's small private practice, as opposed to a large law firm, cannot absorb this loss. Forcing Kendall to provide CART may lead to substantial monetary loss, especially if future legal matters are long and complex. This evidence establishes that CART is a financial burden, which does not support the District Court's findings.

The purpose of the ADA is to prevent discrimination against disabled people while limiting the severity of financial burden on small businesses. The undue burden exception applies differently to large companies and to small business owners. Kendall, as a small business owner, should have to spend only a small sum, such as the cost of an interpreter, and should not be required to pay for CART. The financial burden of CART negates Kendall's obligation to provide it. The District Court's finding that CART would not be an undue burden is clear error because Kendall loses substantial sums of money for every hour that CART is used. Written communication, the auxiliary aid that Kendall has provided, is the best auxiliary aid that Kendall can afford to offer Veditz.

II. The District Court Lacks the Power to Order Parties to Mediate.

This issue is one of law because it can be decided without reference to the facts of the case. Therefore, it is reviewed *de novo*, "that is, with no deference given to the finder of fact." *Reynolds v. City of Chicago*, 296 F.3d 524, 527 (7th Cir. 2002).

Veditz cites several authorities, none of which explicitly provides a court with the power to order parties to mediate. In each instance, Veditz's arguments are based on strained interpretations of words that, read in context, mean something other than what Veditz claims they mean.

Rule 16(a)(5) of the Federal Rules of Civil Procedure allows a District Court to "direct" the litigants to "appear" at a pretrial conference, typically in a judge's chambers, for several purposes, among them "facilitating the settlement of the case." To facilitate means "to make easy or easier." *American Heritage Dictionary of the English Language* 653 (3d ed., 1992). It does not mean "order" or "compel." The plain wording of Rule 16 grants only the power to require parties to appear in a judge's chambers where, among other things, they might choose on their own to negotiate with each other. The words do not grant a court the power to order parties to negotiate with

6

each other, and they certainly do not grant the power to order parties to subject them-selves to a mediation conducted by a mediator. The words "mediate," "mediation," and "mediator" do not appear anywhere in Rule 16.

This Circuit has held that Rule 16 does not grant powers other than those specifically mentioned in the Rule. *Strandell v. Jackson Cnty.*, 838 F.2d 884 (7th Cir. 1987). There, a District Court ordered the parties to take part in a nonbinding jury trial, which is a form of alternative dispute resolution that (like mediation) is not mentioned in Rule 16. *Id.* at 884-86. This Circuit reversed, holding that Rule 16 does not justify "clubbing" the parties into a settlement procedure that one or both parties object to. *Id.* at 888.

Local Rule 16.2(b)(3) of the Southern District of Illinois also does not empower a District Court to order parties, against their will, to mediate. Instead, it provides that certain issues "shall be discussed at the final pretrial conference and shall be included in the final pretrial order," among them "any issue which, in the judge's opinion, may *facilitate and expedite the trial.*" *Id.* (emphasis added). Mediation does not facilitate or expedite trial. If successful, it settles the lawsuit and thus eliminates trial. The primary function of a pretrial conference is to coordinate getting ready for trial. Local Rule 16.2(b)(3) gives only one example of an issue that "may facilitate and expedite the trial." That is "the feasibility of presenting testimony [at trial] by a summary written state-ment." Local Rule 16.3(a) permits a District Court to order "summary jury trial or other alternative method of dispute resolution which the court may deem proper." None of these Rules mentions mediation, and the example of a summary jury trial suggests that the other permitted forms of alternative dispute resolution are limited to adversarial ones.

Although courts have many inherent powers in addition to those provided for in court rules, only one court has ever held that it had the inherent power to compel mediation. *In re Atl. Pipe Corp.*, 304 F.3d 135, 140 (1st Cir. 2002). Another court recognized that it could have that power but declined to use it in part because parties objected. *In re African-American Slave Descendants' Litig.*, 272 F. Supp. 2d 755, 759 (N.D. Ill. 2003).

III. Even if the District Court Had the Power to Order Mediation, It Abused Its Discretion in Doing So.

"To find an abuse of discretion, a court must have a definite and firm conviction that the district court committed a clear error in judgment." *Bell v. Johnson*, 404 F.3d 997, 1003 (6th Cir. 2005). Even if a court has the power to compel mediation, doing so over the objection of a party is a clear error in judgment. Mediation should not be compelled when one of the parties objects.

In exercising its inherent power, the court must use the power with restraint and discretion to enhance its processes. *In re African-American Slave Descendants' Litig.*, 272 F. Supp. 2d at 760. Voluntary participation is the key to mediation's success, and "when mediation is forced . . . it stands to reason that the likelihood of settlement is diminished." *Id.* Further, when settlement is unlikely, the investment of substantial time and money in mediation is inefficient and an undue burden on the objecting party. *Id.*

7

Mandatory mediation can be unfair, inefficient, or uneconomical. Mandatory mediation is overbearing when one party exerts its power over the other party, influencing the outcome of the mediation. Forced mediation also pressures parties to forgo trial and delays a party's day in court. Such a delay may effectively be a denial of justice. *G. Heileman Brewing Co. v. Joseph Oat Corp.*, 871 F.2d 648, 661 (7th Cir. 1987). Moreover, studies have shown that parties who mediate generally do not save time and money, and that courts do not reduce their caseloads, costs, or delays. Holly A. Streeter-Schaefer, *A Look At Court Mandated Civil Mediation*, 28 Drake L. Rev. 367, 388 (2001).

In this case, mediation should not have been ordered because it would not produce a settlement. The likelihood that mediation will resolve this dispute is small because Kendall complied with the ADA and made accommodations for Veditz. Mediation, therefore, will not end the litigation, and the District Court will still have to resolve the case as an adversarial matter. Forcing the parties to mediate merely causes delay and adds to their expense.

CONCLUSION

For all these reasons, the District Court erred in its findings and order, which should be reversed.

Respectfully submitted,

Joanne Olson
Joanne Olson
Attorney for Appellant

Caroline Borden
Caroline Borden
Attorney for Appellant

8

401

# E Document Design

Designing a document is deciding how it should look on the page. Design has nothing to do with the content (your words expressing your ideas). Instead, design creates a visual personality for the document—an attractive appearance that is easy to read. Some documents are unfriendly and difficult to read just because of the way they look. Others appear attractive on a page, seem inviting, and are a pleasure to read.

Layout and typeface are the primary elements of document design. Layout is the arrangement of type on the page so that your organization is clear and the reader is not overwhelmed with text.

Typeface is what the letters and numbers look like: type size, font, and features like *italics* and **bold**. Type size is how large or small the letters and numbers are, measured in points. A font is a group of letters and numbers with a common design (which will become more clear in a moment).

Good document design can help persuade a reader. The Seventh Circuit warns its lawyers thus:

> Judges of this court hear six cases on most argument days and nine cases on others. The briefs, opinions of the district courts, essential parts of the appendices, and other required reading add up to about 1,000 pages per argument session. Reading that much is a chore; remembering it is even harder. You can improve your chances by making your briefs typographically superior. It won't make your arguments better, but it will ensure that judges grasp and retain your points with less struggle. That's a valuable advantage, which you should seize.[1]

---

[1] *Requirements and Suggestions for Typography in Briefs and Other Papers*, at 4, http://www.ca7.uscourts.gov/Rules/type.pdf. *See also* Derek H. Kiernan-Johnson, *Telling Through Type: Typography and Narrative in Legal Briefs*, 7 J. ALWD 87 (2010); Ruth Anne Robbins, *Painting with Print: Incorporating Concepts of Typographic and Layout Design into the Text of Legal Writing Documents*, 2 J. ALWD 108 (2004).

Judge Frank Easterbrook of the same circuit speaks more pointedly: "Why should lawyers think that their [briefs] can be physically ugly and hard to read, yet still go over well?"[2]

If you are running out of time before an assignment is due, *please stop reading this appendix now*. Write the document. Do not spend your limited time trying to enhance its appearance on the page. *Just write it.* Content matters more than document design.

Part 1. Simple Document Design

Your word processor is the software in your computer with which you write documents. It is probably either Word or WordPerfect. What we say here applies to both.

Default font and type size. Your word processor probably defaults either to Times New Roman or Calibri (fonts) and 11- or 12-point (type sizes). The fonts look like this:

Times New Roman

Calibri

Later versions of Word default to Calibri or Cambria. Earlier versions default to Times New Roman, as does WordPerfect. You can change these default settings. Unless they are changed, your word processor will automatically produce one or the other of these fonts every time you start a new document.

Fonts are either *serif* or *sans serif*. In a serif font (like Times New Roman) most letters have little transverse lines called *serifs*. A sans serif font (like Calibri) has no serifs. (In *sans*, the second *s* is silent. *Sans* is French and means *without*—without serifs. *Serif* is pronounced "SAIR-if"—not "se-REEF.")

Look closely at the Times New Roman and the Calibri examples above. Calibri looks streamlined because it has no serifs. Later versions of Word default to Calibri because it looks good on a computer screen. On computer and television screens, on signs, and in advertisements, a sans serif font is usually easier to read than a serif font.

But in a long document printed on paper a serif font is easier to read. The serifs actually help the reader's eyes travel through extended text. Books are usually printed in serif fonts, although in some (including this one) the headings and a few other features are sans serif. In law practice, memos and briefs are printed in serif fonts.

Courts with typeface rules usually require that the text of submitted documents be printed in a serif font. You will not be able to use Calibri for most documents you write

---

[2] Frank H. Easterbrook, Judge, U.S. Court of Appeals for the Seventh Circuit, Speech, *Challenges in Reading Statutes*, Speech to the Lawyers Club of Chicago 16 (Chi., Ill., Sept. 28, 2007).

in a law office. If it is the default font in your word processing software now, you might consider changing it. The easiest choice would be Times New Roman, just because it is commonly used and is the default font in other versions of Word and in WordPerfect. Lawyers use it regularly, and although it is problematic, you will see it in many of the documents that come out of law offices. If you want to consider other fonts, see Part 3 of this appendix.

Near the top of your Word or WordPerfect screen is a small window that tells you which font the word processor is using. Next to it is an even smaller window that tells you the size of the type (a number). In Word, those windows are on the top left, under the "insert" tab. In earlier versions of Word, they are to the right of the top center of your screen. In WordPerfect, they are on the top left.

From each of those windows, a drop-down menu lets you change the font or the point size. To open the menu, click on the little down-arrow next to it. Click on the font you want; then click on the point size you want.

When you create a new document in either Word or WordPerfect, you can set its font and point size by placing the cursor at the very beginning of the document and clicking on the font and point size you want. In Word, you may have to do this before you type anything. To change an existing document's font and point size in Word, you may have to block the entire document and click on a font in the drop-down menu. In WordPerfect, just put the cursor at the beginning of the document and click on a font and a point size from the drop-down menus, and the whole document should change.

It is more complicated to reset your word processor's defaults so that *all* new documents will be in the font and point size you prefer. But if you will be using the same font often in the future, it will take less effort in the long run to change the default once rather than choose the font every time you start a new document. Search your word processor's help function for instructions about changing the default font and the default point size.

Default justification. Justification determines where lines of type begin and end. If your documents are left-justified, the left side of your text forms a straight vertical line, and the right side is ragged because the text lines do not all end in the same place. If a document is fully justified, however, both the left and the right sides of the text form straight vertical lines. Most books are fully justified. The default setting on your word processor is probably left justification. That's fine. Nobody will criticize you for using it, and many readers will prefer it in the documents you produce.

White space. Too much type on a page can make a document difficult and unpleasant to read. Creating white space opens up the page and makes it less crowded and easier on the eye. Your word processor's default margins are probably one inch on each side. You can create white space by moving the left and right margins each a quarter inch toward the center of the page so that each becomes 1.25 inches.

You can also create white space by the way you handle headings. In a single-spaced document, many writers will skip a line above a heading and skip another line below it. Instead, skip two lines above the heading. That will make your organization more visually obvious. The heading will more clearly belong to the text below because twice as much white space will appear above as below. If your document is double-spaced, you can get similar results by pressing the Enter key twice above the heading and once below it. With double spacing, a line is skipped automatically every time you press Enter.

Don't go overboard. Too much white space reduces the amount of text on each page. Avoid adding so much white space that the reader has to turn pages constantly and cannot easily back up to review what you said a paragraph or two earlier.

Adding white space might also increase the number of pages in your document. If your teacher has imposed a word or character limit on document size, increasing the number of pages will not matter. But if you are subject to a page limit, adding white space might put you over that limit.

Part 2. More Advanced Document Design

Headings. Each component of a memo or brief gets a heading, and the component headings are usually the largest in the document.

Office memo components include the Issue, Brief Answer, Facts, Discussion, and Conclusion. Sometimes you will want to break up the Facts or Discussion with additional headings. They should be smaller than the component headings and can be italicized or bolded to set them off from the text. Here is a reasonable way of sizing the headings and text—but it's not the only way:

component headings:	TIMES NEW ROMAN 14-point
lesser headings:	*Times New Roman 13-point*
text:	Times New Roman 12-point

(If your text size is 11-point, use 13-point for the component headings and 12-point for the lesser headings.)

Lawyers have traditionally underlined lesser headings because that is all a typewriter could do. With a word processor, however, you can use italics or bold instead, and italics, especially, are easier on the eye than underlining.

In a persuasive document submitted to a court, such as a trial court memo or an appellate brief, the components would include—among others—the Statement of the Case and the Argument. The Argument is divided by point headings and might further be divided by lesser headings called *subheadings* (see Chapter 33). The Statement of the Case might also be divided by lesser headings similar in size to the

Argument subheadings. Here is a reasonable—*but not the only*—way of sizing the headings and text:

component headings:	TIMES NEW ROMAN 14-point
argument point headings:	**Times New Roman 13-point in bold**
lesser headings:	*Times New Roman 13-point in italics*
text:	Times New Roman 12-point

(If your text size is 11-point, use 13-point for the component headings and 12-point for the point headings and lesser headings.)

Lawyers typically center the component headings on the page. Some do the same thing with point headings in persuasive documents. Legal documents have looked that way for generations, and your readers will expect it. Some document design specialists say that if you left-justify the text, you should probably left-justify headings as well (move them to the left margin, like the section headings in this book). Some lawyers therefore left-justify the point headings. Some lawyers center lesser headings as well, but some move them to the left margin.

Lawyers traditionally all-cap the component headings. That's fine. Component headings are short, usually one to four words, and all-capping them causes no problems. See the memos in Appendices A and C and the brief in Appendix D.

In persuasive documents submitted to courts, lawyers have traditionally all-capped *point headings* as well. You will see that in many trial court memos and appellate briefs. In the typewriter era, all-capping was the only way to make a point heading stand out. Today an increasing number of lawyers use bold print instead of all-caps, which has been done in the office and motion memos in Appendices A and C and the appellate brief in Appendix D.

Because point headings have more words than component headings, they are harder to read when all-capped. Compare two versions of the first point heading in Exercise 33-A at the end of Chapter 33:

all caps, Times New Roman, 13-point:	THE SEARCH OF THE DIGITAL CONTENTS OF PETITIONER'S SMART PHONE EXCEEDED THE BOUNDS OF A LEGITIMATE SEARCH INCIDENT TO ARREST.
bold, Times New Roman, 13-point:	**The Search of the Digital Contents of Petitioner's Smart Phone Exceeded the Bounds of a Legitimate Search Incident to Arrest.**

All-capping makes the first example hard to read. The second example stands out well because it is in bold, and it takes up less space and is more readable because it is not all-capped.

But the second example is not as readable as it could be. That is not the fault of bolding but instead a font problem. The rest of this appendix explains why.

Part 3. The Truth About Fonts

One of the oldest traditions of the bar seems to be that legal documents should always *look* boring. Many readers of legal documents intensely dislike this tradition.

Legal documents should look *professional*. That is not the same as looking boring. Judges spend enormous amounts of time reading briefs and other lawyer-submitted documents, and nearly all the judges who have stated their views on this subject would like to read attractive and readable fonts that reflect good taste.

Should you use a font other than Times New Roman for legal documents?
An advantage of using Times New Roman is that you need not think about it. And in law school you have more important things to do than playing around with fonts to find the one you like best. Unless you really do have the spare time to choose a new font, skip the rest of this appendix.

Times New Roman can be tiring to read. When you compare it with another commonly used font, you can see how its letters are cramped and tightly packed:

> This sentence is in Times New Roman 12-point.
> This sentence is in Century Schoolbook 11-point.

In each of these sentences, the first four words are identical. Notice that the fourth word—*in*—is farther to the right in the 11-point Century Schoolbook sentence than in the Times New Roman sentence. That is because Century Schoolbook inserts more space between letters.

Also notice that 11-point Century Schoolbook is comparable in horizontal spacing to 12-point Times New Roman. Eleven-point type in one font can compete with another font's 12-point type. Century Schoolbook's 12-point might be too big for the text of a memo or brief. It might be more appropriately sized for a heading instead.

The Seventh Circuit has run out of patience with Times New Roman and implores lawyers to use some other font. This appears on the Circuit's website: "Typographic decisions should be made for a purpose. The *Times of London* [a newspaper] chose the typeface Times New Roman to serve an audience looking for a quick read.

Lawyers don't want their audience to read fast and throw the document away; they want to maximize retention."[3]

Times New Roman is a newspaper font. Its letters are crammed close together so they can fit into narrow newspaper columns, on the assumption that most readers will not read much more than the first few paragraphs anyway. It was not designed or intended for long documents like memos and briefs. Even newspapers have been switching to other fonts.

The Supreme Court will reject any brief printed in Times New Roman. It insists on fonts in the Century family, such as Century Schoolbook.[4] "The Justices are tired of bad typography," says Judge Easterbrook of the Seventh Circuit.[5] Many other fonts look professional, and you might like one of them better.

How to choose a replacement font. Choosing a new serif font is not a substitute for studying or for doing a writing assignment. It's a study-break activity.

You will want a font that looks professional, is easy to read, and pleases the eye. Eye appeal is not the same as readability. An attractive font makes a good impression visually by inviting a reader warmly into the document and helping the reader feel comfortable—all by being pleasant to look at. Lawyers might think it odd to consider the reader's pleasure, but the Seventh Circuit recommends doing exactly that.

A safe choice might be Century Schoolbook. If the Supreme Court insists on a Century-family font, you can assume that it is readable, attractive, and professional.

But in case you want more choices, below are some professional-looking fonts, with Century Schoolbook for comparison.

> Bell MT 12-point
> Book Antiqua 11-point
> Calisto MT 11-point
> Century 11-point
> **Century Schoolbook 11-point**
> Constantia 11-point
> Garamond 12-point
> Goudy OlSt BT 11-point
> Goudy Old Style 11-point
> Palatino Linotype 11-point

Book Antiqua and Palatino are similar except that Palatino has more space between the lines. The two Goudys are closely related but are not identical. Goudy OlSt BT is more spacious than Goudy Old Style.

---

[3] *Requirements and Suggestions, supra* note 1, at 3.
[4] Sup. Ct. R. 33.1(b).
[5] Easterbrook, *supra* note 2, at 15.

If you like any of these, take a document you have already written, change its font, and see how it looks. If you are not happy with the result, change it again until you find the font you want. Part 1 of this appendix explains how to change fonts.

Be careful about the point size recommendations in Part 2 of this appendix. If you select a font other than Times New Roman, you should experiment to find the point sizes that work best in headings.

The most attractive fonts were created by artistic people, and some fonts are considered art. In *The Elements of Typographic Style*, Robert Bringhurst wrote that letters on the page "have a life and dignity of their own. . . . Well-chosen words deserve well-chosen letters."[6]

---

[6] Robert Bringhurst, The Elements of Typographic Style 18 (4th ed. 2012) (italics omitted).

Index

Index

Mandatory rules, Ch. 2

Martha Stewart, illustrating parallel construction in lists, § 22.3

Memo, see Office memo and Motion memo

Modifiers, confusing placement of, § 22.3

Monty Python, Argument Clinic, § 32.1

Motion memo, generally, Ch. 28
  example, App. C
  format, § 28.2
  procedural posture, see Procedural posture

Motions, see Procedural posture

Muggles, Nimbus 2000, Harry, when to use *as* and *so*, § 22.3

Objective writing, see Predictive writing

Office memo, generally, Chs. 14, 16
  example, App. A
  format, Ch. 14

Opinions, judicial, see *also* Precedent
  ingredients of, § 5.1
  issues, rules, and determinative facts, apartment example, § 6.1
  parrot, exercise illustrating judicial opinion ingredients, Ch. 5
  policy and, Ch. 7

Oral argument, generally, § 34.2, Ch. 39

Organizing, see *also* CREAC
  outlining, § 12.4; Chs. 13, 20

Packing heat, exercise in statutory interpretation, Ch. 9

Paragraphs, generally, §§ 21.1–21.4

Parallel construction in lists, § 22.3

Parrot, exercise illustrating judicial opinion ingredients, Ch. 5

Passive voice, § 21.5

Persuasive writing, Chs. 27. See also Arguments, Storytelling
  predictive writing, distinguished from, § 1.4

Pirates of the Carribean, Ch. 4

Plagiarism, § 12.10

Plagiarism and the board of bar examiners, exercise on statutory interpretation), Ch. 9

Points and point headings, generally, Ch. 33
  appellate briefs, Ch. 35
  motion memos, Ch. 28

Policy, Chs. 7, 38
  CREAC, Ch. 17
  reasoning in judicial opinions, § 10.3

Pony, don't hide the, § 32.3

Precedent, see also Opinions, judicial

Predictive writing, generally, Ch. 16
  persuasive writing, distinguished from, § 1.4

Probative writing, compared to descriptive writing, § 21.2

Procedural posture, § 28.4

Process of writing, see Writing, process of

Prohibitory rules, Ch. 2

Proposition sentences in paragraphs, § 21.3

Public policy, see Policy

Punctuation, § 22.3; also see *Troublesome Punctuation*, article on this book's website

Question Presented, Ch. 37

Quoting, generally, § 23.3

Reading aggressively, § 5.2

Reconciliation of precedent, § 10.5

Rewriting, § 12.7

Roadmap,
  in Argument, § 32.3
  in CREAC, §§ 19.2, 19.5, 20.2

Rule application, in CREAC, Chs. 17–20

Rule explanation, in CREAC, Chs. 17–20

Rules of law, Chs. 2, 3
  broad and narrow rule formulations, § 6.2
  judicial opinions, rules in, Ch. 6
  organizing the application of, Chs. 17–20
  statutes, in, Ch. 4

Section sign, see *§ and Your Wordprocessor*, article on this book's website

Sentences, §§ 21.3, 21.5

Sexist wording, § 22.3

Statement of Facts, in office memos, § 14.1

Statement of the Case, Chs. 29–31,
  see Storytelling

Statutes, Chs. 4, 9
  selecting most appropriate, Ch. 8

Steps for
  analogizing, § 10.2
  digesting a rule, § 2.4
  distinguishing, § 10.2
  filling gap in law, § 8.4
  making policy arguments, § 38.3
  outlining a statute, § 4.2
  selecting facts to tell the story, § 31.1
  using CREAC to outline and begin first draft, § 20.1
  working with CREAC with multi-issue situations, § 19.5